CONFLICTS OVER LAND & WATER IN AFRICA

CONFLICTS OVER LAND & WATER IN AFRICA

EDITED BY
BILL DERMAN, RIE ODGAARD
& ESPEN SJAASTAD

James Currey
OXFORD

Michigan State University Press
EAST LANSING

University of KwaZulu-Natal Press
PIETERMARITZBURG

James Currey Ltd
73 Botley Road
Oxford OX2 0BS
www.jamescurrey.co.uk

Michigan State University Press
1405 South Harrison Rd
110 Manly Miles Building
East Lansing, M1 48823-5245
www.msupress.msu.edu

University of KwaZulu-Natal Press
Private Bag X01
Scottsville, 3209
South Africa
www.ukznpress.co.za

First published 2007

1 2 3 4 5 11 10 09 08 07

ISBN: 978-085255-881-1 (James Currey paper)

ISBN: 978-1-86914-129-5 (University of KwaZulu-Natal Press paper)

British Library Cataloguing in Publication Data
Conflicts over land & water in Africa
1. Land reform - Africa 2. Water-supply - Political aspects - Africa
I. Derman, William II. Odgaard, Rie III. Sjaastad, Espen
333.3'16

Library of Congress Cataloging-in-Publication Data available on request

ISBN 10: 0-87013-816-2 (Michigan State University Press paper)
ISBN 13: 978-0-87013-816-4 (Michigan State University Press paper)

Typeset in 10/11pt Photina
by Long House, Cumbria
Printed and bound in Malaysia

Contents

List of Tables, Figures, Maps, Boxes & Photographs

Tables

Figures

Maps

Boxes

Photographs

Notes on Contributors

Adano Wario Roba is a lecturer at the School of Environmental Studies at Moi University in Kenya. He holds a masters degree in environmental economics from York University (UK). He has recently completed his PhD dissertation, at the University of Amsterdam, on the dynamics of the pastoral economy, natural resource conservation and livestock management in Northern Kenya.

Kojo Sebastian Amanor is an associate professor at the Institute of African Studies, University of Ghana. He has conducted research, and published extensively, on land issues, forestry and environmental policy processes, peasant agriculture and decentralisation.

Nancy Andrew is a researcher and consultant, whose PhD dissertation in sociology, for the Université Paris V – René Descartes, focused on the rural social conflicts over land in South Africa and Zimbabwe since the emergence of land reform. Other publications and research interests centre on labour tenancy and farm violence, political economy, rural social movements, health and agrarian history. She can be contacted at LARRISA (Land and Rural Research in Southern Africa), email: nandrew@larrisa.eu.

Bill Derman is a professor of anthropology and African studies at Michigan State University and Professor II at the Department of International Environment and Development Studies (Noragric) at the Norwegian University of Life Sciences. He has carried out extensive field work in West and Southern Africa. His most recent interests are in agrarian change, political ecology, human rights and land and water reform.

Quentin Gausset is lecturer at the Institute of Anthropology, University of Copenhagen. He received his PhD from the Free University of Brussels and has since worked on the socio-cultural and political aspects of natural resource management in Cameroon, Burkina Faso, Tanzania, Southern Africa and Malaysia. He has also conducted research on AIDS-prevention in Zambia.

Sten Hagberg is an associate professor at the Department of Cultural Anthropology and Ethnology at Uppsala University in Sweden. He has worked extensively on issues of conflict, violence and interest organisations in West Africa.

Anne Hellum is professor of law at the Department of Public and International Law at the University of Oslo and director of the Institute of Women's Law. She is a lawyer and anthropologist engaging in teaching and research on human rights and legal pluralism in Africa, Pakistan and Norway in relation to gender, health, reproduction, family, water and land. In recent years she has published extensively on land and water rights in Africa.

Kjersti Larsen is associate professor in Social Anthropology and Head of Department at the Department of Ethnography, Museum of Cultural History, University of Oslo. Larsen also holds a professor II position in Development Studies at Noragric, Norwegian University of Life Sciences. Larsen has conducted extensive research on, and produced several books and articles about, the Swahili Coast and Northern Sudan.

Faustin Maganga is a researcher with the Institute of Resource Assessment, University of Dar es Salaam. He was educated in Tanzania, Zimbabwe and Denmark, and has published papers on natural resource management, resource use conflicts, and conflict management. Maganga recently coordinated a research project on implications of customary norms and laws for water management in South Africa, Tanzania and Zimbabwe.

Rie Odgaard is a senior researcher and anthropologist at the Danish Institute for International Studies in Copenhagen. Her recent research and publications have focused on customary land tenure and conflict in East Africa. She is also the coordinator of a network on Custom and Conflict in Land and Water Management in Africa.

Espen Sjaastad is associate professor at the Department of International Environment and Development Studies (Noragric), Norwegian University of Life Sciences. He has conducted research on the economics of land tenure in Southern Africa, Tanzania and Mali. Additional research interests include rural exchange systems and the contribution of natural resources to rural livelihoods.

Camilla Toulmin received her DPhil from Somerville College, Oxford, in 1987, and is currently director of the International Institute for Environment and Development (IIED), having formerly run the Drylands Programme from 1987 to 2002. An economist by training, her work has focused on social, economic and environmental development in dryland Africa. This work has combined field research, policy analysis, capacity building and advocacy.

Poul Wisborg recently defended his PhD dissertation, on human rights and land tenure reform in South Africa, at the Department of International Environment and Development Studies (Noragric), Norwegian University of Life Sciences, where he now works as a lecturer. He has been involved in institutional cooperation with rural development NGOs in Ethiopia, India and Pakistan. Major research interests are land policy, development and human rights.

Karen Witsenburg is currently carrying out post-doctoral research on violent conflicts in collaboration with the School of Environmental Studies at Moi University in Kenya. She has recently completed her PhD dissertation, at the University of Amsterdam, on pastoral livelihoods, sedentarisation and natural resource management in Northern Kenya.

Preface

Most of the chapters in this volume were presented as papers at a seminar held on 28–9 November 2002 in Denmark and organised by the 'Custom and Conflict in Land and Water Management in Africa' research network directed by Rie Odgaard, Danish Institute for International Studies (DIIS). The central theme for the seminar was how conflicts over land and water interact and inform conflicts over identity, citizenship and status in Africa, and how these issues in turn overlay conflicts over resources. The seminar was convened by Christian Lund, Institute for Development Studies, Roskilde University, and by Rie Odgaard, DIIS.

The list of participants included specialists from Africa, the Nordic countries, a number of European countries and the United States. The participants included anthropologists, geographers, legal scientists, political scientists, sociologists and economists, who have all been engaged either in studies related to the understanding of the highly complex situation existing in relation to land and water issues in Africa, or in trying to find policy solutions to the management of what in most African countries are becoming increasingly scarce and conflict ridden resources.

The issue of land and other natural resources is one where political and economic, cultural and legal struggles intertwine, where local powers and less localised power structures interact, and where political and cultural symbols of powers and authority are brought into play. Often people's social identity may entitle them, if not to land outright, then at least to claim it. This means that social identities and the question of citizenship become the objects of intense negotiation and conflict. Categories of citizenship, commoners and nobles, ethnic or regional loyalties, gender etc. create a friction, which challenges legislation, custom and practice alike.

To understand conflicts over land and water in Africa is therefore a highly complex process, which calls for analytical approaches informed by theories and concepts developed by different scholarly disciplines. The studies presented in this volume demonstrate the importance of employing an interdisciplinary theoretical framework in the analysis of land and water conflicts in Africa, and provide examples of how it can be done in practice.

It was the ambition of the seminar to situate land and water struggles within a broader context of social and political struggle and by doing so move beyond simple, unsatisfactory, mono-causal explanations. We hope that the studies presented in this book, which are all based on in-depth field research in a number of countries in different parts of Africa, provide illustrations of this, and that they will stimulate further debate and provoke new research questions.

We would like to thank all the authors who have been willing to rewrite and edit their papers in accordance with the suggestions provided by a number of anonymous referees and the editors. To the anonymous referees we would like to acknowledge their very valuable assistance.

Last but not least we would like to express our gratitude for the grant received from the Danish Council for Social Science Research, which has financed the research network and all its activities, including the seminar.

Rie Odgaard

1

Introduction

BILL DERMAN, RIE ODGAARD & ESPEN SJAASTAD

Africa's rates of hunger and malnutrition remain the highest in the world while the majority of Africans remain dependent upon the production of primary commodities. Agriculture still forms the backbone of many African economies. As wealth from minerals and oil continues to be appropriated by elites, and as promises of industrialisation and job creation fade, the role of land and water in securing African livelihoods is unlikely to diminish. At the same time, Africa has experienced more intra-national violence than any other continent over the last four decades and conflicts over land and natural resources appear to be growing as these resources become scarcer and more difficult to access. The causes and trajectories of these conflicts are not always easy to pin down. Various schools of thought have emphasised increasing resource scarcity, rent seeking, ethnic grievances and state failure as primary causes of violent conflict in Africa. As Berry states, however, 'Competition over land has followed myriad social fault lines, pitting national and local elites against ordinary citizens, neighbour against neighbour, kinsman against kinsman and husbands against wives.' (2002: 639). Camilla Toulmin suggests that across much of Africa enclosures are coming as those with greater resources and wealth have taken the land that poor people have farmed for many years (2005: 1). Understanding conflict – its patterns, causes and outcomes – is an important element in the wider problem of understanding development, particularly on a continent afflicted by much conflict and little development over the last half century. In order to understand conflict, however, it is necessary to go beyond the crude assertions and broad generalisations of universalistic theory and macro-empiricism. Despite substantial literature critiquing the 'tragedy of the commons' narrative it continues to have hold of much contemporary analyses of Africa.

This book examines complex aspects of citizenship and identity in conflicts over natural resources in Africa, as the continent moves towards increasing land scarcity. The different chapters reflect the wide range of contemporary issues in the complex intersections of identity, citizenship, law, scarcity, conflict and land. The introduction serves several purposes: to examine if current general theories of scarcity determining the presence of conflicts can explain African conflicts; to examine theories of the causes of 'ethnic conflicts'; to explore the questions of identities including ethnicity, gender and citizenship in relation to land questions;

to examine the role of hierarchies in understanding conflict; to explore access to land, land law and tenure reform in light of this book's chapters. The introduction is organised into six sections before presenting our conclusions as to why the complex and changing realities of conflicts over land and natural resources in Africa lend themselves to careful empirical investigation rather than to assertions of universal causal pathways or the primacy of one or two causal variables over all others. This has important implications for policy – for citizens, for multilateral and bilateral donors and for African nations themselves. In conclusion we suggest a continued and often increased role for the African state while pointing toward the need to adjust to greater complexity rather than policies that simplify its landscape.[1]

Land scarcity & resource scarcity in Africa

In recent and influential work on the genesis of conflict – and particularly violent conflict in developing nations – increasing scarcity of natural resources is seen as *the* key explanatory factor. In this section we present the underlying theoretical discussion of scarcity in the economic and political science literatures. We suggest that a compelling case can be made that the more contextual and complex analyses in this volume are appropriate for understanding the intersections of land, identity and conflict.[2] The geographical focus of this volume is Africa, in which issues of scarcity may seem particularly relevant. First, many African nations have among the highest population growth rates in the world. Second, Africa has, over the last few decades, probably witnessed more destructive and violent intermediate-level conflicts than any other continent. It might therefore be tempting to conclude that the simple correlation of these two factors – population growth and violence – would seem to confirm recent theories of conflict generation. Land rests at the centre of theories of conflict and scarcity due to its assumed growing scarcity. As the central natural resource along with water in Africa, it makes intuitive sense to expect increasing competition or declining quality to lead a range of conflicts. Even though this is not a theory we subscribe to, it requires attention given the continued use and importance of 'the tragedy of the commons' narrative and potential resource wars.

What is scarcity? According to one of the traditional economic definitions, a resource is scarce when it is useful and exists in limited quantity (Walras 1926, Montani 1987).[3] According to this definition, the scarcity of a resource will thus increase whenever its usefulness increases or when its supply is further

[1] James Scott (1998) among others points to the state requiring legibility and simplicity to function efficiently.

[2] The HIV/Aids pandemic has affected growth rates in selected countries. The rapid increase in urban populations while fuelled primarily by population growth in cities nonetheless has absorbed large numbers of people from the countryside.

[3] According to Walras (1926), a good is useful when it is capable of satisfying a want. As Montani (1987) also notes, the notion of scarcity has been central to many *definitions* of economics, and in particular the influential definitions provided by Robbins (1932) and in the economics textbook by Lipsey et al. (1990). These definitions focus on the study of the use of *scarce* means to satisfy multiple and unlimited wants.

restricted.[4] In Marx's (1848) classification, however, the usefulness – or 'utility' – of a good is considered separate from its scarcity, which then simply refers to its quantity. It is, however, difficult to envisage a resource being scarce without its also being useful.[5] In economic terms, a resource is scarce when demand exceeds supply at a price of zero (when it is freely available). In a free market system, price is thus an indicator of the relative scarcity of good: an increase in usefulness (demand) or a reduction in quantity (supply) will lead to an increase in scarcity (price).

It is thus possible to compare the scarcity of a given resource in different locations or at different times, most easily through its real price whenever the resource is exchanged in markets, or to compare relative *changes* in scarcity across *different* resources, as when population growth causes a relative increase in the scarcity of land relative to labour. But is it, in absolute terms, also possible to assert that one resource is scarcer than another? Homer-Dixon (1995) suggests that absolute scarcity can be measured by the ratio of consumption through time to the total available amount of the resource. Such a measure is broadly compatible with the Walras definition of scarcity but is also very crude, ignoring stock-flow linkages, the distinction between renewable and exhaustible resources, availability of substitutes, and issues of access and control.[6]

Natural resources are, of course, generally provided by nature rather than produced by humans. Some are renewable, and can be maintained at different stocking levels depending on management and use. It is also possible to replace one type of resource with another, for example grazing land with forest or one fish species with another. Broadly speaking, however, natural resources are in absolute limited supply, constrained by available areas and volumes of land, water and air and they will tend to become scarcer through time as global population increases.[7]

It may thus appear that scarcity is an uncomplicated concept and that its calculus is a relatively simple affair. Related to the role of natural resource scarcity in generating conflict and our ability to measure such effects are, however, issues related to spatial and temporal scale and context. Analysis of long time series may yield quite different results from analyses of short time series, and an investigation of fluctuations in scarcity may be fundamentally different from an investigation of trends.

[4] The question of what 'usefulness' actually implies is not so simple, however. The result, for example, of the invention of a technology that permits us to use a resource more efficiently may, depending on the economy and the production process into which it enters, be that the resource becomes *less* useful in the above sense.

[5] There is also a marginalist definition of scarcity, descending from David Ricardo, whereby a resource is scarce if additional units of other factors give rise to diminishing returns.

[6] For example: among two otherwise comparable renewable resources managed according to maximum sustainable yield principles, the one with slower reproduction and lower yield would be the *least* scarce of the two; and, in this conception, raising prices through exercise of monopoly control would in fact *reduce* scarcity rather increase it.

[7] Natural resources thus correspond to Montani's fifth and final category of goods: '... commodities which are useful, scarce and not produced by labour, or produced by labour but without the quantity employed having any necessary relationship with its exchange value.' (Montani 1987: 254). Montani here follows Marx (1867) in treating 'usefulness' as separate from the concept of scarcity.

Resource scarcity & conflict

If humans prefer peace to conflict, and if there is no scarcity of any kind, there would seem to be no reason – at least no *rational* motivation – to engage in conflict. Scarcity of some kind – whether it is scarcity of natural resources, power, or 'living space' – appears to be a necessary condition for conflict. Yet this basic understanding by no means automatically supports the hypothesis that more scarcity means more conflict. To assess this hypothesis, one must first investigate human adaptations to both scarcity and to conflict.

The link between resource scarcity and violent conflict is not a recent 'discovery'. According to evolutionary perspectives of conflict, violent encounters and attendant deaths – or 'subtractions' – are inevitable; a means of redressing imbalances between human populations and their resource base. Nor are doomsday prophesies of very recent date. Thomas Malthus's gloomy predictions about the fate of growing human populations in a finite physical world originated more than two centuries ago and have since undergone endless revision and reinterpretation, especially from the 1960s onward. The 1960s also spawned increased awareness about the environmental effects of industrial resource use, resulting in – amongst other things – the pessimistic 'world models' of the 1970s (Forrester 1971, Meadows et al. 1972).

Choucri and North (1975) specifically assessed the role of environmental change as a cause of conflict. In the late 1980s and early 1990s, a growing concern about global environmental problems and their links with poverty (e.g. WCED 1987), the end of the Cold War, and influential writings in both popular and scientific publications (Westing 1989, Homer-Dixon 1991, Myers 1993, Kaplan 1994) finally elevated the environment to a position as one of the central concerns in international security. Conservationists and the military-industrial complex suddenly found that their interests appeared to be converging.

One of the original features of this literature is simply that it grabbed the attention of politicians to such an unprecedented extent. Another is that it combines *all* of the elements found in its various and varied antecedents: population growth, environmental scarcity and degradation, poverty and deprivation, violent conflict, international security, and – at least occasionally – apocalyptic predictions.[8]

Two large-scale research projects specifically aimed at investigating links between natural resource scarcity and violent conflict emerged in the 1990s: one based at the University of Toronto, led by Thomas Homer-Dixon, and one at the Swiss Peace Foundation in Berne, led by Günther Baechler. Engaged in a smaller but related project, Aaron Wolf of Oregon State University, following a qualitative and historical methodology, has assessed the past and future likelihood of water scarcity causing conflict. Given current emphases upon growing freshwater scarcity, this project has significant implications.

The Toronto project, focusing on renewable resources, considered three sources of increasing environmental scarcity: environmental degradation and destruction (supply-induced); population growth, leading to greater consumption of natural resources (demand-induced); and increasing inequality in access to and control over environmental resources (structurally induced). Scarcity arising

[8] Another body of the literature examines mostly the opposite causal link – what are the effects of conflict *on* the environment? – but this perspective is of less relevance here.

from these sources was in turn hypothesised to generate corresponding processes of acute conflict formation: migration and subsequent group-identity conflicts, international conflicts and wars over natural resources, and economic deprivation and subsequent civil strife and insurgency.

What were the findings of the project? In brief, depletion and degradation of agricultural lands, forest, freshwater sources and fisheries were found to be more important conflict triggers than more dispersed environmental problems such as ozone depletion and climate change. Scarcity was unlikely to produce international resource wars. In contrast, scarcity-induced migration and subsequent group-identity conflicts were widespread. The data produced partial support for the hypothesis that increasing inequality would produce civil strife and insurgency. Conflicts were likely to be most serious when there was interaction between the different scarcity-conflict processes (Homer-Dixon 1991, 1994).

The Berne project produced a different, more exhaustive taxonomy of conflicts. The project also found that migration was capable of causing a broader range of conflicts than the group-identity conflicts specified by Homer-Dixon. However, the Berne project, though more inclusive in terms of variables considered and less rigid in its application, used a comparable theoretical model to that of the Toronto project (Peluso and Watts 2001) and generally reached the same conclusions (Baechler 1998). The environmental security literature has broadly been perceived as advocating two interlinked positions. The first is that environmental scarcity is a key factor in generating conflict. Within this general position, the literature then goes on to thrash out the processes and causal pathways by which scarcity emerges and in turn leads to violence. The second position is that increasing resource scarcity – and the conflicts that this generates – today is approaching some unprecedented threshold; that an upsurge in scarcity-driven conflicts, at levels not seen in the past, is underway, possibly to an extent that raises serious international security concerns.[9]

Significantly, with respect to the first position, both the Toronto and Berne projects reach the conclusion that environmental scarcity can be a deep-rooted reason for violent conflict rather than just an intermediary or intervening variable.[10] This position has been criticised on the grounds that findings tend to be based on cases where both environmental scarcity and violence are known to have been present and that analysis of other potential causes of conflict have been neglected (Levy 1995, Gleditsch 1998, Hauge and Ellingsen 1998, Deudney 1999).

In contradistinction to those of Toronto and Berne, the Oregon State project considering the specific resource of freshwater has reached different conclusions from the other two (Wolf 2001, Wolf, Yoffee and Giordano 2005). Their approach contained three elements: the creation of a deep historical database documenting water relations linked to the intensity of cooperation and conflict;[11] the construction of a Geographic Information System of countries and international basins current and historical with associated indicator variables; the formulation and testing of hypotheses about factors associated with water

[9] It is a weakness of the scarcity and conflict literature that it does not systematically explore how the biases of the international economic system affect internal conflicts within African nation-states.

[10] Baechler (1998) also deals with the role of the environment as trigger, target, channel and catalyst for conflict.

[11] They have compiled all reported instances of conflict or cooperation over international freshwater resources from 1948 to 1999 in a water event database (http://www.transboundarywater.orst.edu).

conflict. Wolf, Yoffee and Giordano conclude that cooperation over freshwater resources far exceeds international conflict. They are cautious with respect to the future of potential water conflicts particularly in light of growing water demands and global climate change.

Yet few would argue against the more general conclusion that scarce resources often play a role in violent conflict in the South. In an extensive empirical survey, Hauge and Ellingsen (1998) found that 'countries suffering from environmental degradation – and in particular from land degradation – are more prone to civil conflict. However, economic factors are far more important in predicting domestic armed conflict than are environmental factors' (p. 314).

The problem with the assertion that particular types of conflict are often linked to different forms of environmental scarcity is, in fact, its blandness (Peluso and Watts 2001). The research undertaken by Homer-Dixon and Baechler here tends to become a victim of its scale and ambition on the one hand and its lack of rigorous quantitative methodology on the other; the need to integrate a wide number of disparate cases while unable to gauge the relative importance of different explanatory variables. There is also little attempt to discuss the socio-political causes underlying resource destruction and unequal access (Hauge 2003) although there have been efforts to examine the extractive character of African states.[12]

This is not to deny, however, that both the Toronto and Berne projects have produced significant contributions in terms of classifying sources of scarcity and conflict, thrashing out alternative causal pathways and setting the agenda for further research. Case studies undertaken in connection with both projects have also illuminated important and interesting processes and methodological problems.

In terms of the second position, doomsday prophecies seem to have become rarer over the last ten years or so of research. Kaplan's (1994) grim travelogue from various conflict hotspots, which incorporated extensive quotation of statements made by Homer-Dixon, seems to have been the high water mark. Baechler (1998), in fact, has been careful to note that '... neither apocalyptic scenarios of environmental catastrophes nor alarmist prognoses of world environmental wars are tenable' (p. 24). Yet the notion that we today are on the threshold of an unprecedented outbreak of scarcity-induced conflicts in the poor countries of the world continues to inform both scientific and political discourse (Peluso and Watts 2001).

In the four cases of violence in this book (Tanzania, Kenya, Burkina Faso and Zimbabwe) none support direct links between resource scarcity and violence. Social inequality, the lack of secure land rights, histories of violent raids and the use of land as a political reward, characterise these cases. Witsenburg and Roba's study (this volume) of pastoralists and conflict in Marsabit, Kenya is discussed in some detail below. This is one case where resource scarcity, namely water, might have been expected to explain violence. In Zimbabwe, the one case where the violence is national and ongoing is demonstrably not about scarcity. The latest instance of burning and destroying all 'illegal' shops and residences in

[12] The structure, policies and actions of African states have been intensely debated in the literature. Some important sources include Chabal (1992), Bayart (1993), Joseph (1997), Sandbrook (2000), Bayart, Ellis and Hibou (1999), Chabal and Daloz (1999), Herbst (2000), Ake (1996), Mkandawire and Soludo (1999).

Zimbabwe's rural areas marks a new chapter in efforts by the ruling party to maintain control and has little to do with resource scarcity and much to do with forcing the opposition out of the cities into the countryside.

Ethnicity & violence

In this section we examine general theories about ethnicity and violence. We find, as in the case of scarcity and conflict, that theories about the deep-rooted link between ethnic groups, ethnic diversity and ethnicity in general does not explain past or current patterns of violence in Africa.

In Africa, the close association of land and identity has received much attention. Land and natural resources are not merely assets, sources of income, and commodities but represent repositories of ancestral spirits, sites for sacred rituals, and historical landmarks that tie the individual to particular locations and landscapes. At the same time, the ethnic diversity and the rich variety of local institutional systems found throughout the continent have provided material for numerous assertions about identity and conflict, and this may in part account for the over-representation of ethnicity in theories about African conflict. At the most vulgar and essentialist level, one simply observes the lack of congruence between ethnic and national boundaries and explains conflict as the result of this. Among more sophisticated and influential scholars, Horowitz (1985) has argued that ethnicity can be seen as the root of violence; ethnic divisions both overwhelm and direct politics and tend to dissolve relations necessary for peaceful coexistence. Ethnic diversity and fractionalisation have also been used to explain a host of African ills, from corruption and lack of investment in public goods to economic stagnation and regression (see Easterly 2001 for an overview). While Horowitz refined his views in 1998 it represents the continuation of the theory that African politics are different from those of other regions. Such theories also have the tendency not to take African strivings for democracy seriously enough.[13]

These views are, of course, not unopposed. One strand of criticism is typified by Braathen et al. (2000), who criticise the ideas of Horowitz on the grounds that he neglects important political, historical and economic factors: '...it is possible, and we would even argue necessary, to accept the presumption that most civil wars in Africa are centred around ethnic identities as the subjectification of power, and still question whether this in itself can explain the causes behind violence' (p. 4). They argue that the very concept of African ethnicity is an overworked legacy of colonial times when the portrayal of local populations as backward and stateless provided grounds for modernising and civilising interventions, in many cases leading not only to the formalisation of ethnic groups and their customs but also to their creation. According to Braathen et al., the 'ethnic' narrative finds its post-colonial counterparts in the perception, typified by the World Bank and its policies from the 1970s onward, of customary tenures and ethnic conflicts as barriers to modernisation (see e.g. Easterly and Levine 1997).[14]

[13] There is not the space here to summarise the multilevelled debates about the African state, the nature of power and the prospects for democracy.

[14] Easterly (2001), in a more recent paper, finds that the detrimental effects of ethnic fractionalisation largely disappear in societies with 'good' institutions.

Braathen et al. emphasise instead the need to consider other underlying factors. In particular, they point to the personal and mercurial (rather than ethnic) nature of African politics whereby leading politicians 'buy' political support for purposes of material gain (see also Bates 1998). These tendencies are in turn challenged by the move towards democracy (Bratton et al. 2005). In times of economic hardship, caused for example by donor-imposed reductions in public spending or by the general reduction in foreign aid that followed the end of the Cold War, African governments that can no longer afford to secure continued support by economic means may increasingly resort to divisive discourses and to coercion or violence (Braathen et al. 2000). The poor and disadvantaged have no choice but to follow their lead.

African ethnicity, however, remains unresolved. For one thing, the paper does not deal with what Chege (1998: 377), in a comment to the paper, describes as '...the most fundamental finding of five decades of anthropological inquiry into the origins of contemporary African ethnicity....' Namely, that '...most African ethnic consciousness, as we know it today, is of colonial-era vintage, the product of cultural entrepreneurship in the crucible of social tensions in the modern sector....' Chege notes the constructive side of ethnic diversity: the problem is how to encourage this while discouraging the destructive side.[15]

As Horowitz (1998) points out, taking advantage of ethnicity for the purposes of cost-saving and recruitment purposes presupposes a latent or active polarisation; on the other hand, others might then ask how such polarisation came to pass in the first place. Neither primordial nor purely instrumental views of African ethnicity seem helpful. Nor can observation of neighbouring groups with strong internal affinities and the simultaneous existence of conflict between such groups explain why they in some cases live peacefully together over long periods. Seeing ethnicity as the cause of African conflict seems, in this sense, no more fruitful than seeing nation-states as the cause of international wars. As noted by Peters (1998), there is a need not only to separate between ethnic identity and tribal politics but also to examine more closely how the one spills over into the other. There is also a need to shift the focus towards other identities than those based on ethnicity and to examine their roles not only in triggering conflict but also in avoiding conflict, ending conflict and sustaining peace.

Having found that the more general hypotheses about scarcity, conflict and ethnicity are currently not adequate to explain the variations that one observes in Africa, we turn to a discussion focusing upon context in the intersections of land, conflict and identities. We return later in the introduction to broader debates about conflict, identity and scarcity.

Identities & land

There appears to be a double movement of identity in contemporary Africa. On the one hand national identities formed through anti-colonial struggles are now being undermined through new transnational forces usually lumped under the

[15] Chege also notes that urban ethnic associations in Africa have mostly been formed for entirely legitimate purposes. His prescriptions for avoiding or resolving ethnic conflict, rather than ethnic consensus, involve improved rule of law, decentralisation, and, interestingly, providing ethnic groups with maximum legal room for political play.

rubric of globalisation. For example, women have increasingly entered the work force while some have joined international struggles for women's rights. On the other hand, the notions of 'culture' and 'tradition' are being reinforced as part of defensive struggles against globalisation. The state can be seen, according to Hagberg in Burkina Faso and Gausset in Cameroon (this volume), as indifferent to local struggles for land, while in Zimbabwe the ruling party has argued that its violence has been to prevent recolonization by the United Kingdom (Derman and Hellum this volume). Race continues to play a central role as a marker of inequality especially in Kenya, South Africa and Zimbabwe.[16]

While international mobility may be reducing ties to land, there continues to be a strong connection between land and identity in much of Africa.

> To an African, land is more than an issue of *jus* (rights) as it is culturally connected to community values. Colonialism sought to erode the land values of African communities with the European land rights philosophy founded upon individual control and ownership. (Livula-Ithana 2001: 13)[17]

We accept that strong connections exist between community and land, but too often what constitutes community and who decides the boundaries of 'community' is left unexamined. This volume demonstrates that the relationship between land and identity is highly varied and often quite complex. The idea that land adheres more to 'community values' oversimplifies the connections between land and identity on the one hand, and tends to narrow rather than open up the discussion of how and why identities are important, on the other. Land remains a key cultural, social and political asset, but like other dimensions of life in Africa, its understanding and uses have changed greatly. Precisely how land and community are linked requires empirical investigation. For example, while land can confer power and authority upon those who control access to this resource, it may be that those who do so are migrants (Toulmin). Alternatively, access to land can be contested on the basis of age (Amanor), gender (Andrew), loyalty to a political party (Derman and Hellum), land use (Maganga et al.), or ethnicity (Gaussett, Hagberg, Wisborg).

African farmers across the continent have had to contend with a variety of new processes that have made continuation of customary practices and relationships difficult. Larsen describes how drought has affected the Hawawir. Toulmin describes how through formal and informal agreements and/or contracts people gain access to farming land outside of their family group. In West Africa the research team, which Toulmin is co-directing, found villages in Côte d'Ivoire and Ghana where 60–70 per cent of land under cultivation was obtained through contracts. In Zimbabwe, access to former white-owned commercial farmland rests upon loyalty to the ruling political party. Amanor examines how chiefs are using (abusing) their positions to increase their wealth by controlling 'their' communities' forest resources. Thus, while we agree that rights to land are indeed a central part of African identity it involves a more complex notion of identities than what might appear initially.

16 There isn't space here to enter into the illuminating debate about race provoked by Omni and Winant (1994) nor the vast literature on race. Omni and Winant argue that race is distinct from ethnicity. With respect to the US they successfully contend that race was and is different. Race, in their view, is 'an autonomous field of social conflict, political organization, and cultural/ideological meaning' (p. 48). This approach can be fruitfully applied to southern Africa.

17 Former Minister of Lands, Resettlement and Rehabilitation, Republic of Namibia. Clearly the Namibian experience is quite different from the West or East African.

In the context of changing rights to land due to increasing scarcity, market influences and changing legal systems, we reject the notion that acquiring land through contract or sale is less African than other means. The oft-repeated assertion that obtaining land through membership in a community is the 'African way' simplifies fairly complicated and often political processes.[18] We find that purchase or transfer of rights, conquest, long-term use, gifting or reward for military or other service confers legitimate land rights along with kin group membership. Rather than privilege ethnicity, we suggest that there are a suite of identities at work in access to, and control of, land. We will briefly consider the following ones: ethnicity, gender, citizenship, religion, race and age. These 'identities' all exist in relation to each other and are held by all Africans.

Rapid social, economic and political changes have destabilised fixed notions of identity. New forms of articulation have altered older identities and are creating new ones. Earlier literatures, which attempted to depict Africa's social map as containing different ethnic groups each with their own homeland has been, we hope, permanently displaced. Conflict as we have contended cannot be reduced to growing scarcity. In addition, the social units faced with 'scarcity' are not stable as patterns of production, migration and political boundaries shift. Efforts to create a single national identity vary greatly from one nation to another. In addition, there are multiple efforts to create broader regional identities and indeed a continental one through the African Union. There are many other identities at play including among others international non-governmental organisations, religions, labour unions, chambers of commerce and multinational corporations. Thus, while identity remains central to Africa's ongoing conflicts, attention must be drawn to new identities not just the classic ones, although it is the latter that are emphasised in this volume.

Ethnicity & land

Debates about ethnicity continue. In our view, ethnicity applies universally to all forms of contemporary humanity. We view ethnic groups as changing and fluid, to be understood in relationship to each other and the nation-state. They are groups, which share selected social, economic and religious features at a given point in time. Surprisingly, 'ethnicity is not a product of isolation, but one of dynamic exchange and conflict with others' rooted in patterns of communication (Bolaffi et al. 2003: 95). Ethnicity, as has been emphasised in the historical and anthropological literatures, changes dramatically over time although many ethnic groups retain their names and identity for generations in new contexts. Common ethnic terms like Hausa, Igbo, Zulu, Shona, Maasai, and hundreds of others denote complex, nested groups whose formation in time and space can be located and are therefore not primordial. While we understand that many peoples – both themselves and their interlocutors – conceptualise ethnicity as 'primordial and essentialised', the chapters in this book view ethnicity as historically created but sustained and changed through practice and ongoing social relations.

While ethnicity remains central to our analyses, privileging ethnicity over other identities in the study of Africa does not fit with growing empirical

[18] There is a series of recent publications examining the complex intersections between politics, property, identity and land including Benjaminsen and Lund (2003), Toulmin, Lavigne and Traore (2002), Juul and Lund (2002).

evidence nor does it take into account how ethnicities are reshaped and reformed by changing circumstances. Thus, we reject the notion that ethnicity trumps other forms of identity or that ethnicity is more important in Africa than on other continents.[19] We adhere to the view that all humans have multiple identities that can be shifted or mobilised depending upon a set of conditions including war, land scarcity, commercialisation, labour migration and drought, among others. Ethnicity also works not just by itself but in combination with other identities including age and gender. Youth can reinforce the importance of ethnic identity but, as Amanor demonstrates, youth's changing position also challenges older ethnic identities. Hagberg, Gausset, Maganga et al., and Witsenburg and Adano detail classical forms of resistance to threats to land and natural resources based upon the assertion of ethnicity. Larsen describes how the Hawawir maintain some elements of their identity, while shedding others, when members are displaced due to drought. Local identity in Komaggas, which took so long to form, retains its strength despite efforts to have it replaced by a national South African identity (see Wisborg).

Gender & land

A second lens through which to examine identity is gender. There is not a single identity for women or men. Other identities including age, marital status (married, widowed, divorced, unmarried), ethnicity, motherhood/fatherhood, religion etc. Women's claims to land generally reflect their broader status and positioning within their social and cultural system. Women's, like men's, rights to land vary depending upon the degree of societal inequality or equality, the presence or absence of slavery or serfdom, patterns of marriage, religion, and more recently the colonial and independent nation-state. While land issues are generally framed within national contexts, the actual access to and use of land is negotiated through existing social systems in which women (and men) have distinct and different positions. It is an often held assumption that only men in Africa hold land rights in their own right whereas women don't. Some recent research is challenging this assumption and demonstrates that in several African communities, patrilineal as well as matrilineal, women are in practice exercising land rights in their own right and are directly involved in the negotiation processes in order to acquire their own land rights.[20] However, in most African communities the general picture is that women's claims to land within local landholding systems or 'socially determined land-use rules' (Lavigne Delville 1999: 99)[21] are usually acquired through husbands or male kinsfolk although it can be through their mothers or maternal kinsfolk. Women's access to land thus often depends upon men who have authority over them, and more often than not women do not inherit land as do their brothers. In addition, it depends upon whether or not women are treated as full adults with equal decision-making capabilities with men.

And it remains true that many women across the continent do not have permanent rights to land but rights through marriage, through brothers or

[19] For a comprehensive account of ethnicity see Banks (1996).

[20] For example Muteshi (1997), Rocheleau and Edmunds (1997), Manji (2000), Englert (2003), Odgaard et al (2005), Odgaard and Bentzon (2007 forthcoming).

[21] We prefer the terms local or socially determined land-use rules to customary. As many authors have commented, customary all too often has the connotation of 'traditional' or 'unchanging'.

through children. While such rights may not necessarily be less secure than rights derived through membership in a kin unit (lineage, clan, ethnic group), historical developments in Africa have implied that especially women's land rights under local landholding systems have been, and are still being, constantly contested. All too often women's tenure and rights to land remain much more insecure than those of men. Wealthier women may therefore benefit from the removal of land from, for example, patrilineal groups into their private hands. While colonialism paved the way for male biased private land rights in large parts of Africa it is, in our view, no longer possible to attribute women's lack of rights only to colonialism. In the present context, the assumption that male elders or traditional leaders would either include or exclude women from land is too broad a generalisation. How elders or traditional leaders operate also depends upon context.

Zimbabwe can serve as an example of how the lower status of women is perpetuated through what were intended to be gender-neutral land reform programmes. Neither the resettlement programme of the 1980s nor the current 'fast track' land reform programme recognised married women's right to hold land on an equal basis with men (Hellum and Derman 2004). Both the earlier and later versions of land reform have reinforced the public/private dichotomy underlying Zimbabwe's land regime by not referring to transfer of land within the family in the event of marriage, divorce and death. Under fast track, lack of clarity has led to confusion, conflict and contestation over the redistributed land. While women lack formal tenure security under both regimes, their *de facto* security has diminished significantly under fast track. With overlapping authority structures in terms of party-loyal chiefs and war veterans, the prospects for women to negotiate their position in the event of divorce or the death of their husbands do not hold great promise in Zimbabwe compared to their position in the 1980s when professional resettlement officers administered the programme.

The Zimbabwean, South African and Sudanese cases demonstrate that using a gender lens means that core assumptions about land tenure can be incorrect, or at best incomplete without incorporating links between gender perspectives and other identities.[22]

Citizenship & land

Globally, virtually all people are now included in state systems. Each nation-state has its own system in place to indicate citizenship including national identity cards, passports, and visas for travelling within and beyond Africa. For many Africans, reference continues to be made to colonial times when Africans were denied citizenship in their homelands. However, as new generations have been born after independence, the history of citizenship denial recedes while the actual

[22] Ikdahl, Hellum, Kaarhus and Benjaminsen (2005) write in summary on women's land rights: 'With a view to the blurred boundaries between state law and various forms of customary law, we find it virtually impossible to come to a conclusion regarding whether state law or customary law provides better protection for women's land rights. In this report we point to strengths and weaknesses of both statutory and customary systems. The added values of the human rights based approach is that it cuts across these divisions. Whether land reform, formalisation or registration is based on statutory or customary, individual or communal ownership, mechanisms that protect women against direct and indirect discrimination have to be put in place.' (p. xi)

struggle for citizenship, as Mamdani argues, has not been completed in many nations. Increasingly however, citizenship and the nation-state are of growing importance for obtaining rights to land. Increasingly land policies are made at the national level especially in the context of land reform. The experience of implementing land reform uncovers the multiple ways by which rural Africans get rights and access to land and raises complex issues as to how to cope with multiple local tenurial rules. The chapters by Toulmin, Wisborg, Derman and Hellum, Maganga et al. and Andrew demonstrate the contentious issues that arise in altering current land tenure. They also point to significant inequalities in access to land based upon how citizenship is constructed and understood.

In West Africa, due to large numbers of migrants, citizenship has been increasingly used to provide formal land rights. In Namibia, South Africa and Zimbabwe past and current racial imbalances require redress in land ownership. Zimbabwe has gone furthest in determining citizenship on the basis of race by systematically forcing whites (whether Zimbabwean or not) off their farms and distributing land to black Zimbabweans only. In general, land constitutes an increasingly significant national resource and a highly political one. This is clearest in southern Africa where efforts at redistribution are under way. Some nations have moved toward restricting land ownership to citizens (e.g. Malawi) while it is under discussion in South Africa. Zimbabwe's recent land reform has been characterised by using land to reward highly placed members of the ruling party and the military. South Africa appears to be continuing a dual system of private lands in the former white-owned areas and communal tenure in the former homelands[23] whereas Zimbabwe is currently moving toward nationalising all rural land.

Within African states there are conflicts between state efforts to control land on the one hand, and the complex and already existing local land tenure systems in place on the other. Wisborg (this volume) examines if and how the representatives of the South African nation-state can define land reform for local areas; in Komaggas, the locals resisted the national conception of land reform and formulated their own. Among the Kwanja, Gausset argues that the Cameroonian nation-state has little interest in protecting their land rights and so they must do so on their own. With respect to gender and increasing women's rights and access to land, male-dominated states hesitate to use power and limited political capital to change discriminating local systems in this respect. This is illustrated in Andrew's paper. Women are not obtaining equal rights to land but it remains unclear if this is due to government's lack of commitment or lack of capacity or some combination of the two. Andrew points to deeper biases toward women reflected in policies which continue to block women's rights to land. Derman and Hellum contend that Zimbabwean citizenship has been redefined in light of the current political, economic and social crisis to favour those who support the ruling party. Those who are eligible for any other national citizenship must prove that they have renounced these possibilities. At the same time, the national government insists that African culture restricts land ownership to men and therefore joint family permits or titles have not been awarded.

Issues of citizenship and nationhood originate from the colonial era. Mamdani

[23] See Ruth Hall (2004) for the most recent figures on the progress of South Africa's land reform.

(1996) contends that many rural Africans remain subjects rather than full citizens in their own contemporary nation-states. He argues for new analyses of rural movements, locating them, for the most part, within broader struggles for democracy rather than ethnic or tribal struggles. In his view then, the independence project has not been completed and will not be until rural Africans have obtained full citizenship rights in their own nation-states. This perspective is taken up directly by Amanor in this volume on rural struggles over land in Ghana and how 'customary authorities' are privileged. Support for Mamdani's general argument can be found in an assessment of African public opinion toward democracy and market reform. According to Bratton, Mattes and Gyimah-Boadi fully '95 per cent of Afrobarometer[24] respondents agree that they feel pride in being a national of their country and 70 per cent agree strongly' (2005: 190). The same overwhelming majority also wants their children to think of themselves as national citizens. They also found that occupational identities and social class identities accounted for 40 per cent of self-defined identity (2005: 188) that is significantly more than the 25 per cent for ethnic groups.

Their surveys are from 12 more or less democratic nations and do not include those from African nations faced with fragmentation, wars to redefine regions and peoples within a nation-state, or wars to force out people defined as 'strangers' or 'not really Africans'. We have not included cases from regions of active warfare but would note that ethnonationalism and racism challenge a common identity in several African nation-states. One of the most extreme examples is Rwanda, which is struggling to create a single nation again out of the two competing racial-ethnic political visions. While it would superficially appear that population density and scarcity produced the extreme conflicts in Burundi and Rwanda, unpublished work by David Campbell demonstrates that other variables are of far greater importance. On the other hand, scarcity can be created through a variety of mechanisms, a theme already discussed. The example of Hutu and Tutsi in Rwanda demonstrate as well the strong links between racism, ethnonationalism and nation-states in combination with new development policies (Uvin 1998, Mamdani 2002). While high population densities and increasing land scarcity are there, it has not been possible to date to demonstrate that these are the driving forces for civil wars and genocide.

The starting point for our analysis is the simultaneous existence of multiple identities without privileging ethnic ones. These can be examined through social identities (household, lineage, clan, ethnic group, region and nation), political identities (faction, political party, nation-state and minority), economic identities (rich, poor, peasant, engineer, business entrepreneur, hunters, etc.), religious identities, generational identity, gender identity, and more. These are categories we can delineate but they are also overlapping and intersecting. Poul Wisborg's chapter from Komaggas in Namaqualand, South Africa, ably illustrates how people with a common ethnic identity resisted inclusion as an urban area rather than a rural area in the land reform process. In addition, the local association, the Komaggas Inwoners Vereniging (KIV), argued that they already controlled and owned the land so that there was no need for any further land reform, even

[24] Afrobarometer is an international survey research project carried out in 12 African nations over time to assess opinions about democratisation and economic reform. The three core partners are the Institute for Democracy in South Africa (IDASA), the Centre for Democratic Development in Ghana and Michigan State University in the US.

if by a new black government. In contrast, Gausset presents a classical case of a small ethnic group trying to keep control of their lands in the face of an influx of new farmers and Fulbe transhumant pastoralists and in the absence of a national government willing or able to protect their rights. They had a profound mistrust of the Fulbe. Amanor explores the complex links between traditional authorities, youth and women in struggles over forests in contemporary Ghana and how all these 'categories' are being reworked in the context of globalisation. In short, even where 'traditional' identities are at play, they have been reworked and reconfigured. In the case of Komaggas, the people known as 'coloured' are adopting one of the oldest identities in South Africa, the Nama. During the years of struggle against apartheid, it was often assumed that older identities would simply become one, black African or South African. The use of Nama however, does not mean that this is an older identity but rather it is a new one in response to new conditions.

Inequality & conflict

In this section we examine general theories about inequality and conflict. We will briefly consider other theories for considering the origins of conflict. Africa, like other continents, has significant social differentiation. As we have contended throughout the introduction, identity cannot be reduced to ethnicity. We find, as in the case of scarcity and conflict, that theories about the deep-rooted link between ethnic groups, ethnic diversity and ethnicity in general do not explain past or current patterns of violence in Africa.

The notion that inequality may cause violent conflict is old. In more recent times, theories of relative deprivation as a cause of conflict have figured prominently (e.g. Gurr 1970, Davies 1972). The literature on greed-motivated rebellion, on the other hand, is notable also for its general scepticism towards inequality as an explanation for conflict.[25] Broadly speaking, substantial income inequality may on the one hand increase the motivation for rebellion; on the other hand, such inequality will also reduce the means (and probability of success) among rebellious groups.

The evidence is mixed. Several studies have investigated, statistically, the role of income inequality as a cause of violent conflict. The lessons from this literature are unclear to say the least. While Muller and Seligson (1987), Boswell and Dixon (1990), and Nafziger and Auvinen (1997) find a positive correlation between income inequality and conflict, Collier and Hoeffler (1996, cited in Cramer 2003) find that inequality reduces the likelihood of civil war. However, in a later paper (1998), with a new model, the same authors find that income inequality has no influence on the risk of civil war. Fearon and Laitin (2003) reach the same conclusion.

A potent critique of this literature is provided by Cramer (2003). First of all, by focusing only on income inequality, many other forms of inequality are neglected. Second, the data used in these models rely on inequality indicators at national levels (Gini coefficients) that disguise local and specific expressions of

[25] Indeed, Collier (2000b) sees the lack of any influence of income inequality as one of three features that distinguish rebellion from organised crime (the two others being rebellion's inverse relation to overall levels of income and the key role of natural resources).

income inequality. Third, conflict may itself be the cause of inequality rather than the other way around. Fourth, the models are static in that they analyse observed inequality rather than changes in inequality, which may be crucial. Fifth, and most importantly, the underlying relations that inform inequality are ignored. Cramer convincingly argues that different types of inequality (inequality of income, assets, power, rights; relative versus absolute; either-or versus more-or-less) and the various correlates of inequality (related, for example, to citizenship, class, ethnicity, religion) are crucial to understanding the role of inequality in generating and sustaining conflict. Macro models will also fail to capture the multitude of small, local and violent conflicts that may simmer for long periods and do much damage to both national economies and local livelihoods.

According to Keen (2000: 31),

> Civil conflicts have typically seen the emergence of groups (often ethnic groups) who can safely and, in a sense, legitimately be subjected to extreme exploitation, violence, and famine. Some groups fall below the law, and some are elevated above it. This process may take place in peacetime as well as wartime, and it can precipitate, as well as shape, outright conflict.

Keen gives Sudan, Sierra Leone, and Ethiopia-Eritrea as examples. Thus, sometimes, groups resort to violence in order to prevent exploitation or extortion and to protect what they believe already to be theirs. The capacity of continued, impending or perceived exploitation to generate emotions and responses that go far beyond what rational calculation would dictate seems undeniable. The portrayal of such conflicts as only greed-motivated or only grievance-motivated is unproductive. As Keen (2000: 32) notes, the point is to understand how economic incentives and grievances interact: '...how it is that particular groups can come to fall at least partially outside the physical and economic protection of the state ... how greed generates grievances and rebellion, legitimising further greed.' In particular, those in power may seek to neutralise and discredit actual and potential opposition by labelling unarmed civilians as rebels, by trying to deflect the discontent of one group onto another, by declaring states of emergency, and by prolonging the armed conflict to the detriment of liberties and elections. At another level, these observations are also relevant to Scott's (1998) analysis of the manner in which states marginalise pastoral and nomadic populations.

A further point is that the term 'greed' cannot be applied generally to violent actions undertaken for the purpose of material gain. The difference between 'grievance' and 'predation' or 'greed' rests in part on the tenuous distinction between protecting legitimate claims and advancing illegitimate ones. That is, even though violence that is motivated by a desire to protect existing rights and freedoms – fighting against dispossession or exploitation – is commonly seen as grievance-motivated (through the influence of real or perceived injustices), such violence is motivated in part also by material considerations. And the distinction between legitimate and illegitimate claims is particularly fuzzy in situations of legal pluralism and overlapping rights, as the chapters in this volume illustrate. In a generous mood, we would describe as mere simplifications the view of inequality as universally irrelevant and the portrayal of rebels as always calculating predators; yet even when material considerations dominate motivations on both sides of a conflict, the term greed is often misleading.

Resource scarcity, inequality and conflict in northern Kenya

If ethnicity itself explains little about conflict let us return to scarcity and examine the chapter by Witsenburg and Roba in this volume because it specifically examines the role of resource scarcity in generating conflict. The context in which they examine the proposition that increased scarcity leads to increased conflict is violent fights over access to water in Northern Kenya. Such skirmishes have a long history in the area, and the data uncovered by Witsenburg and Roba allow them to investigate scarcity-conflict on two levels: first, the frequency of incidents and deaths in relation to *fluctuations* in scarcity – that is, rainfall variability through time; second, conflict frequency in relation to long-term *increases* in scarcity caused by population growth.

With respect to short-term fluctuations, these are recurrent, and one would think that the experience gained through repetition would tend to be resolved over time through institutional adaptations and the evolution of coping mechanisms. The finding of the authors that drought does not cause an increase in conflicts does therefore not seem so surprising. The fact that indeed the opposite seems to be true does, however, bear some emphasis. One of the issues highlighted by this chapter is the way in which scarcity of resources – in this case water – may indeed alter also the conditions under which battles are fought. The ambushes used in Northern Kenya for cattle raids and attacks on enemies demand lush vegetation not found during periods of drought. The issue of long-term increases in scarcity is, however, more complex than that of fluctuations. In Northern Kenya, such change is brought about by population growth rather than by resource destruction or 'discrimination'. Change is cumulative rather than oscillatory and each tightening of the screw leads to a new situation where previous experience may be of more limited relevance, particularly if one – as does the environmental security literature – applies the notion of critical thresholds. The analysis of long-term effects is complicated by the problem of whether conflict is simply one of many forms of human interaction that will increase in proportion to the overall volume of such interaction. If it is, then conflicts will multiply with population growth even if the world and its resources somehow were to expand at the same relative pace – that is, even with no attendant increases in scarcity. Witsenburg and Roba find that violent deaths do not increase through time as population increases, while violent incidents *per capita* decrease with increasing population.

A further point highlighted in the chapter by Witsenburg and Roba is that the organisation and conduct of violent conflict represents a collective action problem. With the exceptions of individual conflict and highly militarised conflict, where incentives are completely or partly internalised, engaging in violence most often involves the voluntary pursuit of a common cause at the risk of individual injury or death. So while avoiding or ending conflict poses collective action problems between opposing groups, initiating or sustaining conflict implies coordination problems within groups. The manner in which communities overcome this collective action problem – through overt sanctions or otherwise – may vary greatly, but issues of citizenship and identity will often be of crucial importance. Moreover, the manner in which scarcity affects collective action mechanisms and associated individual incentives to take part in violence may be highly complex. Environmental stress may reduce the likelihood of peaceful survival while simultaneously increasing the collective stakes over which battles are fought, thereby increasing individual incentives to engage. On the other hand, poor households will under such conditions have less labour and energy to spare for violent activities, and the very mechanisms that may help to coordinate community interaction during times of relative abundance may break down. The conclusions reached by Witsenburg and Roba with respect to these issues might be tentative and conjectural, but point to a much under-researched aspect of mid-level violent conflict.

A focus on 'discrimination' or 'inequality' as a source of scarcity offers a different point of departure for investigation of conflict than does general population growth. The notion of discrimination is essential to several chapters in this volume. While the notion that population-driven scarcity might generate organic solutions be they technical or institutional, it is more difficult to envisage these in the context of inequality-based scarcity increases. A problem with analysing conflict in light of scarcity caused by discrimination, however, can be posed as a question: is conflict caused by the associated scarcity or by discrimination itself? Moreover, the specification of 'discrimination' or 'discrimination-generated scarcity' as underlying causes of conflict overlooks the political and social processes and realities that caused or allowed discrimination in the first place (Peluso and Watts 2001, Hauge 2003). The construction of land scarcity through colonial or racial polices mark Andrew, Derman and Hellum, and Wisborg's chapters this volume. The constriction of pastoralists' space forms the context for Maganga, Odgaard and Sjaastad's chapter on the Maasai.

Issues in access to land

Given both the diversity and complexity of the land-identity nexus we find that the chapters in this volume suggest that the links are highly varied. They suggest that global processes like the market, strategies for development, human rights will be refracted and reshaped by local and national contexts. In the broader trends of increasing competition over land on the one hand and increasing urbanisation on the other, we can continue to look for highly uneven and often contradictory processes whereby progressive, human-rights oriented South Africa has proposed to give chiefs primary control over lands in the former homelands. This would appear to perpetuate the dual tenurial system in South Africa while ignoring competing and contradictory proposals for how to manage land (Cousins and Claassens 2003). In general, we find a shift away from emphasising the rural as a way of life toward seeing the land in more commercial terms, and the location of investment, commodity production, and more specialized producers. This can best be summed up in the phrase 'farming is a business'.

At the beginning of the twenty-first century, the state's role in land tenure and management seems both enhanced and reduced. There are an increasing set of conditions from the Bretton-Woods institutions and UN human rights treaties and conventions that are now part of the broader international environment in which African nations rewrite or implement land laws. Yet, in many local contexts, the reach of the state is often insufficient to guarantee that the laws will indeed be followed. The issues of the state certainly have been well discussed and analysed in the literature. Here we would only point out that state intentions and institutions are inextricably part of struggles over land in either the strong presence of the state, its biases or in its absence. Without strong action by the state, the growth of a market economy may lead to an increasing loss of control over land for women and for longstanding populations (Hagberg, Amanor, Gausset, Maganga, et al. this volume). With respect to women, Andrew finds that the South African government has yet to give women the priority that they deserve, whilst in Zimbabwe, Derman and Hellum find that in the context of lawlessness and violence, women are increasingly disadvantaged in the land reform programme which potentially could have provided a new set of opportunities for them. The role of migrant farmers as described by Toulmin suggests that the labour shortages are partly resolved this way, which in turn reduces the labour burden on women. Despite earlier assumptions about the substitution of national for other identities in African nation-states, this has not occurred at the pace or scale predicted. In the increasing competition for land, multiple forms of identity are called upon to gain access.

How to secure access to land varies greatly from reversals of the massive and historic dispossession carried out by white South Africans from black South Africans, to protecting relatively small groups (minorities) from dispossession (Cameroon, Burkina Faso, Kenya). Hagberg convincingly argues that hunters' associations provide a mechanism to block marginalisation and victimisation. The hunters' association known as Benkadi has been 'reinvented' as a defensive group formed to block Fulbe expansion or appropriation of Senufo lands rather than a continuation of an older cultural institution. In the case presented by Larsen, women hide their animals in the brothers' herds rather than submit them to their husband's authority in order to protect their assets. One could argue that women try to maintain assets to protect them from marginalisation and poverty. Amanor describes how timber-logging companies use the power of the state to gain access to forests while 'customary authorities' receive a share of the royalties. Amanor rightly comments that customary authority is invoked to justify modern forest exploitation that raises far more general and profound questions about how to understand 'new' customary authorities. The place, importance and roles of 'customary authorities' has become an Africa-wide issue. Ruling parties in South Africa, Zimbabwe, Namibia, Ghana and others when in search of political support by chiefs typically offer them increased authority over land ownership or land guardianship. This, in the perspective of Mamdani (1996), demonstrates how rural peoples remain as subjects, very different from urban populations who are no longer subject to chiefs. Customary authorities in both colonial and independent Africa represent some interests (for example, men, royal lineage or ruling party) and not others (former slaves, women, minorities or the landless). They tend to become dependent in varied ways upon national governments and ruling parties. They, like the people over whom they continue to rule, have changed profoundly.

Making claims for land: land conflicts & the complexities of law

Land conflicts occur at all levels – from between individuals and families to international ones. Whether or not there is directionality toward greater land concentration and private holdings in these conflicts remains, for Berry (1993 and 2002), an open question. Peters (2004) on the other hand contends that contemporary land struggles call into question the image of Africa as a place of relatively open, negotiable and adaptive systems of land-holding and land use. Rather, she goes on to suggest that land reveals processes of exclusion, deepening social divisions and class formation. Falk Moore (1999) and Berry (1997) observe that while land rights are embedded in social relations and negotiable not all actors are equally successful when claiming rights. As expressed by Toulmin (this volume):

> So land rights in practice are all about negotiation between different peoples, drawing on whatever resources and bargaining power are at their disposal. Rights are not formally laid down, but in flux, with people engaged in what some describe as 'institutional shopping'. (p. 167)

Land rights are not just present, to be used at any point. Rather access to land depends upon maintaining and reinforcing relationships and claims. How, how often, with whom this is done, and with what type of outcome for the involved parties depends upon context and access to power for the actors involved in the negotiation processes. Exclusion may be the result for some. As referred to above, women's land rights are, for example, generally much less secure than men's, and women are therefore more likely to lose out in negotiation processes. A 'rights-based approach' – that is, the establishment of clearly specified and universal rights and accountable political and legal processes – is claimed by some, especially donors and NGOs, as a possible way of ensuring more fair and equal access to resources for all groups. Bina Agarwal (2003a & b), L. Muthoni Wanyeki (2003) (and the contributors to *Women and Land in Africa*[26]) as well as many other scholars and activists are moving towards a rights-based approach to land access. Cecile Jackson (2003) questions whether or not a rights-based approach will assist women in gaining greater access and rights to land. Her argument rests on the diversity and complexity of ways currently used by women to access land. Land, in her view, may not be of the importance that others have suggested. She urges an ethnographic approach to explore the complex gender dimensions of families, households, and access to land which could lead to more appropriate, locally based, fine-tuned strategies for gender equality. A second line of critique of rights-based approaches can be found in the recent studies by the SLSA team (2003). They stress that vulnerable groups like women and poor people do not have access to the political and legal processes presupposed by 'a rights-based approach'. In addition, the authors warn that 'right-based approaches' often draw heavy inspiration from universalist discourses that see individuals as the bearers of rights and overlook the fact that in Africa rights are often derived from collective identities based on affiliations with, for example, the community, ethnic group or nation.

There have been various attempts to change land rights dramatically through titling and the creation of individual, private ownership on the assumption that this will constitute an important legally recognised asset that can be used, for example, as collateral for obtaining loans to improve production. Formalisation of land rights through titling and more generally creating recognised capital for the poor has been gaining credence in some development circles. There is a long and unsuccessful history of attempting to formalise land ownership in Africa. Once again, it seems that the push comes primarily not from the poor or from

[26] All the authors in this volume (Munyoni, ed. 2003) argue for the use of different international human rights instruments for the realisation of women's rights to land in sub-Saharan Africa.

landowners but from international donors and national governments seeking to simplify and commodify land.[27]

Whose land, whose law?

The history of land in Africa reflects the multiple and often contradictory aims of colonial authorities: creating a class of independent and free-holding native farmers, maintaining large areas under what was regarded as traditional land tenure, forcing the indigenous population to seek employment in urban centres, and holding land in trust for an expected influx of European settlers. A distinction in colonial Africa rests between those colonies where there were relatively large numbers of Europeans, termed settler colonies (Kenya, Namibia, South Africa and Zimbabwe), and those where there was much less land alienation from the African populations. In settler colonies, racialised systems of property rights (and law in general) were contrived whereby non-Africans owned land as private property, in contradistinction to Africans who held land rights as members of groups, communities or tribes usually under the leadership of a colonially recognised chief. In the rest of colonial Africa where there was no large European immigration, land was kept more or less in 'customary' fashion but under the colonial state. In former settler states a dual property regime was established with contractual relations and private ownership in the European areas and customary tenure[28] and leadership in the communal areas. In the non-settler colonies, land was often placed in the hands of chiefly authorities and where there were no chiefs, they were created. There were also other property relations with respect to pastoralists or livestock herders. Pastoralists require access to relatively large areas of land and tend to shift their herds according to seasons, ecology and weather conditions. In general, both colonial and independent states have sought to sedentarise pastoralists (see Larsen this volume). Even where livestock herders have been partially sedentarised their integrated systems require more land than do farmers. However, the land use patterns adopted by pastoralists – and by other non-farming groups including foragers who are attempting to keep their lands (in Namibia, Rwanda, Botswana, Congo, Tanzania among others) – make it very difficult for these groups to have land claims recognised and to sustain whatever land rights they may have been able to obtain with numerous conflicts as a result.[29] In this volume, conflicts between Fulbe mixed farmers and Kwanja and Benkadi (Gausset and Hagberg) demonstrate how volatile they can be.

Regulation of rights to land in Africa takes place within the context of multiple normative orders, which compose the plural legal situations existing in most African countries. With increasing pressure on land resources, rights become an increasingly complex issue to analyse and different analytical approaches are being adopted in the study of them.

Most African rural populations continue to hold their land through the rules and processes of local tenure, but, as mentioned above, in the context of legal

[27] For an excellent summary of the debate and its implications for women see Ikdahl, Hellum, Kaarhus and Benjaminsen (2005).

[28] Perhaps best understood as statutory customary law rather than the range of ways by which various African groups resolved conflicts.

[29] A number of studies from various parts of Africa make this point. See for example IWGIA 1998 and 2001, Tenga and Kakoti (1993), Odgaard (2003b).

pluralism. What has been termed 'customary tenure' rules and norms are not stable or fixed but flexible. And, perhaps most importantly for this volume, 'customary tenure' is a label which includes multiple and diverse forms of land tenure. The nature of local norms and practice vis-à-vis formal legislation and policies is a much-debated issue. Amanor (this volume) criticises approaches, which, he argues, look at 'customary' rights in property as being 'fluid and ephemeral, continually reaffirming social alignments in society and the negotiation between different interests'. Amanor sees customary land relations as rooted in structural power relations and colonial domination, and argues that customary forms of tenure are neither inherently more flexible, egalitarian or dynamic than formal ones. Toulmin comments that the customary is not so much characterized by stability and inflexibility but by representing the interplay of forces between different social groups, generating a shifting set of negotiating positions. Like Peters (2004), Toulmin's work finds that the more powerful groups are winning out and that those people and groups who have secondary rights to land are becoming less secure. She proposes making secondary land rights more secure through a mix of formal and customary processes. The balance should depend upon local structures and contexts. In parallel fashion Andrew suggests that the new Communal Land Rights Act in South Africa will not protect or enhance women's land rights. The World Bank now seems to be of several minds with respect to customary and individual land tenure. While John Bruce and Shem Migot-Adholla (1993) have long been sympathetic to flexibility because individual holdings and titling do not necessarily improve agricultural productivity, they still think that in the long run there will be a move toward individual ownership (Platteau 1996).

It remains debatable whether there is an inevitable and inexorable movement toward private property rights in the westernised meaning of the term, although it is hard to deny that there is a trend that land rights are becoming more and more individualised. Colonialism tended to strengthen chiefly control over land as colonialists sought to keep expenses down on the one hand, and to use chiefs to ensure their authority on the other. While not true everywhere, it was true in Burkina Faso, Ghana, South Africa and Zimbabwe (this volume). Local land tenure could be used to help block the commodification of land and production. Ideologically it was very flexible. It was used to support the notion that African 'traditional cultures' were being protected, or, in the cases of Zimbabwe and South Africa, to suppress African peasant production to prevent them from competing against European settlers. Since the colonial period, there have been experiments in abolishing chieftainship or reducing chief's authority. In most nations, chiefs have to share control of land with representatives from other parts of the political and economic power elites.[30] In either event, the question of the relationship between chiefs, chiefly authority and land remains a thorny and complex issue in most countries where the chiefs are still a recognized authority in relation to land rights. It has become, for example, a highly contentious issue with the new Communal Land Tenure Act recently passed by the South African Parliament. This act, which returns land allocations to chiefs, is being taken to the Constitutional Court by a wide range of civic and women's groups (Cousins 2003; Cousins and Claassens 2003). In Zimbabwe, chiefs have been made part

[30] A situation referred to by Toulmin (this volume). See also, for example, Odgaard (2003a and 2003b).

of the 'fast track' land reform programmes acting more as representatives of government and the ruling party than their populations.

Land tenure for development?

On the surface it would appear that formal law, law existing through the formal legislative apparatus of the state would be easier to deal with than local norms and practices. However, states are quite different from each other in their capacities to develop policies to implement legislation and in how they enforce laws. Derman and Hellum report how Zimbabwe's laws have been deliberately altered to change the bases of land rights. Andrew reports on the gaps between law, policy and realities on the ground for women. Gausset views the Cameroonian state as unwilling or unable to protect Kwanja's land claims while Amanor analyses how the Ghanaian state can be absent when customary authorities make claims upon land and trees. Toulmin documents why there needs to be land rights for late-comers, or migrants, while in many instances there are no land rights for women or long-term residents. While South African land reform rests on three legs – land restitution, land redistribution and security of tenure, there has been no national bill to address the achievement of tenure security. What has been addressed and discussed by Andrew is the Communal Land Rights Bill rather than what had encompassed all land – the Draft Land Rights Bill which has been shelved since 2000. This draft bill attempted to address merging the collective dimensions of social life which are consistent with personal freedom (McAuslan 2000: 91), in short to move South African law forward to genuinely merge multiple traditions rather than continuing to privilege 'European' land law.

Increasingly issues of land tenure have become a central focus for efforts to assist different African nations out of poverty. It is quite surprising that tenure plays such a small role in NEPAD's Comprehensive Africa Agriculture Development Programme (2003), their vision for development through agriculture on behalf of the African Union. Perhaps tenure is too contentious to be included in this document which emphasises markets, technology, water, irrigation and research. Nonetheless, difficult issues include the relative efficiency of large-scale commercial farming versus smallholder agriculture, the degree to which land markets should be promoted and nurtured, and the security of tenure provided by centralised as opposed to various local systems of authority. How to use land most productively, as an engine for growth, dominated discussion during the 1970s and 1980s.[31] The World Bank through its most recent discussion of land policies attempts to redress its own historical biases by emphasising how important land assets are to poor people. Thus, the tenure systems that underlie land need to be carefully adjusted to social, economic and political circumstances. The Bank seems to have moved away from individual title and freehold as the only paths toward increasing investment and producing economic growth. Nonetheless, the Bank argues for the centrality of markets: markets for credit, for collateral, for renting land and for agricultural inputs and outputs. The mix between 'customary ownership', market alternatives and land

[31] The most influential document was *Accelerated Development in Sub-Saharan Africa*, World Bank, Washington, DC (1981). This was followed by a greater emphasis upon sustainability and worries about the environment but still an emphasis upon export agriculture in *Sub-Saharan Africa from Crisis to Sustainable Growth* (World Bank 1990).

reform becomes very complicated especially given the scale of agricultural subsidies in Europe and the US.

We suggest that underlying most issues should be a sense of justice or a normative concern. There should be a close and direct relationship between those who work the land and those who benefit from that work. From a development perspective, the World Bank among many others seeks to increase the value of benefit streams and to maintain a close relationship between those who own and manage the resource. Secure tenure, in most commentators' perspective, remains central to maintaining production. How land rights and/or access is negotiated, controlled or owned is central to most of the authors in this book. The papers are testimony, once again, to the complexities on the ground, and how conflicting interests can be quite difficult to solve. They also point to the difficulties involved in changing land tenure systems (Amanor, Andrew, Derman and Hellum, Maganga et al., Wisborg, this volume). Whether or not any of these systems will be able to adapt in a fair and equitable manner to growing land scarcity[32] where it is present, remains highly problematic.

Lastly, states and donors are always present in the abstract but not necessarily on the ground. Donors were highly influential in trying to create a solution to drought for the Hawawir in Sudan while donors totally lost out in trying to create a viable agrarian reform for Zimbabwe. The series of problems including poverty, violent conflict, deforestation, soil erosion, overgrazing, lack of productivity per unit of labour and/or land sustains the continuing set of interventions to change positively how Africans make a living from the land. The debates have not been resolved and we believe this book adds to the understanding of the complexity that continues to create and shape a modern, commercial agrarian order (Berry 2002: 648). The multiple and complex claims to land access in contemporary Africa has led to significant debates about the politics of rights and power. Who should have authority over access to land and how should that authority be exercised? How will and should the transition from agrarian based economies take place? Will occupational and class identities supplant ones rooted in ethnicity? Can women have equal access to land as men? Africa's rich history, complex social forms, rapid adjustment to changing circumstances gives rise to some optimism despite multiple and well-known problems.

Concluding comments

The writings in this volume illustrate the wide range of conflicts linked to land and natural resources that are found across the African continent. These conflicts differ not only with respect to their intensity and the means by which they are fought but also with respect to the complex and interacting set of motivations that trigger and sustain them. Resource scarcity, different aspects of identity, and land tenure and property rights are critical issues in most of these conflicts. The exact role played by each is, however, highly variable.

A simple hypothesis that emerges is that when multiple forms of inequality coincide, and when these in turn are aligned with divisions along lines of identity, then the probability of violent conflict increases (Hauge 2003). Identity

[32] In many nations faced with high prevalency rates of HIV/Aids labour scarcity has become more important than land scarcity, a return to Africa's classic situation.

need not be the cause of inequality for a combustible mix to emerge; congruence caused by random historical factors may be just as volatile (see e.g. Cramer's (2003) example from Rwanda). A further point that deserves attention, however, is the manner in which tense and volatile situations provide opportunities for manipulation of identities and the wilful pursuit of increased alignment of these and various forms of inequality. Inequality of land holdings, for example, appears as a critical issue in many African conflicts but in the case where the land issue was most touted by the main protagonist and received the greatest media attention, land was little more than a tool conveniently employed in the pursuit of entirely different agendas (see the chapter from Zimbabwe by Derman and Hellum).

Two major points emerge from this volume and our analysis of the literature: First, while much effort has been put into the construction of more or less universalistic theories on the generation of high-level violent conflict with the aid of macro-level empirical tests, these theories appear to be of only limited use when attempting to understand low- and intermediate-level conflicts in Africa. Second, understanding conflict of any type and at all levels demands that attention be given to underlying social and political relations in their specific contexts; resorting to scarcity, ethnicity, greed or income inequality as catch-all explanatory factors obscures rather than clarifies the issues. We find that increasing resource or land scarcity undoubtedly can be seen as either an underlying or contributing factor in many conflicts. Identity is then often used as a symbol or a representation to solidify or shift the fault lines between parties to the conflict. The opposite may, however, just as well be true, with issues of resource scarcity and ownership primarily being used to justify violent struggles and claims to authority and legitimacy. The power to determine access and ownership of resources represents a more fundamental and deep-rooted motive for conflict than the simple distribution of the resources themselves. Land, identity and citizenship are concepts that are so thoroughly interwoven in many African cultures that it becomes impossible to talk of one in isolation from the others. Rigorous study of the isolated effects of a single factor on conflict becomes impossible when interlinkages make nonsense of the assumption that 'all other things remain equal'. This conclusion poses major theoretical and policy issues.

The complex and changing realities of conflicts over land and natural resources in Africa lend themselves to careful empirical investigation rather than to assertions of universal causal pathways and the primacy of a single explanatory factor over others. This has implications also for policy. There is no single menu of instruments that policy makers and bureaucrats routinely can go through in order to identify possible solutions to these conflicts. Indeed, African governments have frequently been seen to contribute to the escalation rather than the avoidance or resolution of conflicts. A weak presence in rural and remote areas is one aspect of this. More importantly, governments frequently give the appearance of taking sides in conflicts, either because of wider objectives (e.g. a move towards more sedentary land use or more privately owned land) or because one of the parties to the conflict has managed to populate the offices in which decisions germane to the trajectory of the conflict are taken.

The first and most important policy move for the state in many African countries is therefore to ensure and fortify its role as a disinterested third party across the range of its involvement, from local to central levels and from law enforcement to environmental and institutional policy. How and if African governments can shift from a unitary perspective on, for example, land tenure systems, to accept and work with the ones existent and functioning well, remains to be seen.

This volume examines primarily the African side of things. We are, with all the authors, cognisant of how land and agricultural issues in Africa, have been shaped and reshaped in the context of colonial and post-colonial relations with Europe and the US. Without profound changes in existing trade patterns, agricultural subsidies and demands for debt payments, there will be little positive change in Africa. There are limits to what fragile, agriculturally based economies can do without a more favourable international climate. It is in this arena as well that attempts to sort out the often difficult questions of conflict, identity, citizenship, historical claims, conflicting land uses, overlapping jurisdictions and sustainable resource management can bear fruit.

Bibliography

Agarwal, B. 2003a. 'Gender and Land Rights Revisited: Exploring New Prospects via the State, Family and Market.' *Journal of Agrarian Change*, Vol. 3: 184–224.

______. 2003b. 'Women's Land Rights and the Trap of Neo-Conservatism: A Response to Jackson.' *Journal of Agrarian Change*, Vol. 3: 571–85.'

Ake, C. 1996. *Democracy and Development in Africa*. Washington, DC: The Brookings Institution.

Baechler, G. 1998. 'Why Environmental Transformation Causes Violence: A Synthesis.' *Environmental Change and Security Project Report*, Issue 4, Spring.

Banks, M. 1996. *Ethnicity: Anthropological Constructions*. London and New York: Routledge.

Barbier, E. and T. Homer-Dixon. 1996. *Resource Scarcity, Institutional Adaptation, and Technical Innovation*. Toronto: The Project on Environment, Population and Scarcity.

Barzel, Y. 1989. *Economic Analysis of Property Rights*. Cambridge: Cambridge University Press.

Bates, R. H. 1998. 'Comment on "Structure and Strategy in Ethnic Conflict: A Few Steps Toward Synthesis,"' by Donald Horowitz, B. Pleskovic and J. E. Stiglitz (eds), *Annual World Bank Conference on Development Economics*. Washington, DC: The World Bank.

Bayart, J-P. 1993. *The State in Africa: The Politics of the Belly*. London: Longman.

Bayart, J-F., S. Ellis and B. Hibou. 1999. *The Criminalization of the State in Africa*. Oxford: James Currey.

Benjaminsen, T. A. and C. Lund (eds). 2003. *Securing Land Rights in Africa*. London: Frank Cass.

Berry, S. 1993. *No Condition is Permanent: The Social Dynamics of Agrarian Change in Sub-Saharan Africa*. Madison: University of Wisconsin Press.

______. 2002. 'Debating the Land Question in Africa.' *Comparative Studies in Society and History*, Vol. 44: 638–68.

Bolaffi, G., R. Bracelenti, P. Braham and S. Gindro. 2003. *Dictionary of Race, Ethnicity and Culture*. London and Thousand Oaks, CA: Sage Publications.

Boserup, E. 1965. *The Conditions of Agricultural Growth: The Economics of Agrarian Change under Population Pressure*. London: Allen and Unwin.

Boswell, T. and W. J. Dixon. 1990. 'Dependency and Rebellion: A Cross-National Analysis.' *American Sociological Review*, Vol. 55: 540–59.

Braathen, E., Bøås, M. and G. Sæther. 2000. 'Introduction: Ethnicity Kills? Social Struggles for Power, Resources and Identities in the Neopatrimonial State.' In E. Braathen, M. Bøås & G. Sæther (eds), *Ethnicity kills? The Politics of War, Peace and Ethnicity in Sub-Saharan Africa*, Macmillan Press.

Bratton, M., R. Mattes and E. Gyimah-Boadi 2005. *Public Opinion, Democracy and Market Reform in Africa*. Cambridge: Cambridge University Press

Bruce, J. W. and S. E. Migot-Adholla (eds). 1993. *Searching for Land Tenure Security in Africa*, Dubuque, Iowa: Kendall Hunt.

Campbell, D. 2002. Unpublished lecture and presentation on Land Scarcity and Conflict in Rwanda. Michigan State University.

Chabal, P. 1992. *Power in Africa*. London: Macmillan, 2nd Edition.

Chabal, P. and J-P Daloz. 1999. *Africa Works: Disorder as Political Instrument*. Oxford: James Currey.

Chege, M. 1998. Comment on 'Structure and Strategy in Ethnic Conflict: A Few Steps Toward Synthesis,' by Donald Horowitz. B. Pleskovic and J. E. Stiglitz (eds), *Annual World Bank Conference on Development Economics*, Washington, DC: The World Bank.

Choucri, N. and R. North. 1975. *Nations in Conflict*. San Francisco: Freeman.

Collier, P. 1998. 'The Political Economy of Ethnicity.' In B. Pleskovic and J. E. Stiglitz (eds), *Annual World Bank Conference on Development Economics*, Washington, DC: The World Bank.

______. 2000a. 'Doing Well out of War.' In M. Berdal and D. M. Malone (eds) *Greed and Grievance: Economic Agendas in Civil Wars*. Boulder, CO: Lynne Rienner Publishers.

______. 2000b. 'Rebellion as a Quasi-Criminal Activity.' *Journal of Conflict Resolution*, Vol. 44, 839–53.

Collier, P. and A. Hoeffler. 1998. 'On Economic Causes of Civil War.' *Oxford Economic Papers*, Vol. 50, 563–73.

______. 2002. 'Greed and Grievance in Civil Wars.' *Working Paper Series 2002–01*. Oxford: Centre for the Study of African Economies.

Cousins, B. 2003. 'The Zimbabwe Crisis in its Wider Context: The Politics of Land, Democracy and Development in Southern Africa.' In A. Hammar, B. Raftopoulos and S. Jensen (eds) *Zimbabwe's Unfinished Business: Rethinking Land, State and Nation in the Context of Crisis*. Harare: Weaver Press.

Cousins, B. and A. Claassens. 2003. 'Communal Land Tenure in South Africa: Livelihoods, Rights, Institutions.' *Development Update*, Vol. 4.

Cramer, C. 2003. 'Does Inequality Cause Conflict?' *Journal of International Development*, Vol. 15, 397–412.

Davies, J. C. 1972. 'Toward a Theory of Revolution.' In I. K. Feierabend, R. L. Feierabend and T. R. Gurr (eds) *Anger, Violence and Politics*. Englewood Cliffs, NJ: Prentice Hall.

de Soysa, I. 'The Resource Curse: Are Civil Wars Driven by Rapacity or Paucity?' In M. Berdal and D. M. Malone (eds), *Greed and Grievance: Economic Agendas in Civil Wars*, Boulder, CO: Lynne Rienner Publishers.

Demsetz, H. 1967. 'Toward a Theory of Property Rights.' *American Economic Review*, Vol. 57: 347–59.

Deudney, D. 1999. 'Environmental Security: A Critique.' In D. H. Deudney and R. A. Matthews (eds), *Contested Grounds: Security and Conflict in the New Environmental Politics*. Albany: SUNY Press.

Easterly, W. 2001. 'Can Institutions Resolve Ethnic Conflict?' *Economic Development and Cultural Change*, Vol. 49: 687–706.

Easterly, W. and R. Levine. 1997. 'Africa's Growth Tragedy: Politics and Ethnic Division.' *Quarterly Journal of Economics*, Vol. 112: 1203–50.

Ellingsen, T. 2000. 'Colorful Community or Ethnic Witches Brew? Multiethnicity and Domestic Conflict During and After the Cold War.' *Journal of Conflict Resolution*, Vol. 44: 228–49.

Englert, B. 2003. 'From a Gender Perspective: Notions of Land Tenure Security in the Uluguru Mountains, Tanzania.' *Journal für Entwicklungspolitik (Austrian Journal of Development Studies)*, Vol. 19(1): 75–90.

Fearon, J. and D. Laitin. 2003. 'Ethnicity, Insurgency, and Civil War.' *American Political Science Review*, Vol. 97: 75–90.

Forrester, J. W. 1971. *World Dynamics*. Cambridge, MA: Wright-Allen Press.

Gleditsch, N. P. 1998. 'Armed Conflict and the Environment: A Critique of the Literature.' *Journal of Peace Research*, Vol. 35: 381–400.

Gurr, T. R. 1970. *Why Men Rebel*. Princeton, NJ: Princeton University Press.

Hall, R. 2004. 'Land and Agrarian Reform in South Africa: A Status Report 2004.' Bellville, South Africa: Programme of Land and Agrarian Studies Research Report No. 20.

Hauge, W. 2003. 'Causes and Dynamics of Conflict Escalation: The Role of Economic Development and Environmental Change. A Comparative Study of Bangladesh, Guatemala, Haiti, Senegal and Tunisia.' Unpublished PhD dissertation. Oslo: University of Oslo, Faculty of Social Sciences.

Hauge W. and T. Ellingsen. 1998. 'Beyond Environmental Scarcity: Causal Pathways to Conflict.' *Journal of Peace Research*, Vol. 35: 299–317.

Hellum, A. and B. Derman. 2004. 'Land Reform and Human Rights in Contemporary Zimbabwe: Balancing Individual and Social Justice through an Integrated Human Rights Framework.' *World Development* 32(10): 1785–1805.

Herbst, J. I. 2000. *States and Power in Africa: Comparative Lessons in Authority and Control*. Princeton: Princeton University Press.

Homer-Dixon, T. F. 1991. 'On the Threshold: Environmental Changes as Causes of Acute Conflict.' *International Security*, Vol. 16: 76–116.

______. 1994. 'Environmental Scarcities and Violent Conflict: Evidence from Cases.' *International Security*, Vol. 19: 1–40.

______. 1995. 'The Ingenuity Gap: Can Poor Countries Adapt to Resource Scarcity?' *Population and Development Review*, Vol. 21: 587–612.

Horowitz, D. L. 1985. *Ethnic Groups in Conflict*. Berkeley: University of California Press.

______. 1998. 'Structure and Strategy in Ethnic Conflict: A Few Steps Toward Synthesis.' In B. Pleskovic and J. E. Stiglitz (eds) *Annual World Bank Conference on Development Economics*, Washington, DC: The World Bank.

Ikdahl, I. A. Hellum, R. Kaarhus and T.A. Benjaminsen. 2005. *Human rights, Formalisation and Women's Land Rights in Southern and Eastern Africa*. Aas, Norway: NORAD Consultancy Report.

Iliffe, J. 1987. *The African Poor: A History*. Cambridge: Cambridge University Press.

IWGIA.1998. *The Indigenous World 1997–98*, Copenhagen.

______. 2001. *The Indigenous World 2000–2001*, Copenhagen.

Jackson, C. 2003. 'Gender Analysis of Land: Beyond Land Rights for Women?' *Journal of Agrarian Change*, Vol. 3 (1–2): 453–80.

Joseph, R. 1997. 'Democratisation in Africa after 1989: Comparative and Theoretical Issues.' *Comparative Politics* 29 (3): 363–82.

Juul, K. and C. Lund (eds). 2002. *Negotiating property in Africa*. Portsmouth, NH: Heinemann.

Kaplan, R. 1994. 'The Coming Anarchy: How Scarcity, Crime, Overpopulation, Tribalism and Disease are Rapidly Destroying the Social Fabric of our Planet.' *Atlantic Monthly*, Vol. 273: 44–76.

Kaimowitz, D. 2002. 'Resources, Abundance, and Competition in the Bosawas Biosphere Reserve, Nicaragua.' In Matthew, R., Halle, M. and J. Switzer (eds) *Conserving the Peace: Resources, Livelihoods, and Security*. Winnipeg: International Institute for Sustainable Development.

______. 2004. 'Forests and War, Forests and Peace.' In *State of the World's Forests 2050*, Rome: Food and Agricultural Organisation of the United Nations.

Keen, D. 2000. 'Incentives and Disincentives for Violence.' In M. Berdal and D. M. Malone (eds) *Greed and Grievance: Economic Agendas in Civil Wars*, Boulder, CO: Lynne Rienner Publishers.

Lavigne Delville, P. 1999. 'Harmonising Formal Law and Customary Land Rights in French Speaking West Africa.' International Institute for Environment and Development (IIED) *Drylands Issue Paper* E86.

Levy, M A. 1995. 'Is the Environment a National Security Issue?' *International Security*, Vol. 20: 35–62.

Lipsey, R.G., Steiner, P.O., Purvis, D.D. and P.N. Courant. 1990. *Economics*. New York: Harper and Row.

Livula-Ithana, P. (2001). 'Land tenure in Africa: From Colonialism to Modern Tenure Systems.' Paper presented at the National Land Tenure Conference, Durban, South Africa, 27–30 November 2001, Department of Land Affairs, Pretoria.

Mamdani, M. 1996. *Citizen and Subject: Contemporary Africa and the Legacy of Late Colonialism*, Princeton, NJ: Princeton University Press and Oxford: James Currey.

______. 2002. *When Victims become Killers: Colonialism, Nativism and the Genocide in Rwanda*, Princeton, NJ: Princeton University Press.

Manji, A. 2000. 'Her Name is Kamundage: Rethinking Women and Property among the Haya of Tanzania.' *Africa*, Vol. 70: 482–500.

Marx, K. 1848 [1977]. *Capital*, Moscow: Progress Publishers.

Meadows, D. H., Meadows, D. L., Randers, J. and W. W. Behrens. 1972. *The Limits to Growth*. New York: Universe Books.

McAuslan, P. 2000. 'Only the Name of the Country Changes: The Diaspora of "European" Land Law in Commonwealth Africa.' In Toulmin, C. and J. Quan (eds) *Evolving Land Rights, Policy and Tenure in Africa*. London: International Institute for Environment and Development.

Mkandawire, R. and C. Soludo. 1999. *Our Continent, Our Future: African Perspectives on Structural Adjustment*. Trenton, NJ: Africa World Press.

Montani, G. 1987. 'Scarcity.' In J. Eatweel, R. H. I. Palgrave, M. Milgate and P. Newman (eds) *The New Palgrave: A Dictionary of Economics*, London: MacMillan.

Moore, S. Falk. 1978. *Law as Process*. London: Routledge and Kegan Paul (repr. 1978, London: Hamburg, Oxford: IAI, Lit Verlag, James Currey).

______. 1999. 'Changing African Land Tenure: Reflections on the Incapacities of the State.' In C. Lund (ed.) *Development and Rights*. London: Frank Cass.

Muller, E. N. and M. A. Seligson. 1987. 'Inequality and Insurgency.' *American Political Science Review*, Vol. 81, 425–451.

Munyoni, L. M. (ed.) 2003. *Women and Land in Africa: Culture, Religion and Realizing Women's Rights*. London: Zed Books.

Muteshi, J. K. 1997. 'A Refusal to Argue with Inconvenient Evidence: Women, Proprietorship and Kenyan Law.' *Dialectical Anthropology*, Vol. 23: 55–81.

Myers, N. 1993. *Ultimate Security: The Environmental Basis of Political Stability*, New York: Norton.

Nafziger, E. W. and J. Auvinen. 1997. War, Hunger and Displacement: An Econometric Investigation into the Sources of Humanitarian Emergencies. Working Paper No. 142, Helsinki: UNU/WIDER.

______. 2002. 'Economic Development, Inequality, War, and State Violence.' *World Development*, Vol. 30, 153–63.

NEPAD. 2003. *Comprehensive Africa Agriculture Development Programme/New Partnership for Africa's Development (NEPAD)*. Midrand, South Africa: NEPAD.

North, D.C. and R.P. Thomas. 1973. *The Rise of the Western World: A New Economic History*, Cambridge: Cambridge University Press.

Odgaard, R. 2003a. 'Scrambling for Land in Tanzania: Processes of Formalisation and Legitimisation of Land Rights.' In T. A. Benjaminsen and C. Lund (eds) *Securing Land Rights in Africa*, London: Frank Cass.

______. 2003b. 'The Struggle for Land Rights in the Context of Multiple Normative Orders in Tanzania.' Paper presented at the conference Competing Jurisdictions: Settling Land Claims in Africa. Amsterdam, 24–26 September.

Odgaard, R. and A. Weis Bentzon, forthcoming. 'Rural Women's Access to Landed Property: Unearthing the Realities within an East African Setting.' In A. Hellum, J. Stewart, A. Tsanga and S. Ali (eds) *Human Rights Interfacing with Plural Inequalities and Gendered Realities*. Harare: Weaver Press.

Odgaard, R., H. Høgh-Jensen, F. Myaka, W. D. Sakala, J. Adu-Gyamfi, J. M. Vesterager and N. E. Nielsen. 2005. 'Integrating Pigeonpea in Low-input Maize-based Farming Systems: A Strategy Towards an Increase in Food Production and Alleviation of Poverty?' Unpublished paper.

Omni, M. and H. Winant. 1994. *Racial Formation in the United States: From the 1960s to the 1990s*. London: Routledge, 2nd Edition.

Peluso, N. L. and M. Watts. 2001. *Violent Environments*. Ithaca, NY: Cornell University Press.

Peters, P. E. 1998. 'Comment on 'The Political Economy of Ethnicity,' by Paul Collier. B. Pleskovic and J. E. Stiglitz (eds), *Annual World Bank Conference on Development Economics*, Washington, DC: The World Bank.

______. 2004. 'Inequality and Social Conflict Over Land in Africa.' *Journal of Agrarian Change* 4 (3): 269–314. London: Blackwell.

Platteau, J. P. 1996. 'The Evolutionary Theory of Land Rights As Applied to SubSaharan Africa: A Critical Assessment.' *Development and Change*, Vol. 27: 29–85.

Richards, A. I. 1939. *Land, Labour and Diet in Northern Rhodesia: An Economic Study of the Bemba Tribe*, Oxford: Oxford University Press.

Robbins, L. 1932 [1952]. *An Essay on the Nature and Significance of Economic Science*, London: Macmillan.

Rocheleau, D. and D. Edmunds. 1997. 'Women, Men and Trees: Gender, Power and Property in Forest and Agrarian Landscapes.' *World Development*, Vol. 25: 1351–71.

Rose, J. 2004. 'Our Present Disillusionment.' *Harpers Magazine*, October, 15–21.

Ruttan, V. and Y. Hayami. 1984. 'Toward a Theory of Induced Institutional Innovation.' *Journal of Development Studies*, Vol. 20: 203–23.

Sandbrook, R. 2000. *Closing the Circle: Democratization and Development in Africa*. London: Zed Books.

Scott, J. C. 1998. *Seeing Like a State*. New Haven: Yale University Press.

Scherr, S. J. 2000. 'A Downward Spiral? Research Evidence on the Relationship between Poverty and Natural Resource Degradation.' *Food Policy*, Vol. 25: 479–98.

SLSA team. 2003. 'Rights Talk and Rights Practice: Challenges for Southern Africa. Cape Town: Programme for Land and Agrarian Studies, University of the Western Cape.

Tenga, R. 1992. *Pastoral Land Rights in Tanzania, A Review*. London: IIED Drylands Programme: Pastoral Land Tenure Series.

Tenga, R. and G. Kakoti. 1993. 'The Barabeig Land Case.' H.Veber, J. Dahl, F. Wilson and E.Wæhle (eds) *Never Drink from the Same Cup*. Copenhagen: IWGIA Document no. 74.

Tiffen, M., Mortimore, M. and F. Gichuki. 1994. *More People, Less Erosion: Environmental Recovery in Kenya*. Chichester: John Wiley.

Toulmin, C. 2005. 'The New Tragedy of the Commons.' *New Statesman Special Issue*.

Toulmin, C. and J. Quan (eds). 2000. *Evolving Land Rights, Policy and Tenure in Africa*. London: International Institute for Environment and Development.

Toulmin, C., Lavigne Delville, P. and S. Traoré (eds). 2002. *The Dynamics of Resource Tenure in West Africa*. Paris: GRET; London: IIED, and Oxford: James Currey.

Uvin, P. 1998. *Aiding Violence: The Development Enterprise in Rwanda.* West Hartford, CT: Kumarian Press.

Walras, L. 1926. [1954]. *Elements of Pure Economics, or the Theory of Social Wealth.* London: Allen and Unwin.

Wanyeki, L. Muthoni (ed.). 2003. *Women and Land in Africa: Culture, Religion and Realizing Women's Rights.* London and New York: Zed Books.

WCED.1987. *Our Common Future.* World Commission on Environment and Development, Oxford: Oxford University Press.

Werbner, R. and T. Ranger (eds). 1996. *Postcolonial Identities in Africa.* London and New Jersey: Zed Books.

Westing, A. H. (ed.). 1989. *Comprehensive Security for the Baltic: An Environmental Approach.* London: Sage Publications.

Wolf, A. 2001. 'Water Conflict and Cooperation in 2020 Vision.' Washington DC: International Food Policy Research Institute.

Wolf, A. T., S. B. Yoffe and M. Giordano. 2003. 'International Waters: Identifying Basins at Risk.' *Water Policy.* 5 (1): 29-60.

World Bank. 1981. *Accelerated Development in Sub-Saharan Africa: An Agenda for Action.* Washington, DC: World Bank.

______. 2003. *Land Policies for Growth and Poverty Reduction: A World Bank Policy Research Report.* Oxford and Washington: A co-publication of the World Bank and Oxford University Press.

Yoffee, S., A. Wolf and M. Giordano. 2005. 'Conflict and Cooperation Over International Freshwater Resources: Indicators and Findings of the Basins at Risk Project. To be published in *Journal of the American Water Resources Association* 39 (5): 1109–26.

Zebrowitz, L. A. 1990. *Social Perception.* Pacific Grove, CA: Brooks Cole Publishing.

I
Conflict & Custom

2

Conflicts & the Reinterpretation of Customary Tenure in Ghana

KOJO SEBASTIAN AMANOR

Recent research on land tenure within Africa has tended to view property rights as the product of a process of contestation and negotiation rather than the outcome of underlying tenure rules (Jul-Larsen and Kassibo 2001). Tenure is seen to be about the ways in which people manoeuvre politically and socially to establish and secure claims in land, or as Berry (2001: xxv) writes: 'Viewed in historical perspective, property appears as a multidimensional social process in which people debate and negotiate the constitution of authority, the distribution of wealth, and the relationship between them.' This approach tends to argue that negotiations over property are never closed but continually contested by investing in social networks as a means of reaffirming rights and legitimacy to resources. Rights in property are fluid and ephemeral, continually reaffirming social alignments in society and the negotiation between different interests. This analytic framework tends to draw its case material from elites in society, disputes between chiefs and other types of traditional leaders, or between powerful lineage heads and wealthy individuals. It does not usually examine vertical power relations between chiefs and wealthy landowners and commoners, or caste-like structures between former conquering groups and the servile groups they conquered who work the land. It presumes that all actors are equally positioned with the power to negotiate and invest in social networks. It does not examine how subaltern, marginalised and oppressed groups in society perceive dominant definitions of tenure and develop their own concepts of the customary. This transactionist perspective tends to root property relations in some specifically essentialist African cultural framework.

Other research tends to equate customary land tenure with civil society (Bruce 1993, Lavigne Delville 2000, Toulmin and Quan 2000, Toulmin et al. 2002). It is argued that customary tenure systems are dynamic, equitable and flexible. These positive characteristics of customary tenure are not recognised by the state, which tends to view customary arrangements as backward and promotes formal land titling programmes. Formal titling is expensive and involves a plethora of bureaucratic procedures which are also time consuming and difficult to negotiate. This deters the greater part of the population from registering their land. Most of the population hold their land under customary forms of land tenure that are not recognised by the state and this promotes insecurity of land tenure. This approach disregards the significant historical literature on the invention of tradition, and the problems of defining a customary sphere outside the realm of the colonial sphere and the colonial ruler's conception of tradition and custom (Ranger 1983, 1993, Chanock 1991). It assumes that there is a unitary concept of customary tenure that is independent of the state and stands against formal state titling programmes.

In this paper it is argued that there are multiple definitions of the customary and that the dominant projection of a unitary customary tenure is dependent upon recognition by the state, and reflects an alliance of rural power elites with the state. Customary land relations are rooted in structural power relations, and the origins of the present configuration and conception of customary land tenure are rooted in colonial domination, the economic and political transformations that occurred in colonial domination and the influence of these factors on the postcolonial world. Asad (1979) argues that one problem with much anthropology is its ideological conception of social structure and culture. Anthropologists have sought to reproduce definitively the authentic discourses of other people as a system of essential meaning, based on an a priori system of authentic culture, rather than taking the production of 'essential meaning' in the form of authoritative discourse as the problem to be explained. Asad writes:

> However much we might, as professional talkers and writers, wish to affirm the profound importance of systematic discourse, it is difficult to avoid the obvious, but by no means trivial, conclusions that political and economic conditions have developed and changed in ways that are rarely in accord with systematic discourse. Or let me put it another way: it is surely neither the power of social criticism nor the relative strength of competing social ideologies within the societies studied by anthropologists (in Asia, in Africa and in Latin America) which explains how and why they have become basically transformed, but the historical forces of world industrial capitalism and the ways these have impinged upon particular political and economic conditions. (1979: 624)

Applied to property regimes, this means that authoritative discourses constructed around customary land tenure need to be understood within the historical, political and economic contexts in which they originated and continue to exist, and within the context of colonial domination and integration into the world market, rather than in a peculiarly African cultural value system. Thus the whole configuration of identities articulated in discourses in customary land tenure are a product of the integration into the world market through the agency of colonialism rather than pre-colonial African cultural systems. The articulation of a concept of land tenure, rights of chiefs, autochthonous people and migrants are a product of the colonial period and the rise of the export crop economy and did not previously exist. In the pre-colonial period, rights in land were frequently intimately associated with rights in people. People were often expropriated to the land as slaves and then incorporated into society as part of the agricultural labouring people (peasantry). Powerful states often raided neighbouring peoples or established tributes in slaves, who were put to work in the agricultural sector and in land colonisation. It was only with the emergence of the colonial economy, with its export crop enclaves and its labour reserves, that the categories of migrant farmers, migrant labourers, and land as a commodity in itself (which could be transacted through sale, leasing or sharecropping) came into being as the dominant social relations of production. However, customary land tenure did not only emerge through the economic changes brought about by the colonial system, but also through the political alliances through which colonial administration was established. This delegated rural administration and regulation of natural resources to chiefs, who in return for their participation in colonial administration were recognised as holding customary ownership of land as well as rights to royalties, fees, taxes and labour services of their subjects. The concept of a customary land tenure related to political authority thus emerged in the context of an alliance between chiefs and the colonial state, and depended upon recognition from the state. Customary land tenure cannot be regarded as representing civil society interests since historically it represented the interests of the colonial state and its political alliances.

This paper explores how structural features define property regimes in the forest zone of Ghana and the group identities, political discourses and processes of negotiation that coalesce around resources within a historical and political economy context, and within the context of exploitation of resources by socially differentiated groups with disparate economic and political power and influence. By comparing the conflicts and processes of negotiation that occur around different natural resources and different types of groups, the paper shows how economic and political interests mediate the concept of customary land tenure in different circumstances. The concept of customary land tenure essentially operates as a political discourse rather than as an essentialist cultural framework. There are many conceptions of customary rights, some of which are subversive and submerged. The paper compares discourses about land and custom in three different production sectors. These include:

- the agricultural sector, where a large number of peasant producers need to have access to land to produce for export and domestic markets, but where the needs of large-scale agriculture by powerful interests may require a process of land expropriation,
- timber resources, which are monopolised by a few large concessionaires with considerable influence for export, and
- charcoal resources, a tree resource with little export value, produced for the urban markets by small-scale charcoal burners with little influence on the state.

Customary land tenure & colonialism

The imposition of colonial rule in Africa continued a process of integration of African peasantry into the world market as producers of primary staple commodities for European industry, which was underway by the early nineteenth century. This involved the opening up of export crop production zones, the movement of a free labour force to these areas to transform the agricultural economy, and the creation of a system of rural administration to regulate and facilitate this process. The earliest forms of intervention into economic life were concerned with regulating labour and the rights of people, banning slavery and developing contractual wage labour as the main labour relation. Difficulties in securing labour resulted in forced labour and taxation policies to encourage migrations of labour to the main colonial enclaves and export crop producing areas.

The free movement of labour transformed the economies of many settlements. Migrants created demands for land and provided various forms of hired labour that allowed citizens and land-purchasing migrant farmers to expand the area they cultivated. In the context of rapidly changing land relations the colonial administration intervened in the land question. Its main concern was to prevent the evolution of land markets which it could not control. To maintain control over land it formed an alliance with chiefs under the Native Administration system and invested trusteeship and ultimate ownership of land rights in chiefs. In this framework customary rights in land were seen as flowing downwards, or as Chanock (1991: 64) writes: 'They were derived from the political authority, rather than residing in the peasantry.' Land was conceptualised as consisting of a number of domains. Allodial rights were vested in chiefs and usufructuary rights were invested in peasant farmers. This meant that the chiefs had powers as trustees of the community to regulate and allocate land. Rights to land were acquired through political allegiance, and this reaffirmed the political order of paramount chiefs, village chiefs, sub-chiefs and family heads. Land rights were acquired through citizenship and citizenship created a series of 'customary' obligations, which were determined by the chiefs. These involved obligations to provide the polity with various forms of revenues and taxes as well as the obligation to perform communal labour.

Since the position of the chief was guaranteed by the colonial authority, trusteeship was ultimately vested in the colonial state. The basis of customary land tenure was reduced to the diktat that land belongs to the community and not the individual. It was asserted that the notion of individual ownership was foreign to native ideas (Cowen and Shenton 1994). The title of the community was essentially a usufructuary right. While the user rights of citizens were guaranteed, they ultimately derived from the paramount authority and, as Lord Haldane, who presided over the Privy Council in London, pronounced that this 'may be extinguished by the action of a paramount power which assumes possession of the entire control of the land' (Sobluza II v. Miller and others 1926 A.C., 518 at 525, quoted in Chanock 1991: 67). This caveat enabled land to be acquired by Europeans as concessions or private farming ventures and enabled the expropriation of peasant cultivators. It also firmly rooted land tenure in the system of administration in which land rights could only be legitimated by the political system of administration.

This proclamation of customary rights as the user rights of the community occurred in a period of rapid social change and commodification of agricultural production, in which increasing numbers of farmers were engaging in export crop production, hiring labour and acquiring new plots of land. In this situation land was increasingly acquired on an individual basis and land transactions continued to grow. Thus, the assertion of communal land tenure by colonial authorities did not take place as an affirmation of existing land relations, but as a struggle to preserve some mythical notion of the customary against violation by African producers infected with the ills of individualism and economic ambition (Chanock 1991). The concept of customary land tenure was not drawn up from empirical case studies, but from the writings of Locke and Maine, and from the empire-wide pronouncements of the Privy Council in London (Cowen and Shenton 1994). It formed part of a moral campaign to conserve tradition against the encroachment of modernisation. This tended to undermine the emergence of land markets and insecurity of individual ownership since the land could be appropriated by chiefly authority or be contested by others who could root their claims on the land in customary rights with reference to the political order of Native Administration.

In Akyem Abuakwa in southern Ghana, large tracts of land were alienated to migrant farmers for export crop production during the nineteenth and early twentieth century, before the creation of a Native Authority system. By the 1920s the Gold Coast had emerged as the largest cocoa producer in the world and most cocoa was being produced by migrant farmers in Akyem Abuakwa on land they had purchased. With the creation of the Native Authority system the Okyenhene, the paramount chief of Akyem Abuakwa, set about preventing the alienation of land by sub-chiefs to immigrants. In a letter to one of his sub-chiefs in 1917 he wrote:

> If in ancient times the responsibility of defending the territory against foreign invaders devolved upon the shoulders of my great ancestors, it becomes an obvious corresponding duty of mine as their humble successor in this time of peace to protect the rights of the Stools of Akim Abuakwa against foreign visitors, who employ modern weapons of civilisation to dispossess the stools of their inherent rights and aim at the confiscation and despoilment of the riches and rights which these Stools should otherwise enjoy for years to come. (National Archives of Ghana, ADM 11/136, quoted in Rathbone 1993: 58–9)

Behind the rhetoric of defending customary Akyem rights in land against land sales lay an attempt to control land and extract revenues from migrants. The Okyenhene was not averse to countenancing land sales by sub-chiefs to migrants provided that his ruling Okyeman council was approached and rewarded with a share of the revenues coming from land sales. During the 1920s and 1930s rules on customary tenure were widely flouted as more land was sold by sub-chiefs to migrants. Rhetoric of the invasion of Akyem land by migrants was used by the Okyenhene to justify attempts to gain greater control over migrants and levy taxes upon them. At the same time that the Okyenhene was claiming to protect Akyem lands from migrants, he was busy selling rights to concessions to mineral prospectors and engaging in legal cases with sub-chiefs on rights to concession fees (Rathbone 1993).

Transacting land with migrants

The concept of customary land tenure facilitated the movement of migrants but also defined them as 'strangers'. Customary land tenure prevented the emergence of internal land markets which were not controlled by chiefs. Since chiefs could sell lands to migrants but not to citizens who had user rights to lands, chiefs were frequently interested in selling large tracts of the uncultivated land in their domain to migrants to gain revenues. This frequently resulted in increased land shortage for citizens, and those who were intent on developing commercial cocoa farming frequently migrated to new frontier areas outside their local states to acquire new lands.

The movement of migrants facilitated both the commodification of land and farm production relations, but also created increasing insecurity in land. Chiefs and sub-chiefs could secure claims to land on their boundaries by giving it out to migrant farmers and caretakers (Berry 2001, Chaveau 2000 also reports similar arrangements in Côte d'Ivoire).This enabled them to establish a priori claims to lands lying on the perimeters of settlements where boundaries were not clear. Chiefs and sub-chiefs also gained important sources of income by releasing land to migrants on various types of sharecropping arrangements. In some areas in Akyem sharecropping became a disguised form of land sale. Chiefs would give out land to migrant labourers who would create cocoa plantations. When the cocoa came into bearing, the land was divided into two; the landlord usually took two-thirds and the tenant one third. Through this arrangement chiefs were able to own large cocoa plantations without investing in labour or seedlings, and the migrants were able to gain land.

These relations were ramified lower down the hierarchy with family heads giving out land to migrants on a sharecrop basis. Family labour based on local youth could be deployed to clear virgin land and create cocoa plantations. Once established, the land was placed under migrant caretakers who were remunerated with one third of the cocoa proceeds. Migrants occupied an ambivalent position in society. Their labour created the potential for the commodification of agriculture and the expansion of agricultural production. They were central to the development of export crop economies and the creation of the necessary infrastructure. However, they also facilitated the expansion into new land by the wealthy (by providing them with access to labour) and brought dangers of land shortage and increasing social differentiation.

Migrants were also socially differentiated. The rich Asante cocoa farmers moving to acquire new lands in Ahafo and the Western Region in the 1940s were worlds apart from the annual labourers who migrated from northern Ghana, Upper Volta (now Burkina Faso), Niger and Mali, but the migrant capitalist farmers were also dependent upon the migrant labourer to provide labour for their expansionist farm strategies. The lowest level of migrants included seasonal labour migrants who came to work during the farm clearing season in labour gangs and then return home to make their own farms in their hometowns. The strategy was premised on the fact that the rainy season occurs later in the north than in the south. The major rains start in March in the south and in May in the north. Some migrants would come down to the south in November and work in the later part of the year until January or February before returning home to their own farms.

Annual labourers came down south to work for a whole year. The landlord provided them with housing, land to make a food plot, implements, clothing and 'chop money'. The annual labourer carried out important services for the landlord in addition to cocoa farm work, such as fetching water and participating in other household chores. The annual labourers were paid a lump sum at the end of the farming season and then returned to their villages. The *abusa* caretakers looked after an established cocoa plantation for a number of years and were remunerated with a one-third share of the harvest. In contrast, the *abusa* tenants created a farm for the landlord using their own capital to purchase seeds and hire labour. In return they took two-thirds of the crop. The *abusa* farmers received a third or two-thirds portion of the cocoa plantation – depending on the locality and arrangements – as their own land, in return for making cocoa farms for the land owner. The landlords became responsible for the maintenance of their portion of the farm once it started fruiting (Hill 1956).

The customary subverted

Within the colonial setting there was no notion of human rights outside the customary setting. Beyond the banning of slavery as a relation of production, the rights of colonial rural subjects were defined in terms of customary rights of preserving moral relationships rooted in cultural values from the impact of the market. While the customary was defined by the colonial authority in terms of the rights of its political allies, the chiefs, the notion of the customary rapidly spread through society as a moral concept, which served to define human rights (Chanock 1991). In this process, subaltern elements often attempted to subvert the colonial conception of the customary, developing their own traditions of checks and balances on the central power authorities which the colonial authority had created and empowered. Given the increasing commodification of land and increasing insecurity of land occupancy as chiefs, sub-chiefs and lineage elders began to transact land with outsiders, commoners (*mmerante*: literally 'young men') began to develop discourses on customary rights to defend their land interests and prevent encroachment by others.

In nineteenth-century Akyem Abuakwa commoners were organised into *asafo* military companies, through which the various settlements and lineage segments within them provided military recruits for the organisation of the state's military campaigns. In peacetime the *asafo* companies played a key role in maintaining the transport and sanitary infrastructure of settlements. In the colonial period they formed important institutions through which communal labour was organised. However, commoners began to transform the *asafo* companies into political organisations which were mobilised to check the abuse of power by chiefs, to make them accountable and to destool (depose) chiefs for violating their responsibilities (Simensen 1975, Addo-Fenning 1997). During the late nineteenth century several chiefs in Akyem were destooled for selling land to migrants (Addo-Fenning 1997, Amanor 2001). Between 1904 and 1944, thirty-five divisional chiefs were destooled in Akyem Abuakwa by the *asafo* (Amamoo 1958, Rathbone 1993). The *asafo* companies also attempted to destool the paramount chief of Akyem Abuakwa in 1918 and 1932 and would have succeeded if not for the intervention of the colonial authority (Rathbone 1993). Apart from expropriation of land and land sales, other major concerns of commoners concerned impositions of communal labour and the collection of arbitrary taxes by chiefs. By the 1950s the *asafo* movement in Akyem emerged as an anti-chief and anti-colonial movement which destooled chiefs for collaborating with the colonial administration (Amamoo 1958, Simensen 1975). Central to the *asafo* movement were concerns about the appropriation of land by chiefs and impositions of forced labour and taxes on commoners.

Customary land rights were also used and upheld in a number of other ways to protect land rights. Within the family, young men could stress the obligations of kinship as a way of defending their rights to land and the obligations of their fathers and mothers' brothers in matrilineal societies to provide them with land. Women would also stress kinship obligations of relatives and husbands to provide them with land. Thus, at the local level the concept of the customary emerged as a moral discourse through which groups identified their interests in land, the major groups with whom they were involved in conflict over land, and the violations of customary norms and morality that were carried out by their protagonists. However, they continued to change and adapt to modern conditions, and their definitions and counter-definitions of the customary reflect these changes.

The customary in the post-colonial setting

By the late 1940s it had become evident that social and economic life had been transformed in the Gold Coast and that the institutional structures of the native authorities were largely anachronistic. Following riots in urban centres in 1948 a Commission of Enquiry was set up under Aitken Watson to examine the underlying causes of the disturbances. Many representatives of the commoners or young men complained of the system of Native Administration, the autocratic impositions made by chiefs and elders on the population at large and the lack of any democratic representation of the commoners. The commoners advocated the establishment of a system of local democracy and the relegation of chiefs to the status of figureheads. The Watson Commission and the Coussey Committee, which was charged with making practical suggestions for constitutional reform based on the findings of the Watson Commission, recommended the creation of some system of democratically elected local government. The Watson Commission and the Coussey Committee were not unsympathetic to the institution of chieftaincy, and they made some provision for chiefs to be represented in local government and to preside over its functioning.

The first national election was won by the Convention People's Party (CPP), which had partly fought the election on an anti-chief and anti-native authority basis and supported the mass movements that had destooled many chiefs. The main opposition parties against the CPP were organised into the National Liberation Movement (NLM), which had a strong backing among chiefs in Ashanti and Akyem Abuakwa. However, the CPP also had backing from chiefs in some regions including the northern regions and the Brong Ahafo region, where the chiefs and people wished to break away from Ashanti overlordship and were demanding the formation of their own region. The CPP was not averse to using chieftaincy when chiefs supported them and whittling down the power of chiefs who supported the opposition. The CPP developed an opportunist strategy playing with both the institutions of chieftaincy and local government to further its own political hegemony. As a result of this, reforms of the chiefly system after independence by the CPP did not lead to a strengthening of popular democracy, but rather to an entrenchment of the CPP party and its allies (Songsore and Denkabe 1995). Kwame Nkrumah, himself, adapted the ritual symbols of chieftaincy, incorporating these symbols into state ceremonies and paraphernalia and adopting the Akyem chiefly title of Osagyefo ('the victor'). Like many other early independence leaders Nkrumah held to a doctrine of African socialism, which stressed the communal origins of African culture and society, the lack of social classes, and the need to preserve African communalism and the distinctive culture of the 'African Personality'. These doctrines reproduced the colonial conception of the communal and customary domains. These concepts did not lead to radical land reform or a questioning of the role of the customary, but consolidated the domination of land by chiefs under a system of party rule and local government, which replaced the native authority.

Legislation, such as the 1962 Stool Lands Act and the Concessions Act, vested the powers of chiefs to appropriate land and natural resources into the hands of the state. The Stool Lands Act enabled the state to expropriate land and expropriate farmers. The basis of this was the ideological discourse that farmers only had user rights to the land and that the ultimate allodial rights lay with the chief. State expropriation of land was carried out through the intermediary of paramount chiefs, and farmers were expropriated by asserting the allodial rights of paramount chiefs to the land and their right to expropriate farmers for the 'national interests'. Farmers only needed to be compensated for the crops they had on the land. Compensation for land expropriated for the state went to the chiefs, the 'rightful' owners of the land, and not to the farmers. This gave the chiefs an immediate interest in expropriating land for the state.

The Concessions Act vested all (timber) trees in the office of the president to manage on behalf of the chiefs. However, in carrying out this action it invented the tradition that all trees were customarily owned by chiefs and that farmers had no rights to exploit them. This enabled the timber resources of the nation to be expropriated for the narrow interests of concessionaires who were invariably political allies of government. The interest of chiefs in this process was secured by allocating them a significant share of the royalties.

Following the 1966 coup d'etat against the Nkrumah regime, subsequent regimes have tended to strengthen the control of chiefs over land and natural resources and to utilise them in development administration. The 1969, 1979 and 1992 Constitutions all make provisions for chiefs in national political life. Chiefs are represented in Regional and National Houses of Chiefs, serve as advisers to central government and are represented on important statutory bodies (Arhin Brempong 2001). Concerns about the implications of chiefly authority for national democratic life have been replaced by debates about the roles that chiefs can play in development administration, in the enforcement of both physical and moral dimensions of law and order in the rural areas, in translating the government development directives to the local population and in ensuring that local customs are in keeping with modern sensibilities. The 1992 Constitution makes provisions for chiefs to 'undertake an evaluation of traditional customs and usages with a view to eliminating those customs and usages that are outmoded and socially harmful' (Article 272c). Chiefs also have important functions in making local bye-laws and enforcing them, particularly in relation to the environment.

With the increasing national prominence of chiefs and their importance in the control of natural resources, many rich businessmen and prominent members of the national elite seek to occupy chiefly stools (Arhin Brempong 2001). Many chieftaincies have created new stools concerned with development (*nkosohene*, chief of progress) that are specifically given to wealthy individuals with no kinship claims on chiefly office. Many chiefs are members of families with significant economic and business assets. Segments of non-dominant royal families often become impoverished while the dominant segments expand their wealth using stool revenues to educate their children and build their own enterprises. Through marriage relations, chiefly families and modern elite families converge. Thus, the high echelon of chiefs often has interests and sensibilities that are firmly entrenched in the national capitalist elite, and their rendition of the customary under modern conditions reflect these interests. From above, the customary reflects the interests of the ruling coalitions of state bureaucracy, private business and chiefs.

Custom from above: the case of forest tenure

Forestry resource tenure affords a clear example of how the concept of the customary is manipulated from above to favour the expropriation of resources by national elites. The forestry sector is organised on a concession basis. Concessions are granted to logging firms in both forest reserves and in farmland. In both areas timber companies have monopoly rights to exploit all timber trees that fall into their concession, including trees that have been nurtured by farmers on their farms and in their fallow land. The timber companies pay a stumpage fee, from which the Forest Service takes a 60 per cent share for its 'management service'. The remaining revenues constitute the royalties. The Office for the Administrator of Stool Lands takes a 10 per cent share from this, and the remainder is divided between the local district assembly, which takes 55 per cent, the sub-chief who takes 25 per cent and the paramount chief who gains 20 per cent. The farmer who works among the timber trees and preserves them gains nothing and has no incentive to preserve timber trees. The stumpage values in Ghana have tended to be low, and this has made timber exploitation a highly lucrative enterprise – one in which industry captures the rents of the value of timber trees which farmers have invested in creating and preserving. Since more than 80 per cent of timber exports from Ghana in the 1990s originated from farming areas rather than forest reserves, the rent capture by timber companies is massive. This has angered farmers in many areas and they have taken to destroying timber saplings that regenerate on their farms (Amanor 1996). Calls for reform to this system have been resisted on the basis that this is interfering with customary and traditional arrangements and would be acting against the national constitution in which these customary arrangements are enshrined.

These arrangements are however quite recent and are certainly not based on any conception of customary rights that was prevalent in the early twentieth century, before the expansion of timber logging companies into the forest interior. At every juncture of development in the timber industry customary tree tenure has been redefined.

During the early twentieth century logging firms were confined to the coastal areas in the Western region and to the basins of the large rivers from which timber could be floated down to the coast. Hauling timber was laborious and it was not until the 1940s that timber trucks and road networks enabled the interior of the high forest to be exploited. During this period the main exploitation of timber was for domestic uses and the main timber exploiters were pitsawyers working in farming areas. Trees were normally transacted between farmers and sawyers and the sawyers provided the farmers with a third of the boards or a third of the remuneration. These arrangements were described by Foggie and Piasecki (1962: 242):

> The small pitsaw gang which buys a single tree, saw it and sells the produce. For the latter, no capital except axes and saws and the picks and shovels to dig the saw-pit may be required, as the trees may occasionally be obtained on a share basis, one third of the planks produced going to the owner and two thirds to the sawing gang.

Accounts and bye-laws from the early part of the century suggest that in the pre-war period farmers had rights to sell timber trees that occurred on their own farm and fallow land. However, they could not sell trees on uncleared land which came under the stool. The town chiefs could sell timber trees on uncleared stool land. Once the land was cleared and farmed, the trees on the land could be claimed by the farmer. In a detailed study of the administration of finances and resources in the Akyem Oda, Field writes:

> The allocation of uncleared land to a townsman gives him no rights over the saleable timber. This remains the property of the town and must be left standing. If a town sells a tree in uncleared land which has been allocated to a townsman he receives no special share in the proceeds. If he wishes to sell a tree on his own cleared land he must ask permission of the chief and part of the proceeds will be claimed by the town. (1948: 72)

Various bye-laws from the 1920s and 1930s show that the chiefs only claimed a share of the extraordinary wealth that farmers were able to gain from the sale of timber, not the actual timber. For instance, the Akyem Abuakwa Stool Land Declaration of 6 July 1931 states: 'A native who fells a tree on farm or *mfufua* (fallow/bush) is liable to pay to the stool one log from each tree' (Ghana National Archives, Akyem Abuakwa Land Law ADM11/1017).

By the late 1940s, with the opening up of the forest hinterland to road transport and the coming of timber-hauling trucks, and the large demands for timber in Europe for post-war construction, logging firms moved into the Gold Coast and timber exports developed rapidly. The regulation of the timber industry now became necessary and a concession act was necessary to enable logging firms to exploit timber on farm land. Potentially large sources of timber existed in the new farming areas into which migrant cocoa farmers were expanding in the Ahafo and the Western Region. However, to successfully bring this timber into the concession system, the rights had to be removed from farmers and pitsawyers. The first attempt at this was the Protected Timber Lands Act of 1959. This enabled the state to declare off-reserve areas as 'protected timbers land' and prevent farmers from moving into the area before timber companies had logged out the desirable timber species. The framework for the Protected Timbers Land Act was addressed by the 1951 Fact Finding Committee on the Timber Industry in the Western Province of the Gold Coast. Playing on well-established environmental narratives about shifting cultivation, the report of the Committee argues that if farmers are to continue to hold onto their traditional rights of cultivation, this will be disastrous for the environment and for the logging companies who will lose large amounts of timber to the cultivator:

> Section 12 (6) of the Concessions Ordinance (19 of 1939) states that a concession will not be validated unless the Court is satisfied that the customary rights of the natives are reasonably protected in respect of cultivation, etc., and concession instruments, therefore, invariably include a clause to this effect. This clause may seem harmless in appearance, but its results in many cases are disastrous for the concessionaire.... Cultivation by and large, means shifting cultivation for food production. The extent and spread of farming is conditioned by the existence of communications and the reasonable proximity of big markets for the farm produce.... In many cases farm clearing and burning is well advanced before roads are completed and in use by the concessionaire for logging purposes.... The result is that this unrestricted shifting cultivation utterly destroys large areas of good accessible forest before the valuable trees can be salvaged by the concessionaire. (Minister of Commerce, Industry and Mines 1951: 10)

The report then appeals to the moral obligations of chiefs as custodians of the environment to honour their (customary) obligations to preserve the forest from farmers:

> There remains only propaganda and Government pressure on Native Authorities to honour their obligation and preserve the forest from indiscriminate destruction at least until the existing valuable timber has been removed. Negotiations between the concessionaire and the grantors in order to define an area or areas to be given up to farming might bear fruit in some cases; such a sacrifice by the concessionaire would require to be met by some guarantee that the remaining forest area would be inviolate for a specified period. It might be possible to confine farming initially to agreed territorial limits and to release, at need, further specified areas from time to time ... the creation of Timber Lands Reserves ... would be the ideal solution and Government's influence might wisely be directed to this end. (Minister of Commerce, Industry and Mines 1951:10–11)

From these two premises the report goes on to recommend that chiefs dedicate uncultivated land as forest reserves, which timber companies can log out, using the 'customary conventions' on which forest reserves were established in the colonial period to appropriate the land of farmers:

> Only by voluntary dedication by Chiefs (Native Authorities or Stools) of forest areas as Timber Land Reserves can any further security be given to unreserved forest. If such action could be achieved, farming would be restricted in dedicated areas for a stated period, possibly 20 years in the first instance, and the forests would still be there for reconsideration of its future at the end of that time. Controlled exploitation could, in the meantime, take place. (Minister of Commerce, Industry and Mines 1951: 2)

Finally, the report attempts to cast doubt on the customary rights of farmers to timber on their land:

> The rights of farmers over land is in fact an agricultural right, but in view of the system of shifting cultivation implies the inclusion of the right to cut down and burn, if required, all standing trees on that area. Whether a farmer has the right to dispose of standing trees by sale is not quite clear but such a sale might conceivably occur with the permission of the caretaker. The disposal of the right of ownership of land together with the usufruct is a practice which has spread over from the Eastern Province. In the Western Province as previously constituted, such alienation of rights came to light in the early 1930s. In some cases the right of ownership of land is not given in such alienations, although some alienations holders dispute this and claim, in addition, complete rights over usufruct. In some cases an alienation implies the disposal of farming rights only, and possibly a share in the revenue from timber trees'. (Minister of Commerce, Industry and Mines 1951: 3)

In contrast with the Eastern Region, the expansion of cocoa farming and migrant cocoa farmers into the Western region took place at a period when the timber industry was rapidly expanding in Ghana. Prior to the arrival of migrants agricultural activities were not well developed in the Western region and the expansion of cocoa farming was largely dependent upon an influx of migrant farmers with capital and labourers. As Hill and McGlade wrote:

> The stranger farmers are opening up the Sefwi area with a vigour quite foreign to the native Sefwi farmers, whose are usually very small (an eighth of an acre is a typical sort of size we have heard). Perhaps in the end the native farmers will come to resent the encouragement given to the immigrants by the chiefs. But for now there is little evidence of a conflict between the chiefs and the people.

> Sefwi chiefs readily released land to migrants on favourable terms, both through sale and *abusa*, in which the tenants provided the chief with one third of the plantation as remuneration. However, in the written documents that accompanied such transactions the chiefs were careful to insert a clause which specified that the timber and mineral rights of the land were not transferred (1957: 9–10).

Thus, the chiefs gained rights to the timber trees on migrants' land. Since considerably more land was being farmed by migrants than locals this effectively gave chiefs new controls over timber resources. Having purchased land, migrants would have to wait for timber concessionaires to log the timber before they could gain access to the land for farming purposes. The chiefs gained royalties from this timber. The sale of land to migrants and the laying of claims to the timber resources on that land gave the chiefs access to considerable revenues and forest rents which they could not have achieved if the land had been farmed by local farmers. The conjunction of the movement of farmers into the Western Region for cocoa farming, the opening up of the Western Region to logging firms, and the Protected Timbers Land gave chiefs the opportunity to redefine customary tree tenure by inserting clauses on timber trees into their agreements with migrant farmers, who were the dominant cocoa farmers in the region. The economic interests that chiefs developed in timber and their willingness to cooperate with government in controlling timber resources created the necessary conditions to ensure that the timber resources of farmland were appropriated for logging companies. These arrangements were probably tolerated by the local population since they saw the expansion of cocoa and the migration of farmers and labourers as opening up their settlements to modernity and creating the conditions for their participation in export crop production.

The differences in the timber tenure of the Eastern and Western Regions reflected different historical patterns of settlement. In the Eastern Region migrant farmers had settled before the consolidation of a timber industry and were able to exploit timber on their farms for local markets. When the timber industry began to expand in the 1950s it focused its activities in the timber rich mature forests of Ahafo and the Western region, rather than in the mature cocoa plantations of the Eastern Region with much lower densities of timber resources. Thus, in the Eastern Region farmers were able to continue to insist on their customary rights to exploit and sell timber during this period, at least until the 1990s. While the logging companies had captured the timber resources of new frontier farming areas, the pitsawyers and the loggers occupied different niches. The pitsawyers worked on farms, extracting Odum (*Milicia excelsa*) and Wawa (*Triplochiton scleroxylon*) for the domestic market. The logging companies mainly worked in the forest reserves and uncultivated protected frontier areas, focusing on redwoods for the export trade.

In the economic crisis of the late 1970s and early 1980s the timber industry nearly collapsed and many logging firms were unable to replace old and dilapidated equipment. In this situation chainsaw operators – who had replaced the old pitsawyers – were encouraged to produce timber for the domestic market and chainsaws proliferated. With the introduction of structural adjustment, donors allocated considerable grants for rebuilding the timber industry as a way of promoting export-oriented growth. Timber exports recovered. By the late 1980s there was overcapacity in the logging industry and the timber resource was seriously under pressure, particularly with the development of new markets for African timber in Southeast Asia. With pressures from donors and the international environmental lobby to introduce sustainable harvesting procedures, the Forest Service rigorously applied an annual allowable cut to the forest reserves and the major zones of timber production became farmland. By the late 1980s there were no new frontier areas of uncultivated forests left which could be declared protected areas until logging companies had finished logging. Timber concessionaires now directly exploited trees on farms. With increasing shortages of prime export timber species, logging companies have diversified into a large number of species, including previously unvalued timber species, which can be exploited as core for particle board. To maximise revenues concessions are being allocated in heavily farmed areas, where previously permits would have been given out for the exploitation of individual trees.

The successful implementation of a concession system on farms requires the removal of chainsaw operators and any notions of ownership rights by farmers to trees on their farms or of rights to transact trees. This has been achieved by a ban on the use of the chainsaw to cut timber trees and a re-invention of customary norms of ownership. This means that the situation that came into being in the Western Region in the 1950s has now become the norm for the whole country, including the Eastern Region, and denies the rights of farmers to transact trees on their farms as they have done in the past. This has been backed up by military patrols in areas in which 'illegal' felling of timber is known to occur. The state has been able to implement this legislation through the ideological construct that customary rights to timber belong to the chiefs. Since the chiefs are seen as representing the community, farmers have no official fora through which they can voice their interests and concerns. Government and development agencies approach rural people through the 'community,' and they approach the 'community', through their chiefs. The customary rights of chiefs in the timber industry have been used by the state to deny the rights of farmers and to assure a monopoly of timber resources for logging companies.

During the 1950s youth in some parts of the Eastern Region began to experience land shortage and difficulties in gaining access to land from their lineages. Lineage elders were able to use the availability of migrant farm labour to extend their farms and to exert increasing controls over young men. Old, well-established farms were often placed under *abusa* tenants and family youth were used with hired labour to create new plantations. Among the matrilineal Akan (the dominant population in the forest zone) the family dependants and family farm labour can consist of the sons of sisters and the children of the men. In return for years of service in working on the plantations of the elders, young men would be allocated some of these plantations in recognition of their service (*som*) to their elders. The land could be transferred through inheritance on the death of the senior (*wofadee/agyapadee*) or through a gift (*akyedee*) before death. In the case of a gift, the recipient of the plantation would make a counter prestation, consisting of a sheep, some drink and money, which was known as *aseda* (literally: 'thank you'), in front of the lineage elders.

Douglas (1969) argued that matrilineal systems work best under economic conditions associated with an abundance of resources and a scarcity of labour, where powerful lineage elders are able to mobilise the lineage youth under their command. This was certainly the case with the matrilineal cocoa farmers described by Hill (1963) in the pioneering phase of the expansion of cocoa in the

Eastern Region of Ghana. Wealthy cocoa farmers would buy large tracts of land and give out many plots to their kin to farm. They would retain the larger part of the land for their own use. Matrilineal kin who had served them well in their previous ventures were rewarded with plots. Presumably, this parcelling out of land to indigent kin guaranteed the cocoa entrepreneurs labour services for creating the settlement infrastructure and also farm assistance. With increasing land shortage and economic recession tensions have been placed on the matrilineal system. In the settlements of Apinaman and Dwenease in Akyem Abuakwa, where I carried out research in 1999, this was very evident in the perception of the residents. As an old man stated:

> The *abusua* [matrilineage] still exists but its effectiveness depends on the abusuapanyin [head of matrilineage]. And how he can organise the family. Because of high birth rates we are now moving over to our children [rather than providing for sisters' children]. The *abusua* system is no longer working because our numbers have increased so one cannot afford to keep your sisters' children and your own children.

This was reiterated by a young man who stated: 'There is no more *abusua* help. Times are difficult and everyone wants to narrow themselves to their own wife and children.'

Other residents pointed out that this struggle was not merely about matrilineal and nuclear or patrilineal family member rights. Economic hardships had resulted in a breakdown of reciprocity and mutual welfare support within all types of families and resulted in intergenerational conflict: because the family cannot take care of the youth they refuse to go to farm with their elders. One young man, of 22 years, elaborated on this: 'If you, a boy, ask your parents for school fees and they refuse you, you may have to work by-day [casual farm labour] to get the fees. The next time your parents ask you to do something for them you may refuse to attend to their call.'

During the late 1960s and 1970s land shortage became more pronounced in the cocoa sector. This occurred in a period of recession, which particularly affected the older cocoa frontier areas in the Eastern and Ashanti regions. Okali (1983) examines conflicts in property rights and access to labour between husbands, wives, children and sisters' children during this period. She argues that the successful cocoa farmer supplements hired labour with family labour from wives, children and matrilineal kin. These people work with the understanding that their hard work will be rewarded in the future with gifts of cocoa plantation that they had been instrumental in creating.

However, in the conditions of recession and the replanting of cocoa on old land, the establishment of a cocoa plantation often takes considerable time. Frequently, the cocoa farmers (who often marry well into maturity) die before the farm investments come to fruition and this leads to bitter disputes between wives, children and matrikin over the rights to the plantation. Those who have expended considerable efforts in the venture may be bitterly disappointed, as the fruits of their labour are usurped by others. This does not only apply to sons who find their rights to the fruits of their labour usurped by the matrikin of their father. Sisters' sons may also find the fruits of their labour appropriated by a senior matrilineal relative. With growing land shortage gifts of land become increasingly contentious and those with power within the lineage attempt to consolidate lineage land under their own authority. Lineage elders may challenge the rights of farmers to allocate matrilineal land to their close kin – those who have served them well. With succession, the new matrilineage head may try to redistribute land allocated by the former *abusuapanyin* to his close kin. Scarcity of land also enables elders to play off youth against each other to gain the most labour service from them. Not all children are assured land. As one elderly man at Dwenease explained: 'I bought my land for my personal use. Although I can give some to my nephews I may not give them any if I so please. I will share my land according to the service and attendance given to me.'

A young man at Dwenease stated:

> Now the youth have no Kwae [uncultivated forest land] on which they can clear their own farms. So it is only their parents who can find them some land. But this depends upon how good or serviceable you have been to your father or your mother before they will give you land.

Faced with growing uncertainties in access for land in return for labour service, many young men began to reject this circuit by the late 1960s and sought to gain their livelihood as farm labourers or as sharecroppers. However, their participation in these two activities was limited by the large number of northern migrant labourers working in the cocoa sector in the forest. An alternative reading of the situation is that the local young men began to feel resentment against northern migrant labourers, whose availability for employment gave elders leverage over the youth and created increasing land scarcity for the youth, since the migrants occupied the established plantations as caretakers.

During the economic recession of the late 1960s the Progress Party government resorted to increasing xenophobia and blamed the woes of the Ghanaian economy on the influx of 'aliens', or nationals from other West African countries. In an interview with Cameron Duodu in the *Daily Graphic* of 19 January 1970, Kofi Busia, the President of the Republic, said:

> ... of the people who have registered for work, one in every four is unemployed. Rising prices and pressures: what were we to do? Then, as you know our estimated population now is about eight million. The aliens also number one million and a half. We know that many of them are in the country without resident permits, because of the policies of the Nkrumah government which seemed to invite everybody at all who like to come and stay in Ghana.... Also a number of people have noticed aliens who were unemployed and engaged in stealing. And some were engaged in petty trading in foodstuffs and the rest. So people began to ask why there were so many aliens here. This is a question that no popularly elected government can ignore. So we said let our laws be fulfilled. We have regulations and those aliens who have come without residence papers must obtain them.

At the end of 1969 an Aliens Compliance Act was introduced which gave migrants two weeks to leave Ghana. Many hundreds of thousands of migrants were expelled and many of them had their property seized. The expulsion mainly focused on petty traders and the informal sector, but the expulsions rapidly moved into the farm labour sector and thousands of labourers on cocoa plantations were forced to leave. This raised great concern from cocoa farmers about how they were to gain alternative cheap labour sources. A report in the *Daily Graphic* of 28 January 1970 with the headline 'Police Probe Aliens Bribe Report' narrates:

> Mr Kofi Genfi III, MP for Atwima Amansie, yesterday called on the government to make it abundantly clear that alien farm labourers were privileged to stay in Ghana. Mr Gyemfi said it appeared the Government Compliance Order was being misapplied by some unscrupulous people in the rural areas. Addressing a news conference in Kumasi, Mr Gyemfi said he had received complaints from some farmers that there were people going around the villages asking farm labourers to leave the country. As a result many labourers have left for their countries and this has put some farmers in a difficult position. 'If the Government does nothing to arrest the alarming situation which is rearing its head, the cocoa industry will seriously be at stake,' he said.

After the removal of the Busia government in 1974, the Acheampong-led National Redemption Council announced that it would review the Aliens Compliance Order. Adomako-Safo (1974) reports that moves to re-instate Sahelian farm labour migration was rejected by many rural youth who demonstrated against the return of 'aliens'.

With the expulsion of migrant farm labour, local youth moved into the sphere of providing commodified labour rather than services in return for delayed reciprocity. The terms on which labour was granted were transformed. Annual labourers and *abusa* caretakers were now largely replaced by casual daily labour and job-lot labour. Increasingly, young men are working as sharecrop tenants. However, the agricultural economy in the Eastern Region has been transformed and food crop production has largely replaced cocoa. In some areas oil palm and citrus cultivation are now the main cash crops.

Agricultural production is increasingly commodified and landowners hire labour for farm clearance and for weeding. Many young men chose to work off their family land, as labourers or as sharecroppers rather than work for their family elders. Growing numbers of elders are increasingly forced to release land on a sharecropping basis to youth since they cannot afford the necessary cost of hiring farm labour. Thus, by supporting the expulsion of migrant labourers and caretakers the youth undermined the farm strategies of the elders. Access to migrant labour enabled the elders to create land scarcity over labour scarcity. By employing cheap labour in the lighter tasks of managing established plantations the elders could demand that the young men in their families perform the hard tasks of creating new cocoa plantations. This became a condition for gaining access to family land. The existence of large supplies of migrant labour also blocked young men from working as labourers. With the expulsion of migrant labour the elders are forced to employ local youth, creating more channels for them to work outside the family sphere. The youth could now demand higher wages than the migrants since there was a shortage of labour. The withdrawal of their labour services from the family sphere also resulted in more demand for hired labour. Elders now relied on hired labour rather than merely supplementing the labour of family youth with that of labourers.

However, this is not a simple struggle with clearly defined cleavages between young men and elders. The cleavages between youth and elders reflect competition between elders for control over land and rights to dispose of land to relatives. Bitter struggles have also developed between family elders about rights to allocate land to one's kin. This happens particularly when it involves highly profitable tree crops which alienate land for considerable periods. This is more evident in the burgeoning oil palm sector in the Kwaebibrem area of the Eastern Region rather than on declining cocoa plantations. In this area, many family members oppose attempts to allocate land by family heads to their sons and nephews for oil palm plantation. They argue that given the scarcity of land, large tracts of family land should not be alienated to support commercial plantation development which locks up land for a long period and intensifies land shortage for food farmers. Cases have occurred where on the death of a lineage head his successor has made sure that his oil palm plantations are uprooted rather than allocated to his sons and nephews and that the land is reallocated to close relatives of the new lineage head (Amanor, 1999). Lineage elders will also attempt to make demands on farmers who have established their oil palm plantations on family land and ensure that parts of the proceeds are given to the matrilineage. Under these conditions wealthy young men wishing to invest in oil palm plantations frequently prefer to gain land under sharecropping arrangements rather than invest in family land (Gyasi 1994, Amanor 1999). A further development from this, is that as sharecropping becomes prevalent and sharecropping land more scarce, sharecropping develops within the family and lineage because it is difficult to get good sharecropping land elsewhere. Fathers gain sharecropping contracts for their sons on the land of their matrilineage. Wealthy enterprising sons use the land of their father or his matrilineage and gives them a third share (*abusa*) or a half share (*abunu*) of the farm proceeds to meet the rental value of the land. This can consolidate the bonds between the son, the father and the father's matrilineage on an economic basis.

At Ntronang in Akyem Abuakwa, Nana Frimpong Manso is a prosperous farmer who is the *abusuahene* (family head) of his matrilineage. He has a farm of about 100 acres from his mother's matrilineage which he shares with three sisters. His father has also left him a farm of 40 acres, but this is farmed on an *abusa* basis since he has no direct rights to the land under the rules of matrilineal inheritance. He has planted cocoa and oil palm on this land. He gives one third of the harvest to the head of his father's matrilineage. He intends to pass the plantation on to his children. They too will continue to pay a third share of the produce to the matrilineage. On his own matrilineal land he has given out 60 acres on *abunu* (a half share contract) to three farmers. By working his father's land he is assured of property (in the form of plantations rather than land) which he can pass on to his children, albeit with a third share rent to the matrilineage. Although he cannot provide them with an inheritance in land he can provide them with an inheritance in valuable plantation. This enables him to work together with his children and assures them of land in the future if they cooperate with him. While he is responsible for his matrilineal land, he chooses to give the majority of it out to sharecrop tenants since he has to share the income with others and his personal rights to the land are not securely defined.

With oil palm sharecrop contracts in the Kwaebibirem area, the norm is that the plantations are shared into two halves when they start fruiting and the landlord selects the half of the plantation they s/he is interested in managing. They then manage their farms independently. The tenant has rights to the land for the duration of the tree crop. When the oil palms become old and unproductive, which is usually after 25 years, the trees are felled, palm wine extracted and the land returned to its matrilineal owners.

In addition to providing the landlord with a half share of the plantation, the tenant also makes an *aseda* payment on negotiation of the sharecropping contract. Although *aseda* payments vary, they can consist of quite substantial sums of money for smallholder farmers. In 2000 farmers could pay the equivalent of US$100 as *aseda* for a four acre plot. The *aseda* deters prospective sharecroppers with insufficient capital to develop oil palm plantations from negotiating a contract, and functions as a non-returnable deposit. The *aseda* payment also serves to justify giving out land to sharecroppers, since any family member wishing to secure land for cultivation must make payment of the *aseda*. High *aseda* payment will be beyond the means of food crop farmers and would deter impoverished farmers from seeking land on which to engage in food crop farming. One young woman at Mamanso bemoaned that she had no land to farm and when she approached her father he demanded an *aseda* payment which she could not afford.

Sharecropping is pervasive at Mamanso. In a survey of 106 farmers (Amanor with Diderutuah 2001), 69 per cent had acquired some land on a sharecropping basis. Of the farms worked by these 106 farmers 65 per cent were subject to share contracts. At Mamanso 44 per cent of share contracts were between relatives. However, this involved many different categories of relatives, including father and children, mother and children, other matrilineal kin, siblings and between married partners (Amanor with Diderutuah 2001). Thus in the Kwaebibirem area, the increase of sharecropping within the family cannot be seen merely as a means of transferring matrilineal land to the children of male members of the matrilineage.

Sharecropping reflects an increasing commodification of agricultural production, of labour relations and land, which dramatically transforms and commodifies family and household relationships. This has resulted from the centrality of labour services to family farm organisation and the erosion of the reciprocity underlying the provision of services by growing insecurity in access to land. As a result of growing insecurity in individual rights to family land, youth have retracted their labour services from the household and sold their labour on the market or negotiated contractual share arrangements for land. However, the insecurity in land relations are underlined by growing competition within lineages and between lineage elders for land and a narrowing of kinship obligations as resources become more scarce. Similarly, young men are also socially differentiated and the lack of access of some youth to family land is a result of the wealth of other youth and their willingness to enter into contractual relations to gain access to sharecropping land from elders in other matrilineal segments. The 'customary' rituals surrounding the contracting of sharecropping land and the payment of *aseda* mask the fact that this is a highly commodified relationship in which the lineage elders are essentially leasing out lineage land. While the first stages in the transformation of agricultural relations of production involved the expulsion of migrant labour by youth taking advantage of misguided government policies, the underlying contradictions were the product of land scarcity, the commodification of agricultural production, conflicts between elders over control over land, and conflicts between young men and elders about rights to land and labour services.

Matrilineal land & matrifocality

The colonial framework of customary land tenure denied women rights in land. This was premised on the customary framework for citizenship, which gave citizens rights to the use of land and in return obliged them to perform communal labour service. Since women did not perform communal labour they did not have full rights to citizenship. Women's rights to land were thus assumed to be based on marriage. However, in matrilineal areas, women frequently had rights to land. These rights were seen by colonial authorities as an obstacle to creating proper systems of land tenure and marriage. For instance, in the colonial period Lambert Stokes wrote: 'The men are a floating population and it is the women who are tied to the land. Family life is unstable and there is no solid ground to build a modern form of land tenure' (quoted by Chanock 1991: 73). In a survey of the Gold Coast carried out in 1946 Meek (1946) noted that 40 per cent of cocoa farmers were women. This was corroborated by Polly Hill (1959) in a survey of Asafo and Maase in the Akyem area where more than half the cocoa plots surveyed belonged to women.

While the women owned more plots than men their plots tended to be smaller. Forty per cent of the men's plots were over five acres as compared with 17 per cent of women's plots. The women interviewed insisted that they were cocoa farmers in their own right and that their husbands did not give them any help in their farm work. The women did the farm work themselves or hired labour. Hill (1959: 3) writes that the women were inclined to employ labour and made 'excellent employers, working alongside the labourers in the forest and providing them with cooked food. One has heard the view expressed that labourers prefer women employers to men.' One of the women interviewed commented that 'in the olden times we used to help our husbands to get big, big farms; and when they died we got nothing' (Hill 1959: 2).

This echoes the research carried out by Okali (1983) in the 1970s, where many women who had worked on their husband's cocoa farms found themselves dispossessed by their husband's matrilineage on his death. Okali (1983) argues that wives in the forest belt are increasingly demanding that the farm services they perform are reciprocated in rights in land for themselves and their children. If these demands are not met they are prepared to divorce their husbands. Another strategy is for women to look for security in property by claiming rights of ownership in their own autonomous land and ensuring that women's land continues to circulate between women rather than be appropriated by men. At Dwenease and Apinaman women articulate a strong matrifocal ideology. Matrifocality is based on a commonality of interest between three generations of women relatives within the family and their joint organisation of independent economic and child rearing activities (Smith 1996). Grandmothers, mothers, and daughters often farm together and grandmothers and mothers pass on their land to their daughters and granddaughters. The basis of the matrifocal ideology is to ensure that women continue to get access to land, since the dominant customary tenure, as constructed within the colonial period, does not recognise their autonomous rights to land. Access to land for women is largely dependent upon its transmission by one generation of women to the next. Daughters help their mothers in farming with knowledge that this will secure land for them in their own right. But women also have sons and a good son will help his mother on her farm and there will be bonds of affection between them. To ensure that they continue to have rights to land, daughters must make sure that their mothers do not go soft on their sons and pass on land to them. This is vital at present, where the cooperation between sons, fathers and mothers' brothers has become strained. Under these conditions, sons may try to gain access to land from their mothers, and this will undermine women's rights to their autonomous land. Thus the matrifocal strategy focuses on preserving women's rights from their brothers; it portrays brothers as imposters, violators of customary norms, and portrays women as the true defenders of the matrilineal principle.

The matrifocal ideology states:

> Women usually pass on lands to their daughters and granddaughters. That is the tradition here because men do not belong to the *abusua* [matrilineage]. If you give land to the son it goes out of the *abusua*, but if it goes to the women it will stay home. If you give land to the boys and they happen to give birth the land will go to the wife's children. A father can always give out his land as a gift to his children. In that case it becomes the property of his children and they can sell it out or develop it for their own use.

The matrifocal ideology draws out the contradictions and ambivalence in the role of men in a matrilineal society. Although they control the matrilineal property, they have conflicting demands from their sons (who are not members of the lineage and have no rights to inherit matrilineal property) and their sisters' sons who are their rightful heirs. One young woman at Apinaman narrated:

> We are three sisters and a brother. Our mother's brother is dead and has left a large tract of land for us, which is lying fallow. We are planning to meet here to share the land among us. We are planning that we will not give our brother any part of the land because it will allow him to develop part of it and leave it to his children. So he has to find his own land elsewhere, since he is not going to marry from our family. We can develop what is there little by little for our children.

Increasing scarcity of land and commodification is leading to increasing conflicts between brothers and sisters, and undermining the sibling bonding which constitutes the heart of the matrilineal system. However, there may be much posturing in the aggressive stance of sisters. The aggressive stance is necessary to ensure that mothers do not give women's land to their sons. And the mothers can develop a less aggressive stance which assures their daughters of land without antagonising their sons. As Hill (1959: 3) reports:

> Apart from the assistance given by school children in their holidays, some women are assisted by their elder sons, though they tended to play this down in an interview. It was mentioned that a particular helpful son might be given a farm by his mother during her lifetime. Usually, of course, a woman's daughter succeeds to her property and it is considered more appropriate that they should provide for her brother's needs from her mother's farm than that the farm should actually pass to him.

The matrifocal ideology occurs in the situation where land is increasingly commodified by men and used for individual farming ventures. It occurs in the context in which women's rights to land are eroded and not recognised in the customary framework as formally constituted under colonial rule. This framework re-invented women as the wives of cocoa farmers who assist them in making cocoa plantations and growing foodstuffs. However, women's rights as wives were not secure and frequently their labour investments in farming were appropriated by male members of the husband's matrilineage. This promoted marital instability and divorce. Fully aware of the difficulty in defending their rights to the land of their husband's matrilineage, women began to reassert their rights to their own autonomous land. In defending their rights to land, they point out the contradictions in the role of men as controllers of matrilineal land, as commercial farmers with interests in commodified land and as husbands with interests in narrowing down their obligations to their matrilineage. They cast doubts on the legitimacy of men's customary rights to control matrilineal property and their transparency in managing matrilineal property. This serves to promote female solidarity within the lineage, and to consolidate women's defence of their property rights in land and its erosion by male control of property and the increasing commodification of agricultural production.

Rights to charcoal & tree resources in the transition zone

Charcoal is mainly produced in the transition zone of Ghana, where the many small fire-resistant woodlands provide the ideal resources for charcoal burning. The fire-resistance of these trees promotes good slow burning qualities. The trees of this zone are also robust, and when cut rapidly regenerate from coppice and root suckers. The main charcoal burners are migrants from the Sissala area of the Upper West Region in Ghana who have mastered the art of making charcoal. They also control a large proportion of the charcoal marketing and transport trade in the major urban areas. The Sissala charcoal burners are socially differentiated. Rich Sissala charcoal traders control transport and hire labour. Poor Sissala charcoal labourers cannot afford to purchase permits or even the sacks for packing charcoal and hire their services out to traders.

The main crop produced in the transition zone is yam, and its production is dependent upon the existence of many small trees, which are used to stake the yams, whose tendrils wind up the trunks of these trees in their search for sunlight. When preparing the yam fields fires are lit under the trees to destroy their crowns, or they are ring barked. The trees will eventually put out new coppice growth or root shoots and regenerate over a few years in fallow land. When the small trees have regenerated the farmers return to the plot to plant yams again. The rights of farmers to these tree resources are not secured under customary land tenure since they are recognised as belonging to the chief. Migrant Sissala charcoal burners wishing to gain access to tree resources in the transition zone visit the chief of the area where they wish to work to gain permission. They make payment to the chief for a permit which gives them rights to exploit trees for charcoal burning within a specified area. This has led to conflicts with farmers, since the charcoal resources they exploit in fallow are the trees that farmers are frequently preserving in fallow land for future cultivation of yams. Since farmers' rights to these trees have not been recognised they have not been able to prevent charcoal burners cutting down fallow trees for which they have gained permits from chiefs.

During the early 1990s the situation began to change. Several local district assemblies, under pressure to create sound environmental policies in the post-Rio world of global environmental conventions, began to introduce bye-laws to ban charcoal production, which they considered to be degrading the environment and resulting in desertification. These environmental bye-laws were quickly rescinded when it was realised that they jeopardised fuel supplies in the large urban conglomerates, where about 90 per cent of households depend upon charcoal for cooking. Tolls on charcoal production was also one of the most important revenue sources for district assemblies in the transition zone. Before these poorly formulated bye-laws were rescinded news of their formulation spread rapidly around farming communities in the main charcoal production zone. These narratives of environmental crisis resulting from the impact of charcoal production resounded well with the young men and farmers who were concerned about charcoal burners cutting trees in their fallows.

While there was not necessarily any evidence of environmental destruction, the farming communities used these environmental narratives to portray the charcoal burners as immoral destroyers of the environment. In settlements like Weila and Mansie in the Kintampo District of Brong Ahafo, the young men also began to study the charcoal burning techniques of the Sissala and to engage in charcoal burning as an alternative source of livelihood to farming. The youth began to engage in verbal conflicts with the charcoal burners and placed demands on the chiefs to control their activities. They began to insist that charcoal burners should not be allowed to cut green wood in fallows but must only use trees that had been cleared by farmers. This became a local bye-law which forced the charcoal burners to negotiate with farmers for access to cleared wood on their farm plots. The local youth also requested that farmers release farm wood to them rather than the Sissala, and frustrated by the lack of access to woodfuel for charcoal the Sissala left. Once the Sissala left the area the youth expanded their charcoal production, now clearing charcoal trees in fallow land. The chiefs at Mansie and Weila had lost valuable revenues from the migrant charcoal burners. As citizens, the local young men were not liable to pay for permits to exploit woodfuel resources. Realising that they had been outmanoeuvred by the youth, the chiefs and elders vowed to enforce the bye-laws against burning outside of cleared farms and to discipline the youth. The struggles between local youth and charcoal burners over tree resources were transformed into a struggle between youth and chiefs and their elders. In these settlements, the migrant charcoal burners may have given up the struggle easily because prime charcoal resources were becoming scarcer and better sources were available elsewhere. The Sissala burners do not stay in one locality, but like shifting cultivators, when the charcoal resources of one locality begin to decline, they move to another area, giving the prime charcoal trees time to recuperate and build up their densities again.

In the thick wooded areas around Nsawkaw a different scenario has emerged. It began in a similar fashion with the youth taking advantage of poorly formulated environmental policies to challenge the rights of migrant charcoal burners to exploit charcoal production in fallow land. The paramount chief, who had gained large revenues from giving permits to the charcoal burners, took a stand in favour of the rights of burners to burn charcoal and his right to issue permits. A bitter conflict developed between the youth and the chief and the chief was forced to leave the settlement. Some youth moved into charcoal production as rivals to the Sissala, but they began to realise that charcoal production is not easy work and best left to the professionals. Charcoal was also an important resource in Nsawkaw and large revenues were collected from road tolls. A large section of the community reflected on the struggles between charcoal burners and youth and insisted that charcoal burners had a right to a livelihood, and that the urban folk needed charcoal for cooking. Nevertheless, they insisted that charcoal burners should not spoil the environment for farmers. An accommodation was reached in which charcoal burners were banned from cutting live green trees in fallow, but must negotiate with farmers for access to trees on their farms. Before the farm clearing season begins charcoal burners seek out farmers to trade the standing trees in the areas they intend to farm, which have potential for charcoal production. On maize farms, the charcoal burners may hire chainsaw operators to cut down the trees and burn the charcoal before the commencement of farm clearing. On yam farms, the charcoal burners wait until the yams are harvested before converting the trees into charcoal. Clearly, if a charcoal burner needs a large number of trees an arrangement can be made with farmers to extend the farm, which will give the farmer access to more capital from the sale of more trees to use for the hiring of farm labour and will give the charcoal burners more charcoal to sell.

By manipulating environmental narratives that are rooted in a discourse of morality and blame, the farmers have been able to gain new rights in trees that they never had before. However, to achieve this they have had to engage in conflict with charcoal burners and the chiefs. They have been able to gain the upper hand through concerted action around a moral environmental code that has manipulated poorly thought out district administrative policies. The farmers have then been able to negotiate a settlement involving the rights to sell trees. However, they have partly been able to achieve this because the Sissala are nationally a weak economic group with little political influence, who unlike timber loggers, cannot call upon the repressive organs of the state to secure resources for them.

Conclusion

Contrary to many current assumptions customary land law is essentially formulated from above. Its origins lie in colonial domination and the desire of the colonial authority to create 'appropriate' systems of land administration for people who had not evolved capitalist relations of production. Customary land law was formulated to facilitate the integration of rural African producers into the markets of empire. It aimed to prevent the emergence of speculative indigenous land markets which could rapidly alienate land to Africans and thus prevent its future utilisation by colonial government and its allies. Customary land law enabled European concessionaires and settler farmers in certain areas to gain land on suitable terms for their ventures. Customary land law appealed ideologically to the notion of preserving a tradition that had existed before the imposition of colonialism. This notion was not based on any empirical evidence but deduced from a body of philosophical work on the evolution of civil society. Thus, empire-wide assertions were made of the characteristics of communal land ownership, and legal precedents were proclaimed with empire-wide applicability to a multiplicity of different societies. These preconceptions were totally inappropriate since most of the colonised societies had been rapidly transformed during the nineteenth century. The imposition of colonial rule had completely transformed rights in people and rights in land. Slavery and many quasi-feudal relations had been abolished by colonial occupations and attempts had been made to create wage labour and capitalist commodity markets, which profoundly altered social and economic relationships.

The customary domain was established by an alliance between colonial government and pre-existing rulers (or newly created 'traditional' rulers fashioned to meet administrative needs). Within a set of basic principles drawn up by colonial authorities on what constituted communal or customary land tenure, these ruling 'native authorities' were to codify what constituted customary practice and to define bye-laws. The basis of this was to deny security of individual land rights and to assert the primacy of the community and its usufructuary rights in land. Chiefs were empowered by colonial rule to act as the custodians of tradition, land and natural resources.

However, the concept of community usufructuary rights limited the extent to which rulers could exploit natural resources through local labour (which had user rights to land and natural resources). The commodification of local natural resources depended upon chiefs transacting local resources with expatriate concessionaires and with migrants. This resulted in the chiefs in export producing zones encouraging migrants to settle in their domain, and allocating land to them through sale, sharecrop arrangements and other types of contractual relations. Without any other framework than the notion of the customary with which to hold their chiefs accountable, commoners within native authorities began to develop their own notion of the customary around conceptions of accountability. The constituents of this are based on an appeal to a moral order, and the identification of others who violate this moral order as violating customary norms and rights. Other moral discourses that allocate blame can also be utilised, such as environmental crisis narratives. Since government policies are frequently promulgated in relation to customary rights, contemporary policies also feature in discourses about customary rights. These discourses are usually articulated around concrete struggles and a conflictual approach to negotiation in which consensus can only be achieved by posturing and engaging in heated dispute with other groups before negotiated settlement can occur. This posturing reflects the lack of clearly defined individual and group rights to resources.

These conflicts are often complex and multi-sided. Since chiefs and elders have often used migrants to bolster their position and to appropriate and commodify natural resources, commoners and young men engage in conflicts with migrants to undermine the basis of power of chiefs and elders, and to negotiate for rights. Thus in the Eastern region young men sought to evict migrants to undermine the power of elders over their labour. In the transition zone of Brong Ahafo, farmers' conflicts with charcoal burners undermine the monopoly claims of chiefs to own natural resources. However, struggles between youth and elders over rights to labour services and rights to land and economic support often reflect a process of commodification. Elders may be struggling among themselves to gain control over land which ultimately enables them to control labour. Wealthy young men who engage in share contracts are also appropriating the matrilineal lands of other sections of the youth and undermining their ability to gain family land. Women point to men as violators of matrilineal principles to safeguard their rights to land in the face of a process of commodification and lack of recognised rights in customary land law. The struggles between broadly defined groups, divided on the basis of generation, seniority and citizenship tend to mask processes of commodification of land and labour which lie at the heart of all these struggles.

The customary is also defined by the state as the domain of chiefly privilege. However, the most powerful chiefs have come to form a part of the political and business elite. Thus definition of the customary from above tends to preserve important resources for the rich and powerful. Where the customary refers to valuable resources that are important to national elites, such as timber, the customary reaffirms the lack of rights of rural people and the expropriation of these resources by the privileged. The customary hardens and becomes less subject to processes of negotiations, and the military and police can be used to defend the rights of the powerful against popular encroachment, such as in the case of timber.

References

Addo-Fenning. 1997. *Akyem Abuakwa 1700–1943: From Ofori Panin to Sir Ofori Atta*. Trondheim: Department of History, Norwegian University of Science and Technology.

Adomako Safo, J. 1974. 'The Effects of the Expulsion of Migrant Workers in Ghana's Economy, with Particular Reference to the Cocoa Industry.' In S. Amin (ed.) *Modern Migrations in West Africa*, London: International African Institute.

Amamoo, J.G. 1958. *The New Ghana: The Birth of a Nation*, London: Pan Books.

Amanor, K.S. 2001. *Land, Labour and the Family in Southern Ghana: A Critique of Land Policy under Neo-liberalisation, Research report no. 116*. Uppsala: Nordiska Afrikainstitutet.

______. 1999. *Global Restructuring and Land Rights in Ghana: Forest Food Chains, Timber and Rural Livelihoods*, Uppsala: Scandinavian Institute of African Studies.

______. 1996. *Managing Trees in Farming Systems: The Perspectives of Farmers*. Kumasi: Forestry Department.

Amanor, K.S with Kude Diderutuah, M. 2001. *Share Contracts in the Oil Palm and Citrus Belt of Ghana*. London: IIED.

Arhin Brempong. 2001. *Transformations in Traditional Rule in Ghana (1951–1996)*. Accra: Sedco.

Asad, T. 1979. 'Anthropology and the Analysis of Ideology.' *Man* (NS) 14: 607–27.

Berry, S.S. 2001. *Chiefs Know their Boundaries; Essays on Property, Power and the Past in Asante, 1896–1996*. Portsmouth, NH: Heinemann, Oxford: James Currey and Cape Town: David Philip.

Bruce, J. W. 1993. 'Do Indigenous Tenure Systems Constrain Agricultural Development?' In T. J. Bassett and D. E. Crummey (eds) *Land in African Agrarian Systems*. Madison: University of Wisconsin Press.

Chanock, M. 1991. 'Paradigms, Policies and Property; A Review of the Customary Law of Land Tenure.' In K. Mann and R. Roberts (eds) *Law in Colonial Africa*. Portsmouth, NH: Heinemann and London: James Currey.

Chaveau, J.-P., 2000. *The Land Question in Côte d'Ivoire: A Lesson in History*. IIED Drylands Programme Issues Paper no 95. London: IIED.

Cowen, M. P. and Shenton, R. W. 1994. 'British Neo-Hegelian Idealism and Official Colonial Practice in West Africa: The Oluwa Land Case of 1921', *Journal of Imperial and Commonwealth History* 22(2): 217–50.

Douglas, M.1969. 'Is Matriliny Doomed in Africa?' In M. Douglas and P.M. Kaberry (eds) *Man in Africa*. London: Tavistock Publishing.

Field, M.J. 1948. *Akim Kotoku: An Oman of the Gold Coast*. London: Crown Agents.

Foggie, A. and Piasecki, B. 1962. 'Timber, Fuel and Minor Produce.' In J.B. Wills (ed.) *Agriculture and Land Use in Ghana*. Accra: Ghana Ministry of Food and Agriculture and London: Oxford University Press.

Gyasi, E.A. 1994. 'The Adaptability of African Communal Land Tenure to Economic Opportunity: The Example of Land Acquisition for Oil Palm Farming in Ghana.' *Africa*, 64 (3): 391–405.

Hill, P. 1963. *The Migrant Cocoa-Farmers of Southern Ghana: A study in rural capitalism*. Cambridge: Cambridge University Press. (repr. 1997, London, Hamburg, Oxford: IIAI, Lit Verlag and James Currey).

______. 1959. *The Cocoa Farmers of Asafo and Maase with special reference to the position of women*, Cocoa Research series no. 12. Economic Research Division, University College of Ghana.

______. 1956. *The Gold Coast Farmer*. London: Oxford University Press.

Hill, P. and McGlade, C. 1957. *An Economic Survey of Cocoa Farmers in Sefwi-Wiawso*, Cocoa Research Series no. 2. Accra: Economic Research Division, University College of Ghana.

Jul-Larsen, E. and Kassibo, B. 2001. 'Fishing at Home and Abroad: Access to Waters in Niger's

Central Delta and the Effects of Work Migrants.' In T.A. Benjaminsen and C. Lund (eds) *Politics, Property and Production in the West African Sahel: Understanding Natural Resource Management*. Uppsala: Nordiska Afrikainstitutet.

Lavigne Delville, P. 2000. 'Harmonising Formal Law and Customary Land Rights in French-Speaking West Africa.' In C. Toulmin and J. Quan (eds) *Evolving Land Rights, Policy and Tenure in Africa*. London: IIED, NRI and DFID.

Minister of Commerce, Industry and Mines.1951. *Report of the Fact-Finding Committee, on the Timber Industry in the Western Province of the Gold Coast*. Accra: Government Printer.

Meek, C.K. 1946. *Land Law and Custom in the Colonies*. Oxford: Oxford University Press.

Okali, C. 1983. *Cocoa and Kinship in Ghana: The Matrilineal Akan of Ghana*, London: Kegan Paul.

Ranger, T. 1993. 'The Invention of Tradition Revisited: The Case of Colonial Africa.' In Terence Ranger and Olufemi Vaughan (eds) *Legitimacy and the State in Twentieth-Century Africa: Essays in Honour of A. H. Kirk-Greene*. Oxford: Macmillan Press.

______. 1983. 'The Invention of Tradition in Colonial Africa.' In E. Hobsbawm and T. Ranger (eds) *The Invention of Tradition*. Cambridge: Cambridge University Press.

Rathbone, R. 1993. *Murder and Politics in Colonial Ghana*. New Haven and London: Yale University Press.

Simensen, J. 1975. 'Nationalism from Below: The Akyem Abuakwa Example.' In *Akyem Abuakwa and the Politics of the Inter-war Period in Ghana*. Basel Africa Bibliography, Vol.12: 31–60.

Smith, R. T. 1996. *The Matrifocal Family*. London: Routledge.

Songsore, J. and Denkabe, A. 1995. *Challenging Rural Poverty in Northern Ghana: The case of the Upper-West Region*, Trondheim: Centre for Environment and Development, University of Trondheim.

Toulmin, C. and and Quan, J. 2000. 'Evolving Land Rights, Tenure and Policy in Sub-Saharan Africa', In C. Toulmin and J. Quan (eds) *Evolving Land Rights, Policy and Tenure in Africa*. London: IIED, DFID, NRI.

Toulmin, C., Lavigne Delville, P. and Traoré, S. 2002. 'Introduction.' In C. Toulmin, P. Lavigne Delville and S. Traoré (eds) *The Dynamics of Resource Tenure in West Africa*. London: IIED, Oxford: James Currey and Portsmouth, NH: Heinemann.

3

Land Tenure & Land Conflicts among the Kwanja in Adamawa, Northern Cameroon[1]

'Our Land is Not for Sale'

QUENTIN GAUSSET

The Kwanja territory

The territory of the Kwanja is traditionally divided among a number of chiefs, who are all independent (there is no paramount chief). The boundary of each territory is firmly established; it follows rivers, ridges, and can be marked by big stones or special trees in the savannah. Traditionally, all 'chiefly' animals (leopards, pythons, bird with red feathers) killed on this territory had to be brought to the chief. Failure to do so could bring mystical sanctions on the culprit, and giving the chiefly animal to another chief could lead to war. The chief also took a leg of all cloven-footed animals killed on his territory (buffaloes, antelopes, etc.). Chiefs usually have dignitaries (notables) who can administer part of their territory and take the leg of animals killed in their territory, but they can never take pythons or leopards. The Kwanja make a strong difference between 'leopard chiefs' (*'chefs de panthère'*) and the other, lesser chiefs (dignitaries of the leopard chiefs) (Gausset 1997a, 1997b).

Many of the Kwanja territories have been conquered either mystically or through war. Kwanja history is filled with stories of great warriors who chased away or subjugated neighbouring communities (Bute, Wawa, Tikar, Mambila) through their courage. As a reward, they were given a dignitary title by the leopard chief whom they served. Territories and power could also be conquered mystically; there are numerous Kwanja myths telling how one chief 'stole' the power of another chief through performing magical tricks or through conquering the heart of the population by being generous and courageous. Only a minority of territories is said to be controlled by their original chief (Gausset 1997b). Therefore, the Kwanja territory is controlled today by a number of chiefs of various origins, many of whom seized the power of another.

It is to be noted here that the Kwanja is a bilineal society (both patrilineal and matrilineal) (see Gausset 1998a). The matrilineages are the primary basis of

[1] The data for this article were collected during two years' fieldwork among the Kwanja between 1992 and 2002. I would like to thank the Cassel Fund of the Free University of Brussels, the National Fund for Scientific Research of Belgium (FNRS), and the council for development research of the Danish International Development Agency (Danida) for their financial support. I would also like to express my gratitude to Robert Gibb for his help in improving this paper.

social solidarity. When someone is sick or has personal problems, he looks for support among the members of his matrilineage. Matrilineages are exogamous and regulate matrimonial alliances and inheritance. Hereditary characteristics (such as 'family diseases' and witchcraft) are also transmitted matrilineally. Patrilineages, for their part, are in charge of rituals and formal power. Ethnic identity is also passed patrilineally. Every individual supports the dignitary or the chief linked to his patrilineage and follows the rituals that his chief organises. Moreover, every individual defines himself as coming from his patrilineal trench (see below) or territory.

All leopard chiefs and many dignitaries have inherited their title patrilineally. However, a significant number of dignitary titles are also inherited matrilineally (Gausset 1997a). In cases in which the group of warriors who conquered a territory was composed of a matrilineage, the title which they were given became inherited matrilineally, and the territory controlled belongs to (is controlled by) the matrilineage. Oral history also tells that some forests, river parts, lakes – places with game or fish – were 'bought' by a matrilineage who 'sold' one of his female members away (although it was more the right to game and fish which was bought than the territory as such, which remained under the control of the chief). Thus, *all* patrilineages and only *some* matrilineages control a territory.[2] A Kwanja can always get land through the chief of his patrilineage, but only some people are lucky enough to belong to a matrilineage which controls some land and can get land through their matrilineal affiliation. Matrilineages therefore play a weak role in the political control of land. However, they do play a role in the choice of residence. Witchcraft is believed to be inherited matrilineally and is often practised within the patrilineage but seldom within the matrilineage. It is typically among the members of their matrilineages that people seek refuge when they want to run away from any kind of problem, or when they want to find social solidarity and physical or mystical protection. Therefore, people often prefer to live close to their matrilineal relatives. When a matrilineage controls a territory, its members often prefer to establish themselves there rather than in their father's village. Even when the matrilineage does not control a territory, its members will always do what it takes to provide land for a matrilineal relative who wishes to stay with them (Gausset 1997a, 1998a).

Until recently, land has not been in shortage (even today, only forested areas are rare; unused savannah is still plentiful). If there were a shortage, it concerned the availability of people. Therefore, chiefs and dignitaries did not compete to control land as such, but rather to control followers. Patrilineages also competed with matrilineages, although they sometimes tried to combine their interests through complex matrimonial strategies. In order to attract followers, chiefs had to be good and generous, and they had to have a firm mystical control over their territory. They had to provide both abundance and protection against witchcraft through their sacred power (see Gausset 1995). Migrants were always welcome, as long as they accepted the authority of the chief who hosted them, and as long as they established themselves in the local community. Those who married a local woman (and inter-marriages with neighbouring groups were common)

[2] Not all matrilineages have conquered or bought a territory. Moreover, as matrilineages have no name, and as the founder of a matrilineage is not remembered, matrilineages tend to split slowly during the course of time. This is not the case of patrilineages in which the descent is much more structured around the name of the first ancestor (which is also the name inherited by the chief or the dignitary) and around the name of the trench.

could always find land through their wives' patrilineages or matrilineages.

So traditionally, land was abundant and its control was not an end in itself. It was not even a means of attracting more political supporters since land was plentiful and people chose their residence on the basis of the strength of the chief and of the number of relatives living in the village. Although land could be conquered through war by dignitaries, it was not done to control the resources as such, but rather the prestige derived from territorial control. Chiefs did have conflicts when they disagreed about the border between their territories, something which happens even today, but these conflicts did not concern the resources as such (they often concerned land which was not used by anybody) and were really about the authority and prestige of the chiefs rather than about the control of the resource. Chiefs competed more over their magical superiority or the control of people than over the control of land (which derived from the control of people and magic).

Fulbe conquest of the plateau, Kwanja conquest of the plain

The Kwanja territory was originally founded on the Adamawa plateau. Villages were surrounded by deep artificial trenches, which were dug to provide protection against assault from neighbours. However, these trenches were unable to protect villages against the aggression of the Fulbe and their local allies, who conquered northern Cameroon, and hunted down Kwanja communities for slaves (Lacroix 1952, Kirk-Greene 1958, Froelich 1966, Mohammadou 1966, 1978, 1981, 1982, 1991, Smith 1966, Büttner 1967, Hurault 1975, Bah 1982, Burnham 1996). The captives were sold as slaves in the markets of northern Cameroon and northern Nigeria (Gausset 1998b, 2003). As there was no unified resistance, the Kwanja villages fell one after the other, and the population fled to the Tikar plain, where they chased away the existing Tikar population further south and created new Kwanja villages. This history is still the source of resentment and tensions between neighbouring Kwanja and Tikar communities, despite the numerous intermarriages which have occurred among them, but again, the conflicts are more about symbolic aspects of land (border between territories, rights to chiefly game) or about the local structure of power (do Tikar dignitaries depend on Kwanja or Tikar chiefs?) than about the control of resources as such. The Fulbe colonisation was circumscribed to the Adamawa plateau and mainly concerned those local populations who had cooperated with the Fulbe. Elsewhere (including in the Tikar plain), the Fulbe did not really control the area (Gausset 1998b), but they did make numerous raids to capture slaves. German colonisation pacified the area and put an end to the violent acquisition of slaves although domestic slaves continued to be provided to the Fulbe sultan until the 1950s. At the same time, the colonial administration relied on an indirect rule which conferred the control of territories to the Fulbe sultan, which he previously only used as a slave reserve without really controlling them. Despite the pacification, the bulk of the Kwanja population remained in the Tikar plain. During the 1950s, when the national road was re-made, people were forced to move their villages close to the road although they kept their fields close to their original villages of the plain.

As a result of all these historical processes, the Kwanja population lives today along the main road linking southern and northern Cameroon. This means that most villages and their chiefs are situated on the territory controlled by another chief. In the plain, the territories situated further away from the main road are still farmed, if they are not too far away, but nobody stays there permanently. On the plateau, most Kwanja territories are relatively abandoned. (All trenches have been abandoned. There are only a few small Kwanja communities living far from the main road and most of the Kwanja territory of the plateau is used as pasture for wandering cattle.) Recently, some newcomers have begun to establish themselves in these areas. As a consequence, chiefly titles which had been abandoned for a long time began being distributed again to the descendants of the forgotten chief, partly as an attempt to reassert Kwanja rights over the areas and to make sure that newcomers would not consider this land as totally 'empty'.

The link with the land of origin is still extremely strong. Every Kwanja knows the name of his trench of origin (defined patrilineally), and people still say that they come from a certain trench, despite the fact that some have never seen that trench and would be unable to find it. Although people are nowadays buried in the village where they die, they still believe that the deceased person's spirit travels and rests in its trench of origin, despite the fact that most Kwanja have converted to Islam or Christianity (Gausset 1999, 2002a). Dead chiefs are still buried in their trench of origin, in the chiefs' collective tomb, or at the very least, even if their body is not buried there, their skull is. A few months after a chief is buried in a sitting position, the skull is taken out of the tomb, washed, and then buried in the trench together with the skulls of the former chiefs. Most major fertility rituals (ancestors' cults organised by the chiefs) and some parts of funeral rituals still take place there, even though it might require a full day's walk to reach the trench. During these rituals, people clear the old cemetery of the chiefs and lay people, organise small offerings to the ancestor's spirits while asking for fertility, good luck or abundance, and consult some local oracles (fish, sources of water, etc.) to know what the future will be like for the living.

So despite the fact that the trenches situated on the plateau have been abandoned for several generations and that most Kwanja have converted to Islam or Christianity and live now in the Tikar plain along the main road (i.e. not on their own territory), people still keep a surprisingly strong attachment to their territory of origin, not just because some of them still farm there, but more crucially because it defines an important part of their identity and because it remains central in their system of beliefs and rituals.

Land tenure & agricultural practices

Today land is distributed by the various dignitaries and chiefs who control it. If someone wants to clear a new piece of land, he just goes to the chief and asks for permission to do so. If the candidate lives in the chief's village, there is a high likelihood that he will be granted the land that he wants. If he lives in another village and intends to travel back and forth to farm there, the chief is likely to be reluctant to give away his land to someone who is living with and supporting another chief. Once again, the key aspect in land distribution is not land availability, but the question of power. Land is given to anybody as long as the person is living in the vicinity of the chief who controls the land. This rule may prevent conflicts from arising; if people are farming in different villages, they can easily be torn apart by a conflict which might erupt between the two chiefs. Farming a piece of land confers user rights which might create conflicts if these rights were used to support a chief situated outside of the territory in question. This may explain why chiefs are reluctant to give land to non-residents.

Traditionally, the land is not bought or sold privately.[3] The chief gives it away and cannot take it back as long as the person who borrows it is using it or intending to use it in the future. If a person moves elsewhere, he loses his land, which reverts to the global pool and can be redistributed again to someone else. Generally, both men and women have their own fields and they keep their own harvest for themselves, separately, even though both work together on each other's fields. A woman usually acquires her right to farming land through her husband, who negotiates this right for her with the chief. This is due both to the fact that men are responsible for finding resources for their wives, but also to the fact that most men live on the territory of their patrilineage and that marriages are patrilocal – women move to live with their husband.

The rights in farming land are usually transmitted from father or mother to the eldest son or from elder brother to the next brother, who becomes the head of the family and has to provide resources for his younger brothers and sisters and their children. In this case, the inheritance of the rights to land is more a consequence of the inheritance of the responsibility towards the extended family. The inheritance of these rights is seldom the object of conflict since land is abundant. As women usually move to live with their husbands, they seldom inherit rights to land from their parents; instead they get these rights through their husbands. Since there is no serious shortage of land (only forests are getting scarce), since women have their own fields (including, sometimes, coffee plantations), and since rights to land are inherited by the children, land is seldom the object of gendered conflict in cases of divorce or death of the husband (see also Hilhorst 2000: 185). In these cases, if the woman stays in the village, she continues to farm her fields. If she remarries or moves away, she then gets access to new land through her husband or relatives.

Kwanja agriculture & 'Yamba' migration

Two types of agriculture are practised locally: shifting cultivation and savannah cultivation. Shifting cultivation is the favoured method. It gives high yields and minimises the labour invested, both in clearing or preparing the fields and in weeding, but the yield decreases in the course of time, and people are forced to rotate their fields. Savannah cultivation can give good yields if the land is managed properly (if the soil is softened with successive types of cultivation, mulched with grass, etc.) It therefore requires a higher investment in terms of time and labour. Recently, in the past 30 to 40 years, people have started cultivating coffee as a cash crop. This trend was reinforced by a wave of English-speaking migrants from the north-west province, situated west of the Kwanja territory, who practise a more commercial type of agriculture than the local one, which is

[3] We have seen earlier that matrilineages could 'buy' forests or lakes, but that this was done collectively and for the game found on it (it was not bought for farming).

more oriented towards subsistence. This has led to the transformation of most of the remaining forests into coffee plantations. In the Kwanja territory of the Tikar plain, few forests situated close to villages are left today, and people are reluctantly beginning to get involved in savannah cultivation, mainly for cassava and groundnuts.

In the past 20 years, there has been an important migratory wave of anglophone agriculturalists from the north-west province. These people, known locally as the 'Yamba', are today spreading all over Adamawa, looking for farming opportunities. They exploit the plentiful and fertile savannah of an area which has a very low population density – Adamawa has fewer than 12 people per square kilometre. They are usually hard working and produce surpluses that feed the local towns. They usually live apart from the local communities and tend to congregate in neighbouring quarters, with their own church (often Baptist) and, when they are numerous enough, their own anglophone schools. (Cameroon is officially a bilingual country.) The Yamba are very mobile and do not hesitate to move elsewhere if the local conditions are not judged satisfactory enough, or if they believe that they have exploited all the potential that the region has to offer. Many of them try to maximise wealth in the short run without investing much in long-term social relations with their neighbours or in long-term environmental conservation.

Since they are used to cultivating savannah and since this type of land is abundant in Adamawa, they do not have any problem in getting access to it. They usually ask the chief or a local person for a piece of land, and they can give him a part of the harvest as a gift, once a year (something like half a bag of maize), although this is voluntary and not part of a contract. When they leave an area, the land reverts back to its 'owner' or to the chief. The land that they get is thus only borrowed, and it cannot be bought or sold. Interestingly, the Yamba residing in the Tikar plain have started adopting the local technique of shifting cultivation. They have started 'working with the machete' rather than 'working with the hoe' since this technique offers advantages in terms of labour, weeding and short-term output. They have also successfully created a number of coffee plantations, as coffee is the main cash crop of the area. The problem with coffee is that it is a perennial crop which requires a significant investment in terms of labour and capital and reaps benefits only in the long term. As a result, those who invest in this type of practice acquire longer term rights on the land than is usually the case with annual crops and shifting cultivation.

The development of coffee has introduced serious and far ranging consequences among the local communities. First, it has introduced a commodification of land. Although the land used to establish coffee plantations is given for free, once a coffee plantation is established, it can be bought and sold. This has become a general practice. Consequently, it has become much more difficult to get access to pieces of forest suitable for establishing coffee plantations. Chiefs become reluctant to give them away; they are under pressure from their own people to keep these areas for the locals. If someone wants to have such a piece of land, he must either be close to the chief or he must make a significant gift to the chief to persuade him to give the land away. Thus commodification begins to spread to the land itself and not just to the coffee plantation.

A second consequence has been a change in inheritance patterns. As discussed above, the Kwanja are a bilineal society, both patrilineal and matrilineal. When someone dies, the inheritance is divided by a member of the matrilineage. The matrilineage usually inherits all the moveable property (money, clothes, tools, weapons, animals) while the patrilineage (the children of the deceased) inherits all the non-moveable property (houses, trees, rights to land). It is preferably a brother with the same father and same mother as the deceased who inherits the moveable property. This dampens potential conflicts since he is both from the same matrilineage and patrilineage as the deceased. Traditionally, when the Kwanja were practising subsistence agriculture and did not produce iron or woven clothes, accumulated moveable property was seen as much more important and valuable than land, which was abundant, or houses, which were easily built. When coffee became equated with money, it became both a moveable and a non-moveable property, which created serious conflicts when sharing the inheritance. In the beginning, coffee plantations were often given to members of the matrilineage (for example, brothers having the same mother as the deceased). However, as the brother who inherited the property often tended to favour his own children, this created many conflicts, both with the children of the deceased and with the matrilineage of the deceased (conflicts often expressed openly as witchcraft accusations). The trend today is more and more for coffee plantations to be inherited by the children of the deceased. The trend is in fact increasingly towards following the wishes of the deceased, which often, but not always, go in that direction. Thus, the commodification of coffee plantations has had far ranging consequences for the social organisation of the community (see also Hilhorst 2000: 187).

A third consequence is linked to the question of autochthony. Commodification of land is considered acceptable when it is practised by members of the indigenous community and totally unacceptable when it is practised by members of the Yamba community. Even houses are not supposed to be sold, as their selling would imply a selling of land. Each time that a migrant sells a coffee plantation or a house, the Kwanja have the feeling that they are losing control over 'their' resources, that they are in fact being deprived of them by people who just think of the short-term interest and who don't want to invest for the future. They blame the Yamba for using Kwanja resources in order to get rich quickly and then leave the area and re-invest this money at home. They resent the fact that many Yamba do not want to integrate into the local society, illustrated by the fact that they have different churches, different schools, are reluctant to speak French (or learn the local vernacular), and they only think of leaving the area once they get rich. Some Kwanja blame the Yamba for felling all the remaining local forest, thereby destroying the last valuable wood of the region. (Most owners of chain saws in the Kwanja region are Yamba.) More generally, the fear of losing control over land goes hand in hand with the fear of being outnumbered by the growing numbers of migrants, who seldom integrate themselves in the local society, and with whom the Kwanja feel they cannot compete as the Yamba are seen as much more hard working and much more successful farmers than the locals. The Kwanja (especially their elites) then react by putting pressure on their chiefs to stop giving land to outsiders, especially forested land, and to prevent the chiefs from selling land away. When they forcefully hammer out the message that 'Our land is not for sale,' it means that they want the Kwanja land to remain in Kwanja hands.

In summary, the introduction of a cash crop has led to a slow commodification of land, first and foremost forested land. It has led to significant change in the local inheritance pattern and it has led to the feeling that migrants are depriving the Kwanja of their own resources, exploiting them in the short-run, for the benefit of another region. This has led to the creation of a feeling of animosity towards the migrants.

Migration from the north & agro-pastoral conflicts

The migration from the north-west province has been accompanied by an independent yet simultaneous migration from the north. The Tikar plain used to be considered unsuitable for cattle production as it was seen as being infested by tsetse flies, the vector of bovine trypaniosomiasis. However, with the progress of veterinary services and the development of fly repellents, pastoralists started to spend the dry season in the plain about 30 to 40 years ago. The success of these pioneers attracted even greater numbers of followers who brought their cattle to the plain in transhumance during the dry season. This movement has been strongly reinforced every year and shows no sign of slowing down. It has brought with it numerous agro-pastoral conflicts. Unattended cattle wander around and eat dry-season crops (such as cassava), destroy young plantations of oil palm, spoil coffee plantations, and eat maize stored in granaries in the bush.

Local farmers have great difficulties getting compensation for the damage that they have to bear (see Gausset 2002b). First, it can be very difficult to find evidence of the identity of the culprit since damage is often done early in the morning when everybody is still asleep; trying to find a herd by following a track might not provide conclusive evidence. Second, the rich owners of cattle hire shepherds who are badly paid and who do not always behave in a responsible manner, either towards their herd or boss, or towards their host community (see also Bassett 1994). Third, many pastoralists refuse to pay proper compensation even though their cattle are caught spoiling a field (see also Harshbarger 1995 cited in Hussein 1998). This might be due to a mere reluctance to pay (stinginess, poverty) or to personal revenge (they might feel that some farmers did them wrong in the past and that not paying them is a just retaliation) or to a more profound feeling of superiority and contempt for local populations. It should be remembered that the Fulbe used to raid the Kwanja region to acquire slaves. The Fulbe's feeling of superiority built in the Pulaaku (code of honour) is therefore reinforced by the fact that they consider themselves the masters of the area and consider the local population to be slaves most of the latter being moreover Christian (Schultz 1980a, 1980b, 1984, Schilder 1994, Burnham 1996, Gausset 1998b, 1999, 2002a, 2003).

The resolution of conflicts should normally start at the level of the local Kwanja chiefs. However, the Fulbe seldom recognise their authority and disregard these chiefs as 'Pagan' and as 'slaves'. Cattle herders prefer to bring their case to the Fulbe sultan of Banyo, the highest level of customary court, but farmers do not like this as they believe the sultan to be biased toward the pastoralists' interests since he, himself, is one of the most important owners of cattle in the region. Since farmers and herders disagree on the legitimacy of customary courts, local farmers end up avoiding the sultan and bring their case to the administrative court system. However, this procedure is long and expensive. The extension officer of agriculture and of animal husbandry must both come to the field and estimate the damages. The gendarmerie transfers it to the court. The decision of the court takes time to be handed down. Therefore, the whole procedure is very costly as it involves much transporting of both the conflicting parties and of many government agents. The cost is usually born by the plaintiff until the case is settled. Moreover, the complexity of the procedure leaves plenty of opportunity for the plaintiff or the accused party to bribe the extension officer, gendarme, clerk or judge (Cameroon being considered as one of the most corrupt countries in the world). The richest people usually win their cases and since the richest ones are the pastoralists (one head of cattle is worth an entire year of income for farmers), they are reinforced, gain self-confidence, and are even less inclined to pay compensation to farmers. Local farmers often complain that the Fulbe prefer to pay ten times more in bribing the administration than in paying fair compensation for the damage done by their cattle, and they explain this by pointing to the Fulbe's feeling of superiority as they are unable to accept losing in front of their former 'slaves' (see also Adebayo 1997: 105–6).

As a consequence of the arrival of pastoralists in the plain, local farmers have had to adapt to the situation, building fences around their fields or spending time watching their fields or else face the risk of suffering severe damage. They seriously resent the fact that they are the ones who bear the cost of change while the pastoralists are seen as reaping all the benefits. They again have the feeling that they are losing control of their own land in the sense that they are powerless to impose their own management of the resources and to get justice for damage done by cattle.

As more pastoralists spend the transhumance in the plain, the competition between farmers and cattle herders becomes slowly about more than the regulation of conflicts and begins to concern the control of and access to the resources. Both herders and farmers begin to have the feeling that the other community is limiting its own future pastoral or agricultural expansion. Herders, therefore, try to secure long-term access to the present pastures while agriculturalists try to limit this and to secure themselves access to land for agricultural expansion in the future. Major political manoeuvres are set in process at the regional level with the Fulbe sultan defending the claims of herders. This makes the local communities even more insecure about their future and reinforces the feeling that they are losing control over their own resources. This in turn feeds the anti-migrant feeling.

Conflict about content & distribution of rights

As we have seen, in the Kwanja region land conflicts are *not* about scarce resources. The conflicts concern rather the *rules* of resource management and of conflict resolution, who should follow them and who can define them. They are therefore about rights, but also about identity and power.

First, conflicts can concern the content of rights only. This is the case, for example, with the shift from matrilineal to patrilineal inheritance of moveable property among the Kwanja. These conflicts can be violent (witchcraft accusations), but they remain limited to a few individuals belonging to the same ethnic group, village, lineage or family, who will always find an equilibrium. This conflict does not concern the distribution of rights since everybody wins and loses in exactly the same way. The rules (content of rights) change for everybody and everybody is equally affected. What is gained patrilineally is lost matrilineally. If people inherit more from their father, they will inherit less from their maternal uncle, and vice versa. Conflicts about the content of rules can also concern the commodification of land. Here again, if it is assumed that people have the same access to land originally, everybody loses as much as they win, in the short run, if it becomes commodified. Everyone can potentially win from selling his or her coffee plantation. What is gained on one side (making money through selling land) is lost on the other (one has to buy land) – except when other ethnic groups begin to sell land as well; see below. This type of conflict might create social tensions within a society and might end up creating significant social changes, such as diminishing the importance of matrilineal filiation, creating a class of landless peasants, etc., but as long as the new rules apply equally to all the members of the society as a whole, it is unlikely to create violent conflicts on a large scale since every economic unit loses as much as it wins in the short run.

Second, conflicts may concern the distribution of rights only. In this case, the conflict does not concern the content of rights, but rather the way they are distributed – what category of people should benefit or be excluded from it. It would be the case, for example, if women started to claim equal rights with men. But if one takes nuclear families as an economic unit, what would be gained on one side (more female independence) would be lost on the other (weaker husband or lineage solidarity). Conflicts between indigenous Kwanja and migrant Yamba farmers are also of this nature. They do not concern the content of the rights, but the distribution of rights (Can the Yamba sell land?). The Yamba are not (or not yet) contesting the authority of local Kwanja chiefs; they just want to benefit from the same rules as the local Kwanja. The conflict takes on a special significance because of the simple fact that they belong to migrant ethnic groups and that the zero-sum game described above (what is taken on one side is lost on another) concerns social categories that are considered as competing rather than complementary. Moreover, local Kwanja feel threatened by the Yamba's success in agriculture, by their increasing numbers and by their reluctance to integrate in the local society, which leads to their organisation in independent political structures. The conflict concerns, therefore, much more than the distribution of rights. It has a political dimension as what might be at stake, in the short-run, is the authority of the Kwanja chiefs over their territory. So in this case, we have a conflict among structurally unequal actors (autochthonous versus migrant populations) who are fighting to maintain or change the distribution of rights and, ultimately, to maintain or change the balance of power between them.

Third, even when there is a consensus about the content and distribution of rights, the actual application of these rights can be problematic. This is what happens when two Kwanja chiefs argue about their territory boundaries, when Kwanja and Tikar chiefs argue about the submission of a Tikar dignitary living on a Kwanja territory, or when the Fulbe sultan claims authority over the plain and the Kwanja chiefs. All actors have competing but *similar* claims to the same territory or dignitary and argue on the basis of historical arguments ('My ancestor set the boundary on this river; my ancestor submitted that chief or dignitary, etc.'). In this case, we have a conflict between structurally equal actors (two chiefs) who are not fighting on the content or distribution of rights, but on the actual application of these rights – on the power hierarchy responsible to manage the content and distribution of rights. As in the case of the Yamba, these conflicts change neither the social structures nor the livelihood strategies – just the balance of power between competing actors. What is needed to solve these conflicts peacefully is a paramount authority able to judge the cases – a difficult role which, so far, is successfully played by the state.

As we can see, conflicts can be described according to two dimensions. First, they differ according to whether they concern the content or the distribution of rights or the actual interpretation or application of these rights (the power hierarchy in charge of managing the rights). Second, conflicts differ according to whether the competing actors are seen as complementary (matri-patrilineages, men-women) or as competing (two chiefs, two villages, two ethnic groups). In the first case, what an actor loses on one side is compensated by what s/he gains on the other. In the second case, what is lost is not compensated and is gained by the competitor. Conflicts among competitors are potentially the most serious and the most violent.

However, the most dangerous of all conflicts are those which combine all these dimensions – conflicts that concern the content, the distribution and the application of rights among actors seen as competitors. This is the case in agro-pastoral conflicts.[4] First, there is not consensus on the content of the rights concerning the management of the resources. What should be fenced? Should farmers get the right to establish new fields in former pastures? Can cattle graze in fallow fields? Can cattle spend the rainy season in the plain? Who controls the 'unused' land? Second, there is no consensus on the distribution of rights and duties. Who should fence the fields? Who should fence the cattle? Who should bear the cost of fields damaged by cattle? Can any herder establish himself anywhere without asking anybody's permission? Can the Kwanja start keeping cattle in the plain, including during the rainy season, when the district officer prevents others from doing so? Third, even though there is a kind of loose *de facto* consensus about the content and distribution of rights,[5] the application of this 'consensus on management' is extremely problematic as there is no consensus about who should judge conflicts or define the rules. The Kwanja chief, the Fulbe sultan and the state all have similar and competing claims, which are supported by different actors. Pastoralists refuse the authority of the local chiefs and support the Fulbe sultan instead; Kwanja farmers reject the authority of the Sultan and support their own chiefs. Both farmers and herders rely on the state when they

[4] In Nigeria, on the neighbouring Mambila plateau, agro-pastoral conflicts degenerated in January 2002 into a small-scale ethnic cleansing. Dozens of people were killed, hundreds of houses burnt and thousands of Fulbe were chased away from the Mambila plateau and took refuge in Cameroon. This type of violent conflict could very well happen in Cameroon if nothing is done to dampen the present agro-pastoral conflicts.

[5] This loose consensus is that, in the Tikar plain, herders should either fence cattle during night time (which they never do) or follow them at all times (which is difficult) and bear the cost of damages in fields (which is often problematic). They have the right to establish themselves anywhere but must inform the chief (which they seldom do). It is generally accepted that one cannot do anything against a herder who uses fallow land for grazing (although farmers are unhappy about it). It is also generally accepted that cattle may not spend the rainy season in the plain (although herders are not happy about this). It is generally accepted that one cannot do anything against a farmer who creates a new field in former pastures (although herders are unhappy about this), and so on.

believe that they can gain something from it – including through bypassing the legal administrative framework with bribes. Since the different actors are seen as competitive rather than complementary, the combination of all conflict dimensions makes agro-pastoral conflicts potentially very dangerous for the peace of the region.

Power hierarchy & state's role

The conflicts that oppose customary authority and the state also concern both the content and distribution of rights and are problematic in all parts of Cameroon. (See also Little 1987: 194, Cousins 2000, Hilhorst 2000, Benjaminsen and Lund 2002.) The state claims to own all the land that is not titled (i.e. most land within the rural areas). The local chief claims to be the only authority able to distribute land. The sultan has the same claim as well, although he exercises mostly his authority in allocating grazing rights. All three actors claim to be the best able to judge local conflicts. In theory, however, the sultan represents a kind of customary court of appeal, one level above the local chiefs, and the state constitutes a kind of court of appeal one level above the customary court system. When it comes to defining the distribution of rights and duties regulating access to resources, there is once more a conflict between local chiefs (who usually support indigenous interests), the sultan (who usually supports pastoral interests) and the state (which tries to accommodate all parties equally).

The state has the ambition to define the content of rights (monopoly of land ownership, justice and force) and the distribution of rights (defining all Cameroonians as equals). This ambition is, today, unrealistic on three different grounds. First, everybody in Cameroon expects customary chiefs to be responsible for distributing resources. Even civil servants, who are generally born and educated in villages, know and accept the authority of local chiefs over their territories, and they know that challenging this rule can create a lot of trouble. The legitimacy of the state in defining rights is therefore challenged by the civil servants themselves. Second, it is very difficult for the state to treat all actors equally and to avoid taking sides. Rules are needed to clarify what should be fenced and who should fence it, whether cattle owners should ask for the local chief's permission in order to graze somewhere, whether the owners of fallow fields can refuse grazing cattle, whether land can be sold, etc. Through refusing to take sides clearly, the state encourages conflicts. Third, the state has the ambition to define the content and distribution of rights, but it does not have the means to do so efficiently. In practice, state law only applies to a limited extent, and the state relies heavily on customary power structures to maintain peace and order and to implement the few ill-adapted state management rules (on bush-fire, on the time of transhumance, on conflict resolution, etc.). So on one side, the state undermines the authority of customary chiefs through defining different rights and through giving a free hand to migrants to challenge their authority. On the other side, the state relies on the authority of these customary chiefs to enact its own rules.

The state focuses more on the distribution of rights (every Cameroonian should have equal rights) than on the content. It tries to support a kind of neutrality in local conflicts. The state wants to guarantee the freedom of movement of all citizens, regardless of their cultural background. The problem is that an equal distribution of rights is impossible if there is no consensus on the content of rights. If everybody is free to establish himself where he wishes and to exploit unutilised resources in any way he wishes, this might challenge the local content of rights and force other people to change their own way of managing their resources. It creates problems, which the state does not or cannot manage. While it guarantees the rights of movement of its citizens, the state fails to specify their duties regarding the respect of local authority and customary law. To say that anybody can establish himself anywhere without saying whether s/he has to respect the local customary authority and the local management rules is a *de facto* challenge to the customary authority and management. Trying to accommodate all parties equally and giving as much weight to local customary authorities as to migrants gives a free hand to migrants to challenge the local rules and power structures. It encourages a permanent renegotiation of rules and therefore permanent conflict between indigenous and migrants communities. The positive side to this is that things adapt slowly to accommodate the new situation. The negative side is that when actors are seen as competitors and when the balance of power changes too quickly, extremely violent conflicts may arise. The migration of people into the area to cultivate or graze unused land would not pose any problem if secure rights and adequate enforcement were present. As we have seen above, local Kwanja chiefs are competing to gain followers and are always eager to welcome more migrants, *as long as migrants support them*. Most migrants are in fact well integrated and do support local chiefs, but a minority creates problems, and these are greatly amplified when the state sides with them, either on the basis of national law, or because state structures are so corrupt that they end up siding with the richest – who are usually the migrants.

The equality of citizens is a well-intentioned principle but is always limited at a certain level. Cameroon, for example, limits the idea of equal rights to its national citizens, and denies this to non-citizens. Foreigners are either prevented from migrating to Cameroon or are forced to accept Cameroonian law while they are prevented from influencing it through having access to power (the right to vote). A share in power is only conferred on migrants who have become integrated (who have taken Cameroonian citizenship). If Cameroon opened its border to unlimited migration, gave the right to vote to all migrants and accepted that migrants would challenge Cameroonian law, this would create important changes in the balance of power, as well as serious conflicts. Yet, this is exactly what the Cameroonian state requires from all the ethnic groups within its boundaries – to be open to unlimited migration of Cameroonian citizens who are free to challenge the local rules and structures of power without having to adapt to and integrate with the local situation. If conflicts are to be managed at a local level, one needs clear power structures, which have the means to define and enforce rules. At present, only local power structures can do this. It is, therefore, important to support them rather than to compete with them.

The challenge for the state is to recognise the existence and legitimacy of customary law – to accept that there exists a variety in the content and distribution of rights within Cameroon, depending on the way each ethnic group or local community defines them. The role of the state should be limited, first to guaranteeing that these locally defined rights apply to all citizens equally, without discrimination between autochthonous and migrant populations, and second to solving conflicts of interpretation (for example, conflicts between different chiefs). I believe that this kind of engagement would dampen down the conflicts between local and migrant communities. It would not prevent migration but would make sure that the newcomers adapt their strategies to local rules. Freedom of movement and equality of rights would not be prevented, but it would be secondary to the respect of local customary rules and power by the migrants. The local communities would retain control over their resources and avoid bearing an unfair load of the cost incurred from the changes brought about by the newcomers. There would be a clearer definition of rules and a clearer separation of power between the state and the local authorities. This would make the situation much less ambiguous as rules and authority would be clearly defined and would not compete with one another. Instead of intervening directly in the local definition of management rules, the state would rather play the role of arbitrator, guaranteeing the equal application of locally defined rights *and* duties to all citizens equally.

References

Adebayo, A.G. 1997. 'Contemporary Dimensions of Migration among Historically Migrant Nigerians: Fulani Pastoralists in Southwestern Nigeria.' *Journal of Asian and African Studies* 32 (1–2): 93–109.

Bah, T.M. 1982. 'Les armées Peul de l'Adamawa au 19è siècle.' In *Études offertes à Henri Brunschwig*. Paris, Éditions de l'École des hautes études en sciences sociales: 57–71.

Bassett, T. 1994. 'Hired Herders and Herd Management in Fulani Pastoralism (Northern Côte d'Ivoire).' *Cahiers d'Études africaines*, 133–5, XXXIV (1–3): 147–73.

Benjaminsen, T. A. and C. Lund. 2002. 'Formalisation and Informalisation of Land and Water Rights in Africa: An Introduction.' In A. Benjaminsen and C. Lund, (eds) *Securing Land Rights in Africa. The European Journal of Development Research* 14 (2): 1–10.

Burnham, P. 1996. *The Politics of Cultural Difference in Northern Cameroon*. Edinburgh, Edinburgh University Press.

Büttner, T. 1967. 'On the Social-Economic Structure of Adamawa in the 19th Century. Slavery or Serfdom?' In W. Markov (ed.) *African Studies*. Leipzig: Karl Marx Universität: 43–61.

Cousins, B. 2000. 'Tenure and Common Property Resources in Africa.' In C. Toulmin and J. Quan (eds) *Evolving Land Rights, Policy and Tenure in Africa*. London: IIED.

Froelich, J.-C. 1966. 'Essai sur les causes et méthodes de l'Islamisation de l'Afrique de l'Ouest du XIe au XXe Siècle.' In I.M. Lewis (ed.) *Islam in Tropical Africa*. London, Oxford University Press: 160–73.

Gausset, Q. 1995. 'Contribution à l'étude du pouvoir sacré chez les Wawa (Adamawa, Cameroun).' *Journal des Africanistes* 65 (2): 179–200.

______. 1997a. 'Pouvoir et bilinéarité chez les Kwanja.' *Ngaoundéré-Anthropos* 2: 89–104.

______. 1997b. *Les avatars de l'identité chez les Wawa et les Kwanja du Cameroun*. PhD Thesis; Brussels: Université Libre de Bruxelles.

______. 1998a. 'Double Unilineal Descent and Triple Kinship Terminology. The Case of the Kwanja of Cameroon.' *Journal of the Royal Anthropological Society* 4(2): 309–23.

______. 1998b. 'Historical Account or Discourse on Identity? A Reevaluation of Fulbe Hegemony and Autochthonous Submission in Banyo (Adamawa, Cameroon).' *History in Africa* 25: 93–110.

______. 1999. 'Islam or Christianity? The choices of the Wawa and Kwanja of Cameroon.' *Africa*, 69(2): 257–78.

______. 2002a. 'The Spread of Islam in Adamawa.' In T. Bierschenk and G. Stauth (eds) *Yearbook of the Sociology of Islam* 4. Münster: LIT.

______. 2002b. 'Is the Field Moving to Meet the Cattle or is it the Cattle that Move into the Field? Agro-pastoral Conflicts in the Tikar Plain (Cameroon).' Paper presented at the seminar on 'Beyond territory and scarcity: Social, cultural and political aspects of conflicts on natural resource management', Copenhagen, 7–9 November 2002.

______. 2003. 'From Domination to Participation: The Politics of Religion and Ethnicity in Northern

Cameroon.' In N. Kastfelt (ed.) *The Bible and the Koran as Political Models in the Middle East and Africa*. London: Christopher Hurst.

Harshbarger, C.L. 1995. *Farmer-Herder Conflict and State Legitimacy in Cameroon*. DPhil thesis. University of Florida.

Hilhorst, T. 2000. 'Women's Land Rights: Current Developments in Sub-Saharan Africa.' In C. Toulmin and J. Quan (eds) *Evolving Land Rights, Policy and Tenure in Africa*. London: IIED.

Hurault, J. 1975. 'Histoire du lamidat de Banyo.' *Comptes rendus trimestriels de l'Académie des Sciences d'Outre-Mer*, XXXV (2): 421–65.

Hussein, K. 1998. *Conflict Between Farmers and Herders in the Semi-arid Sahel and East Africa: A Review*. IIED Pastoral Land Tenure Series No. 10. London: IIED.

Kirk-Greene, A.H.M. 1958. *Adamawa, Past and Present*. London: Oxford University Press.

Lacroix, P.F. 1952. 'Matériaux pour servir à l'histoire des peuls de l'Adamawa.' *Etudes Camerounaises* V (37-38): 3-61 and VI (39-40): 5-40.

Little, P. D. and D. W. Brokenshaw 1987. 'Local Institutions, Tenure and Resource Management in East Africa.' In D. Anderson and R. Grove (eds) *Conservation in Africa. People, policies and practice*. Cambridge: Cambridge University Press.

Mohammadou, E. 1966. 'Introduction historique à l'étude des sociétés du Nord-Cameroun.' *Abbia* 12–13: 233–71.

______. 1978. *Fulbe Hooseere. Les royaumes foulbé du plateau de l'Adamaoua au 19 ème siècle. Tibati Tignere, Banyo, Ngaoundere. African Languages and Ethnography, VIII*. Tokyo, Institute for the Study of Language and Culture of Asia and Africa (ILCAA).

______. 1981. 'L'implantation des Peul dans l'Adamawa (approche chronologique).' In C. Tardits (ed.) *Contribution de la recherche ethnologique à l'histoire des civilisations du Cameroun*, vol. I. Paris: CNRS.

______. 1982. *Peuples et états du Foumbina et de l'Adamawa (Nord Cameroun). Etudes de Kurt Struempell et von Briesen traduites par E. Mohammadou*. Collection Archives Allemandes du Cameroun, No 1. Yaoundé: Centre de Recherche et d'Etudes Anthropologiques.

______. 1991. *Traditions historiques des peuples du Cameroun Central, vol. II. African Languages and Ethnography*, XXIV. Tokyo: Institute for the Study of Language and Culture of Asia and Africa.

Schilder, K. 1994. *Quest for Self-Esteem: State, Islam and Mundang Ethnicity in Northern Cameroon*. Aldershot: Avebury.

Schultz, E. 1980a. 'Introduction.' In E.A. Schultz (ed.) *Image and Reality in African Interethnic Relations: The Fulbe and Their Neighbors*. Studies in Third World Societies, 11. Williamsburg, VA: Department of Anthropology.

______.1980b. 'Perceptions of Ethnicity in Guider Town.' In E.A. Schultz (ed.), *Image and Reality in African Interethnic Relations: The Fulbe and Their Neighbors*. Studies in Third World Societies, 11. Williamsburg (Virginia), Department of Anthropology: 127-49.

______. 1984. 'From Pagan to Pullo: Ethnic Identity Change in Northern Cameroon.' *Africa*, 54(1): 46–63.

Smith, M.G. 1966. 'The Jihad of Shehu Dan Fodio: Some Problems.' In I.M. Lewis (ed.) *Islam in Tropical Africa*. London: Oxford University Press.

4

Adaptability, Identity & Conflict Mediation among the Hawawir in Northern Sudan

KJERSTI LARSEN

This paper explores adaptability and perceptions of identity and belonging among pastoralists in Northern Sudan. Questions to be discussed concern to what extent pastoral livelihoods are able to adapt to recent processes of socio-economic and political change and the kind of identity negotiations and forms of conflict mediations that are involved in constantly producing viable lives in arid lands? The discussion below is based on ethnographic material collected during fieldwork among the Hawawir in Wadi al Mugaddam.[1] I conducted social anthropological fieldwork among the Hawawir from 1997 until 2003, in Wadi al Mugaddam and also briefly in the Nile valley. During my fieldwork I stayed with different families as well as in the guesthouse of an NGO working in the area. Hence, I have visited and lived both with Hawawir who have settled close to their irrigated farms, in the recent settlement area or village, and those who stay far away from the irrigated agricultural project and pursue life as nomadic pastoralists. Over the years I have come to know a relatively large number of families and been able to follow some families in the process of changing their livelihoods – from forced migrants to farmers or agro-pastoralists, or from nomadic pastoralists to agro-pastoralists. Data have been collected through participant observation, including both open-ended and semi-structured interviews, and conversations in daily as well as ritual life, in private and public contexts, as well as with both groups of people and individuals. In writing up this research, I have kept the informants' anonymity. In the beginning of the fieldwork I worked with and was actually totally dependent upon an assistant and interpreter, while over time I could move about more independently and even manage language-wise in day-to-day conversation. Still, throughout the fieldwork I remained dependent upon an interpreter when conducting interviews.

The Hawawir have a history as nomadic pastoralists and their homeland (*dar*) is within the Bayoda desert. The Hawawir refer to themselves as *arab*s. In Northern Sudan the term *arab* denotes 'nomad'. The term opposes nomadic pastoral peoples to sedentary, agricultural peoples (Delmet 1989, Casciarri 1995). According to the 1993 population census the nomadic population of the Sudan

[1] Wadi al Mugaddam is a dry tributary of the Nile and runs in a north-south direction. It begins in Northern Kordofan, moving west of Khartoum to join the Nile in Korti, Northern State. The Hawawir live both in the Northern State and Kordofan State.

was estimated to be about 8.5 per cent of the total population (Eisa 2002).[2] Although the nomadic peoples are pastoralists, they are engaged in several activities in addition to herding. It is important to keep in mind that the so-called 'pure pastoralist' does not exist (cf. Gallais 1975, de Bruijn and van Dijk 1995, Babiker 2002) – not even among those whose livelihoods are characterised as nomadic. This being said, pastoralism is, if not the only, at least the main economic activity for those whose lives remain more or less nomadic. Before entering into the discussion of adaptability, identity and conflict mediation, I will introduce the Hawawir.

The Hawawir – nomadic pastoralists adapting to changing livelihood circumstances

The Hawawir are Muslims and Arabic speaking. They refer to themselves, and are considered by others, to be a *qabil* – a term that should be translated as a 'people' or also, 'tribe'.[3] Being a *qabil* implies that they share a common origin myth; they are of the same people and as the Hawawir claim, they are all descendants from a male ancestor called Malik who is said to have migrated from Arabia.[4] They see themselves as a group of agnatic kin.

The Hawawir have their own social and juridical organisation, and they identify with a certain territory or domicile (*dar*). As a *qabil*[5] they share, as mentioned above, collective ownership of a territory, expressed in exclusive rights over water resources and land for grazing and rain-fed agriculture as well as water. An overall agnatic genealogical system segmented into sub-tribes (*ferha qabil*) and patrilineages (*aila*) form the basis of the economic, social and political organisation. The Hawawir also practise preferential marriage with father's brother's daughter (FBD). This practice produces a tendency towards agnatic endogamy. Marriages across sub-tribes do, however, take place, especially among families who have lived or still live in the Nile valley. As a *qabil*, they also have their own particular juridical and political institutions. The *Nazir* is the official leader of all Hawawir. Below the *Nazir* in the hierarchy there are four *Umda* who are considered the leaders in the different areas where the Hawawir live. The *Umda* rules according to the customary law (*al urf*). Just as with the *Nazir*, the

[2] As Suaad Ibrahim Eisa argues, because of the absence of birth and death registration among all nomadic communities, it is difficult to obtain a reliable estimation of the total nomadic population in Sudan (Eisa 2002:183). Some of the major nomadic communities are the Kababish, the Hassanyia, the Baggara, the Abdallah, the Hawawir, the Rasheyyda, the Kenana and the Rufa'a al-Hoi.

[3] The Sudan, as with many other nation states, is made up of different communities who share values, collective consciousness and common tradition but not necessarily beyond what they identify as their community, or as it is called in Sudan, their *qabil*. A person's *qabil* denotes a significant aspect of her/his social identity associating the person to a certain region or territory within the Sudan or beyond, as well as to a tradition and an aesthetic, a lifestyle and way of being. Although part of a nation state, the various communities often have their own customary laws concerning for instance, management of natural resources and family relations.

[4] The Hawawir narrative departs from the views of scholars who would argue that they are actually of Tunisian Berber origin (Herzog 1955), a point that can only illustrate the mobility of people in this part of the world and the puzzlement their movements provides to scholars eagerly trying to define the 'true' origin of various communities.

[5] For further discussion on the significance of the concept of tribe/people cf. Luc de Heusch 1997 and Lawrence Rosen 2002.

Umda is a position that is inherited from father to the oldest son. The *Sheikh*, seven in all, follow below the *Umda*. The *Sheikh* is the religious leader and supposed to lead and make decisions according to Islamic law (*Sharia*) and tradition (*Hadith*). Following the *Sheikh* is the council of knowledgeable men called *al Agawid*. For all these juridical bodies *al urf*, *Sharia* and *Hadith* are important sources informing the decisions made in situations of negotiation and conflict mediation. Apart from the above mentioned institutions, state institutions also govern the Hawawir as citizens of Sudan. One such institution is the 'Mobile Court'. A judge (*khadi*), learned in Sudanese civil law, Islamic law and *al urf* is the head of the 'Mobile Court'. The Mobile Court is stationed in the town of Korti. The court also moves within the area of jurisdiction. Moreover, when cases are too complicated or too sensitive to be solved by the locally based institutions, people would either wait for the Mobile Court to arrive in their area or approach the court in Korti. There is also an additional government-appointed institution called 'the Popular Committee', which plays the role of a local government in the sense that they have the right to issue fines, arrest people who violate law and order, and establish taxes for running community services. It also keeps records of the number of people as well as the movement of people in the area. Thus customary judiciary bodies co-exist with state law and form a certain kind of legal pluralism.

Securing a livelihood in Wadi al Mugaddam

Within the homeland or *dar* of the Hawawir, rainfall is low, with an average of 50mm per year, concentrated in three months. The rainfall is variable in both temporal and spatial dimensions. Hence, the livelihood of the Hawawir within Wadi al Mugaddam in the Bayoda desert has mainly been based on nomadic herding of camels, sheep and goats although most people are unable to subsist on livestock produce alone and need to obtain cereals to supplement their diet through trading livestock produce and casual labour. Although the Hawawir no longer move outside their *dar* or homeland, they do move within it and migrate to lusher areas during rains, especially in the Kereb Hills, Abu Hasheem, El Kufriga and Kag. During the rest of the year they move between the surface wells and the Nile River (ADRA et al. 1995). Different forms and degrees of mobility are accommodated, and the organisational flexibility of the community makes possible a continuous regulation of the relationship between livelihood strategies and environmental circumstances. What characterises life in arid lands is adaptation to harsh climatic circumstances. In this environment, insecurity is a permanent feature of life, and, thus, flexibility and mobility are components that are integral to social organisation. People utilise a variety of strategies in order to cope with changing circumstances, for instance, herd diversification, adjustment of herd size, increasing or decreasing their mobility, splitting into smaller groups and temporary sedentarisation, as well as involvement in agricultural activities.

Given the minimal amount of rain that falls in the area of the Hawawir, agriculture has never been considered a main subsistence activity. Only approximately every tenth year are the annual rains abundant in areas close by, in the sense that water from the surrounding mountains floods certain valleys (*wadi*). During such years rain-fed agriculture is possible and thus, sorghum is planted. This means that people are familiar with rain-fed agriculture but that the climate is such that it is not a viable livelihood in itself.[6] Within the *dar* of the Hawawir, agriculture can only be made possible through extensive irrigation systems based on the presence of fresh-water aquifers at a reasonable depth.

The severe drought in the region called the Sahel in the 1980s also affected the livelihood of the Hawawir (cf. Larsen 2001). Due to loss of livestock and subsequent starvation most of the Hawawir had to leave their homeland (*dar*). Thus, their lives and livelihoods were affected by forced migration to the Nile Valley, known today as 'internal displacement'.[7] As a response to the situation the Sudanese government, in cooperation with an NGO, the Adventist Development and Relief Agency (ADRA), established an irrigated agricultural project within the Hawawir *dar* in order to facilitate their return. The irrigation project has, as expected, initiated a return process but also new forms of livelihoods and thus resource management negotiations. Following the irrigated agricultural project and other governmental initiatives, there are now three main adaptation possibilities: 1) Nomadic pastoralism moving within their *dar* and between the *dar* and the Nile Valley; 2) Irrigated farming related to the ADRA development project combined with partial settlement in or outside the newly established settlement area called *al gharia* (the model village); 3) Pastoralism and/or small-scale business involvement combined with settlement in a government-initiated settlement called *al Sherian*. Hence, at present, a livelihood in Wadi al Mugaddam is considered viable if based either on livestock and/or irrigated farms. For limited periods it is, in addition, also possible for a restricted number of households to base a livelihood on casual labour on the farms of others, as herders, or on more or less irregular remittances from relatives who have migrated to, for instance, Saudi Arabia (cf. Myers et al. 1995). Most households would, however, usually combine the various possible sources to make a living. Nevertheless, as is common among pastoralist societies, socio-economic stratifications are still based largely on animal ownership.

Customary law: negotiation & conflict mediation

Wadi al Mugaddam is government-owned land communally held and managed by the Hawawir (ADRA et al. 1995) according to their customary law, *al urf*. With regard to land ownership there is, in the Sudan, a system of dual land ownership (Awad 1971, Manger 2001). In the riverine region there is private land ownership mostly individually owned and protected by law, whereas in other regions land is communally held. Communal land is state land and subject to usufruct rights vested in a tribal or village community and thus regulated by customary law (Awad 1971).[8] It is worth considering that customary law is

[6] Recent years suitable for planting were 1978, 1988, 1994 (ADRA et al. 1995) and 1999 (personal observation).

[7] The term 'internal displacement' is legally defined by the UN as the result of people involuntary driven from their original domicile to other areas.

[8] The cultivable part of the country is only 18 per cent. The rest is pasture and meadow (9.6 per cent), forest (36.5 per cent) or, waste land (35.9 per cent) (Awad 1971: 218). In 1970, the 'Unregistered Land Act' instituted a leasehold tenure system, declaring that all unregistred land, occupied or unoccupied, belonged to the state and was deemed to be registrered in the name of the

defined by particular communities and will therefore usually link rights with residence and perceptions of origin. This means that land and water rights are ascribed with reference to ancestral origin and that only persons associated with a particular origin-based identity may, in principle, live and use the land and water resources within a defined area. Furthermore, typical for any customary law is that it is grounded in understandings that define property rights according to culturally constructed concepts that have their basis in moral and ethical universes (cf. Galaty 1998) that are usually different from that of civil law. For instance, the customary law of the Hawawir advocates universal rights to vital resources and emphasises negotiations, compensation and agreements rather than verdicts, prosecution and punishment. *Al urf* is not scriptural and discussed with reference to interpretations of an already existing text but rather recollected, orally transferred and negotiated. Customary law being oral and part of the Hawawir moral system also encompasses *Sharia* and *Hadith*, especially with regard to what is considered family law including inheritance rules, but as mentioned above, as this society is not a literal one, the *Sheikhs* in the various localities not only hold the authority with regard to interpretations of the Islamic law as such, but are also considered to possesses the knowledge of the Koran as a scriptural text.

In principle, *al urf* secures equal rights to water, land and pasture for all Hawawir. This statement of 'universal rights' should, however, be understood with reference to cultural understandings of the person and thus of different kinds of persons and personhood – a theme that is too elaborate to enter into in this article. According to the dominant ideology among the Hawawir, 'universal rights' means all adult male Hawawir who are then responsible for redistributing or providing access to resources to their dependants, be they women or young men. Customary law is often, at least within anthropological writings, understood to protect the rights of communities otherwise perceived as marginal within a nation state. This claim does, however, consider the rights of communities in general and not the rights of the various categories of community members. As already mentioned, customary laws are grounded in given cultural understandings, and as such they also include their own system of discrimination. One concern when considering customary rights is precisely that different rights and responsibilities are usually associated with different categories of persons, for instance persons differentiated by gender and/or age.

The principle and practice of sex-segregation is in the Hawawir society, as in other Muslim societies, important. Sex-segregation both with regard to work, responsibilities, duties and the use of space, means, among other things, that in order to understand management of resources, the gender dimension in all its complexity has to be included, as I will illustrate below.

In Hawawir society formalised authority, decision-making and ownership are associated with men.[9] In most cases, women acquire access to various resources,

[8] (cont.) state (Manger 2001). State ownership has, however, been used primarily to give government a freer hand in land acquisition and the allocation of land to development project areas. Consequently, land outside major development projects has continued to be administered by traditional authorities (ibid.).

[9] Negotiations, and thus conflict mediation according to *al urf*, usually take place when men sit down together in contexts that are more or less pre-arranged. In the area where I have conducted fieldwork, tea-stations (*ghawi*) along the tarmac road from Khartoum till Dongola in the north are, for instance

material or immaterial, through male relatives, fathers, brothers, husbands, sons and grandsons. During her marriage a woman usually receives livestock from her father and/or brothers (*al sharrit*). Moreover, she will also receive livestock from her father as inheritance later in life. According to Islamic *Sharia* law, women inherit from their parents half of what their brothers inherit, and any 'property' (*al haggi*) including livestock given to a woman from her family belongs to her. As Muslims, the Hawawir follow Islamic laws and practices. However, given the fact that the Hawawir in Wadi al Mugaddam are illiterate and, with the exception of the *Sheikhs*, not well versed in the complexity of Islamic theology, their practices may sometimes divert from theological/scriptural interpretation and instruction. For instance, when women inherit livestock, the animals belong to them although the animals will in practice be included in their husband's herd. In principle, a husband should need the wife's consent to sell or slaughter any of 'her' animals. This principle is, however, not followed by men. Thus women usually prefer to hide their livestock with their brother's herd in order to keep them, as they say, 'hidden from their husband's eyes'. This is to ensure that the herd remains under her control. This indicates that women do actually fear that the husband may take control of their property, contrary to both customary and Islamic law. Women's ways of 'hiding their animals' instead of voicing their ownership claims also illustrates that the husband is considered the head of the household, the eldest man in the household and the head of the wider family and thus that their decisions or actions cannot be openly criticised by the wives. According to the dominant ideology and thus existing interpretations of 'the law', men possess the authority and control over resources and may, if a woman's rights are not voiced by her own male relatives, actually decide to take full control of what would otherwise be considered her property. Thus an examination of the gender system in the Hawawir society reveals conflicting interests between women and men as well as between the families of husband and wife with regard to access to and control over resources. Despite this, a woman would hold that she and her husband are sharing the property, including the herd. It is usually only with reference to ongoing negotiations, for instance, with regard to a divorce or when women wish, in front of other women of their same age group, to presents their position as one of strength, that information of individual ownership is heard. Hence, although a 'conflict-gaze' may reveal, for instance, a variety of practical interpretations of ownership, such a gaze may also easily ignore other and maybe even more significant aspects of relationships and situations that would be important in understanding connections between resources, management ideologies and identity. Furthermore, and as I will exemplify below, different kinds of resources are perceived in different ways. While livestock and knowledge related to animals are definitely closely linked to men, other resources as well as knowledge are more often associated also with women. For instance, in principle, in this society there is an understanding that women hold the right to keep their own money if the money is given to them by their relatives or

[9] (cont.) significant meeting-points and political arenas where men from different areas meet. In addition to being places for rest and meals, the tea-stations are also financial and political centres in the sense that people working there would collect money from traders and travelers passing by, for particular causes and for distributing to those in need and centres for problem and conflict solving whether individual or group based.

earned by themselves. This is also an understanding that is advocated, as mentioned above, by the *Sharia*. Let me elaborate this point:

Bahita is an elderly woman who lived with her husband and children for several years in the Nile valley before returning to Um Jawasir. In a discussion with me and other women concerning women's rights to make decisions within the household, she told about the two goats she managed to buy for money that she had earned while in the Nile. Bahita claimed that these were her goats, owned by her only, and that no one, not even her husband, could make decisions concerning these goats without her consent.

Thus, some women do use money to buy livestock and to ensure some property of their own which is directly linked to economic activities. Another practice that may illustrate the cultural understanding and acceptance of husband and wife having, at least to a certain extent, separate economies is that relatives, that is, mostly men working in, for instance, Saudi Arabia who irregularly send remittances to their parents at home will usually send to their mother and father separately, regardless of whether the husband has only one or several wives. To a certain extent women and men are considered to control and have access to separate resources within the household and/or family.

Knowledge is also considered to be a resource, and, usually it is the men who are associated with knowledge and with being knowledgeable. Hence, it is men who hold positions within the various decision-making institutions in the Hawawir community. Age is, however, something that should be taken into account when knowledge is discussed. With age women are understood to become knowledgeable. Thus age is a dimension to be considered with respect to men's formalised control over resources but also with regard to women's more informal authority and control over resources. With age women usually hold significant positions within the life of men – positions that provide them with voices also in matters of politics and economy. *Al haboba* is a term denoting women who are considered to have extensive experience and knowledge with regard to exchange of resources within as well as between households and sub-tribes over time, as well as kinship genealogies which are considered important whenever political negotiation takes place. The position of *al haboba* with regard to knowledge perceived as crucial for conflict mediation according to customary law indicates that although men are considered to be in power in the Hawawir society, women are not seen as powerless.

Customary law (*al urf*) is, as discussed above, not scriptural, and one of its main principles is that of negotiation in order to find a solution to any problem that is morally and contextually acceptable to all involved. Because of the processual, contextual and interpretative character of *al urf*, it is difficult to establish a principal distinction between rules, norms and practices as well as to make a clear definition regarding gender and power. As exemplified above, although men are by the dominant ideology considered to be owners and decision-makers, women may also because of co-existing norms and practices, partake in both ownership and decision-making processes. Hence exploring customary law will, in many cases, show that a definite distinction between rules, norms and practices has limited relevance when it comes to understanding the formulation as well as the application of this form of legal system.

Economic activities & matters of morality

The Hawawir hold that it is possible to cope in the desert for up to three years with minimal or no rain. Within this period they survive by selling livestock and buying their food, sometimes combined with casual labour. Still, during the 1980s where there were no rains for more than four years, some families were able to remain in the desert throughout. They explain that there was, for them, nowhere else to go or also, that their families were too big to move. They did not have the camels and/or donkeys needed for transportation. Still, in most cases, the younger men from these households did migrate to the Nile Valley in search of casual labour. They brought grain, sugar and tea back to their families and kin in the desert although their visits were erratic. Hawawir who migrated to the Nile Valley lived or still live in the outskirts of urban areas where they survived on relief and daily or casual work as agricultural labourers, construction workers or house servants (Larsen and Hassan 1999, 2001, Larsen 2001, Hassan 2002).

The situation of spatial/geographical 'displacement' was, especially when relief activities were phased out in 1986, recognised as a major problem, both by the Nile communities to where the Hawawir and people from other nomadic tribes moved as well as by the government. As a consequence, the planning of a possible repatriation of the nomadic pastoral population was initiated.[10] This resulted in the above mentioned irrigated agricultural project in Um Jawasir[11] in the early 1990s that was eventually established in 1994. The project provides user rights to relatively small plots of irrigated farmland, to a number of people in the community (ADRA et al. 1995, Larsen and Hassan 1999, Johnsen et al. 2000, Larsen and Johnsen 2001, Haug 2002). Decisions concerning the distribution of irrigated farmland are made by the *agawid* consisting of elderly men together with the *Sheikh*s from each sub-tribe and the more recently established Farmers' Committee consisting of Hawawir men who already hold user-rights to irrigated farmland. Returning to Um Jawasir are men with their extended families, elderly widowed or divorced women with children or grand-children as well as newly established nuclear families units, who, for different reasons find life in the Nile Valley difficult, who do not possess any livestock and thus are in need of farmland.

Although the development project is focusing on irrigated agriculture organised as much as possible according to already existing juridical and political practices, its presence also induces more unintended changes affecting the organisation of the physical, social and moral environment. Below I will present some discussions evoked in the wake of the project in order to illustrate the processes of adaptability and how these relate to questions of morality and what are seen as 'habits' or custom (*ada*).

[10] Personnel at the University of Khartoum were contacted by UNEP in 1985 to undertake a feasibility study and found that Wadi al Mugaddam possesses a rich fresh-water aquifer at a reasonable depth and soil of sufficient quality for irrigated agriculture (ADRA et al. 1995).

[11] In the Sudan there is a system of dual land ownership. While in the Nile region private ownership of land is, protected by law, customary and historical rights of the people to land are in other regions, circumvented by legislation– something that is often unknown to the actual user (Manger 2001).

Within the Bayoda desert,[12] the Hawawir have usually lived scattered, and only extended families have composed clusters. The houses/shelters (*kerriga*) of the Hawawir living within the desert are either in the form of tents built from sticks and carpets woven from goat hair, constructions of mud upon a frame built from dry sticks and poles, or shelters built from dry wood only, that is, sticks and poles found in the surroundings. The kind of material people use to construct their shelters is connected to the kind of environment in which they live; in sandy areas with few trees, tents would be most common, while in areas with a lot of trees the wood constructions would be more common. In the case where mud and 'wood' constructions are built the owners will leave these when migrating, taking with them all their belongings, and later on returning to the same constructions. Those who live in tents will always take their carpets with them when they move. People who have recently returned to Um Jawasir and whose main economic activity is irrigated agriculture will usually build square mud houses. An increasing number of the returnees will now settle within the area demarcated as the 'Model Village' (*al gharia*). Until recently hardly any family would settle in this area. They would say the area is *sahara*.[13] that is, an area not liveable for either humans or livestock (Larsen and Hassan 2003). Families who have stayed in the desert throughout do not want to move to the area demarcated as 'Model Village'. Rather, they claim that they already have their own *gharia* (village) using the same word for their cluster, and thus see no need to move in order to live within a more restricted area where, as they argue, even the wells (*mushara*)[14] will be far away from the homes.

The area called Um Jawasir has recently become a centre where a number of families are settling and where several shops, as well as a market operating twice a week, have been established, and a mosque built. These physical changes also have, as shown below, implications for the organisation of the physical and moral environment.

New discussions are brought forward, for instance with regard to what and where young girls should be allowed to move. Girls as well as boys are curious and eager to visit and explore the new shops and marketplace. Simultaneously, adult women as well as men discuss among themselves whether their daughters should be allowed to move within the new areas that are not gender specific, and they express their reluctance according to their notions of sex-segregation and its importance. Following from their understanding of the force of sexual attraction and the moral ideal of girls' virginity and women's chastity, they claim that arenas where girls and boys would meet unchaperoned could easily create situations where girls' respectability is at stake. At present there is a rule that girls can visit the shops, but that they should not be allowed to attend the marketplace. The new themes raised and negotiated and the solutions agreed upon are interesting in the sense that they illustrate well both people's willingness to adapt

[12] This more specifically identified Hawawir area lies within the Bayoda desert south of Debba in the present Northern State, to the Wadi el Malik in the northwest and Wadi al Mugaddam in the northeast. The Hawawis move with their animals to the south to Kordofan State and to an area called El Safia in the northeast of the state (Bushra 2000).

[13] The Hawawir would usually use the term *sahara* to distinguish the liveable from unliveable areas within the desert. While *sahara* denotes the unliveable areas, *khala* is the term used to denote liveable areas.

[14] *Mushara* denotes wells dug and owned by a clan. *Bir* (well) refers to all kinds of wells, including boreholes.

to a changing life-situation and their insistence on certain cultural values. Among the families who did not leave the area during the droughts, many would use the fact that they stayed as an explanation of why they, not the returnees, know life in the desert and that their life-style is more in accordance with Hawawir custom (*ada*). Some would even say that the returnees have forgotten the Hawawir tradition, especially with regard to gender relations and the socialisation of girls and boys. They would, for instance, claim that, 'We are those who never left the land, and we do not want to interact with the people now coming from the Nile Valley (*Shamalia*).' Today those who stayed in the desert despite the drought emphasise that they were always (*daiman*) there, and because of this, they still know life in the desert and the customs (*ada)* of the Hawawir. By saying this, they also indicate that those who now return from the Nile Valley have no right to make decisions on their behalf if these imply a change of life-style.

User-rights to farms within the irrigated agricultural project were from the beginning given to men in their position as 'heads of households'. Among those who have returned from the various towns along the Nile in order to resettle in the homeland as farmers on irrigated land are women who often work on the farms. In many cases, the women are provided with user-rights to certain plots by their male relatives and/or husbands. There is also a tendency that the so-called returnees are eager to send their children, firstly boys but also girls, to the recently established schools in the area. They claim that they have seen that school education is crucial for their children in order to manage in contemporary society. Some men would, however, claim that education is not good for the girls because it will affect their behaviour in a negative way. They exemplify their statement by referring to, for instance, how they have seen girls behave in urban areas: talking and walking with boys in the street. Returning from the Nile Valley, women, in particular, complain that those who have stayed in the desert have not managed to become modern; they have not developed, they claim. Saying this, they refer to discussions with relatives and/or neighbours who have not lived in the Nile Valley and who claim that women should not farm, not go far from their homes, that there are no good reasons why girls should attend school, and that such an activity will only 'destroy their minds' and their behaviour.

In the above-mentioned discussion the community seems to insist on the value of sex-segregation and thus that girls and/or unmarried young women should not move freely within domains where men are present or, rather, in what is considered male space. Nevertheless, a representation of more heterogeneous life experiences among the Hawawir combined with new economic activities and educational institutions provoke discussions with regard to the practical possibilities and moral limitations inherent in existing gender perceptions.

Changing ways of organising everyday life

The presence of the development project has been accepted although the opinion that it brings too many people from the Nile area is from time to time expressed. When people began to return from the Nile Valley, they would say that Hawawir who had lived outside the desert for some time and who had become used to another kind of life would not be able to stay for long in Wadi al Mugaddam. However, as most of the women and men do stay on even, as is said, only to work as casual labourers on the farms of others, some argue that they do not need labourers within their area. By saying this, they are expressing opinions on the present changes in the social organisation of their society – changes that appear to be in conflict with basic values relating to everyday-life arrangements and the formation of social relationships. Let me illustrate:

In most cases the Hawawir still live in clusters (*mushraa*) consisting of a collection of nuclear families (*al ushra*). The clusters are formed around the main *kerriga* of the father surrounded by the *kerriga* of sons with their wives and children as well as the *kerriga* belonging to divorced daughters. The clusters are usually considered to be a household (*al beet*) in the sense that they live together, keep their animals together and have access to land for grazing and cultivation through the father. Each married and divorced woman with children, has her own house where she prepares food for her nuclear family, although the whole household often eat together, especially in the evening. Thus, there is simultaneously a marking of the connectedness of the wider household and the independence of the nuclear unit. The segmentary organisation of the community provides the flexibility needed in order to regulate the relationship between livelihood strategies and environmental circumstances (cf. Stenning 1959, de Bruijn and van Dijk 1995). The mode of management of resources within and beyond the household is thus dependent upon both individual and cultural factors. Thus, the familiar organisation of everyday-life including a division of labour grounded in family and kinship ties is based on perceptions of a sharing of common resources rather than the idea of formalised labour relations between owners and workers.

Furthermore with regard to livelihood sustainability and management of vital resources such as water, land and livestock, the settlement policies of governments are in many ways surprising. For instance, the Sudanese government has established a settlement close to the Hawawir area and next to the new tarmac road stretching from Khartoum towards the northern town of Dongola. The creation of a settlement is negating not only the mode of social organisation existing in the area, but also the dominant resource management system based on mobility in physical space and flexibility of household with regard to the size of the units dwelling together in different periods of the year or according to the environmental conditions. The government-initiated settlement, *al Sherian,* with its newly dug wells is meant to develop into a town. For the time being, *al Sherian* has boarding schools – one for girls and one for boys, a mosque, a health clinic and some shops and 'tea-stations' or cafés (*al ghawi*). In *al Sherian* there is also electricity (*karaba*) or light, *al nur*[15] as the Hawawir would say, as well as a water tank (*sereji*) and taps. Hawawir women and men often refer to *al nur* and *al sereji* as signs of improvement. Hawawir who settle in *al Sherian* receive the sum of 30,000 Sudanese dinars (about 115 US dollars) from the government in order to build their houses when they themselves have already built a foundation and planted trees on one of the plots. One problem with settling in *al Sherian* is that beyond the few shops and the tea-station, there are few possibilities for employment in this area, and moreover, being a settlement and becoming a town, there

[15] In Sudanese Arabic the term *karaba* denotes electricity. The Hawawir, however, use the term *nur* or 'light' when they refer to electricity.

are no possibilities for livestock keeping. So, among those who have moved to this settlement, those who have livestock keep only a few. They say that it is impossible to find fodder and that it is far too expensive to buy fodder. The price of fodder, they say, is so high that if they sell the livestock in the market, the price they get would not cover their expenses for feeding the animals. In their view and according to their economic calculations the input would exceed the output. The employees at the boarding schools and in the health clinic are not from Wadi al Mugaddam. One reason for this is that the Hawawir living in the area are mostly illiterate, and women and men from Hawawir society who live in urban areas and who have received education are reluctant when it comes to returning to their home area in the desert. Hence, those who have settled in *al Sherian* are families where the men work either in the tea-stations, are drivers of buses or lorries, traders, or men engaged in wage work in the Nile area whose wives, children and other members of their households still live in the home area. So, some people do, at least for now, take up a more settled form of housing. Still, in the new settlement, there are no alternative systems of resource management, or for that matter, any alternative livelihoods than pastoralism or trade, or more or less permanent labour migration to urban areas. Pastoralism, seen as an economic activity (cf. Babiker 2002), is still one of the main ways of coping in arid environments (de Bruijn and van Dijk 1995).

Perceptions of belonging & identity

Women and men who return to what they consider their homeland try to establish themselves in new ways in the desert. Their livelihood is dependent upon access to irrigated farmland or the opportunities to become a labourer on somebody else's irrigated farm. Many of the solutions chosen in this critical period diverge from ideal pastoral values with respect to life-style. In this situation people often refer to the advantages of a settled life, including access to modern institutions such as schools, health stations, electricity and water tanks. The possible ways of responding to calamities, poverty or starvation often come into conflict with ideals regarding mobility and what is perceived as the appropriate life-style. In such situations people tend to evoke the values associated with a sedentarised way of life and resource management instead of pastoral values in order to explain their choices and, thus, they become the advocates for change in terms of government promoted modernisation projects. This trend is also observed in other pastoral, nomadic societies (cf. de Bruijn and van Dijk 1995).

Although adapting to new livelihood conditions, livestock and herding is still perceived as the significant economic activity. It is, however, interesting to note that people – even those who for the time being do not possess livestock – do not in matters of identity become 'farmers'. They are, as they say, *arab*, that is, nomadic. This means that the main economic activity is not necessarily, in this society, the sole indicator of who you are. I was often told that it is expected that during one's lifetime a person may have to engage in other economic activities than livestock and herding, such as, for instance, trade, construction work or farming in order to survive. However, I would always be made to understand that the aim was to be able to re-establish a life as a herd owner and/or herder. This being said, it is important to bear in mind that being a pastoralist is, as de Brujin and van Dijk (1995) remind us, not so much a question of pursuing a certain activity, but rather a matter of self-definition, of how someone or a group express themself and of which activities someone or a group aspire to pursue or are prevalent in terms of cultural values. The importance of a nomadic identity and linkages to a certain area of land – of belonging – is expressed in several ways. Let me exemplify:

The Hawawir will always locate their graveyards opposite a well. When asked why, they say that they do this because they need water in order to prepare the body of the deceased for burial. Thus, it is important that the graveyard is situated close to a well. On a more abstract level, I would also suggest that the relation between graveyard and, hence, ancestors and the well and water is another expression of their sense of belonging. Both the well and the ancestors denote the source of life in a particular space. This can be seen, within Hawawir cultural understandings, as a statement of their particular identity and the rights to the land - their homeland - and the natural resources that follow.

An additional example is given by Mukthar, an elderly man, who explained the importance of belonging to a certain place and of being on one's own land as follows:

> It was a long time ago and *Asham* was the most beautiful place that existed. Everybody came to *Asham* and they all wanted to live there. Thus, *Asham* became crowded. In this situation, Prophet Mohammed prayed to God in order to ask God to give people knowledge so that they would understand that their own home area was as beautiful as *Asham* itself, and that everybody should see *Asham* in their own land. God accepted the prayer from Prophet Mohammed. As a result, people started to move back to their own land. After this incident, everybody has seen *Asham* in their own place, just like I see *Asham* in Um Jawasir.

These brief examples illustrate how perceptions of a locality may tie people to place and social relationships (cf. Lovell 1998) not necessarily in the sense of being immobile, but rather as a part of defining who you are. Furthermore, for the Hawawir who have a recent experience of being displaced – of living in a place where they do not belong and are not ascribed any rights – the idea of place also evokes emotions and sentiments of longing to be in a particular location and thus, to return to one's own place.[16]

Negotiating change: coping in arid lands

The Hawawir tend to refer to the natural resources within their *dar* as well as their livestock as property (*mal, sheij* or *hag*). Disagreements concerning interpretations of user-rights to property refer, however, more often to life-style and how communal life should be organised, than, for instance, explicitly to the access and use of land and water as such. Hence the main concern appears to be how to

[16] Land resources are part of conflicts within and between communities all over Sudan whether between farmers or pastoralists. Although political reasons are given as the main reasons for the civil strife that started in 1955 in Torit in western Equatoria, Southern Sudan and which had by 1995 spread almost all over Sudan, conflict over resources remains one of the main root causes (Abu Sin and Takana 2003). This reminds us that despite different forms of adaptation, issues related to land and water are, in general, identity markers in the broad sense of the term and as such, these issues involve political, economic, social, cultural and legal dimensions whether or not people and/or communities are directly involved in ongoing conflicts.

organise user-rights and management systems rather than how much resources or property an individual or family ought to have access to.

The flexibility of the natural resource management system and people's willingness to accept changes related to economic activities even within their *dar* should be seen in relation to the environmental conditions in which they live. In arid areas short-term ecological equilibrium does not exist (cf. de Bruijn et al.). Hence, disequilibrium is expected on a short-term basis – and one may speculate whether such a situation can only be accommodated through an approach to the environment and people that is characterised by flexibility, willingness to negotiate and, as the Hawawir stresses, generosity (*karaan*). Let me give some examples:

The establishment of irrigated agricultural land has been agreed upon, and the present system of distribution and redistribution of farms (*hawasha*) seems acceptable to most people. The issues that trigger disagreements and create division between those who never left Wadi al Mugaddam and those who recently returned, are, as discussed above, rather linked to life-style, mobility, settlement, education and gender relations. Many of these disagreements refer to initiatives raised by the development project. However, Um Jawasir, the area where the irrigated agricultural development project is located, used to be the grazing land of the sub-tribe called Rubab. Only through long negotiation between the Rubab elders (*agawid*) together with the *Sheikh*, representatives from the involved NGO and the *Nazir* was it agreed that this particular site should be the location of the development project. The agreement implied, however, that the Rubab would lose control over the area and thus that the implementation of the project meant that people from all the various sub-tribes, not only Rubab, would have access to land and water in the area. This is an example of the flexibility that characterises political and economic negotiations among the Hawawir. It is a form of flexibility that arises from an emphasis on livelihood security rather than a static and rigid notion of rights.

Negotiations may, however, also result in the formalisation of certain rights. According to the existing resource management system men, as I have already discussed, manage the rights (*al haggi*) to natural resources (*mawalid*) within the Hawawir homeland. Still, some years after the irrigated agricultural project had started a 'Women's Programme' was established. One important component in this programme was farming activities that women performed collectively on farmland put aside as nurseries. After some time women did express a wish for user-rights to irrigated land. Up until this point women had access to irrigated farmland (outside the Women's Programme) only if their male relatives and/or husbands allotted them a part of their farms. In addition to this, in many cases women work the farms with their husbands. However, the issue of women's rights to irrigated farmland was received with surprise because women in this society usually do not have user-rights to land in their own names. The issue was brought to the *agawid* including the *Sheikh*s and discussed thoroughly. The result of the negotiations was based both on customary practices and new experiences. It was decided that certain categories of women should be allowed to have user-rights to irrigated farmland, namely, widowed and divorced women with children as well as women whose husbands were sick or too old to provide for the family. Interesting with regard to this negotiation is that it both opens up change from the previous practice where women had no user-rights to land and, at the same time, remains grounded in customary law that allows for women who do not have male relatives or husbands to support them to be provided for by the group. In this case, an existing yet informal welfare institution is formalised. With rights being formalised women can, at least in principle, voice their demand for support in order to manage the maintenance of themselves and their children when in vulnerable life-situations, instead of waiting for their need to be identified and 're-acted' to.

Formalisation of existing practices may secure certain groups access to vital resources. Still, it seems that practices based on a culturally grounded experience of sharing natural resources is, given the environmental conditions, significant to viability. As mentioned above, the various sub-tribes have user-rights in different areas within the *dar* where they have their shelters, they dig their wells, where they move and keep their herd, where they inherit their rights in relation to grazing and water sources. In 2002 people expressed their worries because of the absence of rains. They said that it was the third year without proper rain. Usually, people and livestock, they explained, could manage up to three years without rain, but that was the most. Then suddenly the various shades of colour of sky indicated that it was raining in certain areas, and several herders and families moved with their livestock in the direction of the rain. Older family members remained, together with a few younger women with their children to care for them and at least one young man to protect them all. To my surprise, they moved with their livestock for grazing and watering to the areas of other sub-tribes. In my ignorance I asked how that was possible and hence if they would be allowed to use these resources. Ali, an elderly man and household head, explained it as follows:

> When it comes to rain (*mattara*) and the rainy season we move with the livestock to the area where the rain falls – even when the rain falls on the land of our neighbours (*majiran*). We are all free to move in order to make use of the rain. The years when the rain falls only in certain areas we have to share the rain and the grass. Some years the rain falls only in our area and the neighbours will come to us with their livestock. Other years the rain falls only in their area, and we move with our livestock to them. This is how it is. The rain is scarce in the desert, and in the rainy season we have to share the rain where it falls.

Customary law, *al urf*, is based on cultural understandings concerning the distribution of what is considered 'property' as well as authority or power within and between the various sub-tribes as well as with regard to the community as such. Still, as the three examples above show, for the Hawawir the two key concepts are 'negotiation' and 'generosity' which can be illustrated as follows: Precarious resources such as rain belong to all, even when it in certain situations means that they have to enter into each others' demarcated areas. Moreover, they hold, for instance, that the idea of punishment (*azadik*) is uninteresting. What is important is honesty (*mazulum*) and justice (*adl*) in order for people to reach agreements with which all involved parties can live. The agreements, they say, will usually involve compensations so that the violated party regains what was initially 'taken from' them. This is, according to both women and men, the only way to manage conflicts (*mashakel*) in a society where people depend upon cooperation and continuous support in times of need.

Living with insecurity and changing conditions, people cannot totally rely on a static, juridical repertoire to cope with the hazards of life. They constantly have to respond in a creative manner to new circumstances or perish, as shown by the example of their ability to accommodate the irrigated agricultural project. They do so as individuals and as members of a group in daily interaction with each other and with outsiders. Multiple normative and legal structures form a matrix in which they orient their claims and decisions with regard to property, tenure rights, access to natural resources and the formation of various forms of social relationships, and in a situation of scarcity, individuals or groups try to manipulate and negotiate to bend property and tenure regimes as well as human relationships in the direction they see as desirable and viable, given their situation as well as their aim.

By way of conclusion

Although the majority of the Hawawir still live within the Bayoda desert, many have had to leave their homeland. It is well documented, with regard to pastoral societies more generally, that the most affluent households usually leave for urban areas in order to live what is considered a 'modern life' while keeping their herds with related families or paid herders in the desert. The poorest and unviable households leave for urban areas in search of employment opportunities. However, due to the severe droughts in the Sahel in the 1980s most households among the Hawawir lost their livestock, and thus the character of the migration process changed. Recently, many people who were forced to leave are returning to their homeland, mainly due to the initiation of an irrigated agricultural project. Women and men who are at present returning from the Nile Valley to their homeland hold ideas of how to organise their community and their economic activities that differ from those who have 'always' lived within the desert and who have only seasonally migrated to the Nile during the date harvest in order to sell their labour. For them a good life is still understood as moving within the desert in ways that mean both humans and animals thrive and for whom the state and its various institutions are not considered either necessary or particularly helpful. Rather, in order to secure their livelihood within the desert *al urf* is considered most adjusted to both the environmental circumstances and their moral 'universe', including perceptions of equality, inequality and the values of generosity and negotiation. Historically, inequality grew out of the internal dynamics of pastoral society itself. At present the situation of inequality may, however, become intensified by the fact that livestock and herding would be combined with unequal access to external resources (cf. Manger 2001). For the Hawawir, resources external to livestock and herding are accessible through their involvement in the development project and thus irrigated farming, employment in other sectors or remittances received from relatives working, for instance, in Saudi Arabia.

Settlement, as well as the need to be more closely linked to the urban centres with regard to marketing of both cash crops and livestock,[17] seems to be the ideal voiced by the Sudanese government as well as many NGOs when it comes to

[17] Babiker argues that 'maybe the most significant change pastoralism is experiencing (...) is the increasing importance of raising animals for exchange rather than for sheer subsistence (Babiker 2002: 4).

development policies directed towards nomadic, pastoral societies. The underlying motivation of these policies is linked to an understanding of pastoralism as a static economic activity embedded in a society of pre-modern values and aspirations. However, despite this view, it appears that pastoralism adapts to new socio-economic and biophysical conditions and does find a niche in the modern world (Babiker 2002) despite the various effects of changing political and economic circumstances.

What is in the Northern Sudanese context considered a nomadic, pastoral livelihood with its particular conceptualisation and organisation of relationships of people to land and water rights is, as mentioned above, usually not seen as adjustable to a modern society. There is, however, in the East African drylands a complex interaction between pastoralism and agriculture, and as argued by scholars, the understanding of this interaction is still incomplete (Toulmin 1983, Babiker 2002). Hence, given this uncertainty, the inducement of too radical a change in resource management may in the long run only cause limitations to the flexibility and thus adaptability of, for instance, management practices in Wadi al Mugaddam; these are environmentally viable practices suited to a socio-cultural context where life and livelihood are still anchored in customary and, it seems, always adaptable understandings and practices.

References

Abu Sin, A.M.and Y.Takana. 2003. 'Civil strife and the environment: the Sudanese case.' In Hassan A. Abdel Ati (ed.) *Sustainable Development in Sudan*. Nairobi: Heinrich Böll Foundation Regional Office Horn of Africa.

ADRA/Sudan and Soil Conservation, Land Use Planning, Water Programme Administration (Ministry of Agriculture, Sudan) and Andrews University. 1995. *Baseline Study of Socio-Economic and Environmental Characteristics of the Um Jawasir Project Area*. Berrien Springs, USA and Khartoum, Sudan.

Awad, M.H. 1971. 'The Evolution of Land Ownership in the Sudan.' *The Middle East Journal*, vol. 25 (2): 212–22.

Babiker, M. 2002. 'Introduction.' In M. Babiker (ed.) *Resource Alienation, Militarisation and Development. Case Studies from East African Drylands*. Addis Ababa: OSSREA.

Bushra, E.2000. 'The Hawawir and the State: An Exposition of Identity.' Unpublished paper, Aas: Noragric, Agricultural University of Norway.

Casciarri, B. 1995. 'The Role of Women in the Changing Family and Social Organization of Ahamda Pastoralists (Central Sudan).' In *Nomadic Peoples* 36/37: 105–18.

De Bruijn, M. and R. van Dijk. 1995. *Arid Ways: Cultural Understandings of Insecurity in Fulbe Society, Central Mali*, Amsterdam: Thela Publisher.

De Heusch, L. 1997. '"L'Ethnie": Les Vicissitudes d'un Concept.' *Arch.Europ.Sociol.* XXXVIII (2): 185–206.

Delmet, C. 1989. 'Sociétés Rurale et Structures Sociales au Soudan Central.' In M. Lavergne (ed.) *Le Soudan Contemporain*. Paris: Karthala.

Eisa, S.I. 2002. 'Nomads' Education and the Mobile School in the Sudan.' In M. Babiker (ed.) *Resource Alienation, Militarisation and Development. Case Studies from East African Drylands*. Addis Ababa: OSSREA.

Galaty, J.G. 1998. *African Law Review*, no.71. Nairobi: Limited.

Gallais, J. 1975. *Pasteurs et paysannes du Gourma: La condition Sahellienne*, Paris: Centre National de la Recherche Scientifique.

Hassan, M. 2002. *Forced Migration and Socio-cultural Change: The Case of The Hawawir, Northern Sudan*. Unpublished Ms. Thesis. Aas: Noragric, Agricultural University of Norway.

Haug, R. 2002. *Forced Migration, Processes of Return and Livelihood Construction among Pastoralists in Northern Sudan, Disaster*, 26 (1): 70–84.

Herzog, R. 1955. 'Die Hawawir, Eine Berbergruppe in der Bajuda-Wuste.' *Mitteilungen des Instituts für*

Orientforschung, Vol. 3, No. 3: 463–78.

Johnsen, F.H., A. Jamal,Y. A. Mohamed, M. M. Mustafa and A. I. El Fadl. 2000. *Evaluation of the Um Jawasir Project*, Aas: Drylands Coordination Group, Noragric, Agricultural University of Norway.

Larsen, K. 2001. 'Forced to Migrate – Told to Return: The Case of the Hawaweer Pastoral Nomads of Northern Sudan.' *NORAGRIC Working Paper*, no. 23.

Larsen, K. and M. Hassan. 1999. 'ADRA's Um Jawasir Project in Sudan.' In G. Berge, K. Larsen and S. Rye, *Synthesis Report and Four Case Studies on Gender Issues and Development of an Improved Focus on Women in Natural Resource Management and Agricultural Projects*, Aas: Drylands Coordination Group, Noragric, Agricultural University of Norway.

______. 2001. *Perceptions of Knowledge and Coping Strategies in Nomadic Communities: The Case of the Hawawir in Northern Sudan*, Aas: Drylands Coordination Group, Noragric, Agricultural University of Norway.

______. 2003. *Sedentarization of Nomadic People: The Case of the Hawawir in Um Jawassir, Northern Sudan*. Drylands Coordination Group, Reprot no. 24. DAC/Noragric, Aas: Rotator.

Larsen, K. and F. H. Johnsen. 2001. 'The Um Jawasir Project, Sudan: Irrigated Agriculture and Repatriation of Displaced Nomads.' In R. Haug and J. Teurlings, *Successes in Rural Development*, Aas: Noragric, Agricultural University of Norway.

Lovell, N.1998. 'Introduction.' In N. Lovell (ed.) *Locality and Belonging*. London: Routledge.

Manger, L. 2001. 'Pastoralist–State Relationships among the Hadendowa Beja of Eastern Sudan.' *Nomadic Peoples*, 5 (2): 21–48.

Myers, M., R. David, S. Akrat and A. A. Hamid. 1995. *The Effects of Male Out-migration on Women's Management of Natural Resources in the Sudan*. London: IIED Report, No. 60.

Rosen, L. 2002. 'What is a Tribe, and Why Does it Matter.' In L. Rosen, *The Culture of Islam, Changing Aspects of Contemporary Muslim Life*. Chicago: The University of Chicago Press.

Stenning, D. J. 1959. *Savannah Nomads: A Study of the Wodaabe Pastoral Fulani of Western Bornu Province Northern Region, Nigeria*. London: Oxford University Press (reps. 1995, London, Hamburg, Oxford: IAI Lit verlag, James Currey).

Toulmin, C. 1983. 'Herders and Farmers or Farmer-herders and Herder-farmers.' *Pastoral Development Network Paper*, no.15d. London: Overseas Development Institute.

II
Land Reform, Policy & Conflict

5

Negotiating Access to Land in West Africa
Who is Losing Out?

CAMILLA TOULMIN

Why does land matter?

Land issues[1] in West and Central Africa are rising rapidly up the policy agenda of governments and donor agencies. Having once seemed in ever-abundant supply, in many areas land is now becoming relatively scarce due to a variety of pressures. Such scarcity brings higher market values and greater difficulties for those seeking access to this resource.

Land is of fundamental importance to the economies and societies of the region, contributing a major share of GDP, incomes and employment in most countries, as well as a predominant share of exports and tax revenue. Such heavy dependence is likely to continue for the foreseeable future in the absence of other major sources of economic growth (Fafchamps, Teal and Toye 2001). Thus, ensuring investment in the long-term sustainable management of land and natural resources will be critical to livelihoods and economic performance, as well as providing the basis for social harmony.

Gaining secure access to land is of particular importance to poorer people, whose livelihoods depend on balancing a range of different activities, including negotiating access to a plot of land and being able to use the local commons. Yet such rights are increasingly subject to threat as land values rise and new interests enter the land arena. The poor tend to be particularly vulnerable in areas undergoing rapid change, such as on the peri-urban fringe (Kasanga and Kotey 2001).

In the past, land in West Africa was often the object of multiple demands and users, depending on the season, nature of use and resource in question. The changing pressures, regulations and mechanisms for gaining access to land are generating increased conflict between user groups as option values rise. Thus, increasingly farmers are pitted against farmers, state and local people find themselves at odds, herders and farmers argue over rights for cattle to pass through cultivated areas, while migrants see their rights whittled away by local people who wish to re-assert control over this resource. Conflict is often violent with clashes between groups leading to deaths and the exodus of refugees.

[1] Here we refer to land in its broadest sense to include natural resources, such as grazing, woodlands, fisheries, and water. This report does not include the commercial forestry sector or mining.

Land constitutes a key political, social and cultural asset, conferring great power and authority upon those who control access to this resource. Business people, customary chiefs and politicians are keen to accumulate and invest in land, as a source of profit for current and future generations, as well as an asset of value in cementing political alliances (Toulmin and Quan 2000). The land issue is open to considerable political manipulation, as we have seen in Côte d'Ivoire, where the very large number of migrants from neighbouring countries seeking land to farm has generated heated debate regarding the issue of who can claim Ivorian nationality and associated land ownership rights. In many other parts of Africa, conflicts over land lie at the heart of local and national political tensions.

All governments in the region have recognised that land lies at the heart of many intractable political and social issues. As a result, a number of new measures have been initiated. Bit by bit and to varying degrees, these initiatives have tried to involve civil society and experiment with alternative ways of addressing land issues. In general, they have gone for greater pragmatism and willingness to try out new methods, learning from local practice rather than assuming that government can do everything (Toulmin, Lavigne Delville and Traoré 2002).

Where do land rights stem from?

In the West African context, there are several arguments that people use to lay claim to land:

1. Customary claims have usually been based on first settlement and clearance of bush land, converting it into farmland and establishing some kind of covenant with the spirits of the area through regular offerings and sacrifices.
2. Claims can also be asserted through conquest as, say, with the expansion of the Ashanti and the Mossi kingdoms who acquired superior rights over lesser chiefs and subject people. Equally, the colonial powers used conquest to justify their assertion of eminent domain.
3. Claims can also be made on the basis of long-term occupation and use of the land, such a basis for claiming rights having often been supported by governments, based on slogans such as 'land to the tiller'. However, such claims are often not granted recognition under customary law. In Ghana, they say 'long occupation can never ripen into ownership'. However long you may have been renting someone else's plot, you can never acquire the full rights over it. Equally, the Bambara of Mali say '*Jiri kuru be men ji la – a te ke bama ye*' which means 'a log of wood may lie a long time in water – but it doesn't turn into a crocodile.'
4. The fourth means by which people can claim land is through direct allocation by government, such as in titling programmes, and in development projects, such as irrigation schemes.

Thus, people use differing grounds on which to lay claim to land. Overall in West Africa, less than 5 per cent of land is formally titled, being concentrated in cities and project areas. The vast majority of land is subject to a variety of local administrative systems, often an amalgam of local, customary and state regulation, but with considerable room for confusion and contradiction between competing claims, leading to negotiation, dispute, land grabbing and conflict.

Why does the distribution of land rights matter?

Neo-classical economics argues that the distribution of land rights should not matter so long as there are perfect markets for trade in all factors, including credit, risk and insurance, which will allow people to reach an optimum mix of factors. Of course, in practice, market imperfections are often very considerable, leading to a wide variety of responses to market failure, as has been recognised by the new institutional school of economics (de Janvry et al. 2001). Thus, for example, poorer farmers cannot easily access credit with which to rent or buy land, and they must seek other means to gain access to land. Unequal land ownership can lead to very imbalanced social and political systems both at local and national levels which do not respond to the needs of the many. Ownership and control over land often are associated with patronage in several other fields because of the primacy of land as a resource on which people depend and interlinkages with other markets. Land rights owners in West Africa can use this power to gain access to a range of other assets and resources and maintain a monopoly of local power.

There is growing evidence to show that countries with a more equal distribution of assets, including land, tend to grow faster, with a broader based pattern of goods and service production (Deininger and Squire 1997, Quan 2000). Thus greater equality seems to be good both for poverty reduction and for economic growth. Access to land and common property resources is of especial importance to poorer groups, such as migrants, women and seasonal users, such as pastoralists, for whom continued and assured access is critical for livelihood security. However, the commons are under threat in many areas, either from enclosure and privatisation, or through open-access situations, in which local communities are unable to assert control. A number of pilot projects to establish and strengthen community management of common property resources show the potential for sustainable management where conditions are right and governments are willing to respect local arrangements (Alden-Wily 2001, Dème 1998, Hilhorst and Coulibaly 1998, Vogt and Vogt 2000).

What are the institutions and structures through which land rights are administered in practice?

There is a multiplicity of institutions and structures through which people gain access to land in West Africa. In many countries, the government formally claims ultimate ownership of all land, such as in Senegal and Burkina Faso, but in practice, much day-to-day administration is actually done by:

- Families
- Local and higher level customary chiefs
- Religious leaders
- Local government, councils/communes
- District or village land boards
- Project staff
- Government officials (district administrators/préfets, police, judges)

'Legal pluralism' is the term often used to describe the West African situation as it relates to land. There is no single set of rules which apply to land – it all depends on who you are and the claims you may be able to assert, where you are, who you turn to and the resources you have available to help ensure a judgement in your favour. A successful claim this year may be overturned next year if changes in the social, political or institutional environment so permit (Lavigne Delville 1999, Lund 1999).

So land rights in practice are all about negotiation between different peoples, drawing on whatever resources and bargaining power are at their disposal. Rights are not formally laid down but are in flux, with people engaged in what some describe as 'institutional shopping' (Lund 2002, Leach, Mearns and Scoones 1999). In many places, this institutional confusion does not matter too much since land is reasonably abundant, and one or other structure for regulating access to land is more or less dominant. However, where land is becoming more valuable, there are rising tensions and disputes regarding land, between different groups, between households, and between family members. Such tensions are particularly marked in peri-urban areas, and those regions which have received high levels of in-migration in the recent past (IIED 1999).

Examining secondary rights to land in West Africa

Having given a broad outline to land issues in West Africa, the paper now turns to look in more detail at issues of secondary, or derived, rights to land and natural resources.[2] Recent research undertaken by IIED, GRET and West African colleagues has focused on derived rights to farm land, these being taken as 'the range of formal and informal contracts through which people gain access to land for cultivation from those outside their family group.'[3] Thus we took these to be all those arrangements of a non-definitive nature to a person outside the immediate family, involving contracts such as tenancy, sharecropping, loans, mortgages and a range of other arrangements, but these European terms are a very pale reflection of the diversity of form, content, clauses and conditions which are found on the ground.

Derived, or secondary, rights to land, while originating in traditional concepts, are themselves very dynamic in form and content. Undergoing transformation as social and economic circumstances change, they constitute an ever-evolving set of arrangements which may be re-negotiated or revoked when one of the parties sees fit. They can thus be seen as a typical form of 'customary' practice, with all the ambiguities that surround such a term. 'Customary' in this sense is typified less by the longevity and stability of the institutional arrangement, and more by the interplay of forces between different social groups, generating a shifting set of negotiating positions.

We wanted to work on these arrangements for gaining access to farm land because so much of the land policy debate focuses on land ownership and establishing title to land. Thus land and property rights are assumed to constitute a single claim which is granted to an individual through the registration process,

[2] This section draws heavily on a joint programme of work carried out in collaboration with English and French-speaking colleagues from West Africa, and coordinated by IIED, London and GRET, Paris.
[3] In order to focus the research enquiry, we chose to exclude the many arrangements by which people gain access to land for purposes other than farming, such as grazing, hunting or collection rights.

conferring absolute rights. In practice, we would see rights over land and resources as constituting a bundle within which different kinds of claim may be held by a variety of people and groups (Schlager and Ostrom 1992). Our interest has lain in demonstrating the considerable significance of this range of land rights and their importance for a large number of people. In general, secondary rights are most important for those social groups who do not have primary rights to land. In the case of West Africa, where patrilineal farming systems have laid claim to much land, those who must depend on secondary rights thus include women, younger men, in-comers and pastoral groups. In addition, the research sought to examine how governments might best treat such secondary rights to ensure their continued contribution to the dynamism of the farming sector.

The significance of secondary rights to land & their evolution

Drawing on field research from a range of sites (see Table 5.1 below) allows for a comparison of derived rights arrangements between settings and how they have changed over time (see appendix for details).

Research sites were chosen in locations where we thought derived rights would be of significance. Thus the sites do not represent a representative sample of places from across West Africa. Sites were also chosen to provide comparable evidence on secondary rights in similar contexts but different countries. Thus, for example, two peri-urban settings were taken in southern Benin and south-east Nigeria, two plantation crop areas in eastern Ghana and centre west Côte d'Ivoire, two irrigation project areas in north-west Nigeria and northern Senegal, and so on.

In almost all sites, the incidence of derived rights was very significant. In the case of Mamanso village in Eastern Ghana, various share farming arrangements made up 65 per cent of all plots surveyed. For the villages in Côte d'Ivoire, migrants made up 70 per cent or more of the population and occupied more than 70 per cent of the land under cultivation. These migrants are both from northern parts of the country and from neighbouring Burkina Faso and Mali. There are an estimated 5 million migrants from the Sahel resident in Côte d'Ivoire, a little less than one-third of the population. They have been key to ensuring the rapid growth of Ivoirian cocoa and coffee production through the 1970s and 80s, but now face great difficulties with the sector in crisis and many Ivoirians seizing back the land which they had formerly lent out or sold to the migrants on a variety of terms. In west and south-west Burkina Faso, there are many areas where more than 80 per cent of the land is in the hands of migrants, such people coming from the drier north of the country, especially the Mossi plateau. In the case of southern Benin, in this highly urbanised region, a large number of people are using land rented from others, often from those who have moved to town. More than 60 per cent of those studied were engaged in one form or another of land transaction, and in many cases were both leasing land out to one person and renting it in from another.

In the case of north-west Nigeria, the irrigated land is part of the Sokoto-Rima scheme and subject to formal tenancy agreements and written contracts. In practice, much of this land is then sub-let to others, although this contravenes

Table 5.1 A comparison of research sites studied

Name of site	Rainfall mm/yr	Population density (people/km^2)	Crops & farming system
Southern Benin	1,250–1,500	250-300	Palms for wine & oil, subsistence maize & manioc, intensive tomato plots.
South-west Burkina Faso	800-1,000	40-70	Cotton, plus sorghum, millet & maize. Small vegetable gardens & fruit orchards near towns
West centre Côte d'Ivoire	1,400	80-100	Coffee & cocoa plantations, rice, bananas, yam, maize & manioc
Eastern Ghana	1,500	90-100	Old cocoa area, now turning to oil palm & citrus plantations, plus food crops
Northern Ghana low density; high density	700-1,000	10-25; 100-200	Grains, yam, groundnuts, cotton, small areas of vegetables
Sokoto, North-west Nigeria	600-800	250-300	Uplands with sorghum, millet, groundnuts & beans. Irrigated lands – rice, vegetables & fruit.
North-east Nigeria, Lake Alau area,	500-700	70	Uplands with sorghum, near Maiduguri millet, groundnuts & beans. Irrigated lands – rice, vegetables & fruit.
South-east Nigeria, Port Harcourt area	2,500	360	Densely settled peri-urban zone, food crops & oil palm
Northern Senegal	400	12-50	Irrigated plots of rice & vegetables, surrounded by dry uplands

the terms of the tenancy. In Senegal, all land within the village irrigation schemes examined is administered by the local cooperative, which took over control of the scheme when the state pulled out in the mid-1990s. Thus, all land is farmed under various delegated arrangements, the local co-op withdrawing plots from those who fail to repay loans and water dues, and reallocating them to others. Only in the case of the low density site in northern Ghana were derived or secondary rights of negligible importance, due to the abundance of land.

Thus these derived rights arrangements are very important in many areas, covering a large percentage of the land area and involving a high proportion of the population under both annual and perennial crops in many parts of the region.

Describing derived rights

Tables 5.2, 5.3 and 5.4 below illustrate the wide variety of institutional arrangements by which people can gain access to land and resources. Some are common to different settings; others are more specific responses to particular constraints and a product of a given cultural setting. Thus, for example, sharecropping is particularly prevalent in the perennial tree crop regions of coastal West Africa, where a considerable amount of effort and capital must be invested in clearing land, planting and maintaining plantations for as many as seven years before the first harvest can be sold. The share of the crop received by the different partners depends on the scarcity of land, nature of the crop, inputs invested and so on. Thus, for example, where the tenant or sharecropper invests his own labour and capital, he gains a greater share of the harvest than when these inputs are provided by the land owner. There is evidence for the existence of *abusa* (division in thirds) and *abunu* (division in halves) share contracts in Ghana from the nineteenth century, and possibly earlier (Hill 1963, Robertson 1987). Comparable arrangements exist in the forest areas of Côte d'Ivoire. Sharecropping is also widespread in the irrigated area of north-west Nigeria, where those with tenancy agreements with the project authority sub-lease land to others to help defray the input costs necessary for irrigated agriculture.

Mortgage arrangements are found where land has acquired a clear market value. In southern Benin, south-east Nigeria, and central Côte d'Ivoire, land ownership has become a means by which capital can be raised for various other purposes. Mortgages are agreed with other local residents and migrants. Land owners do not resort to formal credit institutions to gain a mortgage. However, there tend to be particular difficulties associated with these arrangements due to the lack of clarity regarding the terms and conditions under which the land may be redeemed or acquired by the creditor. As a result, mortgages are rarely transacted between kin since it is recognised that misunderstandings are likely to arise that would damage family relations.

The arrangements available in a particular site are also undergoing change as new opportunities develop and circumstances change, as will be seen later. Equally, the arrangements that a given person can negotiate will depend on their social status and relationships with others. The social origin and relationship between the land giver and taker will greatly influence the terms negotiated, while the maintenance of good relations between the parties is critical to the

Box 5.1 Mortgage of land in Benin

Awoba, or mortgage/pledge of land, involves the leasing out of land for an indeterminate period in return for a cash loan. The land will only be returned where the cash sum is repaid. The land acts as a guarantee for the loan, while cultivation rights serve as a form of interest payment on the capital sum granted. In times of crisis, many turn to pledge of land as a means to raise money. Creditors include urban dwellers (often emigrants from the village), as well as alcohol distillers and fishermen, seeking ways to diversify their assets and activities. The original land owner may repeatedly request further loans from the person who has taken on the land. In some cases, the cumulative total of loans given to the original land owner reaches a sum equivalent to the value of the land and the transaction becomes, in effect, a sale.

The creditor using the land is able to delegate rights to a third party and may also take responsibility for the trees on the land depending on the arrangement. But the creditor faces some insecurity since he must return the land when the loan is reimbursed. To address such uncertainty, one strategy pursued by the creditor is to agree a period in advance as the minimal amount of time before the sum will be repaid. Equally, some creditors make a succession of cash loans to the land owner, thereby making it increasingly difficult for the latter to repay the entire sum. Once the outstanding loan has grown to be broadly equivalent to the sale value of the land, the creditor negotiates the conversion of the *awoba* arrangement to be a sale contract. A particular worry arises with *awoba* when the owner of the land dies, since his heirs may not acknowledge the contract which their father had agreed, nor the size of the outstanding loan to the creditor.

As a result of such concerns, many transactions now take the form of written contracts. All sales of land are now systematically written and taken to the village chief as well as the sous-Préfet for signature and an official stamp. Other transactions are also increasingly subject to written agreement although the pieces of paper concerned are often very scant in details. They usually give the names of the two parties, sometimes accompanied by witnesses, but with little detail concerning the plot of land concerned, its size and location, the period of the contract, nor conditions attaching to its use. Usually there is no validation of the paper from the government authorities, though the *chef du village* now provides a stamp on some contracts in return for a consideration of 2,000 FCFA. Nevertheless, the growing use of paper indicates the value of written testimony in establishing, at the very least, the existence of a contract between two parties. This is of particular use to the tenant in the event of the landowner's death. Such paper does not exclude negotiation nor avoid dispute, but it does make it easier.

Source: Honorat Edja (2001).

Table 5.2 Institutional arrangements for access to land in southern Benin

Contract form & parties to agreement	Type of land, crop	Rights conferred	Other terms & conditions
Zunda, tenancy. Between family members & with outsiders	Land after fallow, often rested for less than 5 yrs	Cultivation, collect palm nuts, clear & sell wood. No rights to tap palm wine. Such rights may often be let out to a third party.	Rent paid at start of farming season, in cash. From 10-30,000 FCFA/ha depending on land quality. For 1–5 yrs.
Lema share-cropping. Usually between old landowner, young tenant	Formerly with oil palm, but now cover maize & manioc	Cultivation, with share after harvest; ⅓ to land owner, ⅔ to cultivator.	Tenants complain of interference & would prefer *zunda*.
Lema tomato, with tenants from Adja plateau	Intensive tomato cropping	Cultivation & share of harvest, usually ⅔ to tenant once cost advance paid off.	Landlord often advances food & other costs to migrant labourers.
Kpama	Palm wine	Extraction of palm wine, for alcohol.	Tenant cuts trees in preparation for tapping, sharing 1:2 with landowner.
Custodian contracts, between former masters & captives	Land under palm trees	Rights to cultivate between trees & to collect nuts. No rights to tap palm wine, nor sell trees. Protection of trees & land from others.	Longstanding relationship between parties, social obligations on both sides. Annual fee in kind or increasingly cash paid by tenant (e.g. 5,000 FCFA).
Awoba, pledge or mortgage	Farm land	All cultivation rights, not including trees, land to be returned on reimbursement of pledged amount. Delegation to others possible.	Means of raising money when urgent need for cash, creditors include urban dwellers, fishermen, alcohol distillers.
Loans of land	Farm land	Cultivation, collection of nuts & wood, no delegation to third parties.	Fee paid annually, formerly symbolic but now up to one fifth of harvest.
Palm contracts	Purchase of young palm trees (6–9 yrs)	Rights to harvest trees on maturity in 5–8 yrs. Land may be farmed below trees by another.	Purchase often by distiller needing assured supply of palm wine.

(Source: Honorat Edja, 2001. See appendix for details.)

Table 5.3 Arrangements for gaining access to land in south-west Burkina Faso

Name of arrangement	Type of land	Nature of rights acquired	Other terms & conditions
Folo siguily, or first settlement of land	Clearance of bush, allocated by *chef de terre*	First settler rights, including farming, investment, tree planting etc.	Participation in social life & meeting obligations of community membership.
Sissa siguily, or recent settlement	Clearance of bush &/or old fallows	Cultivation	Ban on tree planting, well-digging & other permanent improvements without prior agreement.
Singuely, or long term borrowing	Land borrowed from a lineage rather than *chef de terre*	Cultivation, but no permanent improvements, social obligations.	Becoming less common & shift from annual symbolic payment to a cash rent
Dondonly, short term loans, including payment in kind	Farmland & land developed for tree plantation	Cultivation rights for 2-3 years in exchange for ploughing, or help with establishing plantation.	Particularly common between old established migrants & newer arrivals.
Lalle, rental, often by urban dwellers	Farmland in both ZVCA & newly opened areas	Cultivation rights for 2-4 yrs.	Rents from 5-10,000 FCFA/ha for upland fields to 20,000 FCFA/ha for basfonds.
Sany-féré (purchase-sale) by lineage members needing cash	Farm land in both areas	All rights conferred on purchaser.	Prices depend on soils & parties. From 50-75,000 FCFA/ha in uplands to 100-150,000 FCFA/ha in basfonds in ZVCA.*

(Source: Lacinan Paré, 2001. See appendix for details.)
* ZVCA = Zone de la Vieille Colonisation Agricole, the land taken into cultivation with the expansion of ploughs, and opening up of land in the west of the country which took place from the 1960s onwards.

security of the agreement (Paré 2001). Migrants from a distant region will likely face less favourable terms than someone from a neighbouring village. Similarly, those who can establish some kind of kin relationship may find it easier to gain access to land on more favourable terms than those with no such link (Amanor with Didcrutuah 2001). However, in some cases, it is clear that those with land to let out are choosing to avoid contracts with close family or neighbours because

Table 5.4 Institutional arrangements for gaining access to land in Mamanso, eastern Ghana

Name of contract	Land & crops	Main terms & conditions
User rights, from gift & inheritance	33% of farms surveyed	
Leasing	Rare	
Abusa tenant	Cocoa	⅓ of the yield to landlord & ⅔ to tenant. Tenant responsible for tending the plantation.
Abunu tenant	Oil palm, citrus	½ to landlord after six yrs. Plantation divided into two & landlord is responsible for managing his own half.
Abusa caretaker/labourer	Cocoa, oil palm, citrus	Caretaker manages an established plantation & receives ⅓ of yield.
Abusa on GOPDC out grower contract	Oil palm	Tenant receives ⅔ of sale price of fruits & landlord after GOPDC has made deductions for compound interest on the value of inputs & seeds it has supplied to the tenant.

(Source: Amanor with Diderutuah, 2001. See appendix for details.)
* GOPDC = Ghana Oil Palm Development Corporation

of the assumed favour it is hoped this will bring. Thus, people are actively choosing to establish more lucrative contracts with outsiders rather than to negotiate with kin or neighbours who hope to negotiate more favourable terms by playing on the family connection.

Some contractual forms are widespread, such as various forms of rental, whereas others appear to be missing in certain areas. For example, sharecropping appears to be absent from the cotton growing areas of Burkina Faso, probably due to the availability of formal credit systems for cotton farmers and the relatively low demands for substantial capital inputs at the start of the farming season for other crops. Some arrangements which formerly were common have now largely disappeared, such as open-ended loans.

Evolution of these arrangements

While circumstances clearly differ within and between countries in the region, a number of clear trends were found in how such institutional arrangements have been evolving, shown in Box 5.2 below. These are largely a consequence of the widespread shift in perception over the last thirty years that land, though formerly abundant, has now become scarcer and hence more valuable. In many areas, the land frontier has now effectively closed, especially where there has been substantial in-migration. Thus, for example, in many parts of former forest areas of Côte d'Ivoire, local people are starting to feel the consequences of having allowed many people to settle and cultivate their land reserves over the past 20 years. In western Burkina Faso, the combined effects of river blindness control measures, the push to develop cotton production, and in-migration by hundreds of thousands of Mossi farmers from the drought-prone central plateau have led to the west of the country becoming 'saturated'. People are now moving further and further southwards into the remaining low density areas.

Box 5.2 Summary of major trends in land transactions

1. Land labour ratios are changing and the terms on which land is available are becoming tighter. Land which used to be available on long term loan, at little or no cost, is now being rented out for an annual payment (Côte d'Ivoire, southern Benin, south-west Burkina Faso).
2. Land is becoming more monetised. Tribute and dues which were formerly paid in kind are now increasingly demanded in cash.
3. Land is being used as an asset against which to raise credit through various kinds of mortgage arrangements (such as *awoba* Benin). Tenants are pressured by land owners into lending money or face eviction, in a series of loans which over time approach the value of the land itself at which point the tenant will try to force a sale.
4. Land purchases are increasingly frequent, involving local people and a range of outsiders, whether migrants, traders, civil servants, military or politicians.
5. Local people are increasingly assertive as regards their rights over land, although this may be at odds with the legal position. Increasingly government knows it must recognise such indigenous rights, given their own inability to administer land in practice.
6. Contractual arrangements are shifting, from one crop to another, as with share farming from cocoa and coffee to various food crops in Côte d'Ivoire, and into citrus plantations and oil palm in Ghana. New arrangements are emerging and terms within a given contract form are changing.
7. Given the rapid rise in prices, landowners limit the length of tenancies to ensure that their land is not tied up for too long.

Land 'saturation' or scarcity is clearly a relative term, depending on local forms of land use, levels of productivity and market engagement, and patterns of income diversification. Local people in Côte d'Ivoire are feeling the pinch in terms of access to land at population densities of 80-100 p/km^2 because their production system has relied on extensive tree crop plantations. Such densities are substantially below those found in southern Benin where, with 250–300 p/km^2, land is rarely left in fallow for more than a couple of years. Even in areas where population density is much lower, as in central Mali, substantial in-migration and widespread adoption of new technology (such as oxen-drawn plough teams) can render land relatively scarce. In the village of Dalonguebougou, demographic density has tripled from 5–7 p/km^2 to more than 20 p/km^2 over the 20 years from 1980 to 2000. In 1980, villagers confidently asserted that their bush lands were endless, that the bush could never end. Yet now, they accept that, having allowed many families from elsewhere to come and farm their land, the bush had effectively ended, and there is no spare land left. When migrants come seeking land to cultivate, they are told to travel on to the west (Toulmin 1992, Brock and Coulibaly 1999).

In several countries, there is growing interest amongst urban dwellers in acquiring rural land for farming and speculative purposes. Known in Burkina Faso as 'les nouveaux acteurs', these groups include traders, civil servants, retired generals, politicians and professional groups of various sorts. In some cases they have been actively encouraged by government to get involved in farming, to demonstrate 'modern' farming methods and activate agricultural growth (Ouédraogo 2003). Their likely impact is yet unclear, as is whether they have any intention of fulfilling their 'pioneer' function as hoped for by government. In some circumstances, acquisition of land is less for agricultural purposes and more a means to lever credit and other inputs on preferential terms from government. These new actors are an additional source of demand for land, though frequently they seek to buy land rather than rely on a derived right arrangement.

Changes in government policy also have an impact on the strength of claims asserted by different groups and associated land transactions. For example, the land law of 1998 in Côte d'Ivoire has shifted the balance of power over land more strongly in favour of indigenous Ivoirians (Chauveau 2000). Migrants from neighbouring countries can no longer 'own' land, but must lease this from Ivorians. The RAF (Réorganization Agraire et Foncière) of 1984 in Burkina Faso attempted to shift power in the opposite direction and wrest power from local customary chiefs by asserting the state's ownership of all land, with equal access for all Burkinabè regardless of origin. Land issues would be adjudicated by an elected village committee in place of the chief. However, repeated revisions of the legislation have brought about a significant change to the law and re-introduced a role for customary leaders within the land allocation process.

Economic factors and their evolution also help explain the changing pattern of secondary rights. The land rush in Côte d'Ivoire in the 1960s to 80s coincided with good prices for cocoa and coffee on world markets, leading to massive clearing of land, and many farms being set up on sharecropping terms. However, from the late 1980s onwards, the downturn in prices, the broader economic crisis in the country and loss of employment in cities led to the return of younger men to the village seeking land. Immigrants have increasingly been blamed for land shortages and a wide range of other woes. As a consequence, in certain areas, land is being seized back or the terms re-negotiated unilaterally. Political parties have also been active in re-asserting the rights of indigenous people, so that land issues have become highly politicised.

Social factors are also important in understanding the evolutions underway.

The last couple of generations have seen a shift in social and household organisation, particularly a breakdown in the web of mutual expectations and responsibilities within the household between older men and their juniors. Thus, younger men upbraid their fathers and uncles for having sold off the family's land to strangers for nothing, leaving them with little land to inherit. As a consequence, older men and household heads can no longer rely on the labour of their sons, and they must make new arrangements with other sources of labour, such as in-migrants.

The shift in generations over time is especially important in areas of substantial in-migration, such as in southern Côte d'Ivoire or western Burkina Faso. Young men from migrant households increasingly resent always having to be subservient to their 'hosts' to whom the land belongs under customary law. Thus, for example, many Burkinabè migrants in Côte d'Ivoire were born there and may never have visited their homeland. Home for them is Côte d'Ivoire, but they will never be considered natives in the areas where they have settled. They argue that their parents did indeed buy the land which they have worked for a generation or more and that there are no grounds on which they should have to return it. However, local people contest such claims, arguing that the land had been 'lent' to migrants rather than given and that they now wish to terminate the loan (Zongo 2002). Land withdrawals are particularly common on the death of a migrant household head since this prompts an ending of the contract and the re-negotiation with the dead man's heirs of new terms on which access to land will be allowed.

Given the risks of dispute associated with arrangements for gaining access to land, each party tries to make their rights more secure through a variety of means, such as:

1. Drawing up written contracts, to identify the plot of land and some of the terms relating to the agreement, such as the rent payable and date negotiated. There is increasing use of witnesses to such contracts and resort to an official stamp from the local village or government administrator. These pieces of paper have no formal legal value but nevertheless provide both parties with a greater sense of security.
2. Land owners re-asserting their prerogatives, by insistence on payment of a fee, even if only symbolic, since this re-affirms by whom the underlying rights to the land are held. Equally, landlords may insist that tenants spend no longer than two or three years on any single plot of land, to avoid their being able to claim rights based on long occupation, such as 'land to the tiller'.
3. Strengthening social relations, through establishing patron-client relations through which land access can be sought, involving regular gifts to the land owner, visits and help with other chores. Inter-marriage with the local land-owning group is another means used to acquire over time stronger rights to land, especially for children stemming from such a marriage.
4. Developing relations with the local administration to ensure support for land claims in the event of a dispute. Such a strategy is often followed by incoming urban investors who seek to mobilise the power of the state administration to recognise and support whatever land 'purchases' or other transactions in which they are engaged.

Impacts of such changes on different groups

So, with land becoming scarcer and more valuable, who is winning and who is losing out? Are there certain social groups who are becoming impoverished while others are consolidating their wealth? Our research sought to answer such questions. However, we found that the picture across West Africa is highly complex, with distributional impacts depending on setting. Relations between and within families are bound to change with shifts in land and labour availability, and the emergence of new economic opportunities. Thus, for example, in the early years of cocoa expansion in Côte d'Ivoire, it was relatively easy for labour-rich migrants to acquire land for establishing a plantation, with minimal cash outlay. Now, in many areas, land is no longer available either on loan or for purchase.

It is important to recognise that the term 'land owner' or 'landlord' does not necessarily reflect social relations or capture the distribution of power and economic advantage in many West African settings. First, it is probably better to refer to the 'land rights owner' rather than 'land owner' since in many countries ownership of land is a disputed concept. Local people tend to be very clear about who has the right to use land in a particular way, though much statutory legislation contradicts the claims they make. Second, in the negotiations between those seeking land, and those with land to cede to others, the 'tenant' may often be richer and more powerful than the 'land owner'. This is especially the case with incoming urban investors seeking land for farming. Third, many people may both rent in and let out land at the same time, or over their household development cycle.

Despite these qualifications, there are clear trends which are making it harder for poorer groups to gain access to land. The monetarisation of land has meant that negotiating access requires a significant cash payment, even for acceding to a sharecropping arrangement (Amanor with Diderutah 2001). Those without cash cannot meet the terms of the agreement which will include a fee for witnesses, the local government administrator or village chief, as well as purchase of drinks and other items for celebrating and confirming the legitimacy of the agreement. Even where land rights owners do not insist on a cash component to the contract, tenants without some other asset to offer in exchange will be in a difficult position. Those with a good supply of labour, plough team services or specialist knowledge (such as the tomato sharecroppers of southern Benin) stand a better chance of negotiating a contract than those with little to offer.

Ethnic affiliation and identity are becoming of greater significance in determining who gains access and rights over land. In areas of significant in-migration, as land becomes scarcer, new migrants may find it difficult to negotiate access while those who have been settled for some time may find their claims over land in jeopardy as local people try to re-assert control. Although government legislation in some countries may support the claims of migrants to acquire rights over land, such legislation is not enforceable in practice, and in many cases governments recognise the need for greater accommodation with those who claim customary powers over land. Hence, with the withdrawal of the state, migrants are finding themselves and their land claims increasingly exposed to the claims of customary chiefs (such as in the oncho-cleared AVV[4] areas of Burkina Faso). Migrants' land claims are particularly at risk with the appearance of urban investors seeking land since the latter can usually offer a better price to local land rights owners. Thus, in some cases land is being withdrawn from migrants to be re-allocated to a higher bidder (Mathieu et al. 2003).

Other groups losing out include younger men who find that their fathers and uncles have sold off their inheritance to outsiders, leaving them with little land to farm themselves. Equally, poorer women without cash to enter the land market and those whose social networks are weak (widows, divorcees) find it harder to assure themselves a plot of land.

What can government do to strengthen secondary rights?

Secondary rights to land are important, as argued earlier, for several reasons. They provide a significant means by which people can gain access to land, assuring a more efficient allocation of land, labour, capital and other factors than if such arrangements did not exist. They thereby allow for much greater flexibility and adaptation within the farming system to adapt to change over time and to new opportunities in the context of substantial market failure. In the past, they have been particularly beneficial for poorer groups, who could mobilise whatever labour they had in exchange for access rights to land. This valuable set of arrangements is, however, rarely acknowledged by governments. There are even some laws which attempt to ban such transactions. The Land Use Act of Nigeria, for example, makes such transactions invalid unless they have the express consent of the governor of the state. In various countries, there have been attempts to outlaw sharecropping, on the grounds that such arrangements constitute an outdated and exploitative contract.

On land issues there is a large gap between statutory law and what happens in practice. Such a gap generates uncertainty regarding the basis on which land claims may be made and the validity of various land transactions. How might government address this gap between law and practice, and make such transactions more secure?

One option would be for government to draw up a detailed code relating to each and every type of arrangement, specifying the level of rent, period of notice, length of tenancy, terms for sharecropping depending on the contributions made by the different parties, and so on. Detailed codification of this sort has been the approach of many governments in the past, especially but not solely in francophone countries. In the case of Ghana, for example, some of the MPs involved in the debate on land conflicts, sharecropping and tenancy in parliament in 1999 proposed that the government establish a nation-wide level of rent to be paid on all land, and abolish share tenancies on the grounds that they inevitably lead to dispute between the parties (Report of the Committee on Tenant/Settler Farmers 1999).

The second option would be for governments to recognise any contract which people agree to between themselves, subject to it conforming to certain basic

[4] The areas, formerly infested with black fly, have been cleared through spraying since the 1960s, hence controlling onchocerchiasis, and leading to the settlement of farmers in the Amenagement des Vallées du Volta (AVV) – a government sponsored farm settlement project.

principles, such as the need for a minimum period of notice if a tenant is being told to quit. Leaving it up to people to decide on the terms of the agreement should enable local circumstances and cultural arrangements to be built on rather than imposing a standard formula for all such transactions. Government could encourage parties to document these agreements, providing a sample model contract, if need be. This could include ways of handling unexhausted benefits from investment made by the tenant, and establishing a recognised process for settling disputes. This approach requires that governments 'let go' and be willing to devolve power and control to a more decentralised form of land administration, which could grant recognition to locally agreed contractual arrangements.

This second option would seem to be more realistic and better tailored to local needs, if governments are willing to loosen their grip on power. A simple process to formalise secondary rights arrangements might help reduce conflict and encourage people to continue to let land out to others, knowing that their fundamental land rights were secure. For example, with rentals, landowners frequently demand that tenants do not plant trees, dig wells, construct dwellings or make any other major physical investment which might, of itself, provide the basis for a subsequent land claim. Tenants are also discouraged from investing in land (such as applying manure) since the land owner may then find some pretext for early re-possession. A contract with an agreed term, ways of compensating the tenant for investments made and clear recognition of the rights of the land owner could provide the basis for more productive rental arrangements.

Decentralising land administration – but to whom?

The ongoing process of decentralisation under way in many West African countries provides a means by which such a delegation of land rights management might be achieved. This process has been heralded as a means of bringing government and provision of services closer to the people (Manor 1998, Ribot 1999). The experience with these newly elected local government structures has to date been mixed, given their very limited taxable capacity and heavy reliance for funds on central government. Thus, the *communes rurales* of Mali, District Assemblies of Ghana and *communautés rurales* of Senegal continue to find it difficult to establish their legitimacy, whether it be in providing services, managing land or raising revenue. Nevertheless, these local government structures are here to stay and must find a means to establish their powers and legitimacy within an already crowded field.

The powers of local communes to manage land and natural resources are contested by others. Customary structures continue to assert their rights to manage and receive revenues from resources over which they claim management rights. For example, the *jworo* of Mali are the traditional managers of high value flood plain pastures in the inner Niger Delta from which they can earn substantial sums. Newly elected local councils are trying to wrest such management rights away from the *jworo* (so far unsuccessfully) since such management fees would provide councils with a large annual income. Concerns have also been raised about transferring control over land administration to the newly elected communes, since where in-migration has been substantial, these new communes may well be dominated by non-local people.

An alternative structure for land rights management, which has been tried in several places, is a village based committee, on which various social groups have formal representation. These committees constitute an attempt to broaden involvement away from customary leaders and ensure that more marginal groups have a chance to get their voices heard, e.g. women, herders, migrants. Some writers express hesitation about how far these committees can in practice escape being captured by traditional elites (Faure 1995).

Improvements to customary management of land are proposed by the Government of Ghana with the aim of achieving greater transparency and accountability of the land secretariats maintained by a number of Ghana's customary chiefs. It is argued that state structures have failed abysmally to administer land fairly and effectively, hence the need for a return to customary institutions (Kasanga and Kotey 2001).

Reforms to land tenure and administration have major political implications. Choices must be made about attribution of responsibilities and rights, such as between reliance on established customary systems and local elected structures. In each case, there will be pros and cons, with neither choice offering a perfect solution. Thought must, therefore, be given to providing checks and balances on the powers attributed, whichever institutional option is chosen.

Conclusions

Derived or secondary rights to land are very important for many communities and farming systems in West Africa, yet they have been largely neglected by current debate and legislative provisions. Their status needs addressing to deal with disputes associated with such transactions and to ensure they continue to play an important role in future, especially with land becoming scarcer and under greater pressure. The push by some donors and governments in favour of land titling needs to recognise the range of rights associated with land and natural resources in West Africa, and associated overlapping claims. Pursuit of titling risks damaging the secondary rights of less powerful groups.

Making secondary land rights more secure needs to build on the diversity of local practice and the flexibility of such arrangements which allows them to adapt. Detailed codification risks freezing them in a form which would prevent further evolution. The obvious way forward would be to strengthen locally based structures for handling and recognising these arrangements, dealing with disputes and agreeing general principles to which these agreements should conform. Simple model contracts might help prompt explicit treatment of many clauses and conditions which might otherwise form the basis for later dispute.

Such an approach would mesh well with current processes in favour of decentralisation. However, the form taken by such decentralised local structures will depend on context. In Ghana it is planned to work with and render more effective and transparent the land secretariats maintained by many customary chiefs. In Burkina Faso, village level committees are proposed as the primary structure with responsibility for managing land issues. In Mali, the prerogatives of the new *communes* are not clearly established. In Senegal, the *communautés rurales* have been responsible for land allocations for more than a decade. In Côte d'Ivoire the 1998 legislation keeps the process of titling and granting land titles firmly in the hands of government officials. Perhaps the choice of structure may not be too important so long as the processes followed are relatively open and accountable. Of greatest importance is a system of checks and balances which prevents land rights management and resolution of disputes becoming a source of corruption and local patronage.

Appendix

During the period 1996-2001 the British and French governments supported a programme of work to assist in developing and implementing land tenure policies which improve land tenure security for rural people in West Africa. It was funded by the UK's Department for International Development (DFID) and the French Ministry of Foreign Affairs (Ministère des Affaires Etrangères – MAE). The programme on Land Tenure and Resource Access in West Africa has been co-ordinated by IIED and GRET, with technical support from the IRD (Institut français de recherche pour le développement), and guidance from the 'Rural land tenure, renewable resources and development' Steering Committee set up by the French Ministry of Foreign Affairs. The study of derived rights to land in West Africa has involved ten researchers or research teams from seven French and English-speaking West African countries. A final synthesis report from this research was published by DFID (in English) and by the MAE (in French).

People contributing to this research

Case studies:

Kojo Amanor, Institute of African Studies, University of Ghana, Legon, Ghana.
Mark Anikpo, Department of Sociology, University of Port Harcourt, Nigeria.
Saa Dittoh, University of Development Studies, Tamale, Ghana.
Honorat Edja, independent researcher, Cotonou, Benin.
Olivier Iyebi Mandjek, Institut National de la Cartographie, Yaoundé, Cameroon.
Mariatou Koné, Université d'Abidjan/GIDIS-CI, Abidjan, Côte d'Ivoire.
Abubukar Mamman, Department of Geography, Usman Dan Fodio University, Sokoto, Nigeria.
Ibra Cire Ndiaye, Laboratoire d'Anthropologie Juridique de Paris, Paris.
Lacinan Paré, consultant, Ouagadougou, Burkina Faso.
Abba Isa Tijani, Department of Anthropology, University of Maiduguri, Nigeria.

Co-ordination & direction:

Camilla Toulmin, Judy Longbottom, IIED (Great Britain), and Philippe Lavigne Delville, GRET (France).

Technical Advisory Committee:

Jean-Pierre Chauveau, IRD; Jean-Philippe Colin, IRD; Philippe Lavigne Delville, GRET; Camilla Toulmin, IIED.
Etienne Le Roy (Laboratoire d'Anthropologie Juridique de Paris (LAJP) Paris I), Mike Winter (Consultant) and Mike Mortimore (University of Cambridge) also played an important part in launching this programme. Alain Rochegude (LAJP, Paris I) undertook an analysis of the relevant legal texts. We would also like to thank Mahamadou Zongo for letting us use data from his recent study of Bodiba (Côte d'Ivoire).

The complete results of this piece of research are available in:

Lavigne Delville Ph., C. Toulmin, J.Ph. Colin and J.P. Chauveau. 2001. *Negotiating Access to Land in West Africa: A Synthesis of Findings from Research on Derived Rights to Land.* IIED/GRET/IRD, and *L'accès à la terre par les procédures de délégation foncière (Afrique de l'ouest rurale): modalités, dynamiques et enjeux*, rapport de recherche final, GRET/IRD/IIED.

Reports produced for the purposes of this study

Amanor, K. S. with M. K. Diderutuah. 2001. *Share Contracts in the Oil Palm and Citrus Belt of Ghana.* IIED/GRET, p. 28

Anikpo, M. 2000. *Derived Rights and the Security of Tenancy in Oyigbo Local Government Area (LGA), Rivers State, Nigeria. A Case Study of Obigbo and Ndoki Communities.* IIED/GRET, p. 35.

Brégeot G. 1998. *Droits délégués en Afrique noire: revue à partir de la littérature francophone*, preparatory research document. GRET/IIED, p. 85.

Colin J.Ph. and J.P. Chauveau. 1999. *Guide de production des données de terrain*, document concerned with research methodology. IRD/GRET/IIED, p. 9.

Colin J.Ph. 2001. *Efficience et équité des droits fonciers délégués, éclairages économiques.* Contribution to the research. IRD/GRET/IIED, p. 26.

Dittoh, S. 2000. *Agricultural Land Use Arrangements and Derived Rights for Gaining Access to Farm Land in Northern Ghana.* IIED/GRET, p. 35

Edja, H. 2001. *Land Rights under Pressure: Access to Resources in Southern Benin.* IIED/GRET, p. 23.

GRET/IIED. 1999. *Les droits délégués d'accès à la terre et aux ressources: négociation, renégociation, sécurisation*, report on the Accra workshop. GRET/IIED, 1999.

Iyebi-Mandjek, O. 2001. *Dynamique des droits délégués chez les Mafa du nord Cameroun*, preliminary report. GRET/IIED, p. 103.

Koné, M. 2001. *Gaining Rights of Access to Land and Natural Resources in Bodiba and Zahia, Centre-west of Côte d'Ivoire.* IIED/GRET, p. 40.

Mamman, A. B. 2000. *The Incidence and Nature of Derived Rights in the Sokoto Rima Basin, N.W. Nigeria.* IIED/GRET, 83 p. + ann.

Ndiaye, I. C. 2001. *Transferts temporaires et définitifs des droits de la terre à Mboyo et à Guede Wuro (départment de Podor).* GRET/IIED.

Paré, L. 2001. *Negotiating Rights: Access to Land in the Cotton Zone, Burkina Faso.* IIED/GRET, p. 28.

Tijani, A. I. Daura, M. M. and Gazali W. A. 2000, *Derived Land Rights in Lake Alau, North-east Nigeria.* IIED/GRET, p. 37.

References

Alden-Wily, L. 2001. 'Making Woodland Management More Democratic: Cases from Eastern and Southern Africa.' *Drylands Programme Issue Paper 99.* London: IIED.

Brock, K and N. Coulibaly. 1999. 'Sustainable rural livelihoods in Mali', *IDS Research Report no. 35.*

Chauveau, J.P. 2000. 'The Land Question in Côte d'Ivoire: A Lesson in History.' *Drylands Programme Issue Paper no. 95.* London: IIED.

de Janvry, A. et al. (eds). 2001. *Access to Land, Rural Poverty and Public Action.* Oxford: Clarendon Press.

Deininger, K. and L. Squire. 1997. 'Economic Growth and Income Inequality: Re-examining the Links.' *Finance and Development.* March: 38–41.

Dème, Y. 1998. 'Associations locales de gestion des ressources naturelles du Kelka, Mali.' *Drylands Programme Issue Paper 74.* London: IIED.

Fafchamps, M., F. Teal, and J. Toye. 2001. *Towards a Growth Strategy for Africa.* Oxford: Centre for the Study of African Economies.

Faure, Armelle. 1995. *Private Land Ownership in Rural Burkina Faso.* Issues Paper, IIED Dryland Networks Programme, no. 59. London: IIED.

Hilhorst, T. and A. Coulibaly. 1998. 'Une convention locale pour la gestion participative de la brousse au Mali.' *Drylands Programme Issue Paper 78*. London: IIED.

Hill, P. 1963. *The Migrant Cocoa Farmers of Southern Ghana. A Study of Rural Capitalism*. Cambridge: Cambridge University Press (repr. 1997, London, Hamburg, Oxford: IAI. Lit Verlag, James Currey).

IIED. 1999. *Land Tenure and Resource Access in West Africa. Issues and Options for the Next 25 Years*. London: IIED.

Kasanga, K. and N.A. Kotey. 2001. *Land Management in Ghana. Building on Tradition and Modernity*. London: IIED.

Lavigne Delville, P. 1999. 'Comment articuler législation nationale et droits fonciers locaux: expériences en Afrique de l'ouest francophone.' *Drylands Programme Issue Paper no. 86*. London: IIED.

Leach, M., R. Mearns and I. Scoones. 1999. 'Environmental Entitlements: Dynamics and Institutions in Community-based Natural Resource Management.' *World Development*, vol. 27, no. 2: 225–47.

Lund, C. 2002. 'Negotiating Property Institutions: On the Symbiosis of Property and Authority in Africa.' In K. Juul and C. Lund (eds) *Negotiating Property in Africa*, Portsmouth, NH: Heinemann.

______. 1999. 'A Question of Honour – Property Disputes and Brokerage in Burkina Faso.' *Africa* 69 (4).

Manor, J. 1998. *The Political Economy of Democratic Decentralisation*. Washington, DC: World Bank.

Mathieu, P. et al. (2003). 'Making Land Transactions More Secure in the west of Burkina Faso.' *Dryland Programme Issue Paper No. 117*. London: IIED.

Ouédraogo, M. 2003. 'New Stakeholders and the Promotion of Argro-sylvo-pastoral Activities in Southern Burkina Faso.' *Drylands Programme Issue Paper No. 118*. London: IIED.

Quan, J. 2000. 'Land Tenure, Economic Growth and Poverty in sub-Saharan Africa.' In C. Toulmin, and J. Quan (eds) *Evolving Land Rights, Policy and Tenure in Africa*. London: DFID/IIED/NRI.

Report of the Committee on Tenant/Settler Farmers on a Study of Problems of Landlords and Tenant/Settler Farmers in Sefwi-Wiawso and Juabeso-Bia Districts, Western Region. May 1999.

Ribot, J. 1999. 'Decentralisation, Participation and Accountability in Sahelian Forestry: Legal Instruments of Politico-administrative Control.' *Africa* 69: 23–65.

Robertson, A.C. 1987. *The Dynamics of Productive Relationships: African Share Contracts in Comparative Perspective*. Cambridge: Cambridge University Press.

Schlager, E. and E. Ostrom. 1992. 'Property Rights Regimes and Natural Resources: A Conceptual Analysis.' *Land Economics* 68 (3) August: 249–62.

Toulmin, C. 1992. *Cattle, Women and Wells. Managing Household Survival in the Sahel*. Oxford: Clarendon Press.

Toulmin, C., P. Lavigne Delville and S. Traoré. 2002. *Dynamics of Resource Tenure in West Africa*. Oxford: James Currey.

Toulmin, C. and J. Quan. 2000. *Evolving Land Rights, Policy and Tenure in Africa*. London: DFID/IIED/NRI.

Vogt, G. and K. Vogt, K. 2000. 'Hannu Biyu Ke Tchuda Juna – Strength in Unity. Shared Management of Common Property Resources – A case study from Takiéta, Niger.' *Securing the Commons*, no. 2. London: IIED.

Zongo, M. 2002. Étude des Groupements Immigrés Burkinabé dans la Région de Oumé (Côte d'Ivoire): Rapports fonciers avec les Groupes Autochtones et les Pouvoirs Publiques Locaux et Organisation en Migration. IRD-URF Doc. 3, Montpellier.

6

Land Tenure Reform in a Namaqualand Communal Area, South Africa *Contesting Komaggas*

POUL WISBORG

Transformation of Certain Rural Areas Act, Act 94 of 1998 (Trancraa) is part of South Africa's land reform programme and provides for transferring land ownership rights in 23 rural areas from the state to local institutions. During 2001–2 Trancraa was introduced in six areas in the arid and semi arid district of Namaqualand on the border of Namibia. In five of the areas the process went largely according to guidelines, but in Komaggas it ended in a stalemate between local and external actors. This paper explores why it proved impossible to implement an apparently pragmatic and non-prescriptive tenure reform act in a place where there was wide support for community ownership and governance of land.

Towards land tenure reform in South Africa

Land tenure reform addresses rights over resources and therefore the power relations between individuals, age and gender groups, communities and the state. In land tenure reform, state-centric models – socialist or freehold – have repeatedly failed in Africa (Toulmin and Quan 2000). These failures have often involved 'seeing like a state': simplified readings of 'exceptionally complex, illegible, and local social practices, such as land tenure customs' (Scott 1998: 2). Falk Moore (1978: 3) studied tenure and law as process, communicated, reshaped and immersed in 'social reality [as] a peculiar mix of action congruent with rules ... and other action that is choice-making, discretionary, manipulative, sometimes inconsistent, and sometimes conflictual'. As a government initiative, tenure reform may cause suspicion and resistance: 'individual acts of foot dragging and evasion, reinforced by a venerable popular culture of resistance [that] make an utter shambles of the policies dreamed up ... in the capital' (Scott 1985: xvii). The concept of tenure must include meaning, power and contestation because seeing institutions as only 'rules' is 'far too narrow a compass for understanding social dynamics' (Peters 2002). Tenure reform must 'legislate for negotiability' (Cousins 2002).

In South Africa, conquest, colonial and apartheid legislation, forced removals and unequal development excluded the majority from the most valuable land and from institutions of ownership, forcing millions of rural people to live with inequitable and insecure tenure in 'homelands' and other racially defined areas.[1] As elsewhere in Africa the colonial power reshaped local leadership institutions in order to incorporate the majority as subjects rather than citizens, employing a language of 'culture' and 'community' in rural areas and of 'citizen rights' in urban areas (Mamdani 1996: 18). Ntsebeza (1999: 108–9) has shown that this analysis applies to the way apartheid governments co-opted local authorities as appointed agents of the state, shaping their wide-ranging allocative, administrative and judicial powers.

Today the constitutionally mandated land reform programme of restitution, redistribution and tenure reform aims to 'heal the divisions of the past'.[2] Yet, after the first ten years of democracy, inequality in land ownership remains extreme, and only around three per cent of farmland has been restored through restitution and redistribution combined (Hall and Lahiff 2004). 'Communal tenure reform' for the estimated 15 million people in the former 'homelands' is deeply contested with respect to class, gender, race and the role of 'customary' law and 'traditional leaders' (Claassens 2000, Cousins 2002). A draft Land Rights Bill was shelved after a change of minister in 1999 and a new draft bill was published for comments in August 2002 and adopted by Cabinet in a dramatically different version in October 2003. After very critical submissions and hearings in November 2003[3] the Communal Land Rights Bill was approved by Parliament and signed into act in 2004 (RSA 2004).

An earlier case of tenure reform may provide insights into challenges awaiting the implementation of the Communal Land Rights Act. Transformation of Certain Rural Areas Act, Act 94 of 1998 (Trancraa) provides for repealing apartheid legislation, protecting user rights and transferring ownership of 23 'Act 9' rural areas to local institutions (RSA 1998).[4] During 2001-2 the act was implemented in eight rural areas in Northern Cape Province, six of which are in Namaqualand (Wisborg and Rohde 2003). In five of the areas the consultation was fairly successful, but in Komaggas the process ended in a stalemate.[5] The goal is not

[1] Former 'homelands' comprise about 17 million ha (14%) of the country, privately owned farmland about 105 million ha (70%) (Kepe and Cousins 2002).

[2] The Constitution Act 108 of 1996, Bill of Rights, Section 25 (5-7) holds that: 5) The state must take reasonable legislative and other measures, within its available resources, to foster conditions which enable citizens to gain access to land on an equitable basis. 6) A person or community whose tenure of land is legally insecure as a result of past racially discriminatory laws or practices is entitled, to the extent provided by an Act of Parliament, either to tenure which is legally secure or to comparable redress. 7) A person or community dispossessed of property after 19 June 1913 as a result of past racially discriminatory laws or practices is entitled, to the extent provided by an Act of Parliament, either to restitution of that property or to equitable redress.

[3] Legal opinions for the Commission on Gender Equality and the Legal Resources Centre viewed that the Communal Land Rights Bill 2003 was inconsistent with the Constitution (RSA 2003a, PLAAS/NLC 2003, Commission on Gender Equality 2003).

[4] The term 'Act 9 areas' derives from Rural Areas Act 9 of 1987. The 'Act 9 areas' cover about 18,000 km^2 (10.5% of the former 'homelands') and have a population of about 70,000 (0.6% of the former 'homelands') (Catling 1996).

[5] Komaggas is one of two Namaqualand rural areas selected for field study in a PhD research project on human rights and tenure reform (the other was Pella). Working with Francios Z. Jansen, during October 2001 to November 2002 I conducted 80 interviews with households and leaders in Komaggas, and at municipal and district level. I am thankful to everyone for sharing time and knowledge with me.

to assess the Trancraa process, but to learn from an 'extreme case' of contested tenure reform on the geographic and institutional frontier of a new South Africa. I ask why it proved impossible to implement a pragmatic, non-prescriptive tenure reform act in a place where many local actors advocated community ownership and governance of land. I suggest that tenure reform became engulfed in power struggles in a divided community where parties came to see control over the process as more important than widely shared interests in securing rights to land. The Komaggas story shows why it may be difficult to negotiate and change land tenure – and thus heal state-society relations in the bifurcated society when power relations, the freedom of farmers, identities – and perhaps diamonds – are at stake.

Namaqualand & Trancraa

'Act 9 Areas'

The history of the six Namaqualand rural areas is one of conflict over land and resistance to external control. They originated as mission stations for people of Nama (once the major pastoralist group in the area), San and mixed descent who were trying to protect themselves against colonial dispossession (Boonzaier et al. 1996). The colonial government issued 'Tickets of Occupation' to mission stations for temporary tenure security, but later brought the areas under state administration by the Mission Stations and Communal Reserves Act 29 of 1909. This led to protests in Komaggas and other areas, where locally elected councils defied the new government controlled 'Management Boards' then introduced (Hendricks 1995). It speaks about a remarkable persistence that in 2002 some Komaggas residents said that they were resisting new legislation partly because they had never accepted the nationalisation in 1909.

During the twentieth century the areas were labour pools for a cyclical mining and farming economy. Local councils (*Raad*, pl. *Rade*) preserved a certain degree of autonomy despite increasing control by governments through a long list of acts and amendments (Pienaar 2000). As elsewhere (Letsoalo 1987), top-down policies created suspicion of government-driven tenure reforms, seen to force inappropriate institutions, neglect the problem of resource distribution and extend gender biases. In the 1980s government tried to enforce 'economic units', semi-privatised sections of the commons, but the programme was abandoned following a Supreme Court ruling in 1988 (Hendricks 1995). In 1994, women met to discuss legislation[6] which they saw as a threat to their interests, because it aimed to convert family use rights, generally registered in the name of men, to full ownership (Archer and Meer 1997).

Today the six 'rural areas' make up about 14,300 km^2, or some 30 per cent of Namaqualand, and are home to about 30,000 of the 70,000 inhabitants (Table 6.1).[7] During 1995 to 2000, elected Transitional Local Councils governed the areas as distinct political units. From January 2001 they were integrated into larger municipalities designed to break down the institutional and geographical

[6] General Law Amendment Act 108 of 1993.

[7] Namaqualand today is roughly equivalent to the four municipalities of Kamiesberg, Nama-Khoi (where Komaggas falls), Richtersveld and Khâi-Ma. These are part of the new Namakwa District Municipality.

boundaries between 'white towns', 'white farm land' and 'Act 9 areas'. The areas are rural towns within sizeable common lands. An estimated 2,000 households use the commons for livestock and cultivation of dryland crops (when rainfall permits), providing an additional source of income to wage labour and/or state welfare payments. Less than 700 privately owned farms (almost exclusively held by 'whites') comprise about 50 per cent of Namaqualand (DoA 2001).

Many residents in the rural areas remain angered by historical land losses, but an official view has for long remained that 'Namaqualand rural land claims cannot be addressed through the Land Claims Court process because of the Constitutional 1913 cut-off date agreed to for land restitution matters' (DLA 2001). However, in 2003 the Richtersveld community successfully contested this view in court cases against government and a state diamond mining company.[8] Instead the emphasis has been on redistribution. Since 1995, local people assisted by Surplus People Project (SPP), the Department of Land Affairs (DLA) and Legal Resources Centre (LRC) have acquired about 313,000 hectares of former mining or private farm land under the 'municipal commonage programme' (Anderson and Pienaar 2003: 1). Land was purchased by government and vested in municipalities, increasing the amount available to 'Act 9' communities by about 21 per cent. Farmers gain access by applying for temporary grazing licences from municipal committees. Table 6.1 gives an overview of the six areas with the original 'Act 9 area' and the re-distribution land.

Table 6.1 Act 9 Areas' in Namaqualand

	Act 9[1] (ha)	Share %	New farms[2] (ha)	Increase %	Total[3] (ha)	Share %	Residents	Ha per capita
Leliefontein	159,182	13%	32,627	20%	191,809	13%	4,825	40
Concordia	75,693	6%	40,760	54%	116,453	8%	4,564	26
Pella	48,276	4%	34,912	72%	83,188	6%	4,092	20
Komaggas	62,600	5%	27,228	43%	89,828	6%	4,927	18
Steinkopf	329,000	28%	110,023	33%	439,023	31%	7,822	56
Richtersveld	513,919	43%	0	0%	513,919	36%	3,643	141
Total	1,188,670	100%	245,550	21%	1,434,220	100%	29,873	48

(Source: SPP 2003a: 4)
1: Act 9 trust land vesting in the state (to which Trancraa applies).
2: Redistribution farms or 'new farms'.
3: Not included are state farms provisionally allocated to the Act 9 area communities (372,888 ha)

Trancraa

The Transformation of Certain Rural Areas Act, Act 94 of 1998 (Trancraa) grew out of popular pressure and civil society advocacy during and after the apartheid

[8] Based on the Interim Constitution 1993 and the Land Restitution Act, 1994 individuals and communities could seek restoration of land lost due to racial discrimination after 1913. In February 2001, the Land Claims Court dismissed a land claim by the Richtersveld community against the state-owned diamond mining company *Alexkor*, arguing that legal dispossession had taken place through colonial annexation in 1847 (Land Claims Court of South Africa 2001). In 2003, the Supreme Court of Appeal (2003) ruled that the Richtersvelders are entitled to restitution or compensation because they still held rights in land at the time of dispossession (1920s), a judgement confirmed by the Constitutional Court (2003).

struggle.[9] Government stated that the Act should 'bring an end to administrative uncertainty, as the governance of these areas will be done solely in terms of local government legislation' (DLA 1998). The stated purposes are to 'provide for the transfer of certain land to a legal entity', which may be: (a) a Municipality; (b) a Communal Property Association (CPA Act No. 28 of 1996); or (c) 'Another body or person approved by the Minister' (Purpose and definition iii). The transfer applies to 'Act 9' land used in common by the community and held in trust by the state, but not to town areas, which continue to vest in the state (Sections 2 and 3.1). The Minister may only transfer land to a municipality or CPA if she is satisfied that plans and regulations provide for the security and balance of rights between the residents, members of land owning institutions, present and future users and the public interest in access to land (Section 2). The act defines the accountability of a municipality to the right-holders who must get 'a fair opportunity to participate in the decision-making processes regarding the administration of the land' and 'reasonable preference in decisions about access to the land' (Section 4). Apart from a general ban on discrimination (4.b), the act does not mention the protection or promotion of equal rights for men and women.

Implementation of Trancraa only started after a new municipal structure was put in place from January 2001. The experienced land NGO Surplus People Project (SPP) was the official facilitator of the reform process for the six Namaqualand areas and carried out the mandated tasks together with locally elected Transformation Committees. Public interest lawyers from Legal Resources Centre (LRC) provided training, advice and advocacy, civil society thus making up for the more sporadic presence of government. Municipalities, Provincial Department of Land Affairs (DLA) and SPP met in quarterly steering meetings to review and guide progress, and representatives of national DLA (Pretoria) joined occasional meetings. From 2002, ANC at district and municipal level campaigned in favour of municipal ownership of land – some leaders warned that only government-owned commons could expect public support in future. During November 2002 to January 2003, people in five of the six areas – leaving out Komaggas – voted over three ownership alternatives: 1) Communal Property Association (CPA); 2) Municipality; or 3) Option of own choice (including individual title). The results showed a majority for community ownership through CPAs in four of the five areas. The process and outcomes have been thoroughly documented (SPP 2003b). Although national and provincial DLA officials have discussed the follow up of the Trancraa referenda among themselves and with stakeholders in Namaqualand during 2005 and 2006, as per August 2006, the Government has not announced its plans concerning the transfer of land.

Komaggas

Location and land

Komaggas is a rural area, has about 4,800 inhabitants and has been since 2001

[9] A National Rural Areas Committee was established to consult and draft the act. It was headed by Professor Nic Olivier and supported by provincial committees involving the Provincial Department of Local Government and Housing, the Northern Cape Office of the Department of Land Affairs, the Legal Resources Centre (http://www.lrc.org.za) and the Surplus People Project (http://www.spp.org.za). LRC and SPP have been central in land research and advocacy in Namaqualand, including facilitating redistribution after 1994.

part of Nama-Khoi Municipality, though separated by 70 km of rough gravel road from the municipal and district capital of Springbok (Map 6.2). Further west, on the Atlantic coast, diamond company De Beers owns Kleinzee mining town and is the major employer for Komaggas residents. Household incomes vary greatly, but show the highest average among the Namaqualand rural areas.[10]

Komaggas means 'the place where the cattle drink', due to the natural springs there. The land is generally semi-arid (precipitation 200–400 mm/year), combining mountains (*bo-veld*) and coastal plain (*sandveld*). Although most people live in a town, about a fifth of households engage in livestock and dryland farming, which contribute to livelihoods and are cherished as a 'birth right', 'way of life' and a link to the Nama heritage. Land also sustains projects and ideas about future ventures in tourism, conservation and agricultural development. The 'old commonage' (*ou meent*) of 63,000 hectares is used for grazing, cultivation and firewood collection. Scattered around the common land are springs, seasonal streams and boreholes, abandoned mining sites, stock posts (*veepos*), and dryland plots (*droeëlandpersele*) with cultivable fields (*saailande*). Farms purchased by government from mining companies and farmers after 1996 are called 'new commonage' (*nuwe meent*) and make a total of 27,000 hectares. Municipality hold new farms for the benefit of Komaggas residents. The 'average' land endowment is thus about 90 ha of rough, semi-arid terrain per household or about 450 ha for the estimated 200 livestock owning households.[11]

History

According to local legend, a son of a Boer, Jasper Cloete, founded a community in the Komaggas area after marrying the daughter of a Nama chief. She mediated in a conflict between her husband and father and became 'the mother of Komaggas', setting a precedent for women to share in land rights and mediate between male-dominated groups (Sharp 1994). In 1798 the colonial state annexed Namaqualand as far north as Komaggas and in 1829 the London Missionary Society applied to the Cape Governor to secure land tenure for people at Komaggas. An area of 59,000 hectares was demarcated in 1831 and approved with a 'Ticket of Occupation' in 1843. Through generations a contentious issue has been whether an earlier agreement with the colonial government (Queen Victoria) gave Komaggas rights to a larger area. Researchers have not found formal agreements or authoritative maps on which to base larger land claims, but it is well supported that the community historically accessed and controlled much larger areas than the current 'reserve' (Sharp 1994).[12] From around 1843 the state gave lease farms to Boer settlers around Komaggas. In 1851 some of them wrote to the Governor to complain about the large areas 'lost' to reserve dwellers and to protest against extending their rights to the *trek-veld* between mission stations (Van Zyl et al. 1851). By 1915, private farms encircled Komaggas,

[10] In 2000, average monthly income was R 3028 per household and R 590 per capita (Macroplan 2000), concealing great inequalities linked to unemployment estimated at 40 per cent by the municipal office (1 Euro was then then about 8 Rand).

[11] The 200 households owned an estimated 6,200 goats, 4,300 sheep and 370 cattle (Dip figures April 2002. G.J. Fredericks, Chief Animal Health Inspector, Dept of Agriculture, Steinkopf).

[12] Elders presented the historical Komaggas as being five times the size of the present reserve (Oct 2001).

although many of them were neither fenced nor permanently occupied. Komaggas residents could, therefore, still access and cross them (Sharp 1994: 404). In 1925 diamonds were found at Kleinzee on land historically used and claimed by Komaggas people. By the end of the 1920s the state had sold the land to diamond companies. According to elders, during the following decades parcels of Komaggas land continued to be 'cut off' for white farmers, the present boundary being established only in 1947. These experiences nourished resistance to Trancraa for not addressing land losses and scarcity of land.

Trancraa process: the dynamics of standing still

Consultation

The Komaggas transformation process may be seen as a 'failure to implement' the act or a 'success in resisting'. It was thorny from the outset. At a consultation meeting in August 1996 the SPP facilitator, Johannes van Wyk, later a member of Parliament for the ANC, urged the community to contribute its views (Landelike Gebiede Komitee 1996). He then explained – through what is recorded as 25 pages of unbroken speech – the need for a new act because the current 'Act 9' from 1987 conflicts with the Bill of Rights in the Constitution from 1996: the old restrictions on who can settle in the area; the authority of local government to evict people for improper behaviour ('put across the line'); concentration of decision-making power at national level. The facilitator only hesitantly entered the sensitive question of land ownership: 'The land is the matter that is close to our hearts, right, but today we shall not talk a lot about the land.' He did, however, explain that the 1987 'Act 9' placed land 'in trust' by the Minister but made provision for granting individual rights to residential and business plots in 'towns' and sowing or grazing rights in the 'remainder'. The ideas of state ownership and a movement towards privatisation touched the fears of some participants. An elderly man, Joseph Grace, pointed out that many were boycotting the meeting and that it is ominous to be offered something you already regard as yours:

> I deplore the community of Komaggas. We are not here today, Komaggas is not here. We are more or less a committee who are sitting here and I am worried. [...] We have never spoken the truth. As far as I know the people, and if they come, let us hope that a success comes out of this beginning, but then you must not think that it is you who have created it. You must also not think that it is your land that you are giving to us. It is our land, which is just coming back to us. Thank you, Mr Chairman. That was all I wanted to say. (Mr Joseph Grace, Komaggas consultation, 1996)

The Transformation Committee & the transitional phase

After further community consultations and the passing of Trancraa in 1998, communities and SPP prepared for the prescribed transitional phase to begin in January 2001. In Komaggas, as elsewhere, a Transformation Committee (TC) was established to facilitate the process in 2000. After that, however, Trancraa remained at a standstill due to resistance by a powerful residents' association, Komaggas Inwoners Vereniging (KIV). KIV had initially favoured participating in Trancraa, but it demanded a majority of the seats on the Transformation

Committee, referring to an alleged majority support in the community.[13] Other stakeholders, including ANC leaders and SPP, rejected this demand and offered two seats. SPP and TC wrote letters to KIV, consulted the Department of Land Affairs (DLA). Community meetings were held, but due to discouragement by KIV very few residents attended. At a district meeting of all Namaqualand Transformation Committee members in February 2002, the Komaggas TC leader met with only his deputy. His report on 'group work' was a poster asking: 'What can one do when +/– fifty per cent boycott the Transformation process?!'

SPP staff and a local ANC member argued that more active leadership, household visits and community meetings could have broken the standstill, but during early 2002 the conflict intensified. It also related to problems on the 'new farms'[14] and resistance to municipal tariffs. KIV sent an 'interdict' against Nama-Khoi Municipality warning that it was not wanted in the community. The oral version held that KIV would 'chase Nama-Khoi over the mountain' on Youth Day, 16 June 2002, a day symbolic of anti-apartheid struggle. In spite of diplomatic efforts by SPP and DLA, resistance persisted. In June 2002, SPP and DLA accepted that KIV could get the requested majority on the Transformation Committee and agreed to hold a 'community meeting' in which they would respond to people's concerns about the transformation process. Between two and three hundred people participated, KIV had called the meeting so they were mainly from the KIV section of the community (many saw it as a 'KIV meeting'). Government representatives stressed the need to participate in a national legal process, but the meeting ended in disagreement. It became the last effort by DLA and SPP to implement Trancraa in Komaggas. The TC Chair threw in the towel:

> By our Transformation Committee meeting 21 August 2002 we have decided to hereby report to the Municipality that we have done everything within our capacity to bring the disagreement between the Komaggas Inwoners Vereniging (KIV) and the Transformation Committee out of the way (so that the transformation process could proceed), but that we were unsuccessful. It is evident that there is a grouping within the KIV that is not willing to move from its conviction. (Benny Fortuin, Transformation Committee Chair, letter 22.08.2002)

Nama-Khoi Municipality forwarded the case to the Minister of Agriculture and Land Affairs, requesting her to make a decision. Most observers expected that, given the community division, she would transfer the land to the Municipality. Some protested against this prospect and demanded their right to vote. However, while referendums were held in the other areas, Komaggas residents of either conviction started to realise that they had missed that train.

[13] The Transformation Committee was formed by asking the Municipality, a youth group, the Farmers' Association and Inwoners Vereniging, etc., to nominate members. Four out of 12 nominees were women (SPP 2001). KIV not only withdrew its own representatives but convinced others to stay away (TC Chair and SPP, Nov 2001).

[14] A *Meent Komitee* (Commonage Committee) had been established to assist the Municipality with managing the 'new farms'. It had tried to enforce grazing regulations and other rules, including a moratorium on grazing ('to let the land rest') from 2001. Most farmers had moved their livestock back to the 'old commonage', but a few, including a central KIV committee member, refused to do so. He argued that 'new farms' belonged to the community and should not be governed by the Municipality. He referred to the handing over ceremonies in which the Minister of Land Affairs gave title deeds to community members. In 2002 the Municipality launched court action against the KIV member/farmer, which they subsequently withdrew, hailed by the farmer as a proof of the community rights.

The Komaggas divide: conflicting views

The divide

The conflict between the Komaggas Inwoners Vereniging (KIV) and the ANC coalition, which supported Trancraa, related to a history of community division. A divide between 'pioneers/conservatives' and 'newcomers/progressives' was documented in the 1970s (Sharp 1977). It apparently arose when the Rhenisch Mission decided to leave Komaggas and transfer its rights to the Dutch Reformed Mission Church without consulting people. 'That ultimately led to a split within Komaggas in 1950/51 between those who were prepared to work with the Dutch Reformed Church and mission society and those who wanted to be independent. It was a question of the possible dispossession of people, it was the time of apartheid, 1948, and the Nats were busy instituting their apartheid policy, so that sharpened the whole conflict' (Reverend Pieter Grove, Oct. 2001). Protesters against apartheid in the Dutch Reformed Mission Church invited the Calvinist church to Komaggas: 'They went looking for a preacher and came back with a church!,' Benny Fortuin said in a discussion.

Today most ANC supporters belong to the church that grew from the Dutch Reformed Church while members of the Calvinist church are associated with the New National Party/Democratic Alliance opposition (P. Grove, Oct. 2001). People expressed frustration with a division that hampered developments efforts. The Komaggas divide was maintained by withdrawing from committees and projects one could not control, rather than negotiating compromises. KIV boycotted the Transformation process and several other projects, while the ANC ensured that only party sympathisers were employed on a road project in 2002, against official employment criteria about poverty alleviation.[15] A youth forum established to bridge the divide only had eight members left in February 2002: their wish for the future was 'peace in Komaggas'. Terry Grove, activist and teacher, compared the conflict to a 'Sicilian feud where the parties have forgotten the original cause'.

KIV claimed to have broad support in the community and was acknowledged to be effective in mobilising people for meetings. Although KIV had few paying members, it could raise funds on ad hoc basis. The executive committee had seven middle aged and elderly male members and one woman, acting as secretary. KIV had prepared a written 'Constitution' to be able to receive land under the Communal Property Associations Act (1996). The front page logo features loincloth-bearing 'Khoi' and 'San', livestock, grains and the motto, *'Plough forth on our own land'* in Afrikaans. The document notes that 'The members of the community have been alienated of their rights to land and land ownership as a result of the promotion of racially discriminatory legislation and practice. The community has never accepted the alienation and has taken action to get their land rights back.' It states two main objectives:

- To keep, protect and manage to the benefit of the residents and in accordance with the Communal Property Associations Act the land in the Farm Komaggas as it was demarcated in 1843 and adjacent land, with moveable and immoveable properties.

[15] Interviews with ANC member and a member of Komaggas Road Committee, Sept–Nov 2002.

- In the name of residents to make legal claims and demands for reparation and restitution, as already initiated, and to further pursue, maintain and win them: And thereby to facilitate a process of restitution and compensation to the benefit of those who have suffered losses and become impoverished as a consequence of the behaviour of the State (KIV 2002).

These objectives appeared to be shared by most residents and in line with Trancraa. Written rules could have led one to predict a smooth transfer of land rights to a 'constitutionally' minded local organisation, but the reality was a different story.

The Executive Committee of Komaggas ANC, the ANC municipal councillor, the administrator of the municipal ward office, the leaders of the Farmers' Association and other community members expressed support for Trancraa. They said that it was an opportunity to strengthen community land rights. While supporting the Act, the ANC Women's League said that agriculture and land governance was not among their priorities (a few other women criticised this view). Komaggas ANC had received majority support in the elections in 1994/99 (national) and 1995 and 2000 (local), and highlighted this to show that KIV/Democratic Alliance ('they are all the same people') did not enjoy majority support. A supporter of Trancraa said that KIV refused to participate in broader processes of a new South Africa: 'Most of our people have still got this tunnel vision that it is our land, so nobody can come and do anything on it. They feel that the Municipality will come and do things and that we will lose everything. It is a fear of payment, a fear of loosing *baasskap* [control, leadership] over something' (Former Chair, Komaggas Land Committee, Charles Bezuidenhout, Nov. 2001).

The title

Komaggas people have always 'put a different construction' on the Ticket of Occupation than the state (Sharp 1994: 405, 410). KIV argued that Trancraa is wrong in assuming that Komaggas belongs to the state. It held that Komaggas is different from the 'Act 9 areas' because Queen Victoria through the Governor of the Cape Colony granted residents a private, group title to land in the early nineteenth century. No transfer back to the people was therefore required. In the 1996 hearing, *Oom* Joseph Grace explained that the erosion of rights has caused ambivalence about the value of title deeds.

> Sir, I would still like to say, and I have lived a few years too, that title deed [*kaart en transport*] was never anything for this Nama area, for Komaggas. Because title deed was already given to the Nama kaptein who got the land, the leader Luit Morgens. So, title deed, that is hopeless. I have no trust in a title deed. It can perhaps be worth something for someone else who doesn't live in a Nama area. *But for us, the owners of Namaqualand, it was never worth anything.* Because, the surveyor comes, and he comes to cut off parts for his white brother ... There is no help for you there, no help for you. So, Sir, I would really have asked that you do not speak about such a title deed. So long as God wills, the days that God will still grant me, I shall not swallow that one! (J. Grace, Komaggas, 1996, emphasis added)[16]

[16] Another resident pointed out that i) not everyone shared the opposition to 'title' to their property (e.g. houses and residential plots) and ii) a famous photo taken a few years later showed Minister of Agriculture Derek Hanekom together with Mr Grace holding a title deed to a new re-distribution farm over his head in triumph!

Another assumption in the act also caused problems. Trancraa distinguished between town (*dorp*) as municipal land and the 'remainder' (*buitemeent*), the farm and pasture land: only the latter could be transferred under the act (Sections 2 and 3.1). KIV leaders insisted that Komaggas was one property and should be dealt with as a unity. They rejected any previous town demarcation as having 'never been accepted' by local people.[17] They advocated a certain 'flexibility' in interpreting the act:

> There are some articles that fit to other areas, but not to Komaggas. We want to use what is applicable. Komaggas is not a 'certain rural area' [*landelike gebied*], but a farm [*plaas*]. It is actually at the provincial level that they want to make Komaggas the same as the other areas. At the national level, they *do* recognize that Komaggas is a farm, here there is no reference to a reserve with a 'dorp' and a 'meent'. We respect the law, but not the way it is being implemented. We have a right to decide, and we support Option 1 [*CPA*]. We do not speak of 'meent', 'restant' etc. It is our land, and it is *one* farm. The current border defines 'Restant 200' of the Farm Komaggas. The Farm Komaggas includes the white farms, De Beers land etc. (KIV Executive Committee, interview April 2002)

The KIV Constitution also states that 'the Farm Komaggas exists under one title deed [*Een title aktes*] as it was issued in 1843' and requests self-management to '[e]nsure the security of ownership and use rights as per the agreement between our ancestors and the government of the day stipulating that the land must remain from generation to generation eternally unchanged as it is determined in the map from 1843' (KIV 2002). Two residents explained that a map of the original Komaggas land had been removed from the parsonage during the change of churches in the 1950s, but had recently been found again at the Deeds Office:

> Mr Cloete: We knew about [the map] from our parents and grandparents, that the land is unchanged. The land actually belongs to the Cloetes and their offspring.
>
> Ms Cloete: The bond on the land includes the Cloete women, it includes all of them. The mothers' rights too.
>
> Mr Cloete: And fathers' rights too. It is legally so, and the map is legally endorsed by the queen. It is legal. (Interview, 2002)

While linked to the '1843 Ticket of Occupation', community tenure has a deeper source in historical rights, recognition by Queen Victoria and continuity of use, 'from generation to generation'. People experienced their tenure rights as more fundamental than an old permit ('Ticket of Occupation') that requires a transfer of ownership rights by government.

The land claim

In the post-1994 strategising about land reform in Namaqualand, government and civil society stakeholders in consultation with communities decided to prioritise redistribution and tenure reform over restitution (except Richtersveld, see fn. 8). People in Komaggas have a long-standing and reasonable claim to land beyond the reserve boundary (Sharp 1994: 403) but also a debate about how to justify their claim. The dominant view was that claims should be based

[17] According to KIV a 1998 statement from the Deeds Office confirmed the unified title of 'the farm': 'Sertificat van verenigde titel erf 250', dated 02.11.1998, T 10244098.

on the 'Queen Victoria title', while another group supported a claim based on rights of aboriginal title or rights of occupation as acknowledged in Roman-Dutch law (Sharp 1994: 406). People were also aware that they had limited political influence in the new South Africa and feared that 'if they jump the gun with an aboriginal rights claim, they might hinder the chances of appealing to the new government for grants of additional land on other grounds' (Sharp 1994: 412). In 2001 a Trancraa supporter argued that 'Komaggas cannot claim the whole Namaqualand from Springbok and seven kilometres into the sea ... but would only get more land under the laws that are there now' (Bezuidenhout, Nov. 2001).

KIV mobilised people around a claim to historical lands, including the diamond rich coast. It sought legal advice, but appeared not to have found lawyers who were both competent on land reform legislation and willing to work with them over time. SPP saw the moves of KIV as sectarian and maintained that their land claim did not meet formal requirements (interview SPP staff, 2001). KIV leaders said that they had forwarded their claim to government and repeatedly, but unsuccessfully, requested official responses to it. They envisaged the Minister, as land owner, giving her personal attention to the claim and Trancraa:

> We have said we support option 1 [in Trancraa: CPA ownership]. Although the Minister is in Pretoria, if she knows that Inwoners Vereniging will win, why should she waste thousands on a referendum and all that? The Minister has our land claim with 3–400 names as signatories. The opposition did not make a land claim. The Minister might look at the voters roll. Why should she then spend a lot of money on the referendum? If SPP had looked at the options of everybody, and not decided on the Municipality, then it would have gone well. The Minister said in 1998: it is your land. We were told to claim land before the cut-off date [1999] and we have done so. We have written many letters, but they totally ignored them. (KIV Executive Committee, interview April 2002)

KIV implied that Trancraa was unnecessary because the land claim had already demonstrated their support in the community. Some KIV supporters even saw Trancraa as a competing land claim by an ANC leaning group. A KIV sympathiser assumed that only signatories would benefit from a restitution award:

> That 'transformation' is for 'certain rural areas'. It is a new law, a property law. Komaggas is not part of that demarcation. They said before the demarcation [municipal] that you must apply for your land. We did that before the demarcation. Komaggas is not demarcated. They said that if a claim were not submitted, then it would later form part of the greater municipal land ... however, the application has been submitted in time. It [Trancraa] does not apply. The people who have not applied for the land have their own little groupies that they have elected [the Transformation Committee]. And now they want two representatives of some of the residents who have claimed the land [two KIV representatives for the TC]. But *they* did not apply for the land and that is why we are not prepared to support them [although] some of them are of our own people. (Komaggas resident. Farmer and KIV supporter, 2002)

Here, demarcation of the new municipalities, land tenure reform and claim for land restitution are all woven together by an individual who is trying to make sense of land policy and other institutional changes. For example, he sees the land claim as about avoiding enrollment in the municipality. It is the voice of someone who has waited, is poorly informed or misled. He and his wife have placed their stakes with the Inwoners Vereniging, an organisation that is somewhat like the *Raad* (local council) of recent times and which may gain a similar power through a successful land claim.

Contested user rights

Scepticism about Trancraa was linked to people's experience of family tenure. Some farmers have *saailande*, cultivation plots, in areas where rainfall can support the growing of cereals. *Saailande* have been passed from one generation to the next as a respected 'family right', although this required council approval. Komaggas residents stressed that in the past such user rights were reserved for *inwoners*, born members or residents approved after a period of about five years of residence and 'proper behaviour'. Inheritance rules gave preference to sons, so women would mainly become registered right holders upon the death of a husband (Archer and Meer 1997: 92). The current use rights to *saailande* were officially based on regulations from the 1960s and on lease agreements with local councils, but a study showed that payment and registration were highly irregular; it therefore recommended surveying of *saailande* to make future transactions legal and prevent conflicts (SPP 1999).

During the Trancraa process SPP and professional surveyors assisted farmers in other areas with recording and surveying *saailande* rights, using funds allocated under Trancraa (Article 3.16). This confirmed that there were many unclear boundaries and overlapping claims. Draft maps of newly recorded boundaries were posted and discussed at meetings and most of the conflicts resolved. However, in some instances surveyors had been 'persuaded' to mark off unduly large areas of common surrounding these plots (pers. comm. Rick Rohde). When dryland plots were mapped in Leliefontein as part of the Trancraa process, it turned out that considerable amount of what was previously common grazing land became registered as family held plots. A study compared farmers' own drawings with those of the subsequent survey and found an increase of more than 80 per cent in the surveyed plots (Husum 2004: 52–5).

In Komaggas the leaders of the defunct transformation committee prepared a 'rough' list of 29 *saailande* owners (26 men and three women). Some right holders argued that a survey would be useful to clarify disputed boundaries (these were often indicated by natural features such as trees, a stone or a path). However, KIV leaders firmly rejected a survey and argued that it would lead to privatisation of community resources. No survey was done in the transition period 2001–2002, due to the general Trancraa stalemate. In the first half of 2002 residents led by KIV leaders even chased away surveyors who were there to demarcate residential plots as a basis for transferring title to owners (a process outside the Trancraa act). Women had earlier resisted formalisation of rights (Archer and Meer 1997: 92), but that was in the context of late apartheid. Now women missed an opportunity to assert equal rights to family-held resources. In one case in 2002, a woman lost the fruits of the hard work she invested in a tourism and environmental conservation site and orchard, because her relationship ended and her partner was the sole holder of the lease right.

Community & municipality

Tenure conflicts were linked to a struggle over governance. Trancraa was implemented simultaneously with a new local government structure, and for some residents the two were inseparable. A survey in Komaggas in 2000 had found that 69 per cent preferred the existing Komaggas Council as the system of local authority, while 16 per cent preferred the Namaqualand District Council and 14 per cent the proposed new municipalities (Macroplan 2000). That didn't help: from January 2001 Komaggas became a ward in Nama-Khoi Municipality. A resident presented the old *Raad* nostalgically as the provider and protector of user rights:

> Everything we have was installed by the Council [*Raad*]. If you wanted land then you would ask the Council. And then it comes and gives it to you. And you pay taxes. If you want cultivation rights, sowing rights then you ask for it from the Council. And all your complaints are laid down at the Council. My mother, my grandfather and great grandfather, have cultivated this garden I am sitting in. Now tell me how many years is that? How old is my great grandfather and I still have that right! It has been passed on from generation to generation. We have had this land for hundreds of years. Now they want to come and boss us around! (Farmer and KIV supporter)

From this point of view it was hard to imagine that Trancraa was about increasing tenure security. Instead, KIV leaders claimed that the new Municipality aimed to use the act to increase control over Komaggas land and community. Their scepticism hardened when during 2002 the ANC at local and district level started campaigning for municipal ownership of land. Furthermore, KIV complained that concessions to re-work old diamond mines were given to well-connected outsiders rather than Komaggas people.[18] However, it was the incorporation in a new governance system that was problematic for residents and KIV leaders at Komaggas, not conflict with stakeholders in other areas of the Municipality. Private farm owners and mining companies indicated that they regarded the tenure reform as an issue for residents in the 'communal' areas. If anything, it was the fact that municipal integration brought limited benefits of socio-economic integration, but rather new municipal fees and taxes, which caused resentment and fuelled the land conflict. KIV carried out a non-payment campaign and from August 2002 encouraged people to pay municipal fees into a KIV account. The municipal ward office manager estimated that it led to a temporary drop in the payment rate from the normal 50 per cent to less than 10 per cent. Yet, resentment of the new municipality went well beyond taxation:

> This is the only complaint we have: We don't want them here. We have gone to a lot of trouble. We don't have to go to court to get the land, because the state has promised to give us the land back. We have proof that the land is ours, so now we must just wait until it is given back to us. We hate Nama-Khoi, we don't want it here. It does not fit here. (Farmer and KIV supporter who also praised the old Raad above)

Trancraa supporters (generally ANC leaning) accused KIV of advocating a return to the past, seeking 'independence of all government, self-governance ... their own *homeland – tuisland*' (Local NGO staff, Feb 2002). In late 2001, inspired by war in Afghanistan, Trancraa supporters talked about KIV as the *Taliban*. ANC leaders at municipal and district level deplored the lack of progress with Trancraa, and ascribed it to the historical conflict and the illegal claims by KIV, such as for control of the process and ownership of the town area. The ANC

[18] In 2002, the concession to operate a mining dump went to an entrepreneur from another town called by an observer 'the greatest crook in Namaqualand'. KIV leaders protested, pointing out that Section 6 of Trancraa gives residents preferential access to such concessions (the only time during my field work that residents physically produced and pointed to the Trancraa Act).

municipal councillor for Komaggas felt the Trancraa stalemate would exacerbate the isolation of the community. In November 2002, issues that had been subject to the ANC and KIV conflict (including the building of a school hall) were resolved through community voting won by the ANC. An ANC supporter commented: 'So much for the *Inwoners*' claims that they represent two-thirds of the community. It has never been proven at the polls. This again is proof that they merely represent a strident group of people who want to derail development in Komaggas and are merely power hungry.' (Note to author, Nov. 2002). KIV reportedly grumbled that the voting had been rigged. Such is life under the Komaggas divide.

Discussion: contesting Komaggas

Tenure reform in a historical context

In Namaqualand in general, the 2001–2 transition phase of Trancraa was a fairly successful consultation (Wisborg and Rohde 2003; 2005), and as such departed it from earlier apartheid governments tenure reforms and from the prescriptive and state-centric privatisation or nationalisation schemes criticised by Scott (1998). However, in Komaggas 2001–2 Trancraa was not implemented. While many welcomed the Act as a step towards recognition and integration, others felt that it put local governance and tenure rights at risk.

Past exploitation and domination engendered practices of protesting, avoidance and distrust of outsiders and the authorities. The community was transferred from mission station to state without consultation in 1909, from one church to another in the 1930s without consultation, occasionally passed on between different apartheid ministries, and from 2001 integrated in a Municipality against the wish of the majority. Nevertheless, residents in Komaggas and other Namaqualand rural areas preserved a fragile sense of self-governance well into the democratic era, with the locally elected Transitional Local Council running community affairs from 1995 to 2000. Mamdani's concept of 'decentralised despotism' in some ways fits the Namaqualand areas as instruments of patronising control, first by missionaries and then by government. However, these were also rural towns where *inwoners* or *burgers* saw their land rights as a basis for civic rights and collective decision-making (Carstens 1966 and pers. comm. Henk Smith). Thus, Mamdani's dichotomy between urban areas with a 'culture of civic rights' and rural areas with a 'culture of custom and traditional authority' is here too simplistic (Mamdani 1996: 18–19). Trancraa aimed to replace the racial legislation of the past with legislation of general application, giving effect to citizenship in land affairs. Yet, some residents saw land rights associated with the status of *inwoner* as reliable and wanted to preserve and combine them with new legislation and the status as citizen in a constitutional democracy. In defending their rights, they drew both on Nama culture, practices rooted in the missionary era and discourses of the modern state (Robins 1997). An example is the KIV logo that features loin-clad San and Khoi and a motto about 'ploughing one's land', placed on the front page of a 'Constitution' written to comply with the 1996 Communal Property Associations Act.

Rather than normal community heterogeneity, Komaggas is characterised by a deeply entrenched and polarised conflict, exaggerated through manipulation and a paranoid imagination. Instead of bridging the divide, Trancraa got stuck in and probably deepened the conflict. The promoters of the legal reform underestimated the strength of resistance and the tenacity of perceptions of land – and the local opponent was exceedingly difficult to deal with. KIV leaders believed that the act would not further their interest in controlling a future land-owning institution (CPA). They defended a sense of local land ownership against what they saw as illegitimate local government control. KIV saw Trancraa as cementing mistakes of the past (such as dividing town and land) and as a threat to the ultimate community control over family-held resources through surveying leading to 'privatisation'. These concerns were not unique to Komaggas. Several of the arguments and emotions – 'love of the land' and 'fear of payment' – are well-known across Namaqualand. In the intensive late phase in November 2002 an SPP staff commented that 'The contagion is spreading, Taliban is gaining ground', because groups in other areas were threatening a Komaggas-style boycott. And four out of five Namaqualand areas voted for community ownership, against the ANC campaign (local and district level) for municipal ownership. Komaggas resistance was not unique, just better organised.

The Komaggas debacle may be linked to the general tensions between decentralisation and neoliberal economic policy discussed by Hart (2002). Shortage of funding and human capacity have hampered the South African government's emphasis on decentralisation and developmental local government (Bek, Binns and Nel 2004: 23). Trancraa was implemented in the context of government reluctance to support development in the 'communal areas' with investments and training. A Namaqualand researcher said that in the corporate model of governance communal land is no longer 'core business' while a land lawyer thought Trancraa could be 'a chance for the state to bail out'. It appears to be a contradiction that municipalities hold on to land in the privatisation era, but it may not be: A poorly funded local state may be reluctant to let go of land as a source of power.

Rights: Process & impact

The role of democratic rights in the Komaggas process is ambiguous: was it a case of 'failed implementation' or 'successful resistance'? Both sides claimed to support the 'rule of law' and to fight for basic rights. Yet, they could not agree about how to practise democratic principles, for example when establishing a Transformation Committee.

SPP and ANC representatives argued that the act required that diverse groups be represented, and that it would not be fair to accept KIV domination (although they later abandoned the principle, in an attempt to save the process). They also argued that one could not re-negotiate basic provisions of Trancraa and other legislation, such as the apartheid era town demarcation and the current municipal reforms. The right of people to not participate in tenure reform may be an aspect of liberal society: One may argue that it was individuals who have a right not to lend legitimacy to a reform process that preserved what they saw as past violations and which they felt was heading in one direction, rather than being truly negotiable (for example, that demarcation of family plots would lead to 'privatisation'). However, opponents of the act did not have a right to hinder fellow citizens from getting information about national legislation nor to demand to control the process of consultation: Here the authoritarian character of the organisation and the form of resistance was evident. Advocates of the act could therefore argue with justification that the process broke down because some democratic principles are more important than Komaggas.

The impact of the breakdown on residents, including their rights, is also ambiguous. The breakdown violated people's right to be informed and participate in governance. The community missed a chance to debate their contrasting views of history and land: the 'Queen Victoria title', the land claim, 'One Farm Komaggas', etc. These views will remain stumbling blocks for consensus and development. While people in other areas used Trancraa as an opportunity to explore land development options, in Komaggas residents mainly discussed such ideas informally and never across 'the divide'. They will, like everyone else, be subject to the Minister's decision about future land ownership, but the new institutions cannot draw legitimacy from debate and a fair referendum. Relations to the Municipality and the Department of Land Affairs have worsened and may be used to justify a laissez-faire attitude of national government.

Conclusions & implications

When the Transformation of Certain Rural Areas Act 94 of 1998 (Trancraa) was introduced in six areas of Namaqualand during 2001–2, in Komaggas it proved impossible to implement the apparent pragmatic and non-prescriptive tenure reform act, although there was wide support for community ownership and governance of land.

The suggested explanation is that tenure reform became engulfed in power struggles in a divided community: this made control over the process more important than the goal of securing rights to land. While some residents welcomed tenure reform as a measure to integrate Komaggas into a 'new South Africa', a residents' association that represented a significant section of the community strongly opposed it. They questioned the state's underlying claim to ownership of land and rejected the apartheid era division of the area into 'town' and 'remainder' (the commons), which excluded the 'town' from the 'transfer'. Opponents of the Act also expressed mistrust of the new municipality that they had become part of at the same time. They were further provoked by ANC's district level campaign for municipal ownership of land. Paradoxically, a strong local sense of ownership became an obstacle to a reform that aimed to 'return the land'. The outcome is ambiguous. It violated the constitutional right of residents to strengthen and clarify their land rights under new legislation, but also manifested resistance to local government reforms that threaten a sense of self-governance and had brought limited new resources.

Komaggas is a special case, and one I have treated here from a narrow perspective of understanding resistance. One may still ask if it holds lessons for the wider challenge of 'communal tenure reform' in South Africa. Lessons of the Komaggas Trancraa story in 2001–2 are that we must i) recognise the steps and potential conflicts in a transfer of land; ii) read land tenure in its historical context (as land users do); iii) understand the power relations that land is part of; iv) offer legal assistance throughout the process; and v) integrate material support to make land rights secure and economically viable.

The Komaggas case confirms that the 'transfer of land approach' is risky and potentially divisive (Claassens 2000: 254, Cousins 2002: 88–91). The stake of ownership made communication and negotiations difficult. Trancraa also underestimated the extent to which people felt they already 'owned' land (as indicated by Joseph Grace). Residents could have benefited from a gradual expansion and clarification of individual and community statutory rights rather than a 'transfer'.

It is sometimes claimed that the absence of 'traditional leaders' makes the Namaqualand areas institutionally less complicated than the former 'homelands'. However, in both these areas, many actors, including new municipalities, contend for land and other resources. In both, tenure reform may cause resistance rather than mobilise the democratic potential in local institutions (discussed by Claassens 2001: vii–ix). Trancraa was oriented towards democratisation through municipalities, unlike later legislation for the former 'homelands', the Traditional Leadership and Governance Framework Act and the Communal Land Rights Act (RSA 2003b, RSA 2004). However, in Trancraa local government both facilitated the consultation and actively advocated itself as one of the options for future ownership. An SPP staff commented in 2003 that, 'the act puts the municipality in a very central position in which they are an interested party. This was problematic from the word go, and should be avoided at all costs in any further tenure reform consultation processes' (Note to author, 2003).

One may argue that the Act does provide for this: it 'legislates for negotiability' (Cousins 2002), facilitates consultation and the Minister has the power to hold land until she is satisfied with the balance of rights in proposed plans. However, the case illustrates the difficulty of predicting law as process and power struggle. Local groups engaged in land reform as a struggle over economic and political advantages: the tensions, threats, contempt for the law, disintegration of community bodies etc. quickly undermined any notions one might have about a harmonious 'community' and rule-governed behaviour. Nader has written that 'speaking about conflict resolution without speaking to and about power' is inadequate (Nader 2001: 21, 25). The repeated diplomatic efforts by SPP and government were probably unsuccessful because of the underlying power struggle. Seeing land tenure as a set of rules, and Trancraa as a neutral effort to renew those rules was, in Pauline Peters' (2002) phrase, an inadequate compass to understanding Komaggas dynamics. So, the deficiency is one of process in a specific community but also insufficient awareness of how provocative even participatory legislation can be. Land tenure reform is not a neutral legal instrument but depends on trust between residents, local leaders and government.

To realise the socio-economic benefits of legal rights tenure reform depends on wider public investments (DLA 1997; Mayende 2001), which apart from a substantial redistribution programme was lacking. Trancraa offered neither redress for past losses nor development support, and therefore few material incentives for participation. The case holds some warning signals about a land reform programmes that many residents experienced as un-coordinated and poorly funded, problems that have been documented more generally (Turner and Ibsen 2000, Kepe and Cousins 2002, Hall, Jacobs and Lahiff 2003). Measures that could have promoted the rights of residents include more informati on and legal consultation, for example, to secure a correct and timely restitution claim by the whole community.

To create the democratic South Africa of healed divisions and equal opportunities called for in the Constitution, efforts must be made to remove the inequalities of the apartheid land system. To provide secure land tenure in marginalised rural areas requires an ability to read and interact with diverse and historically rooted understandings and practices of resistance and ownership, trying to encourage their democratic rather than the authoritarian potential. And one needs to listen to those such as *Oom* Joseph Grace in the 1996 consultation: 'let us hope that a success comes out of this beginning, but then you must not think that it is you who have created it. You must also not think that it is your land that you are giving to us. It is our land, which is just coming back to us.'

References

Anderson, Megan and Kobus Pienaar. 2003. *Municipal Commonage. Evaluating Land and Agrarian Reform in South Africa: No 5*. Cape Town: Programme of Land and Agrarian Studies, University of Western Cape.

Archer, Fiona and Shamim Meer. 1997. 'Women, Tenure and Land Reform: the Case of Namaqualand's Reserves.' In Shamim Meer (ed.) *Women, Land and Authority. Perspectives from South Africa*. Cape Town: David Philip and Oxfam in association with the National Land Committee.

Bek, David, Tony Binns and Etienne Nel. 2004. '"Catching the development train": perspectives on "top-down" and "bottom-up" development in post-apartheid South Africa.' *Progress in Development Studies* 4, no. 1: 22–46.

Boonzaier, Emile, Candy Malherbe, Andy Smith and Penny Berens. 1996. *The Cape Herders. A History of the Khoikhoi of Southern Africa*. Cape Town: David Philip.

Carstens, W. P. 1966. *The Social Structure of a Cape Coloured Reserve: a Study of Racial Integration and Segregation in South Africa*. Cape Town: Oxford University Press.

Catling, David. 1996. *The 'Rural Areas' (landelike gebiede): Their Current Status and Development Potential. A Socio-economic Study Pepared on Behalf of Independent Development Trust*. Cape Town: Independent Development Trust.

Claassens, Aninka. 2000. 'South African Proposals for Tenure Reform: The Draft Land Rights Bill.' In Camilla Toulmin and Julian Quan (eds) *Evolving land rights, policy and tenure in Africa*, 247–66. London: DFID/IIED/Natural Resources Institute.

______. 2001. *'It's Not Easy to Challenge a Chief": Lessons from Rakgwadi. Research Report no.* 9. Cape Town: Programme for Land and Agrarian Studies.

Commission on Gender Equality. 2003. *Submission to the Portfolio Committee on Agriculture and Land Affairs on the Communal Land Rights Bill [B67-2003], 10.11.2003. With legal opinion by Geoff Budlender*. Cape Town: Parliamentary Monitoring Group. Available at http://www.pmg.org.za [accessed 30 Jan 2004].

Constitutional Court of South Africa. 2003. *Alexkor Ltd and the Government of the Republic of South Africa versus the Richtersveld Community and others (CCT 19/03). Judgement 14.10.2003.* Available at: http://www.concourt.gov.za/ [accessed 15 Nov 2003].

Cousins, Ben. 2002. 'Legislating Negotiability: Tenure Reform in Post-apartheid South Africa.' In Kristine Juul and Christian Lund (eds), *Negotiating property in Africa*. Portsmouth, NH; Heineman.

DLA. 1997. *White Paper on South African Land Policy*. Pretoria: Government of South Africa, Department of Land Affairs. Available at: http://www.info.gov.za/documents/whitepapers/index.htm.

______. 1998. *Cabinet Memorandum on the Transformation of Certain Rural Areas Act (draft)*. Pretoria: Department of Land Affairs.

______. 2001. 'Namaqualand Commonage Investigation.' *Monitoring and Evaluation, Newsletter, Department of Land Affairs No. 3, 2001* .

DoA. 2001. *Namakwaland: Grondbesit patrone (Unpublished overview of land owners and land redistribution in Namaqualand)*. Springbok: Department of Agriculture.

Hall, Ruth, Peter Jacobs and Edward Lahiff. 2003. *Evaluating Land and Agrarian Reform in South Africa: No. 10 Final Report*. Cape Town: Programme for Land and Agrarian Studies, University of Western Cape.

Hall, Ruth and Edward Lahiff. 2004. *Budgeting for Land Reform. PLAAS Policy Brief No. 13, August 2004*.

Cape Town: PLAAS, University of Western Cape. Available at: http://www.uwc.ac.za/academic/indexr.htm [accessed 15 Nov 2004].

Hart, Gillian. 2002. *Disabling Globalisation. Places of Power in Post-apartheid South Africa*. Pietermaritzburg: University of Natal Press.

Hendricks, Fredrick T. 1995. 'Antinomies of Access. Social Differentiation and Communal Tenure in a Namaqualand Reserve, South Africa.' Paper presented at Reinventing the Commons, the fifth annual conference of the International Association for the Study of Common Property, 24–28 May, 1995, Bodø, Norway.

Husum, Hans. 2004. 'Land-based Livelihoods and Land Reform in Kamiesberg Municipality, South Africa.' MSc thesis. Aas: Noragric, Agricultural University of Norway.

Kepe, Thembela and Ben Cousins. 2002. *Radical Land Reform is Key to Sustainable Rural Development in South Africa, Policy Brief No 3 – Debating Land Reform and Rural Development*. Cape Town: Programme for Land and Agrarian Studies, University of Western Cape. Available at: http://www.uwc.ac.za/academic/indexr.htm [accessed Feb 2003].

KIV. 2002. *Grondwet van die Komaggas Vereniging vir Gemeenskaplike Eiendom/Constitution of the Komaggas Residents' Association*. Komaggas.

Land Claims Court of South Africa. 2001. *Judgement in the Case between the Richtersveld community and Alexkor Ltd, 22 March 2001, case no. LCC 151/98*. Cape Town.

Landelike Gebiede Komitee. 1996. *Verbatim notule van die vergadering gehou te Komaggas 24 Augustus, 1996 (Wet 9 van 1987)*. Pretoria: Transcribed and printed by International Data Solutions.

Letsoalo, Essy. 1987. *Land Reform in South Africa. A Black Perspective*. Johannesburg: Skotaville Publishers.

Macroplan. 2000. *Socio-economic Survey of Various Rural Communities in the Northern Cape (Komaggas)*. Upington: Macroplan Town and Regional Planners.

Mamdani, Mahmood. 1996. *Citizen and subject. Contemporary Africa and the Legacy of Late Colonialism*. Oxford: James Currey and Cape Town: David Philip.

Mayende, Gilingwe. 2001. *The Challenge of Land Tenure Reform in South Africa. Issues, Problems and Prospects*. Technical Paper by the Director General, Department of Land Affairs the National Land Tenure Conference, Durban, 26 November 2001 (circulated document). Department of Land Affairs.

Moore, Sally Falk. 1978. *Law as Process: an Anthropological Approach. New Introduction by Martin Chanock*. (2nd ed. 2000). Münster-Hamburg: Lit Verlag and Oxford: James Currey.

Nader, Laura. 2001. 'The Underside of Conflict Management – in Africa and Elsewhere.' In Richard C. Crook, and Peter P. Houtzager (eds) *IDS bulletin. Making Law Matter. Rules, rights and security in the lives of the poor.* Norwich: University of East Anglia.

Ntsebeza, Lungisile. 1999. *Land Tenure Reform, Traditional Authorities and Rural Local Government in Post-apartheid South Africa. Case Studies from the Eastern Cape*. Research Report No. 3. Cape Town: Programme for Land and Agrarian Studies, University of Western Cape.

Peters, Pauline E. 2002. 'Grounding Governance: Power and Meaning in Natural Resource Management.' Tor Arve Benjaminsen, Ben Cousins, and Lisa Thompson (eds) *Contested resources. Challenges to the governance of natural resources in Southern Africa*. Cape Town: Programme for Land and Agrarian Studies, University of Western Cape.

Pienaar, Kobus. 2000. *Index of Acts and Amending Acts Relevant to Namaqualand from 1909–2000*. Cape Town: Legal Resources Centre (unpublished).

PLAAS/NLC. 2003. *Submission to the Portfolio Committee for Land and Agriculture on The Communal Land Rights Bill, 10.11.2003*. Parliamentary Monitoring Group. Available at: http://www.pmg.org.za/ [accessed 20 Nov 2003].

Robins, Steven. 1997. Transgressing the Borderlands of Tradition and Modernity: Identity, Cultural Hybridity and Land Struggles in Namaqualand (1980–94). *Journal of Contemporary African Studies* 15, no. 1: 23–43.

RSA. 1996. *Republic of South Africa Constitution Act 108 of 1996*. Government of South Africa Online. Available at: http://www.info.gov.za/documents/constitution/index.htm [4 Mar 2005].

______. 1998. *Transformation of Certain Rural Areas Act 94 of 1998. Government Gazette No. 19417, 02.11.1998*. Cape Town: Republic of South Africa.

______. 2003a. *Communal Land Rights Bill as approved by Cabinet 08.10.2003. Republic of South Africa, Minister of Agriculture and Land Affairs [B 67–2003]. Government Gazette No. 25562 of 17.10.2003*. Pretoria: Available at http://land.pwv.gov.za/home.htm [accessed 6 Jan 2004].

______. 2003b. *Traditional Leadership and Governance Framework Act, Act. No. 41 of 2003*. South Africa Government Online: http://www.info.gov.za/documents/acts/2003.htm [accessed 2 March 2005].

______. 2004. *Communal Land Rights Act, Act. No. 11, 2004. Government Gazette No 26590, 20 July*

2004. Cape Town.

Scott, James C. 1985. *Weapons of the weak. Everyday forms of peasant resistance.* New Haven: Yale University Press.

______. 1998. *Seeing like a state. How certain schemes to improve the human condition have failed.* New Haven: Yale University Press.

Sharp, John. 1977. *Community and boundaries: an enquiry into the institution of citizenship in two Cape Coloured reserves. PhD thesis.* Cambridge: University of Cambridge.

______. 1994. 'Land Claims in the Komaggas Reserve.' *Review of African Political Economy*, no. 61: 403-13.

SPP. 1999. *Report on the 'Saailand' pilot study in the Rural Areas of Namaqualand.* Cape Town: Surplus People Project.

______. 2001. *Komaggas Transformasie Nuus/Transformation News, May 2001.* Cape Town Surplus People Project.

______. 2003a. *Steinkopf Verslag/Report on Steinkopf.* Cape Town: Surplus People Project.

______. 2003b. *Verslag aan die Minister van Landbou en Gronsake, Wet op die Transformasie van Sekere Landelike Gebiede, Wet 94 van 1998. September 2003.* Cape Town: Surplus People Project.

Supreme Court of Appeal of South Africa. 2003. *Judgement. The Richtersveld Community and others (Appellants) vs. Alexkor Limited (First Respondent) and the Government of the Republic of South Africa (Second respondent), Case No. 488/2001. 24 Feb 2003.* Bloemfontein.

Toulmin, Camilla and Julian Quan. 2000. 'Evolving Land Rights, Tenure and Policy in Sub-Saharan Africa.' In Camilla Toulmin and Julian Quan (eds) *Evolving Land Rights, Policy and Tenure in Africa*, 1–29. London: DFID/IIED/Natural Resources Institute.

Turner, Stephen and Hilde Ibsen. 2000. *Land and Agrarian Reform in South Africa. A Status Report.* Cape Town: Programme for Land and Agrarian Reform, University of Western Cape.

Van Zyl et al. 1851. *Letter from J. A. van Zyl and other Farmers of Ward of Namaqualand to Sir H. W. Smith, Governor of the Colony of the Cape of Good Hope. Requesting that certain land may not be granted to Inhabitants of Missionary Stations at Kookfontein, Pella and Kamaggas.* Cape Archives, Cape Town. Ref Z2. Doc No.TAB496858619.

Wisborg, Poul and Rick F. Rohde. 2003. *Trancraa and Communal Land Rights: Lessons from Namaqualand, Policy Brief No 5. Debating Land Reform and Rural Development, April 2003.* Cape Town: Programme for Land and Agrarian Studies, University of Western Cape.

______. 2005. 'Contested Tenure Reform in South Africa: Experiences from Namaqualand.' *Development Southern Africa* 22(3): 409–27.

Acknowledgements

The Programme for Land and Agrarian Studies (PLAAS), University of Western Cape and Noragric at the Norwegian University of Life Sciences co-operate on the programme 'Human rights, governance and land reform in South Africa', co-ordinated by Norwegian Centre for Human Rights, University of Oslo and funded by the Norwegian Agency for Development Cooperation. I am thankful to the Norwegian Research Council for funding my PhD studies, to Surplus People Project and Legal Resources Centre, Cape Town, for sharing knowledge and helping in numerous other ways. I sincerely thank people and local government officials in Komaggas for discussing and sharing information with me. I thank and remember Francios Z. Jansen from Concordia who contributed greatly as interpreter and whose death in September 2003 was such a tragic loss.

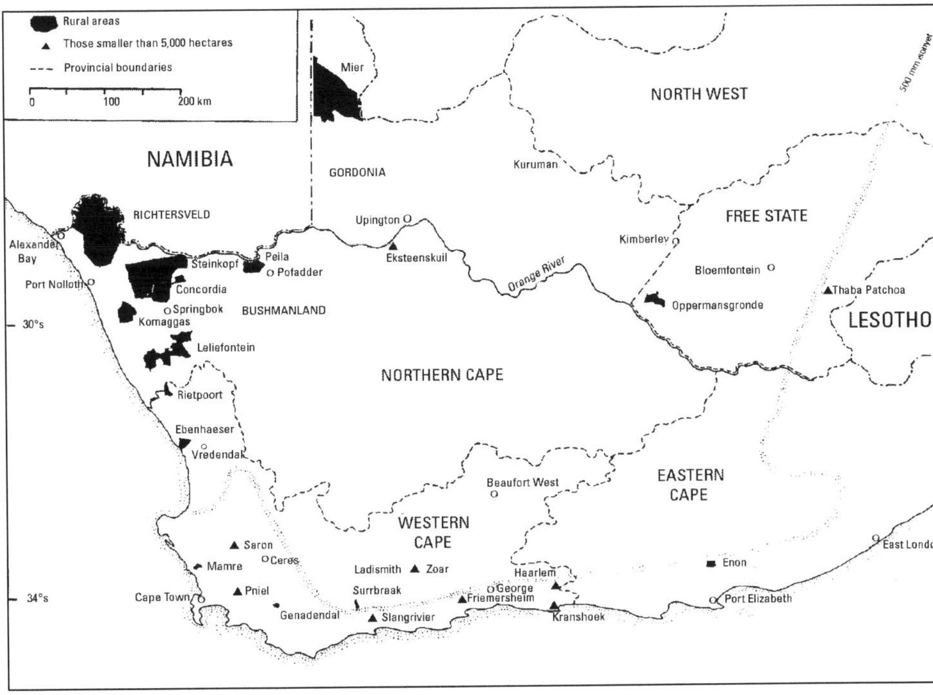

Map 6.1. Areas administered under the Rural Areas Act 9, 1987
(Source: Catling 1996)

Map 6.2. Komaggas in Nama-Khoi Municipality
(Source: Municipal Demarcation Board: Category B Municipalities Northern Cape. NC062, 2000)

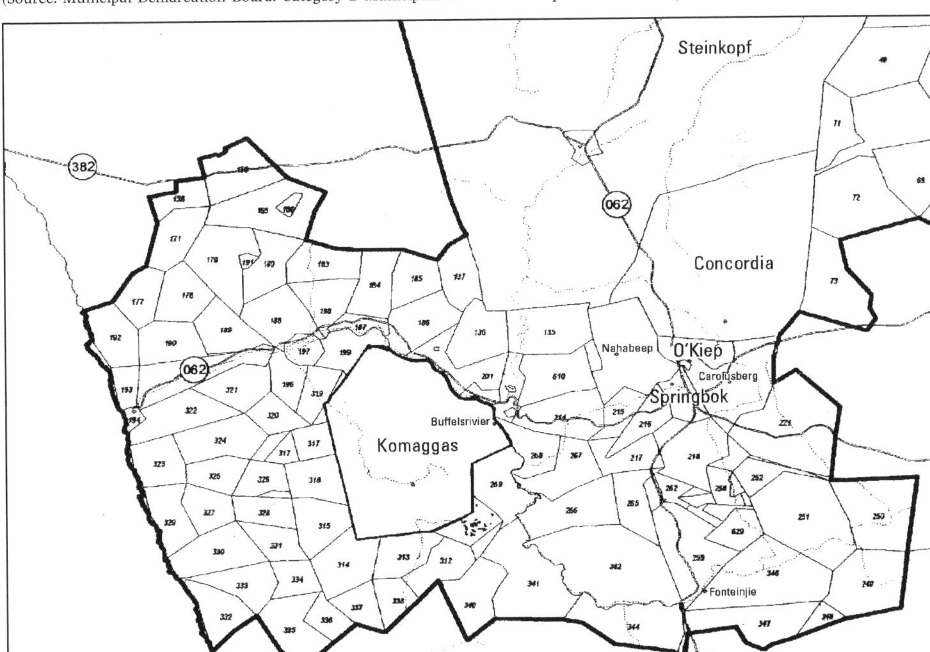

7

Land Reform & the Rekindling of Land Conflicts in South Africa
Rural Women's Access to Land

NANCY ANDREW

Introduction

Despite some initial attempts at modest reform in the early 1990s by the National Party (NP) on the throes of its apartheid deathbed, the land division in South Africa was similar to what it had been for the past several decades under white settler rule in 1994 when a new National Unity government was formed between the NP and the African National Congress. The 1913 and 1936 Land Acts, which aimed to prohibit Africans from holding and owning land, divided the country into areas controlled by the white minority, nearly 87 per cent, while the overwhelming black majority was organised into artificial national states known as bantustans on just 13 per cent of the land. The few exceptions to this were freehold areas referred to as 'black spots', continually whittled away under the massive forced removals by the state in the period of 1960 to 1980. An important percentage of the black rural population remained in the so-called white farming areas in various tenancy arrangements – working as labour tenants on the farm in exchange for a piece of land to cultivate, in rare cases for rent, and increasingly as agriculture modernised, as very low-paid farmworkers, sometimes with a right to land and sometimes not. Dispossession of African land and the corresponding socially engineered territorial organisation of the twentieth century underpinned the entire logic of apartheid colonialism, making the land question a sharp and continual source of conflict throughout South Africa.

How a new government would handle the problem of rights to land and breaking up the white monopoly[1] in the context of the seething land conflict in a racially divided society became a major question from the period of 1992–3 onwards when it became clear that the old state configuration was about to change. Because of the land question's central importance, land reform was an assumption, yet it was also a highly volatile issue from the beginning. International institutions paid considerable attention to influencing policy, in particular the World Bank, which argued for rapid market-assisted reform in

[1] Although in the context of the new provincial spatial configuration official sources are reluctant to establish clear figures, today white farmland constitutes about two-thirds of the total area, with the balance in military land and parks (7%), urban land (13%) and former bantustan areas (13%).

order to avert what they saw as potentially destabilising peasant rebellion in the rural areas (Binswanger and Deininger 1993: 1466).

The Department of Land Affairs (DLA) under the auspices of the ANC within the framework of the National Unity government developed its land reform programme in 1996, finalised in the 1997 *White Paper on South African Land Policy*, which guided policy changes for the first five years. The programme's three main components included: *restitution* of land unjustly taken because of apartheid laws and practices; *redistribution* of land through the market – on a willing buyer/willing seller basis – and third, a *land tenure reform*, which in addition to reviewing customary tenure and private ownership, included improving tenure security for landless peasants working on white farms, that is the labour tenants and farmworkers.[2]

In 1999 land reform was put on hold after a new minister was appointed to head both the DLA and Agriculture. A new orientation prevailed which favoured a small class of emerging black farmers, instead of the rural landless poor as a whole that the 1997 *White Paper* had ostensibly targeted. The new (2001) LRAD programme (Land Redistribution for Agricultural Development) requires higher input by individual farmers in order to obtain state aid to buy land, according to a sliding scale. NGOs and others have criticised it for bypassing the problem of structural inequality in the rural areas and supporting the relatively more established and better-off black farmers (Capps and Batterbury 2000, Nkuzi Development Association 2002: 9).

Conflicts over land were already intense based on the settler colonial organisation of agriculture and the systematic attempts to suppress black independent farming, enforced by decades of forced removals under apartheid as well as evictions of Africans from white farms. However, the introduction of land reform – which posed the question of who should acquire land rights and on what basis – rekindled and refocused these conflicts in a more concentrated way.[3]

Hopes pinned on the ANC

Land reform also revived conflicts because the black rural population anticipated change from a black government despite reservations they might have had about the ANC in particular. The land question was discussed throughout society in numerous forms, including meetings, conferences, debates and polemics in any

[2] For further analysis of labour tenants' and farmworkers' conditions and social relations on the white farms, see FRRP (1995), Ntsedi and Waldman (1997), Andrew (1999a).

[3] My doctoral research focused on the ways in which land conflict intensified after land reform was introduced: how land hunger and demand were expressed, how rights and access to land developed as land reform was implemented – or not implemented – and the nature of the constraints facing the programme due to the major compromises made during the negotiations process. In light of today's conflictual social relations on the white farms, where several million black people are living as part of labour tenant and farmworker families, the study included examining the debate over whether the countryside was still marked by significant pre-capitalist features. Fieldwork was undertaken in the form of discussions with labour tenant men and women on white commercial farms in the northern and southeastern areas of Mpumalanga province (formerly the Transvaal), and with people living in former bantustans or traditional rural areas that comprise another 13–15 million rural African dwellers. Interviews were organised in a resettlement community in the Eastern Cape (Ciskei), amongst families living on trust land in southern KwaZulu-Natal and in a rural township in Northern Province (Lebowa) amongst both longer-term residents and recent arrivals from other towns as well as people evicted from white farms.

sphere related to it, in addition to the media, as it became clear that the spectre of modifying one of the basic pillars of the apartheid system was much more threatening to most of the white population than de-segregating parks and public places.

At the same time the land question had not been a strong card in the ANC's hand, and its rural support was very uneven, partly because it had not carried out much political struggle in the countryside under apartheid and, particularly, not in relation to land hunger.[4]

Despite abundant good intentions and some wishful thinking about rectifying past injustice, land reform was primarily viewed as a necessity for political stability for the incoming ANC ruling circles and for the government of National Unity as a whole. While the transition had lowered some of the important political and legal barriers to Africans, the economic structure and system were essentially left intact. The transition was the outcome of a compromise process of negotiations, closely supervised and to a great extent organised and financed by the Western powers. It was not centred on goals of overcoming the poverty and deprivation of the black population, and especially not the rural component. One-half of the population is rural, but 70 per cent of South Africa's poor live in rural areas, where the poverty rate itself is 71 per cent (May 2000: 23).

A primary symptom of the nature of the transition is the fact that land reform is based on a land market. The ANC accepted this while combining such logic with a public discourse pledging to meet the disadvantaged rural masses' needs and desires for land with a transfer of 30 per cent of agricultural land within five years.

Land hunger is strong amongst the rural Africans for a range of reasons, but their *right* to be granted land is closely connected to the debate in society over many questions, including how much the state should intervene on behalf of the poor and how to challenge the sanctity of private property that was protected in the new Constitution, making expropriation a remote option in a land system still entirely dominated by the white minority. A third issue within the framework of redistribution is what constitutes land 'need'; land-deprived and landless people are being asked to prove this need in a social context of decades of scarcity of resources and lack of infrastructure that have made agricultural production a difficult if not impossible primary livelihood.

The three-year rights-based restitution programme was closed in 1998, although of the modest total of approximately 69,000 claims for land only 20 per cent concerned rural land. The limited framework of restitution and slow pace of claim settlement have provoked tremendous dissatisfaction in that restitution was designed to redress the injustice suffered because of apartheid-related land dispossession. It has been hampered with the institutional weight of its cumbersome and primarily legal procedures, making the process extremely long and producing new conflicts among claimant communities as well as between them and the post-1994 state organising such amends (DLA 2003).

This chapter addresses the central role of land in social reproduction as well as some of the issues underlying subsistence agriculture and food security related to women's demand for land. It then focuses on some of the barriers – legal and social, political and structural – to African women's access to land in South Africa's countryside. This is followed by an overview of some of the shortcomings

[4] See, for example, analysis by ANC writer and sociologist R. Levin 1996.

of the land redistribution programme, whose stated priorities at the outset were the 'poorest of the poor' and women.

The constraints of limited land on rural African women

Rural women are by no means homogeneous even though their situation has many common features, and landlessness or land deprivation is a prominent one. The ensemble of property and of class relations in the rural economy forms the framework for understanding their position overall. Within this ensemble one must look at where women and their families are located within apartheid's land squeeze – on communal 'traditional' land and the few remaining freehold areas, on private white farms, or whether they are trapped in-between in the vast 'holding zones' of resettlement and squatter camps. In addition, factors of social differentiation as well as ethnic and customary practices play an extremely important role, while social profile factors like marital status, position within the family, age and kinship ties all have a bearing on women's access to land.

In the black rural population of some 20 million, African women outnumber men by more than a million and are heads of more than 50 per cent of rural households today (Ndlela 1996: 5). Most of these families survive on a combination of subsistence farming, wages and remittances from jobs in surrounding towns, cities, or farms, and small pensions, as well as activities bringing in supplemental income like brewing beer, basket weaving, sewing and handicrafts. Two households per family are an increasingly common phenomenon, one in town and one in the rural areas, where the women are often left in charge. Since pass laws were lifted in 1986, easing physical movement, there has been some migration to the cities, especially in the Western Cape region, but in fact much less than anticipated. Improved transport links have made visits back home to the rural areas more frequent, however, along with a growing number of men returning there to live, no longer able to find jobs in the cities (Ardington 1995, interview 1996).

Land is central to all aspects of social reproduction, providing a base from which family life is organised, including a place to live, a place for a dispersed family to return to and to retire, raise children, care for the sick and elderly, and meet essential food needs through subsistence agriculture. In addition, land lies at the heart of many cultural and social traditions for communities whose origins are mainly pastoral. Politically, land represents access to property and social status from which women have been excluded – by both white minority and traditional rules.

Food security, subsistence & surplus production

Rural African women's demand and need for land revolve primarily around improving their homestead and the production of food, particularly as a supplement to household consumption.[5] The Land and Agricultural Policy Centre

[5] A national study on land demand was organised in 1994-95 by the LAPC, a research unit active in informing government policy throughout the 1990s. Land demand among labour tenants and farmworkers was evaluated at nearly 100%, whereas in the former reserves approximately 65% wanted more farming land, and nearly 50% more land for their homestead. 71%, including rural township residents, said they preferred to remain in the countryside and not move to urban areas. (NLC 1996: 8)

(LAPC) estimated that women produce 60 per cent of the food consumed by rural households and that they contribute 80 per cent of agricultural labour – principally as unpaid family labour (Ndlela 1996: 5). This is reflected in the fact that women are the backbone of subsistence agriculture – in other words, that most of this type of farming is done by women. If they have access to land, they tend to practise subsistence farming on some level, whether in the former reserve areas, now incorporated into nine provinces, or as farmworkers or labour tenants on the white commercial farms.

Women's earnings from agriculture are nonetheless very low, and surpluses (food they can sell locally) are often quite small, depending on a range of factors from climatic and geophysical considerations to basic infrastructural problems that exist throughout the black countryside, the most critical of which is water. They also suffer from severe constraints stemming from their position in society – lack of capital, bank loans, seeds and other inputs, training and so forth. While capitalism has become dominant in the economy, it has depended in important ways, both socially and economically, upon pre-capitalist social relations, heavily making use of the extended family and the subordination of women, both on the commercial farms and in the bantustans. In both types of areas, control over land is also closely bound up with male-dominated authority structures.

The subsistence production of food by women, along with their informal economic activities and care for the sick, young and elderly have long borne part of the costs of sustaining and reproducing capitalist wage labour. New generations of labourers are raised through kin networks in the bantustans based on this unpaid 'household' or 'domestic' labour, rather than through a wage paid by a capitalist employer (the classic Marxist definition of labour power). Such labour, as part of pre- or non-capitalist relations of production, has been an essential component of the capitalist sector's superexploitation of both men and women – in industry as well as agriculture – paying them far below the value of their labour power (amount required to reproduce the labourer). This has been the key to high profitability that foreign capital has sought in the dominated countries it has penetrated around the world. (As has been widely documented, the land division in South Africa figured heavily in this logic, in which the state aimed its enforced dispossession along with social and influx control of the non-white population first at capturing the know-how and labour of black farmers and then at trying to destroy independent peasant production in order to force men to seek waged work.) The apartheid economy relied on a certain level of rural production in the bantustans, and on migrant labourers and their children having access to these significant forms of sustenance – mainly resulting from women's labour (See Seidman and Seidman 1977, Simkins 1981, Lotta 1986).

This is fundamental to understanding the formal denial of women's access to land and property as well as the exacerbation of traditional forms of subordinating women, which legally and socially limits their voice and role, although with only partial success.

Through the lifting of pass laws and other restrictions the migrant labour system has undergone some transformation. In addition, large numbers of rural dwellers formerly part of the bantustan reserve labour areas are pushed to the peri-urban areas in the hopes of finding work because of lack of land and possibilities for rural livelihoods. Yet, as in many African countries, the poor are not absorbed into the formal economy (and into only a small segment of the informal economy), and this labour supply also exerts downward pressure on wages in all sectors. On top of this, it is the characteristic of 'modern' capitalist sectors relying on the backwardness of the rural areas, in particular women's labour to reproduce the family – including food production, however insufficient – that still operates today as another factor in keeping wages low. This is very clear in the commercial agricultural sector, where wage levels continue to be suppressed (despite the introduction in March 2003 of a minimum wage for farm work), but it is also true in general, even if the edges of rural and urban livelihoods have become less distinct and the need for multiple incomes to survive makes this feature stand out less.[6]

Women interviewed during fieldwork in the Eastern Cape and KwaZulu-Natal testified that not only are food needs still a central concern of most women trying to raise a family, but growing food remains a minor but crucial way of trying to round out an always-short household budget in a climate of widespread rural poverty. This is a primary motive in their desire for more land and access to water and other infrastructures, and in the course of land reform, the conflict over who in the family obtains rights to land and what it will be used for has brought women's frustrations increasingly to the fore.

In the community of Figtree in Eastern Mpumalanga, an LAPC study found that food security is a major issue, but men and women's perceptions of how to use the land to solve it are different. While men were inclined to produce cash crops, women overwhelmingly wanted the land for food, and with the land shortage community gardens are springing up all over in an attempt to handle this problem (interview Madakane 1999).

Land demand

Land demand among women differs according to a number of factors, including their perception of their chances at farming, their family situation, investment possibilities from outside income, their social and physical environment and, if operative, the chief's role. Their political horizons interpenetrated greatly with their aspirations to expand and improve their livelihoods and also with whether they considered land shortage a national or purely local problem. Women we interviewed on the white farms were primarily concerned about stopping evictions and securing their land tenure. Many of those families who had moved to traditional areas away from what they described as intolerable conditions on the farms, or had been expelled and had their land taken by the farmer for ploughing,

[6] Another growing phenomenon is the feminisation of the rural workforce, or semi-proletariat, reflecting the already systematically lower wages paid to women farmworkers (Marcus 1989). A 1996 study of four provinces in South Africa (Gauteng, Free State, North and Northwest provinces) found that the percentage of women permanent farmworkers had risen to nearly half the workforce, primarily in the worst jobs, in harvesting and packaging. Women constitute two-thirds of the permanent workers in the vegetable sector, half in tobacco, flower and fruit and considerably less in the male-dominated maize and livestock sectors. Although reliable cross-regional statistics are hard to come by, for examples of wage differentials between male and female farmworkers, see FRRP 1996 and 1997. This study found that permanent women workers' wages were 57.6% of the men's in the districts analysed. In addition, the women 'received a far lower percentage of their wages in kind (food) than their male counterparts...who ostensibly share their food with the women in their household' (Ndlela 1996: 5, FRRP 1996: 27, 32).

tended to want to launch some level of petty surplus production. In southern KwaZulu-Natal several women were frustrated at the local chief's powers to allocate land, which they said was 'all divided up' (field interviews 1996, 1997).

Women's demand for more arable land along with the inputs needed to produce on it in order to stabilise and improve borderline subsistence farming or to expand or strengthen their position as small-scale farmers sparked debate over its viability. Women have access to very little land in their own right, and other obstacles such as distribution channels and the political will and ability to break through strong socially patriarchal and legal barriers all figure in the quotient. Water resources are more dominated by white farmers even than land.

A study in Northern Province found that most 'women have indicated a strong interest in deriving income from agriculture', but that land access is the major constraint to women farmers, although the authors cite other factors such as domestic responsibilities, decision-making power and legal ownership of assets for married women, the 'under-representation of women' in access to services and inputs, and low levels of education. The authors argue that the situation of women, who are mainly limited to being subsistence farmers, is 'exacerbated by low levels of production due to the small size of their land and the need to produce maize to ensure food security'. They are able to feed their households if subsistence production is based on maize, but this does not allow them to invest, to procure credit (title to the land is held through men in tribal areas, so women have no collateral as such), or to buy other things they need. So there are still striking levels of poverty (Ngqaleni and Makhura 1996: 335–56).

Social & legal barriers

Land-related demands rank high in African women's aspirations to improve and stabilise their lives. They are responsible for rural households, for providing food, and they bear the brunt of raising children and performing the drudgery of domestic labour from fetching water and fuel to making fires, cooking, cleaning, washing clothes, plastering and repairing houses, on top of agricultural labour in the gardens and fields and tending to animals. Yet their being denied formal rights, especially pertaining to ownership or control of land and significant personal property such as houses, cattle and other animals, is not dissociated from the key role of their labour to the overall functioning of the economy. This overlaps with the social functions on a family and community level, economically and particularly in regard to inheritance.

While a new Constitution and land reform programme exist that in theory are committed to helping women attain their rights in land, the pervasive apartheid-era legislation and institutions still very much influence what goes on in the countryside.

With a few exceptions, historically only white male adults could own property, while black people and women in general could not. Although efforts to keep Africans from purchasing land stem back to the late 1890s, (with a brief six-year respite in the Transvaal after 1905 due to a challenge to the law), it was the settler colonial state's 1913 and 1936 Land Acts that laid the groundwork for systematic dispossession of the indigenous people legally and spatially (Letsoalo 1987: 34).

These were supplemented by the 1927 Native Administrative Act, which defined women as subordinate to men and unworthy of owning property. The advent of Roman Dutch law adopted by the settler state regulated ownership of property through marriage, designating men as heads of household, as guardian of the wife's person, and assigning women a permanent legal status of 'minor'. As Section 27 of the Natal Code reads, '... a female is deemed a perpetual minor in law and has no independent powers save as her own person ...' (Qunta 1987: 83). Women of European origin became adults at age 21 or could sign an 'ante-nuptial contract' before a common law marriage, which allowed them to retain their property and legal capacity, but African women could not.[7]

In addition, black women are subject to 'customary law', which as one African historian describes it, was also 'codified to supplement this process of subordination' by 'distorting certain aspects of African law and lifestyles to suit its own purposes', namely keeping women legally subordinate to their husbands or male relatives (ibid.).[8]

Where polygamy is practised, the picture is even more complicated, making land rights for women and the children of several marriages very confusing and conflictual. As is widely known, in traditional agrarian society women represented labour power and property, to be traded and given as tribute and especially to be controlled through marriage, as a way of transferring and accumulating wealth. Traditionally, in the mainly patrifocal societies, married women are 'expected to render life-long service to a wide circle of kin, to move away from their families of origin ... and to settle within easy reach of the husband's people' (Nene 1986: 12). Delius, describing Maroteng dominance patterns in 1860–1870 maintains that 'Access to, and control over, women and cattle were key components in relations of power at all levels of the society.' Men resisted missionaries' insistence on monogamy, because of their need for 'labour and grain' (1984: 52). This was institutionalised by a practice similar to bridewealth (referred to as *lobola* in Zulu or *bohadi* in Sotho) and the shift of often-significant sums in marriage transactions, which continues to some extent today.

In patrilinear societies inheritance takes place through male children, although in some instances a widow is permitted to hold property temporarily in passage from husband to sons until she dies or until the 'rightful' male heir comes of age. Rarely does she have full authority over the land during this period. This follows the logic of maintaining the family name, and in the event of death, the property does not leave the extended family (Marcus, Eales and Wildschut 1996: 92).

The consequences of this mixture of legal traditions on black women are multiple. They endure the worst of both marriage systems and cannot choose the type of marriage they want, with or without community of property, nor

[7] Thus women could not initiate legal proceedings, could not be heard in court and could not be sued without their husbands' permission. In 1953 and 1984, 'matrimonial' laws were passed to ease some of these restrictions for European women, but they specifically did not apply to African women. (ibid.: 82)

[8] Letsoalo (1987: 36–9).underscores the importance of the colonial state's establishment of indirect rule through the restructuring of the traditional tribal system; the Native Administration Act No. 38 in 1927 expanded the powers of the tribal courts and brought the whole tribal system under the control of white officials through the Native Affairs Department.

can they annul or escape from, 'legally' at least, the marital powers of their husbands, except through divorce. For example, even when it became legal for Africans to buy land on a 99-year leasehold basis, women were not eligible for loans (Qunta 1987: 84). Although rural women are responsible for a whole range of decisions associated with livelihood and childrearing, they have not been legally allowed to enter into the most basic of business transactions without the consent of a male relative, or in the modern version of this, in a (more) capitalist setting, as in the case of small sugar cane growers in KwaZulu-Natal, who are 65 per cent women, the husband grants permission for the wife to handle the business, but only because he expects to take the earnings after the work is completed. Some are widows who do not need anyone to sign contracts for them.[9]

Apartheid and traditional law also pressured women to marry rather than being independent: the severely restrictive pass laws meant that women's rights to mobility, jobs and housing were often defined by marriage and the husband's position. In traditional areas, land for residential purposes, grazing and farming has almost invariably been assigned through a husband or male relative. In addition, African women frequently stay in unhappy marriages because they fear they will lose their family homestead if they divorce their husbands (Barrett 1985). The Recognition of Customary Marriages Act passed in 1998, worked to offset these restrictions and began to provide legal protection for women.

Challenging tradition & resistance to change

It is important to stress the self-evident reality that changes in the law do not necessarily mean that they become accepted social practice. In 1987 in KwaZulu-Natal, for example, the law was changed to allow women heads of household to obtain land in their own name, but implementation seems to meet resistance – by both men and women. Customary 'mediation' prevails by male traditional councils. Marcus, Eales and Wildschut (1996: 91) cite the case of Gannahoek farm, a stable farming community in KwaZulu-Natal which labour tenants bought in 1994, but where the transfer of land to women was very controversial and in general people in the community continued to prefer that male heads of household hold the land for the families. In fact, women who hold land today are mainly widows who acquired it when their husbands died. Even in black freehold areas, like Cornfields, also in KwaZulu-Natal, where traditional authorities no longer control land tenure and women can hold land in their own right, such women tend to be widows, and owning land does not assure them a different social status. Women are active in some of the farm's committees, but have reported they do not enjoy the full support of many of the men and some of the women (AFRA 1995: 13).

Women played an active role in resisting forced removal in Mogopa, a community in Northwest Province whose farms were purchased in the name of their Bakwena ba Mogopa tribe back in the early 1900s. Finally forced out at gunpoint in 1984, they reoccupied the land in 1989 and won title to one farm

[9] Marcus et al 1996: 93 citing A. Vaughan in R. Schrire, 1992, *Wealth or Poverty*.

a few years later. Women now participate in the local *kgotla* (community council) meetings on the farm, helping to shape the political direction of land assignment. They proposed that female divorcees along with unmarried women with children have the right to a residential site and that unmarried daughters should inherit their parents' sites, breaking with tradition of access to land through males only (TRAC 1992: 9–12).

Social barriers are therefore not the same as, but are closely linked with legal barriers, even as some of them begin to change. There are some instances of rural African women acquiring land, but the predominant norms governing land access in traditional settings are still highly patriarchal. These practices have contributed to confining women in marriage and binding them further to traditional roles and extended family commitments. The ideas held by both sexes reinforce these institutionalised forms of authority and have been transformed only slowly, often after a new set of codes was established following a successful struggle against the apartheid administration over land rights for the whole community, such as in the black freehold areas. While many women staunchly defend their rights to land and become actively involved in land and community politics, tradition upholding patrilinear inheritance still remains strong, favouring sons over daughters, as does a tendency for women to vote for men in local affairs, when they are included.

At the same time, women's direct involvement tends to accelerate the pace of change. An illustrative example was the participation of the Mmaboi women in the Northern Province in a wave of land invasions after the community became tired of waiting for the restitution process to verify land claims. When the local land committee divided up the land, one of the single women claimed – and received – her own piece of land, equal in size to the men's and began to plough it (before considered 'men's work'). As Mngxitama summarises it, 'The process of land invasions has unlocked a process of land allocation which seeks substantive equality...' (1997: 89). His interviews with community members led him to conclude that most are now in favour of an equal land distribution policy between men and women, some admitting that 'times have changed' and that now 'even women are using tractors for all aspects of farming'.

In some instances ANC policy on the ground is in direct conflict with actually challenging traditional institutions and relations with commercial farmers. A group of women mounted protests against their resident chief over land rights and for allowing neighbouring white farmers' cattle to break down the women's fences and eat their mealies. Furious, they marched down the main street of Buffespruit near the Mpumalanga-Swaziland border without any clothes on. 'We had to do something strange to get his attention, to show him our empty stomachs. 'Naked grandmothers are no more obscene than not being able to feed our grandchildren,' a 70-year old woman said, who still tended her field from 4 am until sunset everyday. After one week in jail, some community members finally posted bail, but the provincial Department of Land Affairs representative merely told the women 'to share' the land with the cattle farmers, while the local land rights organisation said they could do nothing because it was the chief's land and they should 'work it out'. In the face of such ambivalence and aiming to escalate the conflict rather than back down as expected, the women cautioned, 'We don't care ... We won't stop until we are given land to grow our crops' (Shongwe 2000: 18–20).

Land reform – opening the way to land access for women?

References to gender inequality are frequent in the 1997 *White Paper on South African Land Policy* but solutions remain evasive. General goals include supplemental legislation, access to financial assistance and productive farming opportunities for women, capacity-building and project planning, along with monitoring and evaluation of land reform and women's economic and social status. The White Paper promises to facilitate women's land needs in all three areas of the land reform programme: redistribution, restitution and land tenure reform, with the contention that all existing tenure systems discriminate against women. It specifically mentions the need to provide security of tenure for women along with the tangible goal of registering assets 'gained through land reform in the name of women as direct beneficiaries' (17–18, 34, 50). Transferring land to women in their own name has always been a crucial first test of land reform in any country. Examining some of the paradoxes of the land redistribution programme helps to provide an initial perspective on whether and in what way land reform attenuates or aggravates the conflict over rural women's access to land.

Redistribution: limitations of the household concept

The 1996 land reform programme designated women as a priority for redistribution if they are 'marginalised' and 'in need'. They are also a target group for the R15,000 government subsidy called the Settlement and Land Acquisition Grant or SLAG (later increased to R16,000 in 1998) made available to households earning combined incomes of less than R1,500 per month with dependants. Nevertheless, specifically how women's needs would be addressed, and especially how they would become a priority in practical terms, is not indicated in the *Green Paper* draft policy document, making it more a statement of intent than a policy guide in this area.

One controversy that arose quickly was the question of who and what constitutes a household, when it comes to determining who has a right to access the government subsidy for land acquisition. In addition some critics point out that the terms 'beneficiary' and 'household' were used interchangeably in early DLA documents, sometimes indicating individuals, sometimes the whole family.

Even if women head half of rural households or more, UCT researcher Artz (1999: 56–8) maintains that 'female beneficiaries are a misnomer, as men continue to be the legal beneficiaries for the household'. She gives graphic examples of the ways that men often exclude women from economic benefits of any kind, which is the type of social practice land reform must take into account if it wants to improve women's chances to land access.[10]

[10] Artz cites examples of what she calls 'economic abuse', such as husbands withholding money, requiring that their wives first perform 'duties', or sending remittances for the household to the eldest son instead of to the wife, which the son often squandered on alcohol. She details the consequences of errors such as registering in the husband's name the sugar cane fields which the wife works but for which she gets only 10% of what she earned after the cheque comes in his name.

Ngqaleni and Makhura (1996), in the study of black women farmers in the Northern Province cited above, point out that because men have more income from formal jobs, they will be in a better position to benefit from land reform than women. They also contend that if subsidies are assigned by household, this 'will ensure that men rather than women own land, because they are the household heads' (p. 354). In a situation of split or dual households, they warn that men could use the subsidy for urban lodging while their wives get nothing.[11]

One aspect of the problem is the omnipresent lack of information on actual rights. For example, many women were not aware that they could access the SLAG as a separate household if their husbands were polygamous. As a result of men claiming the money for their families but excluding them from any formal rights, registration, etc., NGOs have insisted that the policy be rectified. The government finally agreed and through its Gender Sub-Directorate made clear in its 1999 report that in customary marriages the husband and main wife constitute one household for one subsidy and all the other wives individually qualify for another subsidy.[12]

The land market – neither income nor gender blind

The market-based programme has created numerous constraints on the possibility of viable land redistribution on a scale that seriously challenges and leads to breaking up the old colonial landholding patterns. Opposition has been widespread both because it is premised on land hungry and landless (black) buyers having to purchase land from willing (white) sellers through the market, tending to exclude rather than benefit the poor, and also because the results in terms of land transferred have been, as many feared, quite modest over the first five years. At the end of 1999, the DLA reported that land transfers through redistribution projects amounted to just under 1 per cent of total commercial farmland (Walker 2002: 45). Theoretically the land market could be construed as 'gender blind', and yet as analysis shows, in fact, far from being above or separate from South Africa, the land market mirrors the social and economic exclusion there, doubly jeopardising women. As of 1998, approximately 4 per cent of households benefiting from land redistribution were listed as female-headed (Bonti-Ankomah 1998: 36), while the government cited a figure of 14 per cent for this ratio for redistribution projects approved by the end of 2000.

Aside from the issue of whether there exist willing buyers and willing sellers, and how many, the prevailing idea in the African rural areas is that land reform under a black government would mean granting land rights to the black rural population that has been denied them. As AFRA (Association for Rural Advancement) writer Mkhize puts it, people want land whether or not they qualify for restitution and don't necessarily want to buy it through redistribution. (1998: 10–11). In addition, the very limited and legally unwieldy restitution programme

[11] See also Panther (1998), who argues that a 'gender-neutral' concept based on undefined households will benefit men.

[12] Although initially women wanting land in 'Power Town', a small community of farmworkers in the Southern Cape, were forced to register as dependants of their husbands and partners to get the government grant, they protested to higher levels of the DLA and eventually won the right to be registered as land reform beneficiaries. See Mlahleki (1998).

has neither eliminated this public expectation nor come close to resolving the political problem it represents.

Redistribution, as the main vehicle of land reform, became tantamount to participants' ability to pay; not just pay to purchase the land, even with government assistance, but pay for high transfer fees. In addition they must locate further funds and resources needed to develop the land itself.[13] University researcher Colin Murray, in his study of land reform in the Eastern Free State, points to the credibility gap between the official discourse of enabling the poor to avail of new chances to farm and the real situation, in which people who can buy land are often businessmen, those who have accumulated enough to operate taxis or own supermarkets; poor people who want to buy farming land face huge financial hurdles (1996: 221).

Since the poor have no savings, (or little more than a few cattle), are fundamentally landless (or at least are not defined as property owners in traditional areas) and cannot obtain commercial credit, basically they cannot participate at all in land purchase as individuals, and if they could, high prices prevent them from acquiring a reasonable quantity of land. (Prices tend to be highest in the fruit-producing region of the Western Cape and the KwaZulu-Natal cane-growing area.) So while in poorer farming areas like the Free State, R700 could buy a hectare in the mid-1990s, in some areas of kwaZulu-Natal, R16,000 – or the total amount of one grant – would buy only one hectare per beneficiary household (Bonti-Ankomah, 1998: 31, 34). The poor have, therefore, been encouraged to come forward in groups. If they are able to organise themselves through a chief or some other existing institution or local body, they are obliged to pool their government subsidies in order to even consider bidding as a group for a piece of land.

Many authors have written about the effects of this policy, namely that the pooling of the land acquisition grant has tended to create artificial communities and use up all the funds people have, limiting their ability to develop the land and to build the infrastructure they need for living and carrying out production on it. It also tends to generate social conflict over how to use the land and widen social gaps within the group from the beginning, as the better-off individuals who can invest a little or may have connections to needed forms of assistance generally exert greater power and authority. Women in theory represent 40–50 per cent of the trusts, or Community Property Associations, that are formed, but this is often formalistic, akin to placing names on a list (thus appearing to serve high numbers of women beneficiaries) without consulting or according women any rights (Interviews with Jordaan 1997 (TRAC), McCarthy 1997 (LAPC), Mashego 1999, Madakane 1999, *Agenda* 1999).

Can the market be considered to be a neutral regulator? How is land that has been monopolised by white commercial farmers in mostly racially distinct areas for almost a century neutrally 'freed up' for sale? How should land value be assessed in this volatile situation, and related to that, what is a free market? Is 'available' land transferred in a neutral way to the land needy? Should state land held in Trust but never incorporated into the former reserves be sold to the African population? These are some of the questions critics are posing about the

[13] (Ibid.). Citing a group of 15 people who pooled their subsidies in KwaZulu-Natal, R32,000 was exacted from them in subdivision and survey costs as part of the transfer fee. Later the government initiated a new fund to cover transfer fees to alleviate some of the pressure.

market logic guiding land reform. Many have pointed out that some farmers are indeed not 'willing' to sell even a hectare of their large landholdings for the purpose of redistribution to Africans and argue fervently through the farmers' unions that only state land should be used for land reform (Interview Shone for Kwanalu 1999). Other farmers have agreed to adapt and are on the whole delighted that the land redistribution programme does essentially nothing to contravene their privileged position (Interviews 1996 with Sulphur Springs farm owner and de Young).

As a structured disequilibrium based on the capitalist mode of production, this approach to land transfer inevitably also gives rise to speculation. In the face of the new situation in which the state no longer provides white farmers with subsidies and advantages, some sellers have proved very willing to extricate themselves from poorly viable or non-viable farming operations, especially if it means selling their properties through lucrative deals from state settlements at market rates. There have been complaints of open land speculation as well as press exposures of farmers who have held out for a much higher price than the government offered (Yako and Cook 2001).

Looking at the similarities between South Africa's neo-liberal macro-economic agricultural policy called GEAR (Growth, Employment and Redistribution) and International Monetary Fund type structural adjustment programmes in a number of countries, Mather (*Mail & Guardian* 1997) points to the frequent result of market-led land reform concentrating production and land in fewer hands. In addition, with its accent on developing small-scale farming, GEAR tends to benefit already-established black farmers. Even if it were able to create 50,000 new ones as projected, its assistance will be temporary, and it will not be able to have a serious effect on the rural poor.

African women's dominant position in subsistence rather than commercial farming is one important reason that the land reform approach has had and will continue to have difficulty reaching the large numbers of poor rural women. Nor does GEAR, which encourages growing higher value export crops like vegetables and fruit, and fruit for processing industries like viticulture, reflect an aim to bolster production of crops improving basic food security for that same population such as maize and wheat that are the staples in rural diets (ibid).

In summary, many critics argue that the market is far from a neutral force regulating supply and responding to demand. It tends to reinforce the status quo and to shift property according to laws of profitability and viability and has little to do with the social needs of the rural black population, broadly speaking, including high land demand, much less those of the majority rural poor and the policy's stated aim of curbing poverty and inequality. The poor have no money to develop farming, but white farmers are selling, often at a handsome profit; some are then even able to buy another more promising location or operation, thus ensconcing their already strong position and reinforcing current land and social inequity. Within these parameters women (as well as labour tenants) are not a high priority, but a low one, and if limited to gaining access to land through households defined as male-headed, they may not acquire any (new) land at all (Interviews Madakane, Kariuki 1999; Hlatshwayo 2001).

As Murray's point above about the Eastern Free State and the Eastern Mpumalanga studies discussing the Community Property Associations show, the market approach also fosters greater social stratification among the African population seeking land. One aspect of this, which both scholarly and NGO critics have exposed, is that the Land Redistribution programme has created openings for traditional authorities to benefit from land reform by arranging purchases of large tracts of land under their name or jurisdiction to boost their prestige and strengthen their political grip over their communities and in some cases in order to re-sell pieces of land (Vaughan 1995: 11–15; LAPC, 1995a: 28–32; LAPC Case Studies, 1995b). This also tends to reinforce rather than eliminate existing inequalities within the traditional land tenure system. During fieldwork in Northern Province (Lebowa homeland) we met former labour tenant women who had left the white farms to move to the scattered rural settlements outside Burgersfort and had recently concluded what they considered to be a purchase of a plot of land from the local chief. Yet no one in the area could explain how supposedly communal land was up for sale. It is important to note that in other regions (the former Ciskei and southern KwaZulu-Natal) some traditional leaders were actively attempting to represent their communities for land reform projects and were genuinely motivated by aims of restoring rights to land and enhanced ability to farm.

The official reasoning of the Department of Land Affairs for this approach to redistribution is centred on the need to maintain public confidence in the land market and on the need to transfer land to the poor. (Of course, others reply with the rhetorical question, 'Which public?' since the black majority has never had any interest or confidence in the land market linked to the developed world that has excluded them. In fact the overwhelming concern seems to be averting established white landowners' fears of expropriation.)

In practice redistribution has achieved low results that are heavily gender-biased and inadequate in most every aspect, including land access, livelihood improvement as well as its stated aims to reduce social inequality and discrimination against women. Apart from the great variance between policy statement and its application, redistribution has proved itself nearly irrelevant in terms of changing land relations between whites and blacks, and those involving black women even more so. In the short term some families will gain access to land, but the more disadvantaged amongst them will tend to be increasingly driven off the land and towards the cities and rural towns. This is one of the common livelihood-destroying effects of capitalism in the third world heightened today by globalisation. In South Africa this may likely mean even greater landlessness among the poor accompanied by a further concentration of land in the hands of white farmers and agro-capital.

The widespread concerns among active land experts and scholars over the inability of the land reform to deliver to the poor on a significant scale and to anticipate development needs have given rise to numerous conferences and articles suggesting a range of approaches. These extend from greater state intervention and funds, to more support services and interdepartmental cooperation, to management issues like decentralisation of land reform to the need for renewed widespread social debate to rethink the overall 'vision'. There also remains discussion of the need to discontinue the willing buyer/willing seller notion imposed by the British in Zimbabwe in 1980 and emulated in South Africa.[14] In addition, without recourse to significant expropriation and as long as all available

[14] Wildschut and Hulbert 1998, Capps and Batterbury 2000, Lahiff 2001, SARPN 2003.

funds are funnelled to the purchase of land and to compensating owners rather than building up agricultural production for poorer farmers, it is difficult to imagine any serious potential for shifting the ownership imbalance.

The 2001 LRAD programme mentioned above is the offspring of greater collaboration between the post-1999 DLA minister and established interests in commercial agriculture. Although results from this new version of redistribution are beginning to be seen for a select minority, concerns are widespread that it goes much further in the direction of excluding the poor in favour of those black farmers who can pay their entrance into the circuits of the existing capitalist agrarian economy.[15] While it pledges to transfer one-third of total redistributed land to women, there is little reference to how this would actually materialise, and further, what mechanisms would prevent a small number of economically better-off women, or those with connections to resource advantages, from filling the gender quota by taking over large quantities of land (Walker 2002: 58). The majority of poor women who need land for differing levels of agricultural production from food security to modest exchange, or who aspire to larger commercial activity, will have even less capacity to compete for land grants within this framework.

Conclusion

This chapter has examined some of the ways in which land reform has rekindled and intensified the social conflicts over land, partly as a result of raised expectations of a black government that has promised significant change. The conflict over African rural women's limited access to land and few formal land rights is a particularly concentrated example of this. It reveals strong attachment to as well as need and hunger for land, underscoring the centrality of land as a resource, although by itself clearly insufficient. Hopes have been revived for the right to reclaim lost land, to gain access to new or more land with the chance of improving food security, livelihoods and the quality of rural life in general, including the system of values and cultural references embedded in rural people's relationship to the land. The sober reality is that after nearly a decade of land reform, land redistribution has succeeded in reaching only a limited number of women due to numerous constraints and impediments.

The formal recognition of women's equality in the legal sphere constitutes an important starting point in changing women's status. Removing the legal restrictions on women's rights in order to facilitate their benefiting from land reform is clearly an essential step and helps to undermine both discriminatory 'customary' practices and those in society at large, without in itself ending discrimination against women. Yet the impact of such rights is diminished in light of the dilemma created by the new Constitution's defence of private land ownership essentially as it existed under colonial rule, relying on expropriation only as a last resort. To what degree can African women attain social equality

15 To obtain the land reform grant in the first redistribution programme eligible applicants had to have earned less than R1,500 per month; the LRAD demands a minimum participation of R5,000 from applicants on a sliding scale reaching a maximum of R100,000 for a R400,000 grant. In both programmes the market is regulator of land transfers. See Jacobs et al. 2003 for an initial overview of the effects of LRAD.

in landholding without the right, along with their male counterparts, to challenge and change the property system that has dispossessed them? Some within the DLA have argued that the sharp edges of absolute inequality have been rounded off and the basis laid for future 'de-racialisation'. While it presents a less 'rosy' perspective, the analysis here shows that for understanding the nature of the social conflicts that are developing in the rural areas it is more accurate to emphasise the main trend underlying South African land reform today. The combination of this legal framework and the government land reform based on market sales rather than the needs of the black majority has tended not only to preserve the existing division of the land and its control by a white land-owning minority but to continue to doubly exclude African women from this configuration – as blacks and as women.

Women's labour is not marginal to the functioning of the economy as some contend, and the structural obstacles linked to the way agriculture and land ownership continue to be organised, with some adaptations but many similarities to the apartheid era, still play an important role in preventing the access of African women, demographically dominant in the rural areas, to land as a resource and a means of production. In addition, the gender aspect of land reform has encountered institutional and administrative barriers as well as widespread social prejudice against women's capacities and role in society. Male dominance and patriarchy remain very strong, and not only within traditional communities. However, the problems associated with bureaucracy and reaching women with reform programmes stem not just from organisational difficulties, but from the regret those in the Gender Forum of the DLA have themselves expressed: that is, the fact that despite some progress, 'principles of gender equality still remain no more than a policy' and such policies 'often fall by the wayside' (Govender-VanWyk 1999: 66) amidst the good intentions of many of those involved. The new orientation of LRAD since 2001 has shifted policy even further in the direction, not of official exclusion or awkward sidestepping of gender concerns so widely discussed in the literature, but of harnessing greater land access to resource capacity, thereby reducing the majority of rural African women's ability to participate.

Bibliography

African National Congress (ANC). 1994. *The Reconstruction and Development Programme.* Johannesburg.

ANC Women's League. 1999. *Delivery to the Women, Achievements of Individual Ministries and Departments – Agriculture and Land Affairs,* April, www.anc.org.za/wl/docs.

______. 1993. *Status of South African Women.* Johannesburg.

Agenda (Empowering Women for Gender Equity), 1999, no. 42, issue on Land and Housing:

______. S. Hargreaves. *Land Reform: Putting Gender in the Centre,* pp. 42–8.

______. S. Ngubane. *Title to the Land,* pp. 7–11.

______. T. Mokone, *Baphiring Women Pool the Subsidy,* pp. 39–41.

Andrew, N. 1999a. 'Le conflit foncier sur les exploitations agricoles blanches: le cas des labour tenants dans le Mpumalanga.' In D. Darbon (ed.) *L'après-Mandela, Enjeux sud-africains et régionaux.* Paris: Karthala. Also available in English.

______. 1999b. 'Notes de lecture: *Down to Earth,*' (Marcus, Eales and Wildschut), *Revue Tiers-Monde,* Paris: Presses Universitaires France, no. 159: 702–4.

Ardington, E. 1995. *Return to Nkandla, Third Survey in a Longitudinal Study of a Rural Community in KwaZulu Natal,* CSDS Research Report no. 7, Durban: University of Natal.

L. Artz. 1999. *Shelter in the Southern Cape: Gender Violence undermines Development, Agenda (Empowering*

Women for Gender Equity), 1999, no. 42, issue on Land and Housing, pp. 55–9.

Aryeetey, E. Bortei-Doku. 1997. 'Accès des femmes aux ressources foncières au Ghana.'*Gérer le foncier rural en Afrique de l'Ouest*, Paris, pp. 165–83.

Association for Rural Advancement (AFRA). 1998. (Sihle Mkhize) 'The Land Policy – Why it must change.' *AFRA News* no. 41, July: 10–14.

______. 1995. 'Women and land, the Case Study of Cornfields.' *AFRA News*, 33: 13, May-June.

Barrett, J. et al. 1985. *Vukani Makhosikazi – South African Women Speak*. London: Catholic Institute for International Relations.

Binswanger, H. and K. Deininger. 1993. 'South African Land Policy: The Legacy of History and Current Options.' *World Development*, 21:9: 1451–75.

Bonti-Ankomah, S. 1998. *Land Redistribution Options for South Africa*, Braamfontein: National Land Committee, April..

Capps, G. and S. Batterbury. 2000. *Notes of the Workshop on Politics of Land Reform in the 'New' South Africa*. London School of Economics, June.

Department of Land Affairs (DLA). 2003. Notes on the Indaba: the Restitution of Land Rights Amendment Bill, 26 June, Pretoria, www.land.pwv.gov.za.

______. 1999a. Minister Didiza's Parliamentary Media Briefing, 29 June.

______. 1999b. Annual Report.

______. 1999c. Portfolio Committee of the DLA, February.

______. 1998. Quality of Life Report, I. Naidoo.

______. 1997a. *White Paper on South African Land Policy*, April. 111.

______. 1997b. 'Women's Rights in Land.' *Journal of the DLA*, March/April: 16–17.

Delius, P. 1984. *The Land Belongs to Us*, Johannesburg: Ravan.

Economic Justice Update, May 2002, 'Land, inheritance rights and livelihoods in rural areas, The impact on women in South Africa', Fair Share, School of Government, University of the Western Cape, pp 1– 4.

Farmworkers Research and Resource Project (FRRP). 1997. *State of South African Farmworkers*. Johannesburg, 60.

______. 1996. Farm Labour Review – Farmworkers and Agriculture in South Africa. Johannesburg.

______. 1995. Zaaihoek, South Eastern Transvaal Case Study, April.

Govender-Van Wijk, S. 1999. 'Gender Policy in Land Reform', *Agenda (Empowering Women for Gender Equity)*, no. 42, issue on Land and Housing, pp. 66–9.

Hlatshwayo, Z. 2001. 'Land Reform Policy is in Trouble.' *Business Day*, 5 July.

Horrell, M. 1975. *Brief Guide to Some Laws Affecting African Women*. Johannesburg: South African Institute of Race Relations, May.

Jacobs, P, E. Lahiff, E and R. Hall. 2003. 'Land Redistribution.' *PLAAS paper*, September.

James, B. and S. Ngcobo. 1997. 'Evicted Farmworkers and Gender in the Small Town of Aberdeen.' In S. Meer (ed.) *Women, Land and Authority: Perspectives from South Africa*. Cape Town: David Philip and Oxfam.

Lahiff, Edward. 2001. 'Land and Reform in South Africa: Is It Meeting the Challenge?' *PLAAS Policy Brief* No. 1, University of Western Cape, September.

Land and Agriculture Policy Centre. 1995a. 'Land-Interested Traditional Authorities.' Provincial Synthesis Report *KwaZulu/Natal Province, working paper* no. 24.

______. 1995b. *Case Studies 1 and 2 on Communal areas in former Kwazulu*. Land Reform Area Study Report.

Letsoalo, E. 1987. *Land Reform in South Africa*. Johannesburg: Skotaville.

Levin, R. and D. Weiner.1996. 'Land Reform in South Africa after Apartheid: Perspectives, Problems, Prospects.' *Journal of Peasant Studies* 23, 2/3: 93–119.

Locoh, T., A. Labourie-Racapé, and C. Tichit (eds). 1996. *Genre et développement: des pistes à suivre*, EHESS-INED-INSEE-ORSTOM-Université de Paris VI, CEPED no. 5: Paris.

Lotta, Raymond. 1986. 'The Political Economy of Apartheid.' *Race and Class*, London: Institute of Race Relations, 27:1, Winter.

Madakane, L. and R. Levin. 1997. 'Mpumalanga Lowveld Escarpment District Study'. (LAPC Land Reform Research), July.

Mail and Guardian. 1999. 'We Can't Deliver the Land, Admits the Government.' 21 January.

______. 1997. 'Agriculture Slips out of Gear.' 9 May, based on a paper by University of Wits geographer C. Mather, commissioned by the LAPC.

Marcus, T. 1989. *Modernizing Superexploitation. The Restructuring of South African Agriculture*, London: Zed.

Marcus, T., K. Eales and A. Wildschut. 1996. *Down to Earth: Land Demand in the New South Africa*.

Durban: Indicator Press.

May, J. 2000. 'The Structure and Composition of Rural Poverty and Livelihoods in South Africa.' In B. Cousins (ed.) *At the Crossroads: Land and Agrarian Reform in South Africa into the 21st Century*. Cape Town: PLAAS/NLC.

Mazonde, I. 1995. 'Food Security and Household Labour: Social Transformation in a Botswana Village.' *Journal of Contemporary African Studies*, 13: 1, pp 75–89.

Ministry for Agriculture and Land Affairs. 2001. *Land Redistribution for Agricultural Development (LRAD)*. Pretoria: National Dept. of Agriculture.

Mlahleki, N. 1998. 'Women's Participation in Land Reform and Decision-making Structures.' *Voices from the Field, Development Work with Rural Women*, Johannesburg: NLC, pp. 46–9.

Mngxitama, A. 1997. *Land Restitution: A Judicial Solution to a Political Problem: The Mmboi Case*. Sociology masters dissertation, University of Witswatersrand.

Moyo, S. 1998. 'Land Entitlements and Growing Poverty in Southern Africa.' *SAPEM*, March, pp. 15–22.

Murray, C. 1996. 'Land Reform in the Eastern Free State: Policy Dilemmas and Political Conflicts. The Agrarian Question in South Africa.' *Journal of Peasant Studies*, 23: 2/3 pp. 209–43.

National Land Committee (NLC). 1997a. 'DLA workshop report: Women's rights in land.' *Land Update* 55, February.

______. 1997b. 'Tenure Insecurity Tops Gender Task Group Agenda.' *Land Update*, 55: Feb.:11.

______. 1996. 'Battles over Land Reform.' *Land Update*, 44: January/February: 6–8.

Ndlela, L. 1996. 'Rural Local Government: Women as an Interest Group.' *Land Update*, 52: 4–6.

Nene, S. 1986. 'Women Caught in Between: The Case of Rural Women in KwaZulu.' *Africanus* 16: 10-17.

Ngqaleni, M.T. and M.T. Makhura. 1996. 'An Analysis of Women's Status in Agricultural Development in the Northern Province.' In M. Lipton et al. (eds) *Land, Labour and Livelihoods in Rural South Africa, Vol. 2, KwaZulu-Natal and Northern Province*. Durban: Indicator Press.

Nkuzi Development Association. 2002. 'No Policy for Change.' www.nkuzi.org.za.

Ntsedi, M. and L. Waldman. 1997. 'Women on Highveld Farms: an Outlook for Development.' In S. Meer (ed.) *Women, Land and Authority*. Cape Town: David Philip and Oxfam.

Panther, J. 1998. 'South Africans Do Not Talk about Independent Land Rights for Women.' *Rural Digest People's Policy*, 1: 3 January: 14–15.

Republic of South Africa. 1996. *Constitution of the Republic of South Africa*, <Bill of Rights>.

Qunta, C. 1987. *Women in Southern Africa*. London: Allison and Busby.

Seidman, Ann and Neva. 1977. *South Africa and U.S. Multinational Corporations*, Westport: Lawrence Hill.

Shongwe, N. 2000. 'Women Strip Naked to Show Hungry Stomachs.' African Eye News Service, *Land and Rural Digest*, 10, January/February: 18–20.

Southern African Regional Poverty Network (SARPN). 2003. 'Seeking Ways Out of the Impasse on Land Reform in Southern Africa.' www.sarpn.org.za.

Simkins, C. 1981. 'The Economic Implications of African Resettlement.' *SALDRU Working Paper no. 43*, Cape Town.

Transvaal Rural Action Committee (TRAC). 1992. B. Sechabeng, *A Feeling of Community*, Johannesburg.

UNCHS. 1998. Peace for Homes, Homes for Peace: Inter-Regional Consultation on Women's Land/Property Rights Under Situations of Conflict and Reconstruction, January.

Van Zyl, J., J. Kirsten, J. and H.P. Binswanger (eds). 1996. *Agricultural Land Reform in South Africa*. Cape Town: Oxford University Press.

Vaughan, A. 1995. *Synthesis Report, District Study One, Kwazulu-Natal*. Durban: ISER, University of Durban Westville.

Vogelsang, F. 1998. 'After Land Reform, the Market?' Land Reform:1, Agricultural Development Unit, ECLAC (UN).

Walker, C. 2002. *Agrarian Change, Gender and Land Reform*. UNRISD, April.

Wildschut, A. and S. Hulbert. 1998. *A Seed Not Sown: Prospects for Agrarian Reform in South Africa*, Johannesburg: Interfund/Deutsch Welthungerhilfe.

Yako, S. and L. Cook. 2001. 'Further Expropriations of South African Farmland in Store.' *Business Day*, 29 March.

Interviews

Libby Ardington, University of Natal, Durban, ISER, February 1996.
Ian de Young, direct meat purchaser from S. African farmers, March 1996.
Wayne Jordaan, TRAC, Fieldwork cooordinator, July 1997.
Sam Kariuki, University of Witwatersrand, Sociology Department, February 1999.
Richard Levin, Department of Land Affairs, July 1997.
Lloyd Madakane, LAPC, March 1999.
Tessa Marcus, Rural Sociology Dept., University of Natal at Pietermaritzburg, February 1999.
Signet Mashego, LAPC, head of Monitoring and Evaluation unit, March 1999.
Mampe Ntsedi, Farmworkers Research and Resource Project, July 1997.
Malcom McCarthy, LAPC, July 1997.
Mdu Shabane, Association for Rural Advancement, Pietermaritzburg, January 1996.
Steve Shone, spokesman for Kwanalu (farmers' union in KwaZulu-Natal), in Pietermaritzburg, March 1999.
Dr Sipho Sibanda, coordinator, Association for Rural Advancement, February 1996.
Farmowner, Sulphur Springs, February1996 (name withheld).

Numerous individual and small group interviews were conducted as part of fieldwork in the Pietersburg area (now Polokwane) of the Northern Province, formerly Lebowa (July 1997) and among labour tenant women in southeastern Mpumalanga (February 1996 and July 1997) near Piet Retief and near Belfast in the northern part of the province (March 1999). Other interviews took place in southern KwaZulu-Natal near Richmond and in a resettlement community near Dimbaza and King Williams Town, Eastern Cape Province (Ciskei), (February 1996).

III
Land, Identity & Violence

8

Land, Identity & Violence in Zimbabwe

BILL DERMAN
& ANNE HELLUM

Introduction

Contemporary Zimbabwe has become a flash point for profound disagreements on the nature and character of the regime and its programme of land reform and expropriation of almost all white-owned farm land. This chapter examines how Zimbabwe's fast track land reform[1] has transformed citizen's rights, citizenship and identity. It focuses on the construction of new paradigms of inclusion and exclusion based upon political loyalty and participation in what has been termed the 'Third Chimurenga'[2] by President Mugabe and the ruling political party. Several legal, political and economic instruments have been used to accomplish this transformation but most rely upon violence or the threat of violence. Following its defeat in a constitutional referendum in February 2000, the Government of Zimbabwe adopted a fast track land resettlement programme based upon a series of land occupations of white commercial farms carried out by the National War Veterans Liberation Association supported by various elements of government, the ruling party and the military. Fast track has been based upon the compulsory acquisition of white-owned farms and their resettlement by people generically labelled as landless. From the original 1,417 farms listed for acquisition in 1997, virtually all white-owned land has now been appropriated by the government and most of the former 350,000 farm workers have lost their employment if not their homes.

This process has been subject to different interpretations. African state leaders such as President Chissano of Mozambique support the ZANU-PF government's view that:

> Zimbabwean land reforms have for the first time given the opportunity to millions of people who previously had no land, to possess it and to produce their own food. (Speech to Corporate Council on Africa, 28 June 2003)

[1] It is also known as the Land Reform and Resettlement Programme Phase II. This implies a greater continuity with earlier land reform programmes that we do not find consistent with the way the reforms actually proceeded.

[2] The first Chimurenga was the revolt against the British South Africa Company in 1896, the second, the war of national liberation against the Rhodesian Front government and the third, against the British effort to continue neo-colonialism or colonialism. The president declared this war won in 2003 with the 'completion' of fast track land reform.

This characterisation of Zimbabwe's latest effort at land reform remains highly contested. There is a large body of literature making the point that the land issue has served as a smoke screen for the government's desperate effort to stay in power (Hammar et al 2003). In this chapter we examine how citizenship and identity are being redefined through a revision of Zimbabwean history as being constituted almost exclusively through land and race. In this process of land reform and violent attacks upon the opposition party, the ZANU-PF government has attempted fundamentally to alter and redefine the state–citizenship relationship[3] while cloaking the enterprise as an anti-imperialist and anti-colonial struggle. Democracy, civil rights and the 'rule of law' are now seen as enemies of the new Zimbabwean revolution.[4]

The paper is divided into three main parts. The first part links the different stages in the land reform to the decreasing legitimacy of the ZANU-PF government and the growing opposition whose common denominator is support for basic principles of human rights and democratic processes. The second part explores how gender has been incorporated into the fast track resettlement process in order to address how citizen rights are mediated through patrilineal kinship and allegiance to the ruler in terms of ZANU-PF and President Mugabe. The third part explores the links between the Zimbabwean state's use of violence to emphasise or create the categories of insiders and outsiders, indigenous and non-indigenous, and defenders of African nationalism and betrayers of Zimbabwe. We briefly explore the potential for even further violence, and if and how this process can be brought to an end.

The Land Question in Zimbabwe

Historical background

Zimbabwe's lands have been divided into the following categories: state land (safari areas, forests and national parks), urban areas, large-scale commercial farming areas, small-scale commercial farming areas and communal areas (including resettlement areas). The British South Africa Company, disappointed in its search for gold, colonised Rhodesia and set aside large areas for European farming. When the British South Africa Company was forced out of governance, the colony of Southern Rhodesia was formed. It existed from 1922 until 1980 when it became independent Zimbabwe. Throughout its history a small minority of Europeans owned large amounts of land, had substantial autonomy from Britain, and held the levers of the state.[5] Their lands were often the best, chosen for their high productive potential. These were termed European areas. After independence these were called Large Scale Commercial Farming areas, while the majority of the black population was forced onto the less productive lands called Tribal Trust Lands, now known as Communal Areas. These social divisions often, although not always, paralleled the 'natural regions' based upon rainfall and soils into which the country was – and remains – divided. The best-watered areas (at

[3] In other papers, we have analysed how the ownership of the key natural resources of water and land has been appropriated by the state (Derman and Hellum 2002, Hellum and Derman 2004a and b).

[4] For a thoughtful consideration of how this has happened see Raftopoulos 2003.

[5] Other former settler colonies in Africa include Algeria, Kenya, Namibia and South Africa. These colonies all had difficult and often violent paths to national independence.

Table 8.1 Land Categories in Zimbabwe (as of 1994)

Type of Land	Area (km^2)	% of Total Area	Population
Communal land	163,500	41.8	4,662,000[6]
Resettlement land	26,400	6.7	355,000
Commercial farming land	142,400	36.4	1,713,000
National parks estate	47,000	12.1	—
State forest land	9,200	2.4	—
Urban & state land	2,200	0.6	3,500,000

the core of the Central Plateau and the Eastern Highlands) are classified as Region I while the lowest rainfall areas are identified as Natural Region V. Communal areas are greatly over-represented in the lower rainfall areas.

Table 8.1 shows the type of land, land area and population.

As of the last fully analysed census in 1995, nearly 65 per cent of Zimbabwe's population lived in rural areas. The country generated most of its foreign earnings from agricultural exports including maize, tobacco, cotton, cut flowers, sunflower seeds, sugar beans, sugar, wheat and oranges along with an array of vegetables and wheat. The country has long striven for internal food self-sufficiency combined with high-value export crops, the most important of which is tobacco. Tourism was the second most important foreign exchange earner until the land occupations and invasions, which began in February and March 2000. All indicators of well-being including life expectancy, per capita income, children in school, gross national product have all fallen dramatically in the past five years. The largest sector of formal employment had been farm workers. The number of full-time employed workers has been dramatically reduced (see below). From being a net food exporter Zimbabwe has become reliant upon food imports and international food relief.

Undoing the divide 1980–1997

One of the most important reasons for Zimbabwe's independence struggle, but certainly not the only one,[7] was to end the inequality in land holdings between black and whites (see Martin and Johnson 1981, Lan 1985, Ranger 1985, Kriger 1992). Thus, an early goal of the newly independent Government of Zimbabwe was to resettle 162,000 households on 8.3 million hectares of land by 1985. This goal, while unrealistic, did lead to the resettlement of 71,000 households on 3.5 million hectares of land by 1998. With almost ten per cent of Zimbabwe's total land area in resettlement schemes, this was a major achievement by international standards but one that has not been readily acknowledged. The land was obtained from large-scale commercial farm owners on a willing buyer/willing seller basis.[8]

[6] This figure includes small-scale commercial farmers. Administratively they are considered residents of communal areas.

[7] Bhebe and Ranger (2001) among many others point to a more general understanding of Zimbabwe's struggle for independence including other dimensions of dignity, oppression, lack of freedom, etc. that generated opposition to colonial rule.

[8] Following the end of the war, many farms were taken by peasants or small scale farmers. This pushed the government to rapidly implement a resettlement programme.

More than 80 per cent of these resettlement schemes are based on a formula known as Model A. The Model A type is based on a separation of fields (called arables), homesteads (called residentials) and grazing areas, with homes arranged in straight lines in villages. Each settler and family (it was initially assumed that they would be male-headed) is given 5 hectares for cultivation and 0.5 hectares for their home. It was a permit-based system with resettlement officers having the right to take away permits if the scheme's rules are not followed.[9] The essence of this programme differed little from the colonially initiated Native Land Husbandry programme (Drinkwater 1991, Derman 1997). It was based upon ideas of equality whereby every rural resettlement household would have the same amount of land for cultivation, grazing and living. It was also based on a village model rather than a capitalist or business enterprise model.

Despite the importance of the resettlement programme little empirical research was done on the programme with the marked exception of that carried out by Bill Kinsey.[10] His early work demonstrates that that the welfare of the families that moved into resettlement areas dramatically increased in relationship to families that remained in the communal areas. His studies and others suggests that women's tenure in practice was more secure in the event of death in the resettlement areas he studied than in the communal lands from where the families originated. Widowed and divorced women were often allowed by resettlement officers to stay on the land in the event of death and divorce (WLSA 1994, Jacobs 2000, Kinsey personal communication).[11] In communal areas, where traditional authorities have had greater influence on land allocation registration practices were, with variations, based on patriarchal customary practices (ZWRCN 1998). Upon death and divorce women in communal areas have more frequently than women in the resettlement areas been denied access to land with reference to customary law. This development may be seen as a reflection of the improved status of women. At independence they became full citizens and the courts in a number of cases struck down customary laws in the area of marriage and inheritance that did not conform to the equality principle. The resettlement officers were educated and many of them, certainly not all, saw secure tenure for women as a means of improving agricultural production in a situation where men often were employed elsewhere or were less reliable than women.

The standard history of Zimbabwe recounts that the Government of Zimbabwe was blocked from carrying out far-reaching land reforms after independence in 1980 due to the restrictive constitution agreed to at Lancaster House that limited the state's ability to nationalise commercial farmland for a decade. Land could be bought by government but only through the willing buyer/willing seller system (Moyo 1995). Less standard histories point towards the growing disinterest of ZANU-PF in small-scale agriculture and their growing interest in business enterprises including the financial sector. Throughout the 1980s and 1990s the ruling party and individuals within it developed substantial private business interests.[12]

[9] For an analysis of the continuities between colonial and post-colonial land use programmes see Derman 1997. For a description and analysis of the resettlement programme see Kinsey (1999).

[10] A summary of his research can be found in Kinsey (2004: 1669–96).

[11] Spierenburg reports that this was not the case in the Mid-Zambezi Valley Development Project where local chiefs, to protect women, registered them as widows rather than divorcees otherwise they would not have been allocated land by the project (Spierenburg 2003).

[12] One important example has been the late local entrepreneur and businessman Roger Boka who founded a bank and opened Zimbabwe's largest auction facility for tobacco. He was a major

In the 1990s a series of constitutional and statutory changes that weakened the protection of private property rights were enacted to lay the foundation for a more radical reform the most important of which was the Land Acquisition Act of 1992. This act empowered the President to compulsorily acquire rural land where 'the acquisition is reasonably necessary for resettlement for agricultural and other purposes' (S. 3). The owner was, in terms of section 16, entitled to fair compensation. A Compensation Committee to be composed of the Secretary of the Ministry, the Director of Agricultural, Technical and Extension Services, the Chief Government Valuation Officers and three other members appointed by the Minister was established to determine the compensation payable. While the compensation issue could be appealed to the Administrative Court, no legal remedies were established with regard to the decision to designate land. This reform fell short of human rights standards such as the right to a fair and impartial hearing by an independent tribunal and the right to appeal. It was not used very much despite fears to the contrary.[13]

It appeared that the appointment of The Commission of Enquiry into Appropriate Agricultural Land Tenure Systems (LTC) by the President in 1993 would lead to specific steps to undo the profound divides between the communal and commercial agricultural sectors. Government had already overseen the political amalgamation of the communal areas and commercial farm areas and thus there was the expectation of a more unified approach to land tenure. Rukuni (1994) observed that as of 1994:

> The resettlement programme is severely under funded and beset with planning and administrative difficulties. Government funding for the resettlement programme, for example, is only equivalent to 2.4% of the defence budget for 1994–95. This has resulted in a very poor rate of resettlement since 1990, and any hope that the programme will relieve communal land pressure has been lost. (Vol. II 1994: 223)[14]

The Land Tenure Commission recommended that land settlement be a permanent long-term programme.[15] To increase the productiveness of the agricultural sector the main recommendations were increased investment in water in Communal and Resettlement Areas.[16] Other recommendations included legally secure tenure, improved credit and financial services and comprehensive agricultural support institutions for Communal and Resettlement Areas.[17] It was clear from the Report's conclusions that the major developmental issues then existent in communal areas could not be resolved through the resettlement

[12] (cont.) contributor to ZANU-PF and part of the reason his bank went bankrupt was due to unpaid loans taken out by ZANU-PF luminaries. He became bankrupt, the bank failed and he lost the auction floors.

[13] See Hellum and Derman 2004 for the links between land, land reform and human rights instruments. For example, The recommendations that were made in this document were very much in the spirit of Article 11 of the International Covenant on Economic, Social and Cultural Rights emphasising the States Parties obligations to take steps to ensure the realisation of the right to livelihood by 'reforming agrarian systems in such a way as to achieve the most efficient development and utilization of natural resources'.

[14] This finding has not been emphasised sufficiently and renders moot the government's assertion that land reform will relieve population and land pressure in the communal areas.

[15] Recommendation 8.8.1 of the Commission of Inquiry into Appropriate Agricultural Land Tenure Systems (LTC)

[16] Recommendation 8.8.3 (LTC Vol. I 1994). The reverse was followed. Virtually all the institutional support for resettlement by government was disbanded in the early 1990s.

[17] Recommendation 8.8.4 and 8.8.5 (LTC Vol. I 1994).

programme as implemented in the early 1990s. It proposed instead, much greater flexibility for communities to select their own tenurial options, to greater democratise land-use planning and to increase dramatically assistance to smaller scale farmers. No adequate explanation has been offered as to why the report was so thoroughly ignored.

Accelerated land reform 1997–2002

The recommendations of the Commission of Enquiry[18] were received by Government but never acted upon. Rather, in response to criticisms that the government was moving too slowly, President Mugabe stated shortly after his re-election in 1996:

> We are going to take the land and we are not going to pay for the soil. This is our policy. Our land was never bought (by the colonialists) and there is no way we could buy back the land. However, if Britain wants compensation they should give us money and we will pass it on to their children. (*The Guardian*, 15 October 1997)

After the Edinburgh Commonwealth Summit at which President Mugabe felt antagonism from the new prime minister of the UK, Tony Blair, he announced that the government would be acquiring 50 per cent of the large-scale commercial farming areas for three different types of resettlement (Chan 2002: 111). This announcement came at a time of multiple crises for the Zimbabwe government, its ruling party and for the wider society.

The crises of the late 1990s

The Zimbabwe government had crafted and implemented its own version of structural adjustment during the early 1990s. By the late 1990s it was clear that these policies had failed to stem growing poverty, the decline in real wages of employed Zimbabwean workers, the decline in social services, the increasing enrichment of high party officials and the ignoring of growing corruption. The labour unions were growing in both numbers and militancy, the National War Veterans' Association was becoming more active and there were growing pressures from black businessmen to get more contracts and business. The Zimbabwean Congress of Trade Unions (the ZCTU) and other civil society activists concluded that little real progress could be made in socioeconomic development in Zimbabwe without greater democracy. The response was to form a new civic society organisation called the National Constitutional Assembly (NCA) which began a campaign for a new, democratic constitution. It was officially launched on 31 January 1998 (Kagoro 2004). The result of this activity was the formation

[18] While the LTC made a number of recommendations about securing tenure in the communal and resettlement areas, they did not adequately address women's tenurial concerns or directly respond to presentations made to them by women's groups. The husband's matrimonial power, which is at the root of the unequal distribution of land between married men and women, was not questioned. The customary law that applies to registered and unregistered customary marriages gives him status as head of household and as such the right to hold property on behalf of his family. In communal areas, where land-use rights usually are conferred to the husband as the head of the family women's access to loans by institutions like the Agricultural Finance Co-operation (AFC) is severely hampered (Ncube 1987, ZWRCN 1998: 26). Furthermore, crops are usually marketed through boards in the husband's name and payments received in his name. Women's lack of title deed and income control has given rise to an increasing number of 'harvest suicides'. In a parallel fashion, tenurial issues for women in resettlement areas were not addressed.

in 1999 of a new national political party, the Movement for Democratic Change (MDC) headed by the former President of the Zimbabwe Congress of Trade Unions, Morgan Tsvangirai. As Raftopoulos notes:

> In the space of two decades the labour movement had moved from a weak and divided organization, under the shadow of a dominant nationalist party, to the facilitator of a broad opposition alliance that was challenging for state power. (2003: 228)

In 1997, the National War Veterans' Party turned temporarily against its patron, President Robert Mugabe, with a series of street demonstrations demanding annual payments, free education and health care for themselves and their families, and priority in any new land reform programme. The President agreed to their demands. Less visible, but quite significant was a national farm workers' strike, the first in Zimbabwe's history. In turn, the ZCTU led a nation-wide successful strike.

With these multiple crises and threats of an intensified land reform, the international donor community including the United States Agency for International Development (USAID), the Department for International Development (DFID), the Danish Agency for International Development (DANIDA), the Norwegian Agency for International Development (NORAD) and the World Bank, attempted to confront the land question more seriously. At the International Donor Conference on Land Reform and Resettlement in Zimbabwe in 1998, the donors indicated their concerns for the need for rule of law, transparency and gender equality in the next phase of land reform.[19] At this conference the donors agreed to fund an extensive land-reform programme encompassing 1,000,000 hectares but wanted greater proof that land reform would benefit the poor in a transparent manner.[20] They insisted that compensation should be paid for land to the land owners and a that technical unit organised outside government should administer the resettlement process. The agreement rapidly fell apart for reasons that remain unknown. It is our hypothesis that the party wanted to reserve the land issue for political purposes and was unwilling at this juncture in Zimbabwe's history to have land reform be administered by technical personnel supported by donors.

Along with the growing dissatisfaction with government came the government's decision to send troops to the Democratic Republic of Congo in support of its unelected President Laurent Kabila. In light of growing unrest, an unbudgeted and undeclared war, the emerging opposition decided that one productive way to tackle such a powerful government was for a wide range of groups, including the labour unions, Christian organisations, human rights organisations and women's organisations to align themselves in the NCA, demanding a new democratic constitution making the executive accountable and limiting the President's power that had been increased through 16 amendments to the Constitution. This movement become so strong that the President in 1999 attempted to co-opt the process by appointing his own Constitutional Commission of 4,000 members including all ZANU-PF members of parliament but also

[19] Communiqué Issued at the End of the International Donor's Conference on Land Reform and Resettlement in Zimbabwe. 9–11 September 1998, Harare, Zimbabwe. The human rights obligations of international donor institutions such as the IMF and the World Bank have in recent years moved centre stage in human rights and development discourse (Skogly 2000).

[20] Partly the donors greatly mistrusted ZANU-PF after it instituted a lease policy which gave large amounts of government land to members of government at virtually no cost. The list of beneficiaries was released by Margaret Dongo then an independent member of parliament.

including many independent professionals and some members of the opposition that through a wide consultation process was to write a home-grown people's constitution.

The Constitutional Commissioners attempted to take seriously the charge of listening to the people. Many members criss-crossed the country to engage in dialogue with broad sectors of Zimbabwean society. According to many of the commissioners who participated in the consultation process and the extant written records, there was no outcry for more land among the peasants in the communal lands. Rather small-scale farmers expressed a strong need for better roads, access to markets, affordable and accessible credit systems – in short – inputs that could help them farm the land they had much more effectively.[21]

In the Consolidated Draft Constitution the protection of private property clause was suggested to be upheld in the event of land reform requiring compulsory acquisition of land. In its listing of factors that may be taken into account in the assessment of compensation for the compulsory acquisition of agricultural land Section 57 weakened the owner's right to compensation by adding that compensation would be affected by clause e) 'the resources available to the acquiring authority in implementing the programme of land reform.' President Mugabe rejected the land provision in the Consolidated Draft of the Constitutional Commission. He unilaterally changed it in February 2000 to make the British government responsible for the actual compensation for land of white commercial farmers. Thus, the Final Draft Constitution that the Zimbabwean Government presented to the people for a yes or no during the referendum in February 2000 did not give a right to compensation for land in the event of expropriation. The ZANU-PF party campaigned on returning land to its rightful owners as the most important reason to vote 'yes' on the draft constitution. Nonetheless the government's Draft Constitution was rejected in the vote.[22]

This was the first national electoral defeat suffered by the government since 1980. There was a great deal of blaming within ZANU-PF but agreement followed that it was due to 'the whites'. Jonathan Moyo, the government appointed spokesperson for the National Constitutional Commission stated:

> Preliminary figures show there were 100,000 white people voting. We have never had anything like that in this country. They were all over town. Everybody who observed will tell you there were long queues of whites. The difference between the 'yes' and 'no votes' would not have been what it was had it not been for this vote. (Quoted by Chan from *The Times*, 16 February 2000: 144).[23]

ZANU-PF now realised that they could really lose the scheduled parliamentary election unless changes were made quickly. The defeat of the Draft Constitution was followed within two weeks by farm invasions of white-owned farms organised and orchestrated by the National War Veterans' Association and ZANU-PF. On 2 March 2000 President Mugabe introduced a Constitutional Amendment precisely the same as the one he had just placed in the defeated

[21] Government of Zimbabwe reports on *What the People Said.*

[22] Many explanations are given for the defeat. Our view is that overall the vote was viewed as a referendum on whether President Mugabe should stay in office.

[23] The votes were 697,754 votes against, 578,210 in favour. Subtracting all 100,000 votes from those against would still not have decided the election. There are a total of 100,000 whites in the country. Many of them are not registered (children), and many did not vote. Moyo's comments were both untrue and racist.

Draft Constitution to a lame-duck session of parliament where ZANU-PF had a two-thirds majority. The amendment passed.

At first the invasions were relatively peaceful even if clearly illegal. However in March 2000 they rapidly turned violent which led to many deaths, beatings, rapes, farm closures, expulsion of workers, loss of employment and agricultural production, loss of foreign investment and of tourism, among the more important consequences.[24] The war veteran camps in the different farming areas, it has been documented, were places where people believed to be members of the newly formed opposition party, the MDC, were taken to be beaten and tortured and forced to perform rituals where they promised allegiance to the ruler of Zimbabwe. The electoral violence and the land occupations were closely connected even though this was denied at the time by ZANU-PF.

In the Parliamentary elections that were held on 24 and 25 June 2000, ZANU-PF gained a narrow victory winning 48 per cent of the vote and 62 seats in Parliament against MDC's 47 per cent and 57 seats. This could have been a turning point with ZANU-PF and the President accepting a genuine opposition. This was not to be. In July of 2000 shortly after the elections, President Mugabe stated at a meeting of ZANU-PF's Central Committee about the opposition MDC: 'It is a counter-revolutionary Trojan Horse contrived and nurtured by the very inimical forces that enslaved and repressed our people yesterday' (quoted in Meredith 2002: 192).[25]

Fast Track

As noted earlier, the 'fast track resettlement programme was the name given in July 2000 to the rapid acquisition of large numbers of large-scale commercial farms by government for resettlement. This formalised and legalised the process of farm occupations which had begun in February of 2000. In the early phases of fast track the goal was to acquire 5 million hectares. This amount has been changing so that by 31 July 2003 the large scale commercial area had been diminished by 9.2 million hectares. The percentage of Zimbabwe's land in large-scale commercial agriculture was cut from 30 per cent to 6 per cent and of that land, almost one-half is now owned by black Zimbabwean farmers glossed by the government as indigenous. Current resettlement models include the older Model A, now called A1, and a new commercial model called A2. The A2 model was intended for those with the material resources to run a smaller but viable commercial farm. A2 farms range in size from approximately 40 hectares to 200 hectares (or even larger). As it became clear that there were serious problems in the fast track programme including lack of uptake, cases of ministers taking more than one farm, dispossession of farm workers, lack of women owners, etc., the President requested a member of his own office, Dr Charles Utete to undertake an assessment of the programme. He was to assess the extent to which the policy objectives of the programme and principles underlying it were achieved and implemented and to recommend measures to address its shortcomings. The findings were published (Utete 2003) in two volumes but the Commission did not

[24] See Human Rights Watch, Division Africa, Report of March 2002, Vol. 14, no. 1 (A) *Fast Track Land Reform in Zimbabwe.*

[25] This was part of Mugabe's strategy to present MDC as an agent of British imperialism thus making the conflict between MDC, land reform and ZANU-PF as an anti-colonial struggle rather than one over governance.

address the methods of force and violence used to drive white farmers and farm workers from their lands and homes. They issued more pronouncements about what should be done but with no authority to follow through.

As of June 2005 there are approximately 600 white-owned farms left and most of these are not in full operation. The scale of uptake, the number of highly placed individuals who have more than one farm, the production levels of different farms are not known at this time. There are many stories told by different actors of what has happened to production levels, livestock herds, farm workers, and how ultimately the former owners were forced off their farms. The best account of one farm is to be found in Catherine Buckle's (2001) moving memoir of the year 2000.

The problems with fast track were well known but ignored by President Mugabe. The rapid decrease in agricultural production, the unemployment of farm workers, the decline in irrigation, the loss of seed production, the loss of industrial production related to irrigation, etc. were commented upon by many analysts. However these were blamed upon drought or the growing economic and political boycotts of Zimbabwe. Independent if not sympathetic outside observers like the United Nations Development Programme documented fast track's shortcomings while supporting land reform. The Parliamentary Portfolio Committee on Lands, Agriculture, Water Development, Rural Resources and Resettlement presented a Report to Parliament in June 2003 (Government of Zimbabwe 2003) that documents many of the less political problems also described in the Utete Report. There were and continue to be significant violations of multiple human rights due in part to fast track but integrally linked to the political challenge of the opposition party, the Movement for Democratic Change.[26]

While there are multiple difficulties from the lack of water to the lack of agricultural inputs, we want to focus on the process for how farms were selected to be acquired by government. Farms selected for acquisition were identified by a new organisation and not accountable to any specific Ministry. This new entity was called the District Land Identification Committee (DLIC)[27] chaired by the District Administrator, a political appointee, some, but not all of the Rural District Councillors (all from the ruling party), war veterans, army, police and traditional leadership. The work of the DLIC was partly supervised by the Provincial Land Identification Committee. This new committee was chaired by the Governor, appointed by the President, district administrators, war veterans, police, Central Intelligence Organization (the secret police) and the ruling party. It was also tasked with appraising applications from those seeking to obtain A2 farms. Lastly, there was the National Land Committee whose functions included overseeing the gazetting (formal listing) identified by lower levels for acquisition and resettlement. Senior politicians did not respect the independence of these institutions resulting in farms being taken intact by many or given to senior military and police officials, and there was bias in selection of farmers. There was no formal representation by women, by farm workers, by members of the

[26] These have been documented by the Human Rights Watch, International Crisis Group, Amnesty International, The Human Rights Committee of the African Union, the Zimbabwe Human Rights NGO Forum, Genocide Watch, Zimbabwe Lawyers' Association, and in the book by the outstanding journalist Andrew Meldrum (2004) who was forcibly expelled from Zimbabwe.

[27] There are 57 Administrative Districts in Zimbabwe but not all have commercial farm land in them.

opposition party or by technical experts. The war veterans were unaccountable to any but themselves.[28] Apart from the economic difficulties produced by fast track, it is clear that it was designed and implemented to guarantee political criteria in the selection of beneficiaries. This marked a decisive and political change in comparison to practices and policies prior to 1997 (Sachikonye 2004).

The Government of Zimbabwe has insisted first that the land issue should not be dealt with by the courts and second, that the seizure of land was according to law. In this chapter we unravel some of the identity issues underlying the government's contradictory position. We do, however, refer to some of the human rights conventions and treaties signed by the Government of Zimbabwe which belie the governments' efforts to claim that they were acting legally.[29]

Gender, Identity, Citizenship & the State in Fast Track

A new discourse and practice has emerged under fast track which asserts that land belongs only to the indigenous people of Zimbabwe. Fast track thus provides a window into understanding how Zimbabwean state and citizenship are being changed by the ruling party. The process of designation and redistribution of land illustrates the exclusion of a wide range of Zimbabweans to the full rights (formal and informal) of citizenship. We suggest that there are links between how the state regards women, whites, farm workers, and black members of the 'opposition'. Out of fast track emerge new paradigms of inclusion and exclusion not only in relation to land but also in relation to citizenship. We begin by examining the strong continuities between past gender policies and the present ones in fast track.

Implications for women

Empirical evidence has demonstrated that women do much of the work in communal areas and they have not been able to gain land rights on an equal basis with men. Maintaining that women always have had access to land without necessarily owning, controlling or benefiting from it, organisations like the Women and Land Lobby Group have called for incorporation of the non-discrimination principle embedded in Convention for the Elimination of all forms of Discrimination Against Women (CEDAW) and the Protocol to the African Charter on the Rights of Women in laws and policies concerning land reform (Women and Land Lobby Group 2001).

As a means of putting women's rights under the CEDAW and the Protocol into practice, the Zimbabwean government is obliged to ensure women's right to participate in the structures set up to allocate and manage land. Article 14 of CEDAW places an obligation on states 'to take measures ensuring that women ... participate in the elaboration and implementation of development planning at all levels'. In fast track, as in land allocation in general, there are no clear government policies with respect to having women represent themselves in decisions regarding land. Empirical work to date demonstrates that whether land is

[28] Amanda Hammar (2003) provides the most systematic effort to examine how war veterans have affected local government.

[29] For an elaboration of this argument see Hellum and Derman 2004.

allocated through customary or state structures, women's organisations and women's representation are not formalised, nor are there any institutions to represent them.

In practice, who undertakes the selection and resolves disputes concerning land is all-important whether the land is in resettlement areas or in communal lands.[30] In fluid and violent land-grabbing situations, as under fast track, women are particularly vulnerable. Research has shown that resettlement officers in the 1980s and 90s often allowed women to stay on the land in the event of the death of a husband or divorce (WLSA 1994, Jacobs 2000, Kinsey, pers. comm.). In communal areas, where traditional authorities have greater influence on land allocation, registration practices have been based on patriarchal customary practices (ZWRCN 1998). Upon death and divorce, women in communal areas have more frequently been denied access to land with reference to customary law than have women in resettlement areas. There is reason to believe that the removal of the resettlement officers and the strengthening of customary authorities in adjudication of family disputes and land allocation that has taken place through fast track mean a setback for women. Chiefs regard themselves, despite some variation, as guardians of customary values and patriarchal law.

In three villages in Mhondoro Communal Land where we have studied water and land reform over the last three years, almost all the recently widowed wives have had to leave their homesteads. The most recent case was a widow who had to leave because the Assistant Headman, who already had a homestead, wanted her property as well. With an increasing number of headmen and chiefs being connected to the party, the disappearance of an independent judiciary and with a police force working with war vets and party militia, women's bargaining power is considerably reduced in comparison to the 1980s. In fast track, war veterans have maintained their positions of political and social dominance in the newly resettled areas. They have a record of violence and sexual abuse against white women, farm worker women, and men and women belonging to the political opposition.

To insure greater equality between men and women, the Women and Land Lobby Group entered into dialogue with the government about the fast track programme, claiming that 30 per cent of the land to be distributed should be allocated to women and be registered in their own names, regardless of marital status. The only available figures for the number of women who actually received resettlement land is in the Presidential Land Review Committee report, more generally known by the name of its Chairperson, Charles Utete. The information collected by them suggests that the number of women allocated land under fast track was very low country wide. Women-headed households who benefited under Model A1 constituted approximately only 18 per cent while women beneficiaries under Model A2 constituted only 12 per cent (Volume I: 40). It is most likely that these beneficiaries are connected to the ruling party or to government.

To obtain secure tenure for women there has been a long-standing call for joint registration of title and joint permits in resettlement schemes by

[30] The recommendations made by Shivji, Gunby, Moyo & Ncube (1998) in their *National Land Policy Framework Paper*, which the authors hoped would serve as a model for the next phase of land reform, suggest that 40 per cent of the membership of an elected village council be women. In their model of villages they would be more self-governing under Village Assemblies. These Assemblies would be made up of all adults in a village. They would vote for a Village Council. These recommendations have not been accepted by government.

organisations like the Women and Law in Southern Africa Research Trust (WLSA), the Women's Action Group (WAG) and now the Women and Land Lobby Group.[31] The Women and Land Lobby Group has also lobbied for joint registration in resettlement areas. They have called for repeal of Section 23 of the Constitution that places customary law before principles of gender equality in family and inheritance matters. This section has been used to prevent legal change enabling women to obtain equal property rights with their husbands during marriage and in the event of divorce and death. One barrier rests in that property is held jointly but the husband, by virtue of his matrimonial power, is the one who disposes of assets, including, most importantly, land, on behalf of the family. This practice has been interpreted by different institutions in such a way as to deny married women access to credit and to lead to highly unequal divisions of landed property in the event of divorce or the husband's death.

Abolishment of Section 23 in the Constitution and joint registration of marital property was the demand faced by Vice-President Joseph Msika when meeting women stakeholders present at the Women's Lobby Group meeting in Harare in August 2000. In response, he argued that ZANU-PF was pro-woman, but that it always had to take black Zimbabwean culture into account in its land policies. Although the Deeds Registry Act allows joint registration of property, Msika stated that such a practice would not be pursued by the fast track programme because it undermined customary values. Fast track leaves in place the old division whereby married women, unlike those widowed and divorced, are not full citizens. While widows, divorced and single mothers can be given resettlement land in their own right, married women cannot. Moreover, even when married women are given land, it will become subject to the husband's control due to the customary notion of matrimonial power protected by Section 23 in the Constitution. This continues to be the case in 2006.

Widows and divorced women eligible for fast track lack the resources they would need to build new lives as comfortable as those they were forced to leave. Access to resettlement land under these circumstances means a denial of rights to the land they had worked. What they need is to retain land rights where they are and not to have to search for new ones in the former commercial farms. Without schools and clinics, children of both new settlers and former farm workers have been put at increased disadvantage and risk.

The government through its fast track programme thus sides with those men who assert the right to retain the deeply patriarchical elements of Shona customs and customary law. This static notion is a departure from the way in which many people, through their customs and practices, have adjusted to changing social, economic and legal conditions and have moved towards greater equality between men and women. Empirical research referred to above has, for example, shown that widowed and divorced women in the 1980s and 1990s were often allowed to stay on the land in the event of death and divorce by resettlement officers. The fast track programme is also a departure from the government's own Draft Constitution of 1999 which suggested that Article 23 of the Lancaster House Constitution, giving customary law privilege when it comes to the equality principle, be abolished.

The findings from the Utete Commission that examined the implementation of

[31] The first statements were in response to the failure by the Commission of Inquiry into Appropriate Agricultural Land Tenure of 1994 to address women's rights.

fast track make clear that its policy towards women, who play a key role in agriculture as farmers, leave a lot to be desired. The Commission concludes that land leases should be registered in the names of the husband and wife. It also suggests that a quota of at least 40 per cent of the land allocations should be made to women and that a quota of 40 per cent funding reserved by the Government of Zimbabwe for women for credit and other purposes should be made available. In cases of widowhood the commission suggests that widows should have first option to take over the lease provided they can work the land (p.163). These recommendations are in consonance with both the CEDAW and the Protocol to the African Charter on Human and People's Rights on the Rights of Women in Africa. However, no explanation was provided as to why this did not occur or any mechanism suggested ensuring that it will. As of August 2006 no attempt has been made to implement the conclusions of the Utete Report with respect to women.

Making the point that women's human rights stretch beyond equal access to land under the fast track programme, the Women's Lobby Group for Land also argued that adequate health services, schools, water sources, credit schemes and agricultural extension services must be put in place by the government to ensure women's, children's and families' right to livelihoods. The view that the fast track programme falls short of the minimum standards provided by the International Covenant on Social, Economic and Cultural Rights is clearly formulated in a communiqué on the implications of the fast track resettlement programme.[32] This communiqué states:

> Civil Society was also concerned that the current approach to land reform would threaten food security at household and national level as well as the country's international obligations which will have an adverse effect on the country's gross domestic product and the inflow of the much needed foreign currency.

and

> Government should make provision of input supply, farmers' training and basic infrastructure should be a priority as the programme might lose one of its objectives which is poverty alleviation.

In its examination of the implementation of fast track, the Utete Report emphasizes women farmers' need for greater opportunities in terms of access to inputs and labour-saving technologies, land ownership, information and extension services and education (p.146). This recommendation resonates with the Protocol to the African Charter that in Article 19c on the Right to Sustainable Development requires States Parties to 'promote women's access to credit, training, skills development and extension services at rural and urban levels in order to provide women with a higher quality of life and reduce the level of poverty among women'.

In the Utete Report, women appear as a homogeneous group while within fast track, it is important to have in mind that women are not just discriminated against 'as women'. Women, like men, are not a homogeneous category; they belong to different classes, ethnic groups, races, political parties and professions. The fast track programme, as pointed out in the section above, has ended employment for large numbers of women farm workers, both full time and

[32] This document was written by the Women and Land Lobby Group and other unnamed organisations known collectively as 'Civil Society'.

seasonal. The programme proceeded with virtually no attention paid to who is already working on a given farm: the number of women, the number of children, where they will be moved to or how alternative employment will be found for them. Internal displacement has, according to the Norwegian Refugee Council's report of July 2003, negatively affected female-headed households that do not have resources to get resettled and are not attractive as labour for the new commercial farmers. This calls for special attention to regularise this group of women's access to land in consonance with the right to livelihood. It also draws attention to procedures that will ensure that working conditions on the 'new' commercial farms are in consonance with International Labour Organisation standards and the Protocol to the African Charter.

Farm workers

Farm workers, whether male or female, have been driven off the farms without any consideration of their formal citizenship. The commercial farms of Zimbabwe are often portrayed as empty spaces. This is not accurate since the farms are filled with farm workers and their families. Typically they live on the farms with their families. It is difficult to establish the numbers of farm workers rendered homeless or jobless because of resettlement. According to the Utete Report and the Farm Community Trust of Zimbabwe (Magaramombe 2003), approximately one per cent of resettled people were farm workers.[33] From the inception of the land occupations, the government demonstrated, at best, complete indifference to what was happening to farm workers. Sachikonye (2003) carried out one of the few field-based surveys of farm workers in early 2003. He estimated that the number of farm workers varied between 300,000 and 350,000 or between 20 and 24 per cent of the national workforce up until fast track. This farm work force supported a population of approximately two million. At best, a third of the original work force was still employed but farm occupations and appropriations are continuing. He found for those who lost work a situation of ever-increasing poverty and often displacement.

The fast track programme largely ignores farm workers' rights to livelihood in terms of 'adequate food, clothing and housing' embedded in Article 11 of the International Covenant on Economic, Social and Economic Rights. No consideration has been given to the government's obligation to 'take appropriate steps to safeguard the right to work' of the farm workers who lose their jobs (in terms of Article 6 of the International Covenant on Economic, Social and Economic Rights). Most of farm workers' civil and political liberties have been lost. Because they are assumed to be non-Zimbabwean, migrant labourers, who were not fully supportive of ZANU-PF in both the referendum and Parliamentary election, they have been targeted for political violence. A great number have been forced from their employment and homes without any provision made to assist them or to find them places in resettlement schemes. The leading role played by war veterans increases the continuing threat of violence toward these same workers, especially if they disobey orders to leave the farms.

Farm workers' vulnerability to malnutrition, illness and insecurity is

[33] Chambati and Moyo ('The Impact of the Fast Track on Former Farm Workers in Utete' Report 2003: 136–54) estimated that percentage to be higher based upon extrapolating their results from Chikomba District. Without doubt there is significant local variation in the numbers of farm workers included in the resettlement schemes (Utete Report, Vol. II: 145).

dramatically intensified. As full-time farm workers lose their jobs due to fast track resettlement, no provision has been made for their children to continue schooling, to receive medical care or food while their parents search for new lodging. This neglect is in clear violation of Article 27.3 of the Child Rights Convention obliging states to take appropriate measures to assist parents in ensuring the well-being of their children and in 'the case of need provide material assistance and support programmes, particularly with regard to nutrition, clothing and housing'.

We have been surprised at the lack of concern for the farm workers. In discussing farm workers' issues with many Zimbabweans, we find that the consideration of farm workers is dismissed for several reasons: (1) the issue is only now being raised by farm owners to prevent land resettlement; (2) it is argued that farm workers can join the queue for resettlement just like everyone else; and (3) they are not real Zimbabweans. In the words of former Minister Eddison Zvogbo at a 2001 conference in Copenhagen, they have 'a farm worker culture' and thus they are not indigenous.[34] The farm workers, according to Zvogbo, are not really integrating into genuine Zimbabwean culture. Former Minister Zvogbo, like many others, wants to freeze the farm workers in time and place without considering generation, education and gender. They are apparently viewed as non-indigenous no matter what their citizenship (Rutherford 2001a). They are not seen to be among those whose property rights or land are to be restored because their identity as farm workers displaces all others. By virtue of marriage to a male farm worker whose family does not originate in Zimbabwe, a Zimbabwean woman may in practice lose her citizenship.

What is happening in the domain of citizenship and land illustrates the narrowing of boundaries and eligibility, with the state making the final determination as to who may be a citizen and who may own land. Constitutional Amendment No. 14 was a turning point in blocking both male and female spouses of Zimbabwean citizens from obtaining citizenship through marriage. It mandates that the Immigration Department shall determine whether any individual spouse can or cannot become a citizen. It replaced the right of Zimbabwean men to pass on citizenship to their foreign wives with a gender-neutral provision whereby neither men nor women can pass on citizenship. Under the present constitution, both male and female alien spouses can obtain citizenship only through the discretion of the Immigration Department.

The new citizenship law further undermines who is and who is not a citizen of Zimbabwe. The law requires that those with potential dual nationality renounce their other citizenship according to the laws, not of Zimbabwe, but of the other country from which they could claim citizenship. The law makes no distinction between those who sought dual citizenship or actively maintained it and those who merely possess it by entitlement from another country. Citizenship had to be renounced by January 2002 or else would be lost automatically. Once lost, restoration of citizenship demands Z$25,000 and a wait of some one-and-a-half years. Without citizenship, hundreds of thousands of people can be forced out of the country, denied land and denied voting rights. The law is also a further attack against farm workers, although it was initially understood as forcing white Zimbabweans to choose between Britain and Zimbabwe. The law can be read as

[34] 'Rethinking Land, State and Citizenship through the Zimbabwe Crisis', Research Conference and Seminar in Copenhagen in September 2001 hosted by the Centre for Development Research (CDR).

an effort to reduce the potential number of voters against the President and to reduce the number of claimants for redistributed land. It also continues the long-term trend of enhancing executive power.

New loyalties & the 'Third Chimurenga'

In this chapter we have argued against viewing Zimbabwe's crises as rooted in land but rather in the political domain. We have pointed toward the use of current land reform by the ruling party and President to hold power against those that they have defined as their enemies. If fast track had been about land then the process would not have ignored the long lists of people seeking resettlement on land held by local leaders – chiefs and rural district council heads. Resources to assist new farmers in access to land, capital and good advice sufficient for most of them to become successful farmers would have been made available.[35] The pace and scale of fast track meant that it was carried out with minimal government assistance and with a maximum amount of political interference. The consensus of virtually all observers, inside and outside Zimbabwe has been that the massive taking of all white commercial farm land from February 2000 to June 2003 has intensified Zimbabwe's economic crisis and led to increasing hunger and impoverishment.

Given the negative consequences of fast track we ask what might have been ZANU-PF's objectives for which it was worth destabilising if not wrecking large parts of Zimbabwe's economy? Six important objectives were accomplished: 1) The removal of voters from the farms – farm owners and farm workers; 2) The removal of the farm owners as financial backers of Movement for Democratic Change; 3) The renewal of an ideology promising a return to socialism and the restoration of land to its rightful owners; and 4) The use of the appropriated wealth and property that could be given to party followers at a huge cost to MDC supporters who would not receive land designated for resettlement; 5) The reinvigoration of ZANU-PF itself after it lost the constitutional referendum of February 2000, and 6) The creation of a new cadre of 'revolutionary followers'.

In a major event, President Mugabe pronounced on Heroes Day in August 2002 that those who were involved in the seizure of white-owned farm land and in the re-election of ZANU-PF candidates to parliament are, in his words, 'the new war veterans...' (quoted by Hammar 2003: 129) This then solves two issues

[35] In June 2003 the FAO and World Food Program commented on Southern Africa: 'As a whole, the region has produced enough food to meet more than two-thirds of its food requirements, with the general food security situation improving regionally helped by the increased production in Zambia and Malawi. Production, however, has been uneven, with Zimbabwe producing barely enough to meet 40 percent of its needs.

Acute food shortages in Zimbabwe

Zimbabwe faces acute food shortages with some 5.5 million people in need of food aid. Food production in Zimbabwe has fallen by more than 50%, measured against a five-year average, due mostly to the current social, economic and political situation and the effects of drought. The situation was compounded by the marked reduction of the large-scale farm sector, which produced only about one-tenth of their 1990s output. As a result, about half of the regional food deficit of some 2.65 million tonnes is in Zimbabwe.

The shortfall means that Zimbabwe will need to import almost 1.3 million tonnes of food, either commercially or through food aid, to meet the minimum food needs of its people.' *http://www.fao.org/english/newsroom/news/2003/19403-en.html*

– the death of many real war veterans and the fact that many war veterans disagreed with the land invasion strategy. Those war veterans who did not support the land invasions did not receive land and many of them have lost their benefits from the government. And, as Hammar observes, it continues the support for violence against those who oppose the Third Chimurenga.

In the new Zimbabwe, post-referendum, the emphasis on loyalty and subjugation cuts across race, class, gender and ethnic dimensions. Allegiance to the ruler becomes central in understanding why and how members of the MDC are excluded from receiving land under fast track and how if they own commercial farms they will have their farms expropriated. Member of MDC are no longer part of 'the people' by virtue of their opposition to the ruler and their liaison with 'whites'.

Fast track, while surrounded by revolutionary rhetoric, masks patrimonial practice where belonging is defined not by patrilineal blood ties but by allegiance to the ruler.[36] These processes may be understood as the emergence of a new form of patrimonialism. There is a narrowing of political power in the hands of a small number of men who are deciding: who has the right to protection by the state legal machinery and who does not; who has a right to benefit from land reform land and who does not; who has the right to defend themselves when their property, life or freedom of expression is threatened and abused and who does not, and indeed, who has the right to life and who does not.[37] There is a shift from citizen to subject to use Mahmood Mamdani's term. And as ZANU-PF controls much of the countryside but very little of the cities, it has recreated zones where the state has been subordinated to the party. Thus when foreign-based food assistance arrives it comes from the party, not from donors and certainly not from the government. The modern state in Mamdani's framework is not reachable by most rural citizens of Zimbabwe. It is in Zimbabwe once again 'a despotic power that governed peasant subjects' (Mamdani 1996: 136).

Fast track is indeed a political process but not a process of giving land to the poor, landless and deprived masses in the way the Government argues. The process is about the recentralisation of power and resources. The ruler and his followers claim to speak for 'the people' or more appropriately 'his people' and those not following are viewed as 'alien'. The ruler rewards his followers with land and punishes those who don't by taking their land – black and white. The restoration of land becomes a 'male' issue since it is only men who can be genuinely landless and only men who own land and pass it on to their heirs. It becomes a mobilising device overwhelmingly for male citizens.

Table 8.2 below summarises the radical change in landholding in Zimbabwe with the ending of the large-scale commercial farms and their transference to either A1 or A2 resettlement models. The tenurial status remains undetermined as of writing this paper (July 2006). For the moment the government owns all land resettled through Fast Track as either A1 or A2 (as it does communal areas, national parks, resettlement areas and state farms). Whether government will continue as the land owner remains uncertain. It certainly represents radical

[36] A major spokesperson and Minister of Information is Jonathan Moyo, an Ndebele not a Shona. Ibbo Mamdaza, part of the so-called technocratic ZANU-PF is not Shona. Accounts attempting to tribalise the current government are off the mark in our view.

[37] For details on threats and actions against farm workers and farm owners see Holtzclaw 2004; Commercial Farmers' Union Situation Reports from 2000—2003 [no longer available on line].

Table 8.2 Changing Land Tenure in Zimbabwe 1980–2002

Land category	1980 (million hectares)	1997 (million hectares)	2002 (million hectares)
Large-scale commercial farms (white-owned)	15.5	12.1 1	(this is uncertain, it could be 0)
Large-scale commercial farms. A2 model. No comprehensive list has been made public of numbers & size of farms	0	0	2.0
Communal areas	16.4	16.4	16.4
Small-scale commercial farming areas	1.4	1.4	1.4
Resettlement areas – in terms of governance. Have become like communal areas	0	3.6	11
State farms – Agriculture & Rural Development Authority	0.3	0.8	0.6

departures from the past with uncertain directions and implications for land tenurial systems for the future.

Law & the New Zimbabwe

Recent legal developments are a far cry from the developments of the 1980s and mid-1990s. Due to the centralisation of executive power and the dominance of ZANU-PF in Parliament, the judiciary bore the major brunt of defending human rights. The Zimbabwean state ratified a wide range of human rights instruments, which, even if not incorporated into law by the government, were mainly adhered to through the judiciary.[38] The judiciary did not shrink from its confrontations with the executive on matters of law and constitutionality. On a number of occasions the Supreme Court struck down discriminatory customary laws

[38] Zimbabwe has signed the Universal Declaration of Human Rights of 1948, the International Covenant on Economic, Social and Cultural Rights of 1966, the International Covenant on Civil and Political Rights of 1966, the African Charter on Human and Peoples' Rights, the International Convention on the Elimination of All Forms of Racial Discrimination of 1966, the African Charter on the Rights and Welfare of the Child of 1990, the Convention on the Rights of the Child of 1988 and the Convention on the Elimination of All Forms of Discrimination Against Women of 1979.

originating from the colonial era as well as government's abuse of citizen's civil rights (Gubbay 1997, Ncube 2001). Women's right to access land on an equal basis with men was enhanced through a series of cases striking down discriminatory provisions in marriage and inheritance law (WLSA 1994, Hellum 2000). A similar development took place at the level of the lower courts, in administration of resettlement programmes and in family practice. The WLSA research on widows' inheritance rights demonstrated how customary norms were changing in this broader national and social environment. At the constitutional and legislative level, the Supreme Court exercised a strong legal presence by striking down provisions of national laws that came into conflict with international law. At the level of legal science, feminist scholarship creatively merged and mixed international, national and local norms, which in its turn gave rise to legal reforms where international and customary understandings were merged.[39] The boundaries between international, national and local identities, values and norms became blurred, as did, the African versus Western divide.[40]

The terrain of law, land and citizenship has dramatically shifted since March 2000. The recent developments in relation to land, citizenship and how to deal with a widely supported opposition party set the current government's policy in an opposite direction to where it appeared to be heading To attempt a preliminary analysis of this new process we suggest linking our understanding of transnational law, legal pluralism, land and citizenship to theories of racial and ethnic violence and globalisation.

While the terms ethnic and racial are used, we wish to insist that neither are fixed, unchangeable or unchallengeable categories. Who is in and out of these major categories has shifted over time and depends upon context. It is usually in the interest of those in power to insist that these are primordial categories and cannot be changed. This is what Hutu extremists have done in Rwanda (Mamdani 2001) and this is how ZANU-PF ideologues characterise 'whites'. It has become the practice in many contemporary nation-states to use state violence against those ethnically, culturally or racially stigmatised. In the case of Zimbabwe, those identities are both separated and merged. Sometimes it is 'white farmers', sometimes it is farm workers, other times it is the British, or members of the opposition party. ZANU-PF extremists including the President have attempted to portray white Zimbabweans as non-Africans and members of the opposition as not really African. In short, they are preparing the way for ethnic cleansing or politicide, or both. While Appadurai has linked his theory of violence to a 'growing sense of radical social uncertainty about people, situations, events, norms, and even cosmologies' (2002: 286), he does not directly address the organised violence of police, thugs and paid militias unless it involves those who are social intimates (p. 287). In the case of Zimbabwe, it does involve both. Indeed, it is one of the puzzles of contemporary Zimbabwe to ask what are the origins and causes of contemporary violence? How much comes from deep political and economic conflicts and how much is orchestrated and planned by the ruling party? It is probably too early to reach definitive conclusions but let us just look briefly at the role violence has played in Zimbabwe.

[39] These developments took place in the context of growing presidential power through constitutional amendments and the dominance of one party in the political system.

[40] It does not follow that this process is either acknowledged or described by many Zimbabwean lawyers and scholars.

The creation of Southern Rhodesia (as most colonies and empires) was based upon the use of force and the imposition of political control first through a private company and then through colonial authorities – both always identified with 'whiteness'. The war for national independence which lasted throughout the 1970s and 1980s was fought between white and black on one side, and black on the other. More recent discussions have commented on the widespread use of violence often directed against a 'caught' civilian population and the use of para-militaries (Kriger 1992, Bhebe and Ranger 1995: 22–3, Alexander, McGregor and Ranger 2000). Aside from the struggle for national independence, the Zimbabwean state prior to fast track only used substantial force and violence to end a minor revolt in Matabeleland from 1982 to 1987. While the nature and size of the threat posed by a dissident group in Matabeleland is subject to dispute, the brutal nature of suppression is not. The Zimbabwean National Army systematically used techniques of torture and terror against civilian populations. A favourite, for example, was to shoot people in their toilets so that filth would rejoin filth, or use bazookas to kill families in their huts to scatter body parts as a warning.[41]

The army was overwhelmingly Shona, the area overwhelmingly Ndebele. Certainly there were clear and powerful elements of ethnic dislike even if both categories – Shona and Ndebele – were products of colonial rule. Did the use of violence mark a growing uncertainty over national and regional identities in a rapidly changing world or was it the effort of a new national-state to demonstrate its power or some kind of mixture? We suspect that it was a complicated mixture including the real threat from apartheid South Africa in support of a secession movement in this part of Zimbabwe. Much of the violence and practices associated with the war against the Rhodesians were deployed against civilians.[42]

Between 1988 and March 2000 the state refrained from employing much violence and never on the scale of Matabeleland from 1982–1987. The threat, however, always remained. We have already documented how the political terrain shifted in February 2000 with the decisive defeat in what was a non-binding referendum. It did lead, however, to a radical shift in discourse and practice. Many questions arise. Was the Zimbabwean state weakened or just the ruling party? Were the institutions and ministries of government really weak or were they weakened deliberately by ZANU-PF in order to bypass the norms and procedures that the state was, under law, required to follow? Can we link the possibility of multiple identities weakening commonly held norms, cosmologies and events, or was it the narrow political base and profound corruption within ZANU-PF that led to the threat and then the use of violence? Having come to power through force of arms, having stayed in power through the threat of force and violence, was ZANU-PF reacting in a defensive way toward globalisation, economic deregulation and democratisation? What alternatives were available to

[41] The most brutal part of the army though was the Fifth Brigade. They entered the Lupane and Nkayi areas of Matabeleland in 1983. Alexander, McGregor and Ranger (2000: 217) write:

> The Fifth Brigade's exercise of violence was concentrated within a relatively short period – just under a year – and was perceived as unique. The Fifth Brigade overtly justified its violence in political and tribal terms. It not only systematically attacked ZAPU and other community leaders but it also attacked civilians at large, civil servants and even other ZNA units and the police.

[42] The Catholic Commission for Justice and Peace in Zimbabwe (1997) after a thorough investigation estimates that over 3,000 civilians were killed by either the police or army, over 8,000 were detained and at least 7,000 tortured.

ZANU-PF? In any event, and no matter what alternatives might have been available, ZANU-PF chose land and race as their response to the multiple threats and alternative possibilities to their continued rule and domination of Zimbabwe.[43] Like the Hutu extremists in Rwanda they sought to portray themselves as potential victims of a broad plot to restore, in this instance, the Rhodesians backed by Great Britain, colonial rule. Thus, on the one hand they are the victims of a vast conspiracy against them led by formidable enemies and on the other, they are aggressors, defending their revolution and attacking all enemies. The party insisted on the myth, that it and it alone was responsible for Zimbabwean independence and that it, and it alone, knows the wishes, feelings and aspirations of the Zimbabwean people.[44] The corollary of this is that anyone who opposed ZANU-PF policies and ideology is seen as 'an enemy of the people'. In this manner, ZANU-PF has attempted to destroy the credibility and legitimacy of the opposition by eliminating any ambiguity about who they are. For example Jonathan Moyo the former Minister of Information in responding to a report that the opposition party continued to question the legitimacy of the President's election stated:

> The time has come for the British media mouthpieces and puppets that are being used by the Rhodesian Selous Scouts[45] running the MDC to get it in their thick heads that President Mugabe's legitimacy as Head of State is not subject to any negotiation. (*The Herald,* 18 June 2003)

President Mugabe never refers to Morgan Tsvangirai by his real name. He always says Morgan Tsvangirson to emphasize that he is just a front for the British. ZANU-PF strategy has to continuously claim that the opposition party is basically white and colonialist, acting in the interests of the British and whites. ZANU-PF does not even address the question of whether or not there is evidence that anyone wants to recolonise Zimbabwe except to assert that MDC represents such interests.

What characterises Zimbabwe is the ruling ZANU-PF party's combined use of law, land and biopolitics to attempt to redraw the boundaries between the new category of 'indigenous people of Zimbabwe' and their betrayers, the white colonialists and their followers – farm workers, the MDC and members of a self-defined Civil Society. Women, who would be otherwise considered indigenous, are viewed as non-indigenous if they cross boundaries and marry farm workers and those in the opposition.

Conclusions

There would be no Zimbabwean crisis if it were not for the growing opposition of workers and farm workers' unions, women's rights organisations, human

[43] They also used Parliament to pass a new series of repressive laws including 1) The Public Order and Security Act (POSA) which requires notifying the police of political meetings, with police having the right to reject proposed meetings or to shut them down at any point, and 2) The a control of media through the Access to Information and Protection of Privacy Amendment Bill (AIPPA) which gives the Minister of Information the right to control the media. The titles of both bills are Orwellian – attempting to mask their true purpose of silencing all dissent and criticism of the ruling party.

[44] This perspective has been developed by Raftopoulos (2004) and Ranger (2004). We wrote this section before having seen either work.

[45] The Selous Scouts were a white-led but mainly black force used by the Rhodesians in the war against ZANU and ZAPU.

rights organisations, church organisations, youth organisations, the National Constitutional Assembly and the MDC.[46] This broad resistance movement is, as we see it, an expression of a struggle for life, dignity and justice under a corrupt, repressive and totalitarian political regime. The way in which these movements frame their quest for democracy, accountability, transparency and rule of law as necessary for a just distribution of basic resources such as land and food can not be reduced to externally imposed principles fashioned to fit western donors, the IMF and the World Bank. These principles have, under the violent and unjust Mugabe rule; become more than abstract human rights talk. They have become a site of African resistance to African misrule.

It is within this central statist, neo-nationalist and neo-patriarchal legal framework that the ZANU-PF government positions itself as restoring the land to what it defines as its rightful indigenous owners. Yet, the political opposition and civil society have resisted. International human rights values embedded in the Constitution such as freedom of speech, free elections, freedom from torture and protection of property (both private and common, like community-owned wildlife) has been at the core of this resistance.

Our analyses point to an essentialising of categories of race, nationality and ethnicity and arguably gender. This essentialisation is a key ideological component in maintaining ZANU-PF's control of the state to determine who can gain access to crucial resources such as land and water. When faced with a large opposition party such as the MDC and a host of civil society organisations uniformly demanding democracy and good governance based on international human rights principles Mugabe and his supporters claim that the opposition are acting on behalf of foreign powers. The government's legal rhetoric emphasises the difference between African and western interests, norms and values. The government's justification of a whole series of laws that undermine its opponent's right to life, integrity, property, livelihood as well as citizenship rights are cast in an anti-racial, anti-globalisation and anti-imperialist language suggesting that the Zimbabwean nation is under attack. In short, Mugabe has wrapped himself in a nationalist blanket and asserts that he can determine who is, and who is not a true Zimbabwean national:

> And how do you work with an opposition which is not itself? An opposition which really is kind of an agency for a country outside or a nation outside. They must be themselves, they must be Zimbabweans in spirit. Zimbabweans not just in terms of their colour or origin but in terms of their thinking. (*The Herald*, 24 April 2003, interview)

As Chanock has observed 'It is internal conflict about ways of doing things far more than any conflict with outsiders that has led to the essentializing of cultures' (2002: 45) to which we add that the creation and naming of an external enemy can be of equal importance in creating internal categories of indigeneity.

The appropriation of commercial farmland by the state and transferring it to different types of resettlement schemes does not fit with local understandings of

[46] Neither should we underestimate the ways in which international law, most often through the lenses of national constitutions, is used as a basis for contestation. This is, for example, the case with movements such as the National Constitutional Assembly, the multiple court actions taken by MDC to contest the rigged elections, or the court cases individual farmers supported by Justice for Agriculture have filed to contest a process that neither is fair, transparent nor due. In understanding the dynamics of law's mobility across local, national, regional and international borders attention should be paid to the two-way flow and the power relations that underlie the flow dynamics.

land and land tenure. The essentialised notion that the President and his party can decide who is and who is not entitled to land and who is and who is not a 'real Zimbabwean' has in many instances been contested not just by the MDC but by local villagers making claims with reference to ancestral links to the land government has given to its followers. The idea that land is redistributed to those in power or to the kin of those in power does not sit well intensified as it is by the profound economic crises. The continued violence and repression have spread, rather than limited, the appeals of human rights discourses. While justifying its claims and actions through manipulations of law the government is also making itself subject to the counter-hegemonic rights discourses of its contesters, at international and national levels. It is possible that Zimbabwe can spiral into uncontrolled youth violence fuelled by the arms, training and empowerment given to the ZANU-PF youth militias. We think it more likely that human rights discourses and organisations will succeed in restoring a new and different Zimbabwe.

References

Alexander, J., J. McGregor, T. Ranger. 2000. *Violence and Memory: One Hundred Years in the 'Dark Forests' of Matabeleland.* Oxford: James Currey and Portsmouth, NH: Heinemann.

Appadurai, A. 2002. 'Dead Certainty: Ethnic Violence in the Era of Globalization.' In A. Hinton (ed.) *Genocide: an Anthropological Reader* Malden, MA and Oxford: Blackwell.

Bhebe, N. and T. Ranger (eds) 1995. *Society in Zimbabwe's Liberation War, Volume I.* Harare: University of Zimbabwe Press and Oxford: James Currey.

Buckle, C. 2001. *African Tears: The Zimbabwe Land Invasions.* Weltevredenpark: Covos Day Books.

Catholic Commission for Justice and Peace in Zimbabwe and the Legal Resources Foundation. 1997. *Breaking the Silence, Building True Peace: A Report on the Disturbances in Matabeleland and the Midlands 1980 to 1988.* Harare: Catholic Commission for Justice and Peace in Zimbabwe and the Legal Resources Foundation.

Chan, S. 2002. *Robert Mugabe: A Life of Power and Violence.* London and New York: Tauris.

Chanock, M. 2002. 'Human Rights and Cultural Branding: Who Speaks and How.' In Naim, A. A. (ed.) *Cultural Transformation and Human Rights in Africa.* London: Zed Books.

Derman, B. 1997. 'Nature, Development and Culture in the Zambezi Valley.' In Barbara Rose Johnston (ed.) *Life and Death Matters.* Lanham, MD: Altamira Press.

Derman, B. and A. Hellum. 2002. 'Neither Tragedy nor Enclosure: Are There Inherent Human Rights in Water Management in Zimbabwe's Communal Lands?' *The European Journal of Development Research* Vol. 14 (2): 31–50.

Drinkwater, M. 1991. *State and Agrarian Change in Zimbabwe's Communal Areas.* Basingstoke/London: Macmillan.

Government of Zimbabwe. 1999. *What the People Said. A Report of National Commission of Inquiry into the Establishment of a New Democratic Constitution.* Volumes I–III. Harare: Constitutional Commission of Zimbabwe.

______. 2003. Parliamentary Portfolio Committee on Land and Water. Harare: Government of Zimbabwe.

Gubbay, A. R. 1997. 'The Protection and Enforcement of Fundamental Human Rights: The Zimbabwean Experience.' *Human Rights Quarterly* Vol. 19, No. 2: 227–54.

Hammar, A. 2003. 'The Making and Unma(s)king of Local Government in Zimbabwe.' In A. Hammar, B. Raftopoulos and S. Jensen (eds) *Zimbabwe's Unfinished Business: Rethinking Land, State and Nation in the Context of Crisis.* Harare: Weaver Press, pp. 119–54.

Hammar, A. B. Raftopoulos and S. Jensen (eds). 2003. *Zimbabwe's Unfinished Business: Rethinking Land, State and Nation in the Context of Crisis.* Harare: Weaver Press.

Hellum, A. 2000. 'How to Improve the Doctrinal Analysis of Legal Pluralism: A Comparison of the Legal Doctrine About Custom and Local Law in Zimbabwe and Norway.' *Retfærd* 89: 40–62.

Hellum, A. and B. Derman. 2004a. 'Land Reform and Human Rights in Contemporary Zimbabwe: Balancing Individual and Social Justice through an Integrated Human Rights Framework.' *World*

Development 32(10): 1785–805.

______. 2004b. 'Re-negotiating Water and Land Rights in Zimbabwe: Some Reflections on Legal Pluralism, Identity and Power.' In K. King and A. Griffiths (eds) *Remaking Law in Africa: Transnationalism, Persons and Rights*. Edinburgh: The African Studies Center, University of Edinburgh.

Holtzclaw, H. 2004. *The Third Chimurenga? State Terror and State Organized Violence in Zimbabwe's Commercial Farming Communities*. PhD. thesis. Michigan State University.

Human Rights Watch, Africa Division. 2002. *Fast Track Land Reform in Zimbabwe*. New York.

Jacobs, S. 2000. 'The Effects of Land Reform on Gender Relations in Zimbabwe.' In T.A.S. Bowyer-Bower and C. Stoneman (eds) *Land Reform in Zimbabwe: Constraints and Prospects*. Ashgate: Aldershot.

Kinsey, B. 1999. 'Land Reform, Growth and Equity: Emerging Evidence from Zimbabwe's Resettlement Programme.' *Journal of Southern African Studies* 25 (2): 173–96.

______. 2004. 'Zimbabwe's Land Reform Program: Underinvestment in Post-Conflict Transition.' *World Development* 32 (10): 1669-96.

Kriger, N. 1992. *Zimbabwe's Guerrilla War: Peasants' Voices*. Cambridge: Cambridge University Press.

Kagoro, B. 2004. 'Constitutional Reform as Social Movement: A Critical Narrative of the Constitution-Making Debate in Zimbabwe, 1997–2000.' In B. Raftopoulos and T. Savage (eds) *Zimbabwe: Injustice and Political Reconciliation*. Cape Town: Institute for Justice and Reconciliation.

Lan, D. 1985. *Guns and Rain: Guerillas and Spirit Mediums in Zimbabwe*. Los Angeles and Berkeley, CA: University of California Press; Oxford: James Currey.

Magaramombe, G. 2003. 'Farmworkers: The Missing Class in Zimbabwe's Fast Track Resettlement.' In M. Roth and F. Gonese (eds) *Delivering Land and Securing Livelihood: Post-Independence Land Reform and Resettlement in Zimbabwe*. Harare and Madison, MI: Centre for Applied Social Sciences, University of Zimbabwe and Land Tenure Center, University of Wisconsin.

Mamdani, M. 1996. *Citizen and Subject: Contemporary Africa and the Legacy of Late Colonialism*. Princeton: Princeton University Press; London: James Currey.

______. 2001. *When Victims Become Killers: Colonialism, Nativism the Genocide in Rwanda*. Princeton: Princeton University Press; Oxford: James Currey.

Martin, D. and Johnson P. 1981. *The Struggle for Zimbabwe: The Chimurenga War*. New York: Monthly Review Press.

Meldrum, A. 2004. *Where We Have Hope: A Memoir of Zimbabwe*. London: John Murray.

Meredith, M. 2002. *Robert Mugabe: Power, Plunder and Tyranny in Zimbabwe*. Johannesburg: Jonathan Ball.

Moyo, S. 1995. *The Land Question in Zimbabwe*. Harare: SAPES Books.

Ncube, W. 1987. 'Underprivilege and Inequality: The Matrimonial Property Rights of Women in Zimbabwe.' In A. Armstrong and W. Ncube (eds) *Women and Law in Southern Africa*. Harare: Zimbabwe Publishing House.

______. 2001. 'The Courts of Law in Rhodesia and Zimbabwe: Guardians of Civilisation, Human Rights and Justice or Purveyors of Repression, Injustice and Oppression?' In Ngwabi Bhebe and Terence Ranger (eds) *The Historical Dimension of Democracy and Human Rights in Zimbabwe*. Harare: University of Zimbabwe Press.

Raftopoulos, B. 2003. 'The State in Crisis: Authoritarian Nationalism, Selective Citizenship and Distortions of Democracy in Zimbabwe.' In Amanda Hammar, Brian Raftopoulos and Stig Jensen (eds) *Zimbabwe's Unfinished Business: Rethinking Land, State and Nation in the Context of Crisis*. Harare: Weaver Press pp. 243–62.

______. 2004. Nation, Race and History in Zimbabwean Politics in B. Raftopoulos and T. Savage (eds) *Zimbabwe: Injustice and Political Reconciliation*. Cape Town: Institute for Justice and Reconciliation.

Ranger, T. 1985. *Peasant Consciousness and Guerilla War in Zimbabwe: A Compartive Study*. Los Angeles and Berkeley, CA: University of California Press; Oxford: James Currey.

______. 2004. 'Historiography, Patriotic History, and the History of the Nation: The Struggle over the Past in Zimbabwe.' *Journal of Southern African Studies* 30 (2): 215–34.

Rutherford, B. 2001. *Working on the Margins: Black Workers, White Farmers in Postcolony Zimbabwe*. London and New York: Zed Books.

Sachikonye, L. 2003. *The Situation of Commercial Farm Workers after Land Reform in Zimbabwe*. Report prepared for the Farm Community Trust of Zimbabwe. Harare: Farm Community Trust.

______. 2004. 'The Promised Land: From Expropriation to Reconciliation and *Jambanja*.' In B. Raftopoulos and T. Savage (eds) *Zimbabwe: Injustice and Political Reconciliation*. Cape Town: Institute for Justice and Reconciliation.

Shivji, I., D. Gunby, S. Moyo and W. Ncube. 1998. *National Land Policy Framework Paper*. Harare:

Government of Zimbabwe, Ministry of Lands and Agriculture.

Skogly, Sigrun I. 2000. 'From Human Capital to Human Rights: The Human Rights Obligations of the World Bank.' Doctoral thesis, Faculty of Law, University of Oslo.

Spierenburg, M. 2003. *Strangers, Spirits and Land-Reforms: Conflicts about Land in Dande, Northern Zimbabwe.* PhD thesis: Amsterdam School for the Social Sciences.

Utete, C. 2003. *Report of the Presidential Land Review Committee (2 Volumes).* Harare: Government of Zimbabwe.

Women and Land Lobby Group. 2001. The Impact of Section 23(3) of the Constitution on Women, Land and Property Rights, Analysis of Gender Gaps in the Land Reform and The Importance of Urban Agriculture. Workshop held in Harare, February 2001. Mimeo.

Women and Law in Southern Africa. n.d. *Women and Land Rights in Resettlement Areas in Zimbabwe.* Harare. (approximately 1994)

______. 2000. *Women and Land in the WLSA Countries* (e.g. Botswana, Lesotho, Swaziland, Zimbabwe, Malawi, Zambia and Mozambique) Harare: WLSA.

WLSA Zimbabwe. 1997. *Paradigms of Exclusion. Women's Access to Resources in Zimbabwe.* Harare: WLSA Trust

______. 1994. *Inheritance in Zimbabwe.* Harare: WLSA Trust.

Zimbabwe Women Resource Centre and Network (ZWRCN).1998. *Beyond Inequalities: Women in Zimbabwe.* Harare: ZWRCN/SARDC.

9

The Authority & Violence of a Hunters' Association in Burkina Faso
'Each Bird is Sitting in its Own Tree'

STEN HAGBERG

Introduction

In this chapter I address how authority and violence are experienced, exercised and legitimised in the context of the traditional hunters' association Benkadi in Western Burkina Faso. Since its creation in the mid-1990s, Benkadi has become a main actor in local politics, notably because the association recruits adult men of many rural villages to ensure protection against banditry; the hunting of game has given way to the hunting of thieves. However, Benkadi is not officially recognised by the Burkinabe state. The main reasons are, first, that it challenges the state's monopoly of legitimate violence, and, second, that the association is largely seen as a supra-ethnic armed movement of mainly farmers more or less associated with Senufo peoples fighting against Fulbe agro-pastoralists. No official state representative has been ready to take the responsibility to issue the 'birth certificate' (Hagberg 2004a) to an association that may develop into a militia and, at worst, engender civil war.[1]

Leaders of Benkadi stress that hunters are protecting society's marginalised and victimised, sometimes leading them to take the law into their own hands. Yet while Benkadi is composed of young men, who carry out the actual hunting of thieves, the master-hunters (*donsokuntigi*) insist that they control the potentially destructive force of male youth and turn it to society's advantage. The discourse on marginalisation and victimisation serves to legitimise the hunters' association in general and the master-hunters' capacity to contain the youth's force. That is why notions of authority and violence are central to the legitimising process of hunters' current practice. First, the association Benkadi bases its legitimacy on the glorious past of hunters, but it also needs state recognition to be legitimate as a civil defence force in present-day Burkina. Second,

[1] Since 1988, fieldwork has been carried out in Western Burkina for a total of five and a half years. The research on hunters and their association Benkadi was particularly in focus in 1996, 1999 and 2001 onwards. In addition to all informants – hunters and others – I am particularly grateful to the late Ernest Yao for the ongoing conversation about hunters and Karaboro society more generally over the years, a conversation that was painfully ended by his untimely death in March 2003. Earlier drafts of the paper have received valuable comments from many colleagues, including Mirjam De Bruijn, Christian Lund, Rie Odgaard, Han Van Dijk, and two anonymous referees.

master-hunters have a locally legitimate authority over young hunters, but often they do not seem to control the violence that these hunters use. Third, the celebrated unity of Benkadi is constantly challenged because different master-hunters seek to impose their respective authority. Fourth, hunters justify the violence inflicted on Fulbe agro-pastoralists by referring to recurrent crop damage caused by Fulbe cattle and, more generally, to what they perceive as Fulbe arrogance.

I will first review the cultural and political contexts within which the hunters' association need to be located. In particular, I will look at how networks of hunters' brotherhoods have become instrumental in present-day political struggles. In the next section I will dwell upon how to conceptualise authority and power in the context of the hunters' association and argue that the very tension between authority and power is a critical locus of investigation. In the subsequent section I will demonstrate how authority and violence have become contested issues that shape Benkadi in two specific ways. Externally, notions of authority and violence are shaping Benkadi's ambiguous relationship with the Burkinabe state. Internally, master-hunters hold that they maintain authority and control the violence of the young hunters. In the concluding discussion I will reflect upon how notions of authority and violence express hunters' experiences of marginality and victimisation, on the one hand, and of power and rights, on the other. While hunters put an emphasis on unity and discipline, each master-hunter is struggling to have his authority respected because 'each bird is sitting in its own tree'.

The cultural & political contexts of Benkadi

The emergence of hunters' associations in Mali, Côte d'Ivoire, Guinea-Conakry and Burkina Faso can be understood in relation to the context of culture and that of politics. The cultural context is that of the historical tradition of hunters, including the ideals and epics, and the claims of present-day hunters to be carriers of that tradition. Hunters' brotherhoods are well known in West Africa. As kings, initiates and powerful magicians and diviners, hunters dominated from the tenth century onwards the regions of the Mali Empire that emerged in the thirteenth century (Thoyer 1995:11). Hunters have played a central role in wars and political resistance, and the hunters' brotherhood is a political and military organisation that excludes any notion of tribe, class and caste and which is founded on a common cult of all its members (Cissé 1964:176). To become a hunter, each apprentice has to be accepted and initiated into the common cult. The apprentice is assigned to a master-hunter, who will teach him the secrets of hunting and all that surrounds it. The relationship between the master-hunter and the apprentice lasts for life, and it takes the form of a father-son relationship, but the initiation itself is said to last seven years.

The term 'hunter' (*donso, donzo* or *dozo* in Dyula/Bamana) in this chapter does not merely describe someone who practises hunting but is also associated to cosmology, behaviour and identity. Hunters are not only specialised in hunting game, but in other activities as well. Certain hunters are very skilled in herbal medicine and divination. Hunters are feared for their spiritual strength because they are generally seen as sorcerers. So, hunters are simultaneously feared and admired. They wear hats and clothes made of *bogolan* (yellow-brown mud-dyed cloth painted in black geometric patterns). They have amulets and are equipped with a fly-whisper (*ku*) and a whisk (*filén*). Some hunters are renowned for possessing 'medicine' (*fura*) against bullets; others are renowned for mastering techniques of invisibility. There is an important bulk of research oriented towards epics, myths and hunters' ideals, focusing on the cosmology of hunters and the meanings of their initiation (cf. Cissé 1964, 1994, Cashion 1984, Thoyer 1995, 1997, Traoré 2000, Hellweg 2001).

Power and knowledge are important to *donsoya* ('the affair of hunting'). Hunters are compared according to what extent they possess 'knowledge', often vaguely expressed, 'He knows [a lot of] things' (*a bi feenw lon*). Knowing here includes especially secret knowledge and sorcery, allowing the hunter to avoid dangers, notably the vital force (*nyama*) of the game. The hunter, therefore, has to behave morally well and to live a healthy life. Hunters are circumscribed by sexual taboos to preserve the purity and combat the vital force of the animals that they have killed.[2] In other words, the individual responsibility of the hunter is stressed by various moral and magical prescriptions that, taken together, demonstrate the ambiguity of the hunter. While the hunter is exposed to the dangers of the bush, belonging to the bush he is himself a challenge to the established social order.

The second context within which to understand hunters is that of politics and the emergence of the hunters' associations. There are hunters' associations in Mali, Côte d'Ivoire and Burkina Faso (Hagberg 1998, 2004a, 2004b, Bassett and Zuéli 2000, Hellweg 2001, Bassett 2003, 2004, Traoré 2004), whose main objective is to fight against banditry in the countryside; farmers cum hunters organise themselves to protect their village. In Sierra Leone, Guinea and Liberia hunters have engaged in military and political conflicts (Richards 1996, Muana 1997, Peters and Richards 1998, Leach 2000, 2004, Ferme and Hoffman 2002, 2004). The egalitarian ideals of hunters are part of the legitimising process that makes the association and its leaders significant political actors. Yet in hunters' associations, emphasis is put on the collective endeavour in contrast to to the individual responsibility of the hunter. Although the courage, strength and morality of the sole hunter continue to be celebrated virtues, the collective political project is now moved to the fore. Politicians seek support from renowned traditional hunters, who often demonstrate their arts at public events, such as political rallies and the launching of a development project (Jonckers 1987, Sanou 1995, Ouédraogo 1996, Hagberg 1998).

It is my contention that the hunters of Benkadi need to be simultaneously understood within these two contexts, that is, the cultural context of the sole hunter and the political context of hunters' associations. A cultural analysis of hunters' ideals is necessary for understanding current political and military usage of *donsoya*. Political conflict is deeply experienced through, and legitimised by, tradition. However, the strong mobilising force of hunters cannot solely be explained by such a political project. The associations simultaneously respond to daily experienced local needs. Threatened by banditry, rural people seek to resist by using the cultural resources at hand.

[2] Youssouf Tata Cissé describes how, for Malinké hunters, the most important means to combat the *nyama* (vital force) of the animal is 'purity' (*sanuya*, which also signifies 'state of gold'). Purity is the central notion: in the sentiments, thoughts, relations, gestures, acts, etc., towards one's likes, and in sexual life. Such 'purities' preserved and even granted the human being the force of *fanka* or *barika* (Cissé 1994: 88).

The hunters' association Benkadi in Western Burkina was created on the initiative of Tiéfing Coulibaly, a well-known hunter in Dakoro in present-day Léraba Province, in the mid-1990s. It was a response to security problems on the countryside. Tiéfing's idea of creating the association came from Côte d'Ivoire, where hunters have been fighting against banditry since the 1980s (Bassett 1988, 1994, 2003, 2004, Diallo 1996, Bassett and Zuéli 2000, Hellweg 2001, 2004). The written constitution of Benkadi was indeed taken from a brother organisation there and slightly adapted to the Burkinabe context (Hagberg 1998: 227–9). The creation of Benkadi was motivated by the fact that there were 'too many thieves' and 'too many losses' in rural areas. Thieves could 'take it all' before the police and the gendarmerie were informed. Therefore, Benkadi included rural men regardless of whether they were traditional hunters or not. Initiation was drastically simplified and shortened, from a seven-years' initiation to a 'modernised initiation' of one day! The growing number of new hunters has also been criticised internally. Some traditional hunters complain that these new hunters 'cannot even shoot a rabbit'. Yet a leader of Benkadi explained how he saw the difference between hunters of game and hunters of thieves:

> The hunter of game and the hunter of thieves, they are not the same thing. The hunter of thieves is stronger because the hunter of game has to hide in a tree or behind a tree. But if it is a thief it is face-to-face.

Hunters of Benkadi clearly state that most thieves are Fulbe herders that steal cattle with which they cross the Ivoirian border to sell them. Therefore, Fulbe are not welcome to join Benkadi, and it is to a large extent seen as an anti-Fulbe organisation. Male local farmers are members of Benkadi, whereas groups of 'strangers', notably Fulbe and Mossi, are not. While the rationale for taking things in their own hands is easy to understand, the process of exclusion of certain categories of people, notably 'strangers' such as Mossi and Fulbe populations, sharpens conflict. In other words, Benkadi is organising local farmers in villages to comprise a civil defence force in a context of state disengagement with few police officers and gendarmes patrolling in the rural area.

However, Benkadi is still not recognised by the state and its different leaders lament this lack of official status. The graziers' trade union repeatedly stress that the hunters' association has no legal existence (cf. SEOB 2001). The president-founder, Tiéfing Coulibaly, died in January 2002 at the age of 70, and although the new president cum master-hunter had not yet been nominated, Benkadi is likely to remain a central actor in local politics.[3]

Authority & power

Hunters of Benkadi say that there is one single organisation that works in different districts, provinces and even countries. While hunters of Léraba Province work together with hunters of the Comoé Province, since 1996 they have been divided by new provincial boundaries, due to a new territorial division, reshuffling the country's 30 provinces into 45 (Hagberg 2004b). They have

[3] Although Benkadi has never been given state recognition, in Comoé Province, in late 2003, Benkadi was replaced by Faso Donso, and this association was rapidly recognised by provincial authorites.

deposited the demand for official, legal recognition according to provinces, but they still consider there to be only one Benkadi. In 1999, Tiéfing Coulibaly stated that Benkadi is united but that the hunters work in small groups: 'Now there is a division into new provinces, but there is no division in the association.' I asked him to clarify whether there is one association named Benkadi or several ones. Tiéfing Coulibaly replied:

> It is the same association. We simply work in small groups. It is the same thing for hunters (*donsow*) in Mali, who are presently here to get explanations, learn and then return to Mali [he pointed at a group of hunters sitting next to us]. All of them who live in the region are my hunters-apprentices. It is the same association.

Tiéfing Coulibaly is recognised locally to be the one who united hunters all over the region. He created the association on the basis of dual membership. It is an association moulded out of the legacy of French organisational culture, but it also unites hunters through a common cult. While the membership fee to Benkadi is 1,000 FCFA (approx. US$2), one also has to be initiated into the cult (Hagberg 1998, see also Ouédraogo 1996). As such Benkadi is a case of different normative orders simultaneously at work. Tiéfing Coulibaly's exercise of power drew on different sources of legitimacy and, particularly, on the combination of these sources in specific situations. Although I have previously analysed power struggles related to farmer-herder conflicts (Hagberg 1998, 2001a), the actual exercise of power is not really the focus of this chapter. Instead I am interested in how, in the case of Benkadi, authority is constructed and the extent to which locally legitimate authority can incite, direct and control violence, particularly that practised by young male farmers.

In political anthropology the issue of coercive power has been a central theme for a long time, especially in accounts of politics in so-called stateless societies (cf. Fortes and Evans-Pritchard 1940, Horton 1985, Gledhill 1994). How is power exercised and by whom? What violence is legitimate and what is not in a society without a centralised power? What poles of power exist and how are they interacting? Postcolonial studies have furthermore assessed the colonial impact on authority and power in African societies. Anthropological descriptions have often come to challenge the Weberian typology that distinguished three forms of authority. First is the traditional authority that is based on the legitimacy of a set of fixed and sacred norms. Second is the rational-legal authority, which is impersonal and resides in the office, not in the person. Third is the charismatic authority, which depends on the characteristics of an individual leader (cf. Morrison 1995). One anthropological objection to this typology is that it emphasises ideal-types more than practices. Another objection is that authority in so-called stateless societies has not so much to do with a fixed set of norms but emerges out of a process of social interaction and dialogue (Seymour-Smith 1986:19; see also Gledhill 1994).

In the introduction to a 1999 volume on the anthropology of power, Angela Cheater highlights the fact that there has been a shift away from the Weberian distinction between power as the ability to elicit compliance against resistance and authority as the right to expect compliance. 'This shift owes much to Michel Foucault and postmodernism, and possibly reflects the ongoing loss of State authority to both sub-national and global organisations' (Cheater 1999: 2). Cheater notes that Foucault's distinction between central regulated and legitimate forms of power, and capillary power at the extremities, refracts somewhat differently the old distinction between a 'formal organisation', on the one hand, and 'informal relationships' underpinning its operation, on the other. In drawing upon examples from Ghana, Slovakia, South Africa and Lebanon, Peter Skalník maintains the distinction between authority and power, but he gives it other distinguishing features than Weber did. Skalník regards authority and power as fundamentally opposed principles, relating to mutually exclusive 'ideal types' of arrangements of public affairs. While he conceptualises power as closely identified with the state and its monopoly of organised violence, authority is legitimate without the backing of power and is voluntarily recognised by all people. 'While authority is gained by free public support and works by vote or consensus, power is a result of the use or threat of physical force and operates without specific recourse to the people's wishes' (Skalník 1999:164). Skalník nonetheless argues that in actual politics both authority and power are present, and what matters is 'the tension between them'.

To my mind, the distinction between authority and power is important, even though the close identification of power with the state is problematic, especially in postcolonial contexts where important domains of power reside, at least officially, outside the state realm. Moreover, the recognition of authority by 'all people' is, at best, exaggerated. At worst, it may lead to a homogeneous conception of society according to which 'all people' agree upon the basis of authority. At least in post-colonial contexts it is clear that 'all people' simply do not tend to agree on the basis of authority. Yet while it can be argued that authority must be related to its implementation – that is, the exercise of power – I find it important to scrutinise authority as the attribution of the right to control other people's actions or decisions in the context of the hunters' association. It is furthermore relevant to investigate notions of authority due to the fact that in Burkinabe French the term 'authorities' (*autorités*) in plural is used to label administrative representatives of the state as well as traditional leaders. Hence, 'authorities' is here an analytical as well as an empirical concept, but what matters, and here I follow the track of Skalník, is the tension between authority and power. This tension shapes, I argue, the political space in which Benkadi must be located. In the next section I will therefore describe different expressions of authority in the hunters' association Benkadi.

Contesting authorities, controlling violence

Benkadi was created in the mid-1990s as a response to security problems in the countryside. While the idea came from Côte d'Ivoire, it rapidly spread mainly because it addressed locally perceived problems. The mixing of organisational structures – a written constitution built upon the French legacy and the initiation into a common cult – made Benkadi particularly appealing for male farmers belonging to 'local ethnic groups'. To get a 'modernised initiation' and rapidly obtain knowledge and power further induced many farmers to join the association.

Benkadi came to organise people in villages across Comoé Province. It was especially in the context of violent conflicts between farmers and agro-pastoralists that the organisation developed (Hagberg 1998, 2001a). When Benkadi spread to the Sidéradougou district most people saw it as an organisation defending farmers' interests. Hunters asserted their presence in the public sphere as young hunters wore their hunting dress even when they went out to the marketplace. However, critics told me that Benkadi was an organisation that aimed to scare people, especially when the dress was worn in public and not merely for hunting. And despite the fact that officially Benkadi is open to all, neither Fulbe nor Mossi are members.[4]

Tiéfing Coulibaly based Benkadi's legitimacy on a combination of different sources of authority. First, the president of each district-section was to be a traditional hunter or master-hunter (*donsokuntigi*). While they are not necessarily those who do most of the work, they are emblematic figures that ritually and morally guide Benkadi's activities. Second, locally influential people were involved regardless of whether they were traditional hunters or not. These people were thought to do much of the practical work to mobilise support and organise meetings. Third, people with reading and writing skills in French were brought in to facilitate writing letters and protocols and to formulate demands to state services. Fourth, some politicians entered the association. They represented the necessary 'long arms' to reach into state administration, but local representatives of the state, notably the police officers, gendarmes and the *préfet* (i.e. head of *département*, 'district'), did not become members. While most leaders repeatedly stressed that Benkadi collaborates with the police and the gendarmerie, the association's challenge to the state's monopoly on legitimate violence posed problems for the involvement of local government officials.

The 'separatist' character and the violent actions of the association have meant that Benkadi has not yet been recognised by the state. While I have elsewhere amply demonstrated how Benkadi has become an anti-Fulbe association (Hagberg 1998, 2001a, 2004a), I will now turn to how the state has shaped the political space in which different master-hunters work today.

Initially, combining his traditional authority with skilful political play, Tiéfing Coulibaly travelled around in the region to get people mobilised. In every district he tried to get a traditional hunter as president, while in practice another dynamic person often took the lead. Two logics of authority are at work here. On the one hand, hunters remained under the authority of the master-hunter, who had initiated them. As the leader of the hunters' association Tiéfing Coulibaly was the supreme master-hunter, and he was respected for that too, but, on the other hand, hunters were organisationally under the authority of their respective local president. They may have generally respected Tiéfing Coulibaly, but it was their own master-hunters who led them. These two logics were in the beginning perfectly complementary and represented two different faces of the hunters' association. Benkadi seemed to unite local farmers across territorial, ethnic and linguistic boundaries. Yet these complementary logics of authority were soon contested.

The contest was mainly linked to the decentralisation policies and territorial reshuffling when Comoé Province was divided into two in 1996.[5] The western part of the province became the new Léraba Province, while the central and eastern parts remained Comoé Province. Tiéfing Coulibaly lived in Dakoro, a

[4] To my knowledge, the only exception is a Fulbe master-hunter in Koloko district in Kénédougou Province.

[5] For a more detailed analysis of political decentralisation and traditional leadership, see Hagberg (2004b).

district of the new Léraba Province, and his grip over the remaining Comoé Province diminished. Tiéfing Coulibaly remained the president of the hunters in Léraba Province, but in Comoé Province, Nianyoro Diao, a master-hunter in Tengrela village of Banfora district, became the new president at the constitutive assembly in Banfora in July 1996. This territorial reshuffling considerably restrained the political space of Tiéfing Coulibaly. He was still respected, but he could not really pretend to represent the hunters of former Comoé Province. In 1999 I asked a hunter leader in Comoé Province if Tiéfing Coulibaly was still visiting the area. He replied: 'In the past, we worked together, but today they have made their place apart. That is why we have nominated Nianyoro as our chief in the region of Banfora.'

In 1999, Nianyoro Diao himself told me, somewhat vaguely, that hunters helped each other, but that Tiéfing Coulibaly was no longer president of the hunters in Comoé Province: 'The power of Tiéfing is limited to Dakoro, Kankalaba and Sobara.' With these words, Nianyoro Diao contested that the authority of Tiéfing Coulibaly reached beyond the boundaries of the new Léraba Province. While the new provincial boundaries had negative effects for Tiéfing Coulibaly's authority, Tiéfing Coulibaly himself explained that these new boundaries did not change much. Nianyoro Diao also declared that this law was something good:

> It is good because of languages. We do not understand them. We the Karaboro, Gouin and other peoples here [in Comoé Province] we understand each other but not them. We are the same group due to *donsoya*, we are the children of the same person and come and go by the same door. [...] But the government has regrouped us. Now we are divided and it is not bad. We are too many.

Nianyoro Diao added that each ethnic group has its villages and rituals. The way the Karaboro hunters do their rituals is not necessarily similar to the ways the Mossi, the Dyula or the Fulbe hunters do theirs. Nianyoro Diao continued:

> If we accept them and say that these are the laws here and they do not follow them it is as if we make them join for nothing. [...] There are plenty of birds in the sky, but each bird is sitting in its own tree. That is why we are like this.

Nianyoro Diao claimed that hunters of Benkadi must be local people who are anchored in a specific village. Even though the sky is full of birds, each one should sit in its own tree. However, in addition to the law of new provincial boundaries – that is, the impact of the postcolonial state – the statement reveals the rivalry between master-hunters (*donsokuntigiw*). Each master-hunter struggles to make his authority respected. Nianyoro Diao told me for instance that he knew more of hunting and had killed more game than Tiéfing did. At public events hunters seek to show their arts and show their skilfulness, and in serious crises such as outbreaks of violence, the authority of the specific master-hunter is at stake.

Let us, therefore, move a step further and explore the tension between authority and the actual exercise of power. To what extent do master-hunters control violence practised by the male rural youth? The Burkinabe state's main reason for not recognising the association is that it challenges the state's monopoly of legitimate violence, but the authority of master-hunters is ambiguous. In the following I will analyse how some key leaders of Benkadi refer to outbreaks of violence in Comoé Province. The narration draws mainly on articles published in Burkinabe newspapers (*Journal du Jeudi* 2–8 August 2001: 3–4;

L'Événement 25 July 2001: 10–12; *Le Pays* 26 July 2001: 16), but in September 2001, I also interviewed some of the key actors in these violent events.

The violence is said to have started with a quarrel between a Fulbe herder and a Karaboro farmer in the village of Kankounadéni on 6 June 2001 when the farmer and his son encountered a Fulbe herder with a cattle-herd in their field. They asked the Fulbe herder to go away and the quarrel alerted other farmers around. When the Fulbe herder was about to leave a stone from a slingshot hit his head. The herder riposted with his firearm and shot at the son of the farmer. He was wounded on the cheek, but it was not a deadly wound. Now the group of farmers attacked the herder, hit him and bound him, but the field-owner stopped the others who were ready to 'finish with the Fulbe man' and told them to bring the herder to the village health-station. They also alerted the gendarmes in Banfora. In the afternoon two gendarmes arrived in Kankounadéni together with a then Member of Parliament and the *préfet* of the Tiéfora district. They transported the Fulbe herder back to Banfora. The son of the farmer cum field-owner was also brought to Banfora. Later, however, the wounded farmer was transferred to the hospital of Bobo-Dioulasso.

The same evening, farmers of Kankounadéni elaborated a plan for attacking the Fulbe camp. Emissaries were sent to mobilise people in neighbouring villages. On 7 June in the morning, somewhere between 200 and 700 hunters encircled the Fulbe camp and sent an emissary to ask a young Fulbe (let us call him 'Siaka') to walk out from the camp. However, 'Siaka' refused to come out, and when the hunters' emissary was back from the Fulbe camp the attack began. In the following events six Fulbe men were killed, including a man of 76 years and a young boy of 11. Other Fulbe found refuge at the blacksmiths' (*numuw*) homestead some four kilometres away, the blacksmiths being Fulbe's joking partners (*senankunw*). The gendarmerie in Banfora was informed and sent two agents to the village. These two gendarmes succeeded in convincing the hunters to cease fire. The hunters then attacked domestic animals of the Fulbe: cattle, sheep and guinea fowls. The granaries were emptied and the houses looted. Later, four other gendarmes came to reinforce the first two and stayed there until eight o'clock in the evening. On the following morning, a group of Fulbe, escorted by four gendarmes, buried four of the victims; the two other corpses were found several days later in a state of advanced decomposition.

According to different sources, during the following weeks the hunters continued to try to chase away the Fulbe definitively and, indeed, many left the region. Yet the administrative head of Comoé Province, the High-Commissioner (*Haut-Commissaire*), intervened to calm the situation. The Minister of Security Djibril Bassolé also effectuated a mission in the region.

When I interviewed the leading master-hunter of the area in September 2001, he denied any responsibility for the violent events in Kankounadéni:

> I heard there was a quarrel between graziers and farmers. They asked me to mediate and I did so to stop the quarrel. I do not know the cause of the quarrel. People told me that a Fulbe shot with a firearm on a farmer when he was in his field. But I did not witness this and cannot tell you why it happened. The authorities [state representatives] came to inform me and I went to stop the quarrel. I told them that it was Satan that took the people.

This master-hunter sought to show that this was really the result of Satan and that no one could stop violence breaking out, but when I asked him to expand on this, he said, 'That a grazier with a firearm goes out with his cattle herd and finds a person in his field and shoots at him, if that is not the effect of Satan he should have gone to the bush and let his cattle graze there.' The interesting point is not whether or not this master-hunter was present when the Fulbe were attacked, even though it is likely that he was involved in the attack on 7 June 2001. What interests me is how he justifies the violent actions of those mainly young hunters that he is supposed to control. It is a fact that violence broke out and that he was unable (or unwilling) to prevent killings:

> Master-hunter (B.S.): The hunters' association was not created for shooting at people. It is because of the conflict that the hunters stood up to organise that people should be defended against looting. That is the role of the hunters. The conflict is a problem between farmers and herders. Was it the hunters who stood up to provoke the quarrel?
>
> Sten Hagberg (S.H.): OK. But one cannot ignore that the action of the hunters favoured the farmers?
>
> B.S.: The hunters, aren't they farmers? Can you make a difference between a hunter and a farmer? In this case they acted as farmers.
>
> S.H.: What impact did these events then have on the hunters' association?
>
> B.S.: The hunters are the same people as the farmers. They have the *daba* [hoe] and the firearm as working instruments. They are not only members of the association. They do not only work as hunters.
>
> S.H.: Have you held any meetings with the hunters since the conflict?
>
> B.S.: We held a meeting where we said that no one should start quarrelling. This has been done and the authorities should not come here and find us quarrelling. But if, however, a quarrel would start, you would find out that the instigator would neither be a farmer nor a hunter. The graziers cause the conflicts.

The ways in which the master-hunter denies the responsibility of farmers cum hunters are striking. According to him, it is really a problem of graziers, and they are responsible for the violence. This version is not really contested by many politicians and intellectuals of the region. One reason is that, contrary to the Fulbe, the hunters carry weight in the ballot box. Another is the resurgence of a discourse on autochthony in Banfora, simultaneously expressing sentiments of belonging. People of Banfora are contrasted with strangers and, in particular, the strangerhood of the Fulbe becomes a boundary of exclusion (Hagberg 2000). However, the master-hunter's attempt to locate the responsibility for the violence on the Fulbe themselves contrasts to the description of the events not only by the Fulbe and the trade union for graziers (*Syndicat des Eleveurs de l'Ouest du Burkina*) but also by the newspapers and other outsiders. The graziers' trade union talked about the outbreaks of violence as aiming at ethnic extermination. In a letter on 16 June 2001 to the Minister of Security the trade union holds that the hunters' attack is beyond traditional farmer-herder disputes. Instead it has escalated into an ethnic conflict or even an operation effectuated against one ethnic group (SEOB 2001). It is, indeed, astonishing to witness how, according to the dominant version provided by the hunters, the Fulbe were responsible for the violence inflicted upon them and, ultimately, for their own death! The marginalisation of local farmers is here used to justify the killings.

As a consequence of these outbreaks of violence, two hunters cum farmers who participated in the killings were arrested in January 2002. It was the relatives of the Fulbe victims who had identified these two men. Yet some relatives of the arrested men in turn formulated a written ultimatum to the *préfet* of Tiéfora in March 2002. In the letter it was stated that their 'brothers' should be released by the latest on 8 March 2002 (*Le Pays* 20 March 2002: 20). According to the newspaper, the master-hunter of the area (B.S.) was to be received by the High-Commissioner in order to solve this new problem. Hence, the authority of B.S. is recognised, but it is also feared. He denies any responsibility for the killings and lootings, but he simultaneously accuses the Fulbe of arrogance and provocation. In outbreaks of violence, he has played on the tension between authority and power.

Discussion

So far, I have described the emergence of the hunters' association in Western Burkina and how hunters formed a civil defence movement in the form of the Benkadi association with tremendous spread and impact in the region. Local notions of authority and violence are central to the hunters' association because they articulate the tension between authority and power with respect to the knowledge of hunting skills, to the capacity to mobilise people and to the territorial reshuffling. The control over the violence of the male youth emerges as central in order to understand the multiple sources of authority in Benkadi. In this final section of the paper I will discuss how these notions of authority and violence express hunters' experiences of marginality and victimisation, on the one hand, and of power and rights, on the other. While the hunters put emphasis on unity and discipline, each master-hunter is struggling to make his authority respected because 'each bird is sitting in its own tree.'

Hunters represent themselves as victims who have taken action to fight against banditry and corruption. Instead of waiting for state representatives and other outsiders, the hunters are defending their rights. While all master-hunters hold that they bring the thieves to the police and the gendarmerie, hunters sometimes act without the consent of any state authority. Many rumours circulate that hunters kill thieves in the bush, sending them to an 'unknown destination'. Hunters say almost unanimously that the thieves tend to be Fulbe. This perceived connection between Fulbe and thieves legitimises violent actions against the Fulbe, even when they are not, strictly speaking, suspected of theft. Crop damage is regarded as a form of theft – the cattle belonging to the Fulbe are 'stealing' the food of farmers.

For the hunters, Fulbe cattle are causing crop damage and still the Fulbe behave arrogantly. Fulbe are also said to resort to violence in disputes. The hunters say they are merely defending themselves when using violence. In these politicised representations, the marginalised and poor farmers, relying on their own subsistence production are contrasted to the rich, cattle-owning Fulbe, who are said to bribe government officials. The hunters therefore claim their right to defend themselves. When I have asked people if crop damage can justify the killing of a person, many hunters say that Fulbe herders let the cattle graze the fields and without fields the farmers cannot live. Accordingly, it is the Fulbe who threaten the lives of farmers in the first place!

The farm fields are central to the identity of these Karaboro farmers. The fields are the material expression of a man's independence and ability to sustain himself by his own actions. This contrasts to traditional notions of poverty where poverty is closely linked to the lack of strength or force and of capacity to work. In the regional lingua franca Dyula the word for poverty is *fangntanya*. It originates from the word *fanga* ('force,' 'strength') or *fama* ('power,' 'government'), and *ntan* ('without'). The word *fangntanya* stands literally for the state of being without power; poor people are those who lack the force to sustain themselves (Hagberg 2001b). In line with this reasoning, farmers' violent reaction to crop damage is not proportional to the economic loss but crop damage is seen as an attack on the person himself and on his wealth. Apart from the physical violence inflicted upon Fulbe individuals, the hunters' slaughtering of cattle, being the prime wealth of the Fulbe, could be seen as a symbolic riposte to crop damage. The excessive meat consumption reported after lootings further emphasises this symbolism (cf. Ouédraogo 1997).

The tension between authority and power is evident in relation to the new provincial boundaries. While Tiéfing Coulibaly maintained a certain authority recognised by all hunters who had been initiated under his command, his authority over the hunters in present-day Comoé Province radically diminished when the new provincial boundaries were drawn. Rhetorically, the hunters are 'united' because there is one single Benkadi. In practice, however, there is a multitude of political factions and rivalry between different master-hunters. The traditional image of the sole hunter roving the woods is difficult to connect to the collective endeavour of the hunters' association, but Tiéfing Coulibaly succeeded in combining individualism and the collectivism. Local farmers were organised in a way that, at least to my knowledge, no development project had ever managed. However, when the new provincial boundaries were drawn, he found himself separated from the followers in Comoé Province. Tiéfing Coulibaly's power nonetheless remained in the new Léraba Province and he maintained an influence in Kénédougou Province. He was the president-founder of Benkadi and as such he was still an authority, although with less actual power than earlier. Although Tiéfing Coulibaly later became the president of the Federal Board of Traditional Hunters of Western Burkina, covering the Léraba, Comoé, Houet, Tuy and Kénédougou Provinces, his death in January 2002 redrew the map of power relations of Benkadi (Hagberg 2004b: 63–5).

The involvement of a master-hunter (B.S.) in the outbreaks of violence in Kankounadéni points towards another feature of the hunters' association. This master-hunter used his authority to justify violence inflicted upon Fulbe, arguing that they provoked the farmers cum hunters. The hunters then sought to solve the problem themselves. The master-hunter cautiously avoided addressing the issue of his own acts during the killings. He was away, he said, and did not even know what caused the conflict. Satan must have entered people, he continued, because otherwise he could not explain why the Fulbe acted the way they did.

Once again there is a tension between authority and power but this time with respect to young men. The potentially creative and/or destructive force of youth in Africa has been much debated in the 1990s (cf. Richards 1996, 2005; see also Finnström 2003, Utas 2003; Ferme and Hoffman 2004). With the increasing number of child soldiers in war-torn areas, societies' capacity to control the violence of young men – and also, but to a far lesser extent, young women – has come to the fore. In the hunters' association, the capacity of the leaders to control the violence of male rural youth is central. Yet while the master-hunters do not necessarily stop violence, they use violence to assert their own authority. Hence, they are using and directing the violence exercised by young hunters. The master-hunter may say he seeks to stop violence while in practice he incites the young hunters to use violence against Fulbe agro-pastoralists. Violence thereby becomes a means by which the authority of the master-hunter is backed by power. Although some master-hunters say that they 'strip' (*déshabiller*) young hunters who use violence by taking the law into their own hands, these cases merely seem to be exceptions.

To conclude this chapter on how authority and violence are experienced, exercised and legitimised in Benkadi in Western Burkina, I would like to argue that the justification of violence results from the combination of experiences of marginalisation and victimisation within a discourse of rights and self-defence. However, the tension between authority and power in Benkadi cannot be understood independently of the Burkinabe state. It is in the contexts of culture – hunters as carriers of a glorious 'autochthonous' tradition – and of politics – hunters as vigilantes taking up the challenge where the state has failed – that the tension of authority and power is articulated. The authority of a particular master-hunter is simultaneously the cause and the effect of his actual exercise of power. The master-hunter who accused the Fulbe of provoking violence had his authority increased among the disciples, while it decreased in the Burkinabe public space, but due to his authority among hunters, he was later called in to negotiate with the first representative of the Burkinabe state at the provincial level (the High-Commissioner). This, in turn, increased his authority among the hunters even more and, consequently, his power, and so the tension between authority and power continues to shape the political space in which the hunters' association claims its rights in the name of victimisation and marginalisation.

This leads to more general theoretical insights into the ways in which the tension between authority and power is mediated by violence. Instead of focusing on traditional authorities per se, such as 'the paramount chief', 'the master-hunter' or 'the earth priest', more attention should be paid to how authority is exercised and practised situationally. Skilful combinations of different bases of legitimacy emerge as particularly successful for exercising authority and legitimising violence in post-colonial contexts, but as I have shown in the case of hunters' association, the use of violence is double-edged. Violence may, on the one hand, express the power to back up authority, and therefore, in practice, challenge the state's monopoly on legitimate violence. However, violence may, on the other hand, purport the erosion of authority if used for what is considered as illegitimate purposes. The real or fictive control over the violence practised by young male farmers is key to understanding the dynamics of the master-hunters' authority. This theoretical insight has also a clear policy implication in that 'traditional institutions' such as hunters' brotherhoods are not merely remnants of the past, but are actively interacting in contemporary politics. The wave of decentralisation and the increased donor support to civil society organisations have in the 1990s opened up a political space for 'traditional institutions'. While some of these institutions may well become voluntary associations in line with western ideas of civil society, others may develop into militias, fuelling xenophobia and ethnic exclusion.

References

Bassett, T. J. 1988. 'The Political Ecology of Peasant-Herder Conflicts in the Northern Ivory Coast.' *Annals of the Association of American Geographers* 78: 453–72.

______. 1994. 'Hired Herders and Herd Management in Fulani Pastoralism (Northern Côte d'Ivoire).' *Cahiers d'Etudes Africaines* XXXIV (1–3), 133–5, 147–73.

______. 2003. 'Dangerous Pursuits: Hunter Associations (*donzo ton*) and National Politics in Côte d'Ivoire.' *Africa* 73 (1): 1–30.

______. 2004. 'Containing the Donzow: The Politics of Scale in Côte d'Ivoire.' *Africa Today* 50 (4), Summer 2004: 31–49.

Bassett, T. J. and K. B. Zuéli. 2000. 'Environmental Discourses and the Ivorian Savanna.' *Annals of the Association of American Geographers*, 90: 67–95.

Cashion, G.A. 1984. *Hunters of the Mande: A Behavioral Code and Worldview derived from the Study of Folklore.* PhD thesis. Indiana University.

Cheater, A. 1999. 'Power in the Postmodern Era'. In A. Cheater (ed.) *The Anthropology of Power: Empowerment, Disempowerment and Changing Structures.* London and New York: Routledge.

Cissé, Y. 1964. 'Notes sur les sociétés de chasseurs malinké.' *Journal de la Société des Africanistes* 19: 175–226.

Cissé, Y. T. 1994. *La confrérie des chasseurs Malinké et Bambara: Mythes, rites et récits initiatiques.* Ivry and Paris: Éditions Nouvelles du Sud and Association ARSAN.

Diallo, Y. 1996. 'Paysans sénoufo et pasteurs peul du nord de la Côte d'Ivoire: Les questions de l'accès à la terre et de l'ethnicité.' In T. Bierschenk, P.-Y. Le Meur, and M. von Oppen. (eds) *Institutions and Technologies for Rural Development in West Africa.* Weikersheim: Margraf Verlag.

Ferme, M. and D. Hoffman. 2002. 'Combattants irréguliers et discours international des droits de l'homme dans les guerres civiles africaines: Le cas des 'chasseurs' sierra-léonais.' *Politique africaine* 88, décembre 2002.

______. 2004. 'Hunter Militias and the International Human Rights Discourse in Sierra Leone and Beyond.' *Africa Today* 50 (4), Summer 2004: 73–95.

Finnström, S. 2003. *Living with Bad Surroundings: War and Existential Uncertainty in Acholiland, Northern Uganda.* Uppsala Studies in Cultural Anthropology 35. Uppsala: Acta Universitatis Upsaliensis.

Fortes, M. and E.E. Evans-Pritchard (eds). 1940. *African Political Systems.* London: Oxford University Press for the International African Institute.

Gledhill, J. 1994. *Power and Its Disguises: Anthropological Perspectives on Politics.* London & Boulder, CO: Pluto Press.

Hagberg, S. 1998. *Between Peace and Justice: Dispute Settlement Between Karaboro Agriculturalists and Fulbe Agro-pastoralists in Burkina Faso.* Uppsala Studies in Cultural Anthropology 25. Uppsala: Acta Universitatis Upsaliensis.

______. 2000. 'Strangers, Citizens, Friends: Fulbe Agro-pastoralists in Western Burkina Faso.' In S. Hagberg and A. B. Tengan (eds) *Bonds and Boundaries in Northern Ghana and Southern Burkina Faso* Uppsala Studies in Cultural Anthropology 30. Uppsala: Acta Universitatis Upsaliensis.

______. 2001a. 'À l'ombre du conflit violent: règlement et gestion des conflit entre agriculteurs karaboro et agro-pasteurs peul au Burkina Faso.' *Cahiers d'Etudes africaines* XLI (1), 161: 45–72.

______. 2001b. *Poverty in Burkina Faso: Representations and Realities.* Uppsala-Leuven Research in Cultural Anthropology 1. Uppsala: Department of Cultural Anthropology and Ethnology, Uppsala University.

______. 2004a. 'La chasse aux voleurs! Une association des chasseurs et l'administration de l'Etat dans l'Ouest du Burkina Faso.' In S. Latouche, P.-J. Laurent, O. Servais and M. Singleton (eds) *Les raisons de la ruse: une perspective anthropologique et psychoanalytique.* Révue du MAUSS. Paris: Editions de la Découverte.

______. 2004b. 'Political Decentralisation and Traditional Leadership in the Benkadi Hunters' Association in Western Burkina Faso.' *Africa Today* 50 (4), Summer 2004, 51–70.

Hellweg, J. R. 2001. *The Mande Hunters' Movement of Côte d'Ivoire: Ritual, Ethics, and Performance in the Transformation of Civil Society, 1990–1997.* PhD thesis. University of Virginia.

______. 2004. 'Encompassing the State: Sacrifice and Security in the Hunters' Movement of Côte d'Ivoire.' *Africa Today* 50(4), Summer 2004: 4-28.

Horton, R. 1985. 'Stateless Societies in the History of West Africa.' In J.F.A. Ajayi and M. Crowder (eds) *History of West Africa.* New York: Longman Inc.

Jonckers, D. 1987. *La société Minyanka du Mali: Traditions communautaires et développement cotonnier.* Paris: Éditions L'Harmattan.

Journal du Jeudi. Weekly newspaper, Ouagadougou.

L'Événement. Monthly newspaper, Ouagadougou.

Le Pays. Daily newspaper, Ouagadougou.

Leach, M. 2000. 'New Shapes to Shift: War, Parks and the Hunting Person in Modern West Africa.' *The Journal of the Royal Anthropological Institute* 6: 577–95.

Leach, M. 2004. 'Introduction to Special Issue: Security, Socioecology, Polity: Mande Hunters, Civil Society, and Nation-States in Contemporary West Africa.' *Africa Today* 50 (4), Summer 2004: viii–xvi.

Morrison, K. 1995. *Marx, Durkheim, Weber: Formations of Modern Social Thought.* London, Thousand Oaks & New Delhi: Sage Publications.

Muana, P. K. 1997. 'The Kamajoi Militia: Civil War, Internal Displacement and the Politics of Counter-Insurgency.' *Africa Development* 22: 77–100.

Ouédraogo, J.-B. 1997. *Violences et communautés en Afrique noire: La région Comoé entre règles de concurrence et logiques de destruction (Burkina Faso).* Paris and Montréal: L'Harmattan.

Ouédraogo, T. O. 1996. *Identification des maîtres chasseurs et leur zone d'influence dans la province de la Comoé.* Bobo-Dioulasso: École Nationale des Eaux et Forêts de Dinderesso, Ministère de l'Environnement et de l'Eau.

Peters, K. and P. Richards. 1998. '"Why We Fight": Voices of Youth Combatants in Sierra Leone.' *Africa* 68: 183-210.

Richards, P. 1996. *Fighting for the Rain Forest: War, Youth and Resources in Sierra Leone.* Oxford: James Currey and Portsmouth, NH: Heinemann in association with The International African Institute.

______. (ed.) 2005. *No Peace, No War: An Anthropology of Contemporary Armed Conflicts.* Oxford: James Currey and Athens, OH: University of Ohio Press.

Sanou, K. B. 1995. *Structuration-organisation des associations villageoises dans la protection de la faune dans la province de la Comoé. Rapport de stage* Bobo-Dioulasso: École Nationale des Eaux et Forêts de Dinderesso, Ministère de l'Environnement et du Tourisme.

SEOB. 2001. 'Situation des Eleveurs dans la province de la Comoé.' Letter to the Minister of Security on 16 June 2001. Banfora: Syndicat des Eleveurs de l'Ouest du Burkina.

Seymour-Smith, Charlotte 1986. *Macmillan Dictionary of Anthropology.* London and Basingstoke: Macmillan.

Skalník, P. 1999. 'Authority versus Power: A View from Social Anthropology.' In A. Cheater (ed.) *The Anthropology of Power: Empowerment and Disempowerment in Changing Structures.* London and New York: Routledge.

Thoyer, A. 1995. *Récits épiques des chasseurs bamanan du Mali.* Paris: L'Harmattan.

______. 1997. *Le riche et le pauvre et autres contes bamanan du Mali.* Paris and Montréal: L'Harmattan.

Traoré, K. 2000. *Le jeu et le sérieux: essai d'anthropologie littéraire sur la poésie épique des chasseurs du Mande (Afrique de l'Ouest).* Köln: Rüdiger Köppe Verlag.

______. 2004. 'The Intellectuals and the Hunters: Reflections on the Conference "La rencontre des chasseurs de l'Afrique de l'Ouest".' *Africa Today*, 50(4), Summer 2004: 97–111.

Utas, M. 2003. *Sweet Battlefields: Youth and the Liberian Civil War.* Uppsala University Dissertations in Cultural Anthropology 1. Uppsala: Uppsala University.

10

Contested Identities & Resource Conflicts in Morogoro Region, Tanzania[1]
Who is Indigenous?

FAUSTIN MAGANGA, RIE ODGAARD & ESPEN SJAASTAD

Introduction

On 8 December 2000, 30 people were killed at Rudewa-Mbuyuni village in Kilosa district, Morogoro, during clashes between cultivators and livestock keepers. A number of reasons were put forward for this tragic event, which has tarnished Tanzania's image as an island of peace and tolerance in a region where intolerance and inter-ethnic strife is the order of the day. Some commentators blamed government leaders for failing to resolve minor disputes before they escalated into unmanageable proportions. These commentators pointed to killings that happened before 8 December, where adequate investigations were never carried out and suspects were allowed to go free. In apparent agreement with this point of view, the government transferred the police chiefs in the area. The District Commissioner was also transferred before being sacked. Other commentators alleged that pastoralists deliberately invaded farms to graze their cattle, then bribed government leaders, police, and magistrates whenever legal action was about to be taken against them (see e.g. Komba 2000, Eneza 2001, Ubwani 2003).

According to one newspaper, the immediate cause of the fight was 'a planned revenge of Maasai pastoralists, following the farmers' attack on two Maasai women on December 6. It is ... alleged that the two *nditos* (young, unmarried Maasai women) were also raped' (Komba, 2000). It is alleged that the two women were beaten by people belonging to the farming community, using their militia defence group, the *Sungusungu*. The women sustained head and body injuries and had to be admitted to the Kilosa District Hospital where they stayed for several days receiving treatment.

An examination of newspaper coverage of the Kilosa killings reveals the social, cultural and legal explanations of the conflict according to conventional wisdom. Most newspaper reports were biased in favour of cultivators and portrayed the

[1] The research project upon which this paper is based was supported by the Evangelical Lutheran Church of Tanzania (ELCT), Morogoro Diocese, and the Tanganyika Christian Refugee Service (TCRS). We wish to thank the villagers of Kambala, Sokoine, Mvuha, Melela, Sangasanga, Mbwade, Twatwatwa, Kwambe, Mabwegere and Kiduhi for responding to our various questions. Also, we thank Rev. Pastor Hebb Hafemann of the ELCT, Mission District Mkuyuni, in Morogoro, and Mrs Ruth Shija of TCRS for logistical support. Last, but not least, we also wish to thank Pastor Jacob Mameyo for facilitating the village visits and assistance in conducting some of the interviews.

livestock keepers as 'aggressive Maasai pastoralists' who were pitted against the normally peaceful village cultivators: 'Maasai attack in Kilosa: Villagers demand regional leaders to be sacked'; '419 flee homes in Kilosa, fearing new Maasai attack: 29 killed, 30 arrested'; 'Kilosa killings: Maasai planned revenge'; 'Hundreds seek police protection after midnight attack'; 'Maasai – villagers conflict: Kilosa MPs, DC form peace team.'

Other journalists tried to remain impartial, while some appeared to take the side of the livestock keepers: 'Pastoralists flee Kilosa after bloody clash with peasants'; 'Killings in Kilosa: Maasai blame members of sungusungu defence group'; 'Kilosa massacre: Maasai warriors, Sungusungu heighten tensions'.

Regardless of the specific casting of villains and victims, however, all of these reports portrayed livestock keepers in Morogoro as 'Maasai pastoralists'. It was also generally implied that these pastoralists were 'outsiders' rather than 'indigenous' to Morogoro Region.

There are a number of pressing and interrelated questions in relation to this event which have as yet been insufficiently addressed, namely: Who are the 'indigenous' and who are the outsiders in the area in question? Are the 'Maasai pastoralists' the only livestock keepers in the area? And what are the root-causes of the conflict?

'Indigenous' & 'Outsiders' in Kilosa

In order not to confuse the term 'indigenous' with issues related to the debates about Indigenous Peoples in Africa[2] we shall immediately introduce the Swahili terms *wenyeji* and *wageni*[3] used generally by local people in Tanzania to refer literally to 'those who are in their home area' (*wenyeji*) and 'guests' (*wageni*). So let us first look at the *wenyeji*.

Changing rural livelihood patterns, warfare and colonial as well as post-colonial interventions have meant substantial population mobility in many parts of Africa, so boundaries between neighbouring peoples have generally been fluid and defined by these people's respective ability to, or interest in, defending specific boundaries between the areas they were occupying.[4] However following various historical sources, the people most often referred to in early writings as occupiers of what in pre-colonial times was referred to as Ukaguru and Usagara, which compose a large part of the area covered today by Kilosa district, are the Kaguru and the Sagara (see e.g. Moffett 1958, Beidelman 1967, Iliffe 1979).

However, tribal boundaries are, as so often shown, more of a colonial construct and the result of external influence than something inherent to the peoples of Africa (illustrated in, for example, Iliffe 1979). Moreover, colonial policies and local interactions between neighbouring peoples have led to an amalgamation of certain

[2] The term indigenous peoples (IPs) is very sensitive in Africa and until recently most African countries claimed that there are no IPs in Africa. See, for example, Tong (2002). We shall not enter into that debate here, but stress that definitions of IPs emphasise aspects of marginalisation in political, economic, cultural and social terms rather than, for example, the issue of 'first-comers' versus 'late-comers'.

[3] In some places *wageni* are referred to as *wahamiaji* stemming from the Swahili term to migrate *(ku hama)* and literally meaning migrants.

[4] Examples of peoples living in the area in question and surrounding areas are found in Sayers (1930), Redmeyne (1968), Rigby (1969), Beidelman (1967) to mention just a few.

sections of different groups, for example the Sagara with the neighbouring Hehe (Redmayne 1968) and sections of the Kaguru with neighbouring Gogo (Rigby 1969).

Other population groups have also since the early1800s found their way to Kilosa district. Kilosa town was situated strategically in relation to the Arab caravan routes to both Tanga and the Southern Highlands (Iringa/ Tukuyu) and emerged as a trading centre in the early 1900s. Some of the first cotton and sisal estates were established in Kilosa district during the German colonial period, and large numbers of workers were brought to the Kilosa estates. Many have stayed there as farmers, and many Indian and Arab traders settled there early in the twentieth century (Sayers 1930, Beidelman 1967).

The Central Railway line, constructed during the period 1905–14 from Dar es Salaam to Lake Tanganyika, goes through Kilosa, and together with the caravan routes and later the Dodoma/Iringa road, this has meant that Kilosa has for a long time been easy for people to access from outside.

Immigration to Kilosa of groups of people referred to as pastoralists is not a new phenomenon, as early historical records from the area indicate. In Sayers (1930), it is mentioned that during the nineteenth century the Maasai[5] '...were pushing south ... as far as Ugogo and Usagara'. According to Beidelman, the Baraguyo (today they are referred to as Ilparakuyo Maasai) began to move southwards long before 1840. Beidelmann (1960) wrote that the 'Baraguyo have resided in parts of Gogo, Sagara, Kaguru and Nguu for far over a century.' However, their movements into these areas accelerated around 1890 due to famine, when the Maasai moved southwards pushing their southern neighbours, the Baraguyo, even further south.

There has been a lot of confusion about the identity of various Maa-speaking communities, as noted by Beidelman (1960):

> Much of the confusion in the various historical sources and in Government reports dealing with Masai and related groups lies in the indiscriminate application of the terms 'Masai' and 'Kwavi' to any Masai-type people. Usually 'Masai' is reserved for those who appear to fill the classic Masai stereotype of the observer and 'Kwavi' is applied to those people who do not quite fit this stereotype but who speak languages similar to Masai, such as Arusha, Meru, Baraguyu, Taveta, Njemps, etc. Often 'Kwavi' merely refers to any Masai-like group observed tilling land. (Beidelman, 1960: 246)

The above noted confusion may have contributed to the lumping together of all livestock keepers in Morogoro as 'Maasai pastoralists'. Bertelsen and Jørgensen (1996) made the following categorisation:

> The term 'Maasai' refers to identity and shared cultural and organizational characteristics, but the sections are separate communities in terms of territorial residence and social affiliation. Most Maasai in Tanzania belong to the Kisongo section ... Other Maasai sections in Tanzania are Ilparakuyo, Siringet, Salei. Some sections such as Purko, Lookokilani, Matapato, Loita and Laitaoik are located both in Tanzania and Kenya. (Bertelsen and Jørgensen 1996: 3)

[5] Sayers uses the general term 'Masai'. However, there are several Maa-speaking peoples who are not necessarily identified as 'Masai', either by themselves or by others. In the case of the immigrants in Kilosa we are mainly talking about the Ilparakuyo Maasai – also referred to as the Baraguyo (who are also Maa speakers and who are identified with a similar livelihood pattern as people known as the Maasai. More details about the distinction between the different Maa-speaking peoples are found in Beidelman (1960).

Many studies and analyses have reinforced a number of misconceptions about the reality and identity of livestock keepers in Morogoro Region: that livestock keepers in Morogoro Region are 'Maasai pastoralists'; that these pastoralists are recent immigrants in the region, who have migrated from a core 'Maasailand'; that these Maasai are pure pastoralists who move from place to place, hence not interested in activities such as farming or contesting for local leadership positions. However, evidence from literature and experience from two recent research projects (Maganga 2002a and 2002b) challenge the validity of these perceptions.

Noting that 'the Baraguyu are perhaps the most dispersed people in East Africa,' Beidelman (1962) constructed a 'demographic map of the Baraguyu'. Among other things, he noted that:

> Much of the Baraguyu population is concentrated in three separate areas: the Kaguru-Nguu area of northern Kilosa and western Handeni districts, the Gogo-Irangi area of north-western Dodoma and south-eastern Kondoa districts, and western Pare District where their paramount leader resides. (Beidelman, 1962: 8)

In other words, we have to move more than a hundred years back in history to find only Sagara and Kaguru people in the area.

So the question, 'Who are *wenyeji* and *wageni?*' is not easy to answer. Among both farmers and pastoralists there are people who have arrived quite recently and people who have resided in the area for a very long time. But is the question of being *mwenyejie* or *mgeni* important in relation to the conflict or is the conflict related more to other factors referred to in the public discourse and reflected by press coverage, namely the competition between crop cultivators and pastoralists? And, if so, are the Ilparakuyo Maasai the only pastoralists in the area? In order to answer such questions we need to look into the history of farming as well as pastoralism in the area.

Farming & livestock-keeping in Kilosa district

The climate in Kilosa is of a semi-arid type with rainfall ranging from 800 mm in low-lying areas to about 1300 mm in high altitude areas. Vegetation in the district is characterised by *miombo* woodland in the hilly areas and grassland in the alluvial plains. Ranging from a large plateau, characterised by dissected hills and seasonally flooded plains, to areas with altitudes of up to 2,200m, Kilosa district offers a variety of agro-ecological conditions for farming as well as livestock-keeping (Mung'ong'o and Mwamfupe 2003).

Based on observations and literature about the area, it is hard to avoid the conclusion that the vast majority of rural households in Kilosa at present are involved in both farming and livestock-keeping activities. However, emphasis on these main production activities for different groups of people has differed over time depending on culture and on changes in availability of resources.

While livestock keeping still forms the main basis of the livelihood for the majority of Ilparakuyo Maasai, it used to be an important part of the traditional economy for both the Kaguru and the Sagara (Beidelman 1967, Iliffe 1979). However, although livestock is still important and a highly valued asset, cultivation of crops has increasingly gained in importance in the economy of both the Kaguru, Sagara and other groups now living in the area. Sisal and sugar cane continue to be the most important cash crops, but several food crops are also grown both for home consumption and for sale. Such crops include maize, beans, sweet potatoes, finger millet, cassava, cowpeas, bananas, and recently also pigeonpeas (Mung'ong'o and Mwamfupe 2003, Odgaard et al. 2005).

The establishment of large sisal estates and production of sugar cane, and a gradually increasing emphasis on crop cultivation among smallholders, caused increased demand for arable land. According to Iliffe (1979: 348), land cases were brought to the native courts by Africans in one of the chiefdoms in Kilosa as early as in the 1930s, and the Africans were said to be land hungry. The population in the area has been increasing for a long time due to importation of large numbers of agricultural workers for the sisal estates during the colonial days, natural population increase and the arrival of new immigrants. Since the 1967 population census the population of Kilosa district has grown from 193,810 persons to 489,513 (United Republic of Tanzania 1973). This has led to increasing pressure on natural resources and cultivation has been steadily expanding into areas previously used as pastures.

Within Morogoro Region, Kilosa district has the highest number of livestock, accounting for around 69 per cent of the total cattle population (URT 1997). Morogoro rural district (including Mvomero district) accounts for 23 per cent of the region's cattle population. The annual number of cattle brought to market generally varies between 4,000 and 8,000, while the number of marketed goats varies between 1,000 and 2,000 per year (URT 1997). These figures, representing between 0.5 and two per cent of total animal stocks, show that the number of sales through official markets is relatively low in relation to the number of livestock in the region. Reasons for this include the social and cultural values of livestock and an associated reluctance to sell animals, the role of livestock as a storage of wealth and the long distances to markets. However, in all the study villages (except the remotely situated Sangasanga), villagers said they participated regularly in cattle markets.

Livestock-keeping plays an important role in the economy of Tanzania. Apart from the supply of meat and other animal products, the activity makes productive a large percentage of the available dry land with few alternative uses. In spite of allegations that they are not good land managers, livestock keepers in Africa have generally been active and prudent managers of their natural resources. They do not simply exploit these resources, but manipulate their stock and rangelands in order to sustain an adequate level of productivity in essentially marginal environments (Mung'ong'o and Mwamfupe 2003).

Until fairly recently, most of the livestock-keeping communities in Tanzania practised transhumance, which was made possible by the abundance of land, and low human and livestock population levels. This land use type made effective use of large tracts of land, while at the same time maintaining its productivity. Transhumant herding patterns were in tune with the ecological realities of dry-land areas, where grazing and rainfall are subject to high risk and seasonal variability. Transhumance allowed regeneration of vegetation, since livestock keepers resorted to seasonal migration. This practice was essentially a drought-coping strategy attuned to the physical environment.

In recent times a number of interventions have interfered with transhumance as practised traditionally by livestock-keeping communities like the Barabaig and the Maasai. State intervention has reduced the livestock keepers' land by converting much of it into national parks and game reserves. In addition to land alienation, other factors have also contributed to destabilise the pastoral economy, such as increasing population densities. Cattle diseases and drought have also negatively affected the pastoral economy, with cattle numbers failing to keep pace with the growing human population. Livestock keepers have tried to cope with these stresses and shocks by migrating to other areas, including areas which were not originally classified as pastoral areas.

Regarding availability of labour for transhumance, there have been drastic changes. As noted by Scoones (1998), human capital represents the skills, knowledge and good health that together enable people to pursue different livelihood strategies and achieve their objectives. At the household level, human capital is the amount and quality of labour available; this varies according to household size, skill levels, leadership potential and health status. Data obtained from the field indicates that human capital is undergoing major changes in the study area. In the old days, livestock-keeping communities were seen as resistant to modern education, preferring to send their children to look after livestock instead of sending them to school. This stereotype is changing rapidly, and it was found that primary schools were among the first institutions to be set up, even in 'new' settlements like Sokoine and Sangasanga. With children going to school and young people looking for alternative economic opportunities, labour for herding is getting scarce. Until recently, cattle were herded by young boys and the *morani* warriors. Calves were separated from adult animals and were herded by women and girls. This was to ensure that calves were not exposed to some of the diseases carried by adult animals. The shortage of herding labour has made it necessary for women and young girls to become more involved in herding activities, increasing their workload. Moreover, as calves are now grazed together with the rest of the herd, they are increasingly exposed to diseases.

Morogoro Region is generally not regarded as a livestock region in comparison to regions such as Mwanza, Shinyanga and Dodoma. However, a considerable number of cattle, sheep and goats are kept by the Maasai, Sukuma and Barabaig communities in the region. These groups comprise the recent 'environmental refugees', and they have reinforced the perception that 'pastoralists' are recent immigrants into the region. However, as mentioned above, historical records indicate that Ilparakuyo Maasai (also derogatorily referred to as Wakwavi, Baraguyu, etc) have been in Morogoro since the nineteenth century, when most 'indigenous' groups were forced to remain in their present areas due to European pacification (Fosbrooke 1948, Beidelman 1962). The Kaguru and Sagara ethnic groups also rear some of the livestock.

Livestock mortality in Morogoro Region is high, especially during drought and periods of increased disease levels. Commercial livestock production is relatively new in Morogoro Region, and it is limited to a few ranches such as Mkata (fattening ranch), Ngerengere Dairy Farm (dairy and fattening), Kingolwira Prison Farm (dairy and fattening), Dakawa (dairy and fattening), Wame and Idete. In addition to these government-owned ranches, there is the privately owned Sangasanga Dairy Farm.

Two of the state ranches, Mkata and Dakawa, are situated close to the study villages. Mkata is the oldest, having been established by the colonial government in 1956. It has a total area of 74,295 ha. and it is situated 60 kms from Morogoro town. It can accommodate up to 16,000 heads of cattle, but currently it has only 1,800 heads. It has 25 employees, and a number of buildings, including a primary school, a garage and some old machinery. Dakawa Ranch, which is situated close to Kambala, Sokoine and Sangasanga villages, was established in 1975, and by 2001 the ranch had only around 1,000 heads of Boran cattle for beef and 13,000 other types of cows, which was well below its capacity. By then the ranch had 16 employees, taking care of its seven ponds, four charco dams (for watering livestock) and two dips. Considerable investment in the ranch has been undertaken by the government including the construction of eight permanent houses, seven offices, a dispensary and a primary school.[6]

Livestock figures among small-scale pastoralists are uncertain since livestock keepers often try to dodge the numerous taxes that are imposed on them by the government. Nevertheless, according to URT (1997), the number of cattle in Morogoro Region rose gradually from around 332,000 in 1984 to around 398,000 in 1992. The number of goats increased from around 140,000 to 205,000 during the same period.

According to URT (1997), the incidence of livestock diseases is high in Morogoro Region. The high level of subsistence animal husbandry and animal movements make high vaccination coverage or economic bush clearing almost impossible. Dips are insufficient in number and often far away, and tick resistance to acaricides and lack of water for replenishment of dips hamper adequate tick-control coverage in the region. According to URT (1997), the cattle mortality rate is between 25 and 30 per cent. The main causes of livestock mortality in the region are frequent occurrences of common cattle diseases, including anaplasmosis, East Coast Fever (*ndigana*), babesiosis, and foot and mouth disease.

Recent research in other parts of Kilosa has shown that, for example, while many Kaguru now put their main emphasis on cultivation activities, there are some for whom livestock is still a major economic activity. In some villages this has given rise to the same type of tension between different groups of Kaguru as those existing between farmers and pastoralists more generally. Problems arise because of differing interests between farmers and livestock owners. Villagers find it difficult to agree on plans and mechanisms to prevent the destruction of crops by roaming livestock (Odgaard et al., 2005). Clearly, conflicts of interests with regard to land use exist not only between *wenyeji* and the Maasai *wageni,* so there must be other factors behind the recent conflict that culminated in such a disastrous outcome.

Language usage & identity

A people's identity is closely related to language usage, both in relation to how they perceive themselves, as well as how they are perceived by other people. A number of studies have noted how language usage and identity can reflect tension between different social groups in Tanzania (e.g. Schultz 1971, Maganga 1995). In the former Mbulu district cultural diversity is illustrated by the fact that representatives of four quite different linguistic groups are found in close proximity, including the Cushitic speakers (Iraqw and Gorowa), Nilo-hamites (Barabaig), and Bantu (Wambugwe) and Khoisan (Hadzabe). The tension generated by the rivalry between different ethnic groups can be illustrated by the

[6] This information was obtained during a field visit to the ranches in 2002.

Table 10.1 Derogatory ethnic terms

What they call themselves	What others call them	Notes
Gorowa	Fiome/Fiomi	Fiomi used by neighbouring Bantu groups. Meaning not known
Hadzabe	Tindiga/Kangeju	Meaning of 'Tindiga' not obvious, but used derogatively by the settled agricultural communities to denote the 'backward' life of hunting and gathering practised by the Hadzabe
Barabaig	Man'gati (Ol'mang'at)	The Maasai labelled the Barabaig 'ol'mang'at', meaning 'enemy', possibly due to their rivalry over livestock and pastures
Iraqw	Mbulu	'Mbulu' used by the neighbouring Bantu groups, meaning people who speak 'with a babbling tongue'

fact that ethnic groups frequently refer to each other through more or less derogatory terms, as shown above (adapted from Maganga 1995).

A more serious example of how language usage can reflect social tensions and even result in tragic outcomes is cited by Beidelman (1960), referring to a clash in the study area between the Maasai and Kaguru in the early 1880s:

> The term 'Wahumba', evidently a derivative, appears in the texts of Burton and Stanley in reference to Baraguyu in Sagara, Kaguru and Gogo territories. The Kaguru and Gogo insultingly refer to Baraguyu as Wahumba. Last provides an excellent example of a kind of incident not unknown even today: 'One day two Masai (Baraguyu?) came to the village, and a native (Kaguru) came out and insulted them by asking, "What kind of a Masai are you? You are not a Masai, but Wa-humba." This is a great insult to the Masai, as they have the bitterest hatred to a Wa-humba, and cannot bear to have the name of Humba mentioned before them. The Masai did not say much, but they went home and reported how they had been insulted. The men at once took arms and went to the village to demand an explanation. The man who committed the offence came out again bravely enough, but was at once speared, as was also another man who came to help.' (Beidelman, 1960: 246, also quoting Last 1882)

In contrast to the popular view that there is a core 'Maasailand' somewhere within the present Arusha and Manyara regions, writers such as Bertelsen and Jørgensen (1996) note that recent studies have challenged the general assumption that the historical process of present 'Maasailand' is the history of a distinct ethnic group that has expanded southward by conquest. They also argue that the highly specialised Maasai pastoralism is not an ancient form, but that it emerged in the eighteenth or early nineteenth century. Before that, communities with a mixed economy of livestock and crop cultivation dominated the present 'Maasailand'.

The Maasai are surrounded by a number of myths about their culture and lifestyle. One persistent myth is that the Maasai diet consists purely of milk, meat and blood. Writing about the Ilparakuyo, one of the Maasai sections, Beidelman (1960), challenges the dietary stereotype in the following way:

> Baraguyu supplement their diet of meat and milk with the following foods: *ugali* flour (chiefly maize), beans, squash, cassava, potatoes, bananas, rice, sugar-cane, groundnuts. These are purchased or begged from local Bantu neighbours. The major vegetable food is *ugali*. Most Baraguyu have a 'relationship' with some households of their Bantu neighbours. During the dry season when milk is scarce, vegetables and grain may comprise the bulk of Baraguyu diet. At such times Baraguyu could not exist without these non-pastoral foods. (Beidelman, 1960: 246)

In addition to dietary changes, evidence from the study villages clearly show that the Maasai and other livestock-keeping communities practise agro-pastoralism rather than pure pastoralism.

Tenure security & political power

We have already noted how the Tanzanian press makes a distinction between 'villagers' and 'Maasai pastoralists'. This distinction arises from a perception of livestock keepers as pure pastoralists and is further nurtured by stereotypical notions of pastoralists as invasive nomads, forever in search of grass and water for their livestock, ignorant of property boundaries and oblivious to the demands of the modern state.

The perception is, however, challenged by findings from a number of villages in the study area, such as Kambala, Mabwegere, Twatwatwa and Kiduhi. In these villages livestock keepers have successfully combined traditional leadership structures and modern village structures. Rather than pure pastoralism, residents in these villages successfully combine livestock-keeping with cultivation of various crops and vegetables.

The nature of land invasion is also often the reverse of that assumed by the media. In villages dominated by livestock keepers, residents are struggling with boundary transgressions by people from surrounding villages. The cultivating communities invade arable areas in these villages in order to cultivate rice and maize, without seeking permission from the village leadership. The scramble for land is partly caused by increasing demand from urban dwellers in Morogoro town and Dumila. These often buy or rent land from villagers attached to communities of cultivators, who in turn must seek new land for their own cultivation. Alternatively, urban dwellers are given direct access to grazing lands, although this is less common due to the understandable reluctance to pay rent for contested lands.

Encroachment of rangeland is aided by, in particular, two factors. First, in the absence of formal property rights, customary claims remain more conspicuous on cropland – through their clear and individual assertion, through their continuous use and through the presence of annual crops and investments – than on grazing land. Second, and perhaps for reasons associated with the above, formal delineation of village lands in Morogoro region is far more common in villages dominated by cultivators than in villages in which livestock keepers are in a majority. The only two 'pastoral' villages with delineated village boundaries are Kambala and Mabwegere, and even in these villages encroachment by cultivators is currently taking place. The value of formal village boundaries to the livestock keepers is, perhaps, summed up in a statement from one of the high-ranking district leaders who is cultivating in Mabwegere without the permission of the village leadership: 'There is no Maasai with land here. The Maasai are not the indigenous people of this area.' The implications of these developments concern not only the dwindling land base available for grazing; encroachments have already led to the effective closing off of corridors for movement of herders and their stock.

Proper representation could enable livestock keepers to defend their customary rights to land. Until recently, it was generally assumed that security of land tenure for livestock keepers in Tanzania was very shaky. However, the country has undertaken some reforms which could ensure security of tenure if villagers know what opportunities are open to them. The National Land Policy (United Republic of Tanzania 1995) sets the direction for land reform that has been followed up by new legislation. The land reform distinguishes between land under the authority of central government and land now under the authority of village governments. Elected village councils are now the land managers charged with the supervision of adjudication and registration of village land within their respective village spheres. Consistent with the Land Policy, provisions of the Land Act (United Republic of Tanzania 1999a) and Village Land Act (1999b) and related regulations recognise customary rights in land and allows for registration of these rights. Customary rights as provided for in the new laws specifically include the right of households, groups or communities to hold commons as registered common property.

The implications of new legislation are, however, as yet unclear. The picture presented by the wording of the new acts must be interpreted in the light of the stifling limits on implementation and follow-up set by available government resources, as well as the frightening prospect that decentralisation of responsibilities and devolution of power will be used to create a stage for the acting out of old grievances. Livestock keepers have tried to contest for political positions, but they have been met with obstacles, possibly because they are not regarded as 'indigenous'. An example of discrimination against livestock keepers and their lack of representation in local government organs was reported by the Kilosa livestock keepers to a meeting held in April 2001:

> Livestock keepers have no representation in local government – the District Council. The special seats allocated for women representatives have been given to those from the group of cultivators. The livestock keepers prepared their representative to contest for the post of Councillor for the Rudewa ward, and he was approved by the residents of Rudewa ward, as well as at the district level, but his name was deleted at the regional level. The runner-up, who is from the community of cultivators, was approved and elected councillor. This is the real situation – the cultivators, who control the administrative ranks, don't want the livestock keepers. The result of this arrangement is that the livestock keepers are not involved in development planning, although they are bona fide citizens in the concerned council. This shows that the livestock keepers

> will never achieve representation through legal means since the children of cultivators, who are learned, are the ones holding administrative posts, therefore they will continue to favour their people and to discriminate against the livestock keepers, hence promoting enmity and hatred between the two communities. (Author's translation of document written in Kiswahili)[7]

Discussion

What were the Kilosa killings really about? A superficial view would ascribe the tragedy to the incompatibility and eventual clash of different ethnic groups and their associated livelihoods. The cultivation of stereotypes – in the press, among politicians and among the protagonists themselves – furthers this interpretation. These stereotypes operate on several levels: the roving herders versus the sedentary farmers; the recent immigrants, or strangers, versus the original and indigenous; the backward, primitive and authority-defiant versus the modern and stable; the land-intensive and inefficient versus the prudent and industrious. This is, of course, the retelling of a familiar tale, a narrative that is ancient and revered but also often flawed and oversimplified.

The reality is very different. The livestock keepers of Morogoro Region are seldom pure pastoralists, but instead people who combine animal husbandry and crop cultivation, as well as other livelihoods, in a diverse portfolio of income-earning activities. They are not recent immigrants but, to the extent that the tracing of ethnic origins is at all possible over such a time span, a people who have lived and made their living in the area for well over a century. How long must a people live in an area to be considered indigenous? Nor are they ignorant of or indifferent to authority; any disaffection with local politics stems from their exclusion from political processes and lack of representation. And, finally, rather than simply wasteful and destructive, the husbandry practices of livestock keepers in Morogoro Region can largely be seen as a rational adaptation to their local environment and an efficient utilisation of land poorly suited to other uses.

Matters of ethnicity and land use in the region are complex rather than clear-cut, but when violence breaks out there is a tendency, across the board, to focus on a single dimension of multi-dimensional identities and livelihoods. Also, the type of violence witnessed in Kilosa in December, 2000, is not a new phenomenon but has been played out, with variations, throughout the twentieth century. The rivalry and animosity between different groups has long been manifested in language usage and terms used to denote each other. On the other hand, violence is the exception rather than the rule and examples of peaceful coexistence over very long time spans are much more common than examples of violent incidents.

Recent developments have, however, contributed to heightened tensions. A demand for land from urban dwellers and encroachment by cultivators on grazing land has increased the pressure already present with regard to availability of sufficient grazing lands. At the same time, livestock keepers are denied access to understocked and adjacent state farms and must face the prospect of privatisation of these farms. Exclusion of livestock keepers from local political forums has not helped.

[7] Minutes of a meeting of livestock keepers from Kilosa and Morogoro rural districts, held at Sokoine village, 28 April 2001.

In contrast to what most of the media coverage would seem to indicate, there is no obvious villain in the clashes that took place in Kilosa. The conflict concerns the continued ability of poor people to maintain their way of life and to eke a living from scarce natural resources. Increasingly, however, the conflict is being portrayed in terms of ethnic stereotypes that bear little resemblance to reality.

The 1999 Village Land Act is intended to facilitate the establishment of village titles to land. The act fits into broader plans of devolution and decentralisation of executive powers to local levels in Tanzania. In the past, many small enclaves of livestock keepers were insufficient in number to form separate villages and were thus incorporated as sub-villages into larger settlements controlled by other groups. The outcome of decentralisation processes with respect to peaceful coexistence among resource users in Morogoro Region will depend on the extent to which these processes provide sufficient opportunities for all groups to take an active part in decision making.

References

Beidelman, T. O. 1960. The Baraguyu. *Tanganyika Notes and Records*, 55: 245–78.

______. 1962. 'A Demographic Map of the Baraguyu.' *Tanganyika Notes and Records*, March and September 1962, Nos 58 & 59, pp. 8–10.

______. 1967. *The Matrilineal Peoples of Eastern Tanzania (Zaramo, Luguru, Kaguru, Ngulu, etc.)*. London: International African Institute.

Bertelsen, P. and M. Jørgensen. 1996. *When Pastoralists Become Irrigators. Maasai people Combining Irrigation and Transhumant Livestock Keeping in Northern Tanzania*. Working Paper. Ålborg: Institute of Development and Planning.

Eneza, M. 2001. 'Kilosa Murder Episode: Demarcating Land for Grazing and Farming is Naïve.' *Guardian*, 1 January 2001.

Fosbrooke, H.A. 1948. 'An Administrative Survey of the Masai Social System.' *Tanganyika Notes and Records*, 26: 1–50.

Illife, J. 1979. *A Modern History of Tanganyika. African Studies Series 25*. Cambridge: Cambridge University Press.

Komba, A. 2000. 'Kilosa Massacre: Maasai Warriors, Sungusungu Heightened Tensions.' *Guardian* 25 December 2000.

Last, J. 1882. 'A Journey into the Unguru Country from Mamboia, East Central Africa.' *Procedures of the Royal Geographical Society*, IV.

Maganga, F.P. 1995. *Local Institutions and Sustainable Resource Management: The Case of Babati District, Tanzania*. PhD thesis. Roskilde University Centre.

______. 2002a. *Planning Sustainable Livelihoods for Livestock Keepers in Kilosa District*. Report Prepared for Tanzania Christian Refugee Service, Dar es Salaam, November 2002.

______. 2002b. *Planning Sustainable Livelihoods for Livestock Keepers in Morogoro Rural and Mvomero Districts*. Report Prepared for Tanzania Christian Refugee Service, Dar es Salaam, October 2002.

Moffett, J.P. (ed.). 1958. *Handbook of Tanganiyika*. Dar es Salaam: Government Printer.

Mung'ong'o, C.G and D.G. Mwamfupe. 2003. *Changing Livelihoods of Migrant Maasai Pastoralists in Morogoro and Kilosa Districts and their Impact on the Environment*. Report Submitted to REPOA.

Odgaard, R. J. Adu-Gyamfi, F. A. Myaka, W. D. Sakala and H. Hoegh-Jensen. 2005. 'Some Reasons Why Pigeonpea Has the Potential of Improving People's Livelihoods in Africa – with Special Reference to Malawi and Tanzania.' In H. Hoegh-Jensen (ed.) *Pigeonpea-based Cropping Systems for Smallholder Farmers' Livelihood*. Copenhagen: KVL.

Redmayne A. 1968. 'The Hehe.' In A. Roberts (ed.), *Tanzania Before 1900*. Nairobi, East African Publishing House.

Rigby, P. 1969. *Cattle and Kinship among the Gogo: A Semi-Pastoral Society of Central Tanzania*, Ithaca, NY: Cornell University Press.

Sayers, G.F. 1930. *The Tanganyika Handbook*. London: Macmillan.

Schultz, J. 1971. *Agrarlandschaftliche Veranderungen in Tanzania: Ursachen, Formen und Problematik Landwirtschaftlicher Entwicklung an Beispiel des Iraqw-Hochlandes un Seiner Randlandschaften*. Munchen:

IFO Afrika Studien No. 64.

Scoones, I. 1998. *Sustainable Rural Livelihoods: A Framework for Analysis*. Brighton: IDS Working Paper No. 72.

Tong, M. 2002. The UN Special Rapporteur on the Situation of Human Rights and Fundamental Rights of Indigenous People: Benefits for Indigenous People in Africa. In *Indigenous Affairs* 1/02. Copenhagen: IWGIA.

Ubwani, Z. 2003. 'Kilosa Patoralists, Farmers Heading for Violent Conflict.' *Guardian* 30 August.

United Republic of Tanzania. 1973. 'The Population of Tanzania: An Analysis of the 1967 Population census.' Dar es Salaam: Bureau of Resource Assessment and Land Use Planning and Bureau of Statistics.

______. 1995. 'National Land Policy.' Dar es Salaam: Ministry of Lands and Human Settlement.

______. 1997. *Morogoro Region: Socio-Economic Profile*. Dar es Salaam: Planning Commission and Morogoro: Regional Commissioner's Office.

______. 1999a. 'The Land Act. Supplement No. 6, 21 May 1999.' Dar es Salaam: Gazette of the United Republic of Tanzania.

______. 1999b. 'The Village Land Act. Supplement No. 7, 21 May 1999.' Dar es Salaam: Gazette of the United Republic of Tanzania.

11

The Use & Management of Water Sources in Kenya's Drylands
Is There a Link Between Scarcity & Violent Conflicts?

KAREN WITSENBURG
& ADANO WARIO ROBA[1]

Introduction

This study explores the link between violent conflicts and scarcity of water in Marsabit District in Northern Kenya – a region characterised by aridity, unreliable rainfall patterns and a dispersed population. This region is inhabited by a large number of different ethnic groups, most of them pastoralists, who have moved across the present border with Ethiopia for centuries. The Boran, Gabra, Somali, Dasenetch, Burji, Garri, Ajuran, Sakuye, Sidamo, Konso and Waata are just a few of the ethnic groups with close kin living in both Kenya and Ethiopia. Ethnic groups are dynamic, in the sense that individuals can identify themselves with different ethnic groups. Equally dynamic are the relationships between groups (Schlee 1989). These groups have histories of animosity, friendship, temporal alliances and violent conflict. Present-day relationships can be described as an oscillation between war and peace, avoidance, integration and coexistence. However, owing to the violent wars in Ethiopia and Somalia over the past decades and the cross-border family ties, the concentration of weapons and migrants in northern Kenya is growing. In the context of increasing insecurity, violence and ethnic diversity we studied the use and management of local water sources.

Water is a crucial, yet very scarce resource. The water sites in an arid environment are extremely important elements that necessarily attract a great number of people and their animals who need to visit the place for their water use. Water sites, although not permanently retaining water, are permanent features in the landscape where many pastoralists live a mobile life, and to which herders have to (re)negotiate access with every move they make. Not only mobile pastoralists need to do this; also settled (livestock-keeping) farmers need to renegotiate access

[1] The authors wish to thank AMIDSt and WOTRO (Wetenschappelijk Instituut voor de Tropen) for research grants. We thank Paul Baxter, Alan de Brauw, Ruth Noorduyn, Mirjam Ros, Cynthia Salvadori, Fred Zaal and an anonymous reviewer for valuable comments and advice on earlier drafts. Part of this paper was presented at the seminar 'Conflicts over land and water management in Africa' organised by the research network 'Customs and conflict in land and water management in Africa', Centre for Development Research, Copenhagen, 28–9 November 2002. We are very grateful for the support and hospitality we received at the Centre for Development Research, Copenhagen.

to water sources every season, because their livestock is usually not 'sedentary'. How people acquire access to water resources in areas facing recurrent drought and rapid population growth is an important issue in the Marsabit mountain area. Access rights to the traditional man-dug shallow wells are especially crucial for the survival of households and the family herds. Although ownership of wells seems to be defined along ethnic lines, ethnic identity plays a role in access rights to these wells.

Using case study material and historical data on violent conflicts in the region we will investigate whether violent conflicts are related to ethnic identity and access to water resources. In addition, we will look into the possible relationship between resource scarcity and armed violence in the region.

The chapter reads as follows: first the study area, population figures and trends in resource availability are described. In the second section, we will look at the statistical data on armed violence and case study material from Marsabit district. Third, we will link the outcome to the discussion on the scarcity of natural resources and question whether environmental factors play a role in the armed violence in the district.

The study area

Marsabit mountain is a high *inselberg* of volcanic origin, rising to an altitude of 1,700m out of the surrounding semi-desert at 400m altitude. A dense mist forest grows on its peaks and is responsible for the cool and sub-humid climate on the mountain. The average rainfall on Marsabit mountain ranges from 800–1,000 mm annually, dispersed over a bimodal rainfall pattern. Rainfall drops to 200 mm, on average, in the surrounding lowlands. Vegetation growth in large parts of the district is scanty due to low rainfall and high salinity of soils and water resources.

Marsabit mountain is a high potential area, where farming can be successful in years of normal rainfall (Map 11.1). Since the English colonial era, pastoralists were attracted by the green mountain, but were not allowed to settle (Adano and Witsenburg, 2005). However, after independence in 1963/64 a large movement to the mountain started in the 1970s as a result of the Somali secessionist war, large losses of livestock and the droughts of 1973/74. The Ethiopian war also caused widespread immigration into Kenya. Marsabit mountain has become an area of refuge for victims from war and droughts.

Indications of increasing resource scarcity

Population growth has been spectacular, especially since 1960.

Figure 11.1 shows that the total population in Marsabit District has almost doubled in the last twenty years. At present, more than one-fifth of the population in the district has tried to establish a livelihood on the fertile slopes of Marsabit mountain. The population pressure on the mountain has increased from 1 person per km^2 in 1959 to 18 persons per km^2 in 1999. Impoverished pastoralists of Rendille, Samburu, Gabra, Boran and Turkana origin, as well as Ethiopian migrants with a farming background are presently living close to each other, trying to establish new livelihoods in an insecure environment. It doesn't take much imagination to guess that the population pressure on land, vegetation and especially water resources has increased tremendously.

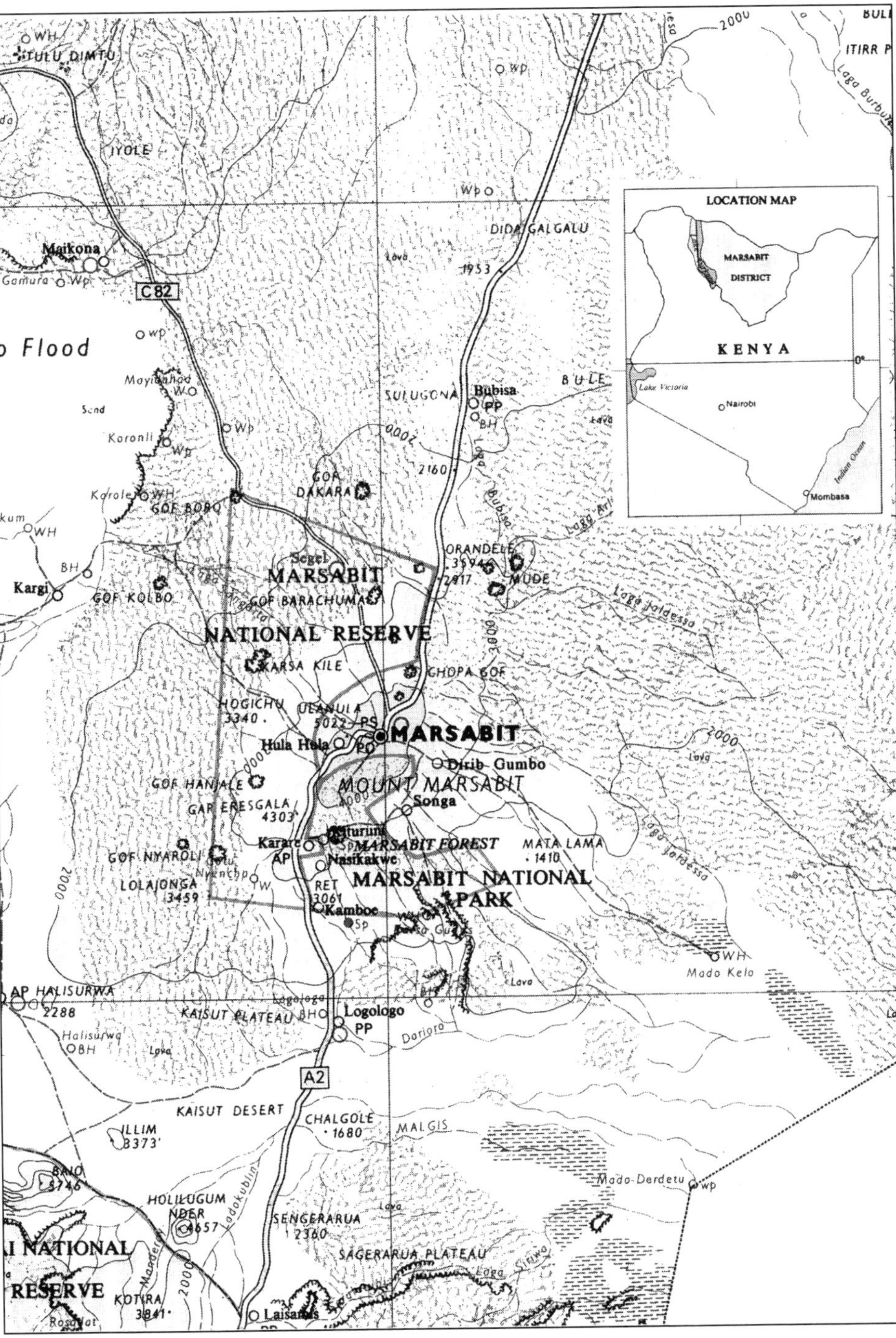

Map 11.1 Marsabit mountain & surroundings
(Adapted from Map 1 Survey of Kenya, GTZ/MDP 1988)

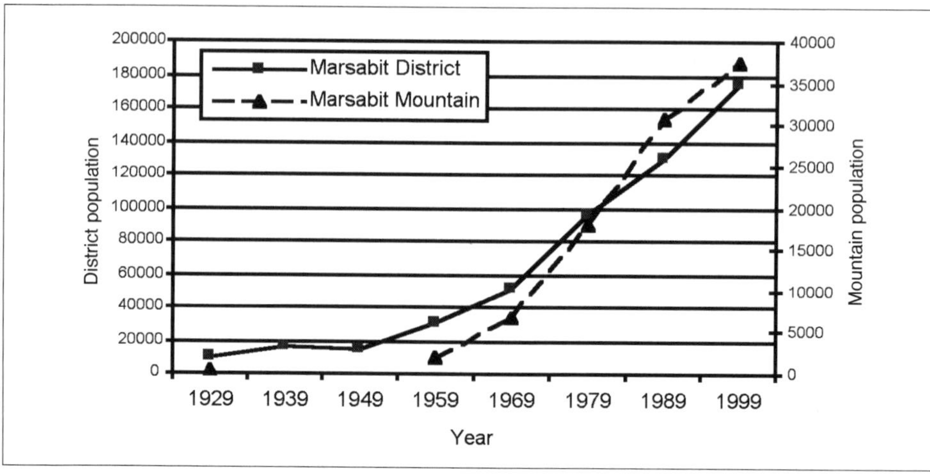

Figure 11.1 Human population trends in Marsabit District and Marsabit mountain[2]
(Sources: Marsabit District Handing Over Report 1922; MDARs 1931, 1935, 1937, and GoK, 1969, 1979, 1994)

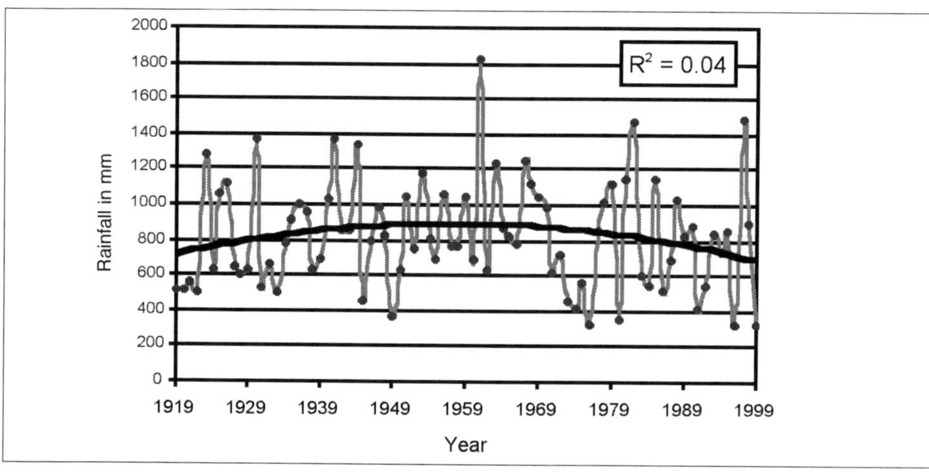

Figure 11.2 Rainfall, Marsabit mountain from 1919–99
(Source: compiled from Marsabit Meteorological Station 1960-1999)

While the population increased, some trends in resource availability were negative. A crucial variable that has a direct impact on resource availability is rainfall. As the following precipitation figures show, ecological features are very variable indeed.

As the trend line suggests, average rainfall figures slightly increased at the beginning of the last century and decreased again after 1960. This pattern was also observed in other parts of Sub-Saharan Africa. Figure 11.3 shows that the

[2] At the time of the British colonial administration, Marsabit and Moyale Districts together were part of the Northern Frontier District. Until 1995, Marsabit and Moyale together formed one district. For these reasons, all data referring to Marsabit District also include present day Moyale District.

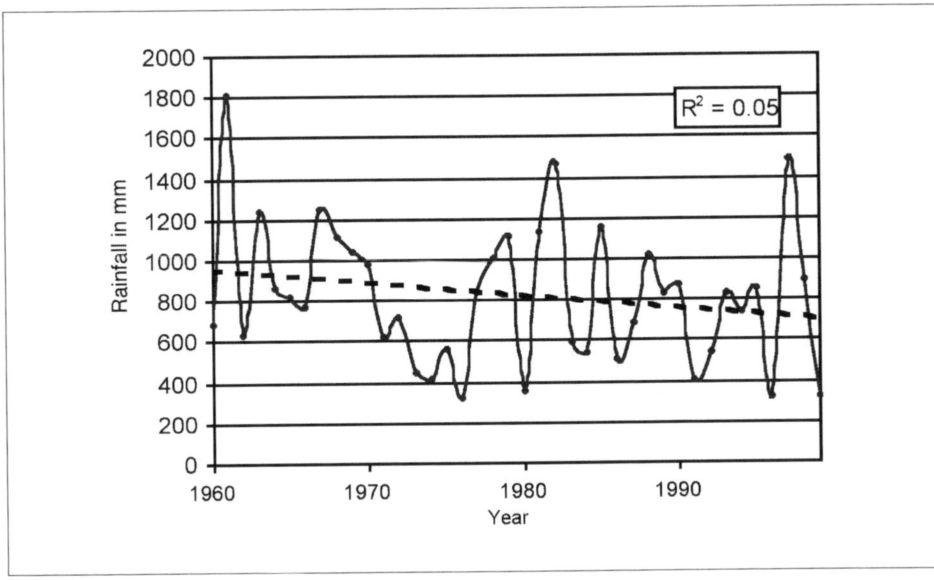

Figure 11.3 Rainfall, Marsabit mountain after 1960
(Source: compiled from Marsabit Meteorological Station 1960–99)

Table 11.1 Human population and TLU measures in Marsabit District

	Rendille Country[3]		Recent survey figures	
	1932	1984	1998	2000
Population	7,250	24,501	2,036	1,901
TLU	106,118.3	129,554.2	4,278.8	3,498.2
TLU/cap	14.6	5.3	2.1	1.8

(Source: authors' surveys 1998 and 2000)
Notes:
Rendille country data adapted from O'Leary (1990).
Recent survey figures are based on the author's household surveys in 1998 and 2000. The 1998 figures are for mobile pastoral households in the lowlands and Marsabit mountain. The 2000 figures refer to settled households in the lowlands and Marsabit mountain. The lowlands data are based on households at Korr and Maikona centres during both survey periods.

last 40 years showed an increasing number of extreme dry years. Even though both trend lines are not significant, severe drought years were more frequent in the second half of the century. Before 1960 only two years had below 500 mm of rainfall, while after 1960 there were seven years when the rainfall had been below 500 mm.

In Kenya's drylands, and certainly in many other areas in sub-Saharan Africa, drought years are generally times of environmental and economic scarcity. The decline in rainfall over the last 40 years caused worsening environmental stress, especially in the face of continued human population growth.

[3] Rendille country is part of Marsabit District and is inhabited by Samburu and Rendille.

The absolute numbers of people and also livestock have increased over the last century. Whereas rangelands have had to support a larger number of animals, the number of animals (expressed in tropical livestock units TLU[4]) per person has decreased tremendously over the years.

In 1984, the measured TLU per capita of 5.3 was already insufficient to support the population.[5] The recent survey figures give similar values. In 1998 we measured 5.3 TLU per capita in the lowlands among the mobile pastoralists at Korr and Maikona centres of Marsabit district. The settled households on the mountain had 1.3 TLU per capita both in 1998 and 2000, and settled households in the lowlands had 3.4 TLU per capita in 2000. This clearly shows that settled households have much lower levels of TLU per capita. Other studies show similar results. Fratkin and Roth (1996) found a decline in the average TLU per household of about 36 per cent between 1976 and 1985 among Samburu Ariaal – from 12.7 TLU per capita in 1976 to 6.4 TLU per capita in 1985. In a recent study, McPeak (1999) reports average household herds of 6.9 TLU per capita in Chalbi and 3.9 TLU per capita in Dukana. Since many inhabitants of Marsabit district are presently living a settled life, we can assume that the TLU per capita ratio for the district is far below 5.3 TLU. This suggests that livestock as productive capital has become increasingly scarce in relative terms in the course of time, even though livestock is still the most important and prestigious household capital in the district.

The natural resources that became increasingly scarce during the drought of 2000 were obviously water and forest resources. Many people with large herds moved away from the area in 2000 to escape local drought effects, and in so doing, relieved the pressure on water and pasture. One could argue that the demand for water thus decreased, making the resource less scarce. Still, people and animals had to queue for long hours to get access to water. During the drought of 2000, old water sources were rehabilitated and NGOs helped to repair piped water systems in villages.

In general, inputs of time, labour and money to extract resources like water and forest resources have increased over the last century. So we discerned a trend of increasing scarcity as people had to walk longer distances to find firewood (Adano 2000), more people were needed to water cattle, and more labour was needed to meet the demands for these resources.

At present, we can see that an increasingly sedentary population with a history of violent encounters live in each other's vicinity closer than ever before. They currently have to share scarce renewable resources like water, pasture and farmland. In addition, the Marsabit mountain population is a society in transition due to the shift from nomadic pastoralism to a more sedentarised way of life, which involved changes in traditional norms and values, loosened family ties and less social control. Intuitively one would expect more violent encounters between people.

[4] 1 camel = 1.2 TLU, 1 large stock unit = 0.7 TLU, 1 sheep or goat = 0.1 TLU (Lusigi 1983: 243).

[5] Based on a study in the district, Fratkin and Roth (1996) observe that 8 TLU per capita is generally considered sufficient for subsistence livestock production as pure pastoralists. Furthermore, it is recommended that a threshold of 4.5 TLU per capita is minimally needed to generate subsistence production (mainly comprising of a diet of milk and meat). Dietz et al. (2001) estimate this minimum value at 4 TLU per capita, or an equivalent of five head of cattle, for full dependency on animals for all food (meat and milk) requirements. This low figure is based on different TLU values (suitable for other parts of Kenya). In addition, these figures do not incorporate the livestock requirements needed to support a social network.

Current authors suggest (see KHRC 2000, for instance, and Mkutu 2002) that violent encounters in Northern Kenya have become more frequent and intensive, with higher numbers of casualties per incident, because contemporary weapons are more lethal than the arms of the past. Population growth, environmental scarcity and violent ethnic conflicts are manifest phenomena in Marsabit District.

In this chapter, we intend to detect whether there is a trend of increasing conflict in Marsabit District. It was initially assumed (partly based on reports and literature about the area) that the increase in violent encounters between ethnic groups was related to scarce natural resources.

Scarcity & armed violence

Development workers and scholars expressed fear of increasing tension between different groups in societies in degrading environments (Kaplan 1994) and in competition over access to resources (Homer-Dixon 1999). This fear is in line with mainstream thinking about the relationship between environmental scarcity and violent conflicts. It is widely assumed that in less developed countries environmental conflict is likely to happen because there is high population growth and high dependency on renewable natural resources. Moreover, as is argued in the current 'scarcity-causes-violence' thinking, poor countries cannot allocate (enough) wealth to research and development to invent new techniques to produce or substitute for scarce resources. In addition, it is argued that developing countries lack well-defined or enforceable property rights to govern renewable resources, as common property resources are used as open-access resources (Homer-Dixon 1999, Maxwell and Reuveny 2000: p.301–2). These arguments are based on the neo-Malthusian assumption that food production cannot cope with population growth, leading therefore to all sorts of problematic events, including violent conflict. At the core of this thinking lies the assumption that poverty is related to a lack of the social institutions necessary to deal with increasing scarcity, which will inevitably result in violence. As Homer-Dixon asserts:

> Poor countries start at a disadvantage: many are underendowed with the social institutions that are necessary for an ample supply of both social and technical solutions to scarcity... (Homer-Dixon 1999: 108)

Thus, violence that results from competition over scarce resources would be triggered by failures in governance such as unequal access to resources and social exclusion, misuse or overuse of a common property resource and free riding problems.

However, numerous studies have falsified some of the hypotheses in the 'scarcity-causes-violence-paradigm'. In the first place, most common property resources are not used as open-access resources and are in fact used in a sustainable way (see Berkes 1989 and Bromley 1992). Second, Platteau (1996) showed in his critique of the 'Evolutionary Theory on Land Rights' that well-defined and enforceable property rights in the form of title deeds in sub-Saharan Africa are not always a solution to insecurity of land tenure, and can eventually lead to violence. Third, widespread resource degradation is not always unidirectional as is shown by Fairhead and Leach (1996) and Tiffen et al. (1994). West African forests seemed to be much more resilient than was assumed and resource productivity in semi-arid Machakos increased with rising population numbers.

A completely opposing view in the debate on violence and natural resources is presently investigated; the relationship between resource abundance and violence. A thorough analysis by de Soysa (2002), which is one of the few studies using statistical data on the number and intensity of conflicts in relation to socio-political, economic and ecological variables shows that there are indications that not resource scarcity, but abundance might be related to armed violence. In a 2003 study, World Bank researchers also explored whether grievance or greed explains armed violence. Availability of easily tradeable and valuable resources like diamonds and arms would correlate stronger with violence than scarcity of natural resources (Klem 2003, World Bank 2003).

This view is now gaining in importance, as it is very difficult to prove the relationship between violent conflicts and population growth-related environmental problems. Markakis (1997), for example, stated that 'the Horn of Africa is a textbook case of environmental degradation and conflict' in his book titled *Resource Conflict in the Horn of Africa*, in which he convincingly quantified the trends of population growth, resource degradation and increasing food insecurity. The part on 'conflicts' in the book remains, however, largely descriptive, showing how tribal and descent groups and cultural movements confront each other or the state in different ways. There are no data on how violent these conflicts were, how many people were killed and injured, and what has been the trend over the last century. Mkutu (2002: 4) also states that 'violent conflicts involving pastoralists have become widespread and increasingly severe throughout much of the Horn of Africa' without listing any trend in numbers. An interesting study on state-sponsored violence in Kenya by Kahl (1998) shows indeed how trends in population growth and increasing scarcity of resources seem to have contributed to widespread politically motivated ethnic clashes in Rift Valley, Nyanza and the Western Provinces. The reported number of deaths was 1,500 from 1991 to 1993 (Kahl 1998: 7), implying an average of 500 deaths per year, while about 300,000 displaced people were counted in the same period. But how large was the population on which these numbers are based? It has been suggested that Kenya has long been a relatively calm country, but we have no proof of population growth-related ethnic violence in the past. As de Soysa has observed, despite a large number of studies on the causes of civil war and an intense debate on environmental effects on social relations, few have systematically tested environmental scarcity and violence utilising hard data on large-N samples (2002: 2).

However, despite the lack of evidence, it seems that armed violence is regarded as a typical characteristic of Kenya's drylands, or of the Horn of Africa in general, that it is more often assumed than validated.

> ... in the Horn of Africa in recent times, conflict among pastoralists has taken on new, exaggerated dimensions. A shrinking resource base has provoked a desperate struggle for survival in which the existence of some groups is threatened. (Markakis 1993: 13)

> The most obvious threat to pastoral survival is the increase in violence in the sparsely populated pastoral areas: warfare and raiding have been constant features in the lives of most pastoral peoples, but automatic weapons and grenades have revolutionised the

intensity and deadliness of conflicts and quite altered their nature. (Baxter 2001: 236)

These statements appeal to many people who have been to the Horn. It is true that modern weapons have a different level of destruction, causing more deaths in a short time. Yet, to avoid misinterpretation of the present, it is necessary to look at the past. One can only claim 'an increase of violence' when there is evidence of a trend in violent incidents over time. Moreover, a trend in incidents should be related to population growth. Absolute numbers of incidents do not say much in an area where population growth is high. It has been suggested that Kenya was a relatively calm country, but we have no proof of population growth-related ethnic violence in the past. Also Hussein et al. (1999) noticed that recent literature claiming 'increasing conflict' in West Africa fails to give evidence of trends.[6]

Another way of thinking about violence in relation to increasing scarcity of resources refers to alternating stages of conflict and response. As resources become scarce, the incentive for conflict increases; but, because conflicts are 'costly', so does the incentive for conflict avoidance and resolution. Therefore, it is interesting to distinguish responses to short-term scarcity situations and long-term trends. Increasing resource scarcity could lead to increasing violence in the short term, in both frequency and intensity. However, violence could eventually generate institutional changes that reduce conflicts. That means that an analysis on the link between resource scarcity and violence should focus on short and long-term responses to scarcity in the form of institutional change.

In this study, we will discuss the trend in violence according to the reported incidents and violent deaths, and try to link the outcome to environmental factors using our own research result. Social institutions that govern natural resources, ethnicity, scarcity of resources and poverty in Northern Kenya are key issues in the Northern Kenyan context that will be addressed in this paper.

Research methods

In order to find out if violence had increased, and whether violence was related to increasing competition over resources, both quantitative as well as qualitative data were used.

With the purpose of investigating whether there was tension over access rights to scarce water resources and, if so, whether this was related to increasing population pressure, we did an elaborate study on the use and management of wells. Ownership and access rights, allocation of water, repair after damage and the use of water during droughts, were the main topics of this investigation that was carried out between 1997 and 2000. Since ownership of resources seemed to be ethnically linked, we were particularly interested in how newcomers or people belonging to different ethnic groups who did not own a well were treated at the well site. We made case studies of the wells and their use, for which we

[6] It is indeed very difficult to find this kind of information. Conflict-ridden areas are notorious for their missing documents, misinterpretation of incidents and government institutions ignoring or denying killings. However, Marsabit District is considered a 'hardship area' by the National Government, which means that civil servants get a 'hardship bonus' on top of their salaries. It does not benefit the police to under-report ethnic violence and raids, as that would reduce the chance that their area of service earns 'hardship status'.

interviewed the well owner and all the important elders related to a particular well. Groups of well users were interviewed at the spot, while individuals were interviewed in their houses. A structured household survey on water use was conducted in the villages.

To find out how ownership and use of wells were organised in the past and whether violence had increased over the past century, a number of reports and books were reviewed. The main sources of secondary information were the annual reports and intelligence reports of the Northern Frontier District and Marsabit District in the British colonial era until 1960, and the Kenyan Human Rights publication of 2000 on Marsabit and Moyale Districts. Other sources were historical overviews from Tablino (1999) and Sobania (1979). For this study, all the incidents and killings that were reported by the colonial government in the first part of the century were listed and compared to the number of incidents and loss of life in the last decade. The annual reports of the present-day government do, however, not systematically list incidents and numbers of people killed in armed conflicts. Unfortunately, we had no data at our disposal referring to the period from 1960 to 1989, which was an extremely violent time due to the Somali secessionist war.

In this study we distinguish between short-term and long-term resource scarcity indicators. A drought year is taken as a short-term water scarcity indicator. However, as years of low rainfall usually result in scarcities of other resources as well, like reduced vegetation and pasture for animals, lack of surface water in pools and wells, lack of milk and harvest and starvation of animals, a drought year can as well be a general short-term environmental scarcity indicator. Data on rainfall and population numbers were obtained from the Marsabit District Annual Reports from 1924 to 1999 and from the Marsabit Meteorological Station on Marsabit mountain. Population figures over the last century indicate long-term increasing environmental scarcity in general. These figures were obtained from the Marsabit District Annual Reports 1929–1999.

Armed violence & reconciliation in Marsabit District

As we indicated earlier, it seemed that the late 1990s showed a particular increase in armed violence. In 2000, the Kenya Human Rights Commission published a report *The Forgotten People Revisited* in which most, if not all, armed incidents that took place between 1992 and 1999 in Marsabit and Moyale districts were described in detail. In this report, 24 armed incidents were registered in 1998, in which at least 93 people were killed and 12 people were wounded. There were 50 incidents in 1999, with 38 people killed and 69 people wounded. These were years in which tension and fear were almost palpable in Marsabit town. In 1998 and 1999 it was hardly possible to walk outside after six o'clock. Most economic activities were seriously undermined, as the road from the farms to the market was continuously under threat. To us and the people in Marsabit town, it looked like an escalation of ethnic violence. In these years, the local residents talked about nothing but raids and killings, and we were seriously hindered in continuing our research. Our assistants refused to go to certain watering places. Everybody was afraid to travel on the roads, especially after some banditry attacks on the main roads and murders on the forest road between

Songa and Badassa (two farming villages on Marsabit mountain). It was absolutely impossible to ask people questions on ethnically delicate topics and to get reliable answers. In such a situation, it was tempting to interpret the violent conflicts in this ethnically diverse area as arising from competition over scarce resources.

In 2000, the severe drought situation seemed a 'good' opportunity to us to find out how the 'traditional ways of resource management' would deal with this increased scarcity situation. To our surprise, we found a peaceful atmosphere on the mountain, even though the severe drought had caused widespread starvation of animals due to lack of pasture. People with large herds had moved away from Marsabit, northward to places in Ethiopia, or southwards to Waso, Isiolo, Wamba, Maralal and Garba Tula. The pressure on Marsabit wells from large herds had thus reduced. However, thousands of poorer households with small herds, who could not afford to move away, still had to use the mountain water holes. The small wells, with little water and a very low water table were avoided, and only large waterholes with a greater capacity were used. This resulted in a situation whereby people of different ethnic groups were all depending on a few waterholes. Contrary to what we expected, the situation around waterholes was one of cooperation and mutual understanding.

Clash at Bakato well

A case in point was the temporary reconciliation around Bakato wells. Bakato is a watering site in a grazing area between Badasa and Songa, exactly on the boundary between the Rendille/Samburu and Borana-speaking communities. In 1998, the place was the arena of fighting and shooting, killing and raiding. It was impossible for us to visit that well site because of the fights. The result of the violence in 1998 was that Bakato dam, the nearby wells and the surrounding pasture were not used for a long time. However, with the onset of the drought, pasture on the mountain deteriorated and the number of usable wells decreased. Herdsmen of both Rendille/Samburu and Borana-speaking communities met, and agreed to stop fighting in order to use the wells and pasture of Bakato. This was the same well site where members of the same ethnic groups had killed each other two years earlier!

We saw Rendille and Boran herdsmen watering each other's animals, and both were willing to talk about the violence that occurred between them in the previous years. They said that violence occurred more often in wet years and they used to reconcile in drought years for sheer survival. Although fights often happen around water places, people do not fight over access to water, as is often reported, but they fight to raid cattle, they said. Raids happen at water places because so many animals are accumulated around a watering point. Well sites are profitable places to raid when there is a concentration of people and animals, because such sites are usually situated in bushy depressions in the landscape, where it is easy to surround the enemy and attack. If people want to acquire access to a certain well site, they usually reconcile and negotiate, as they said. That is traditionally the way to acquire access to water.

In times of ethnic tension, Boran and Rendille/Samburu herdsmen claim ownership over well sites that lie on the border between the groups, like Hula Hula wells on Marsabit mountain, and the Bakato water site. Also Medatte/Maidahad oasis in the nearby Chalbi desert on the border between Rendille and

Gabra rangelands is a place that has been used and claimed by both Gabra and Rendille interchangeably. During times of reconciliation, ethnic groups admit that they understand why the enemy has a rightful claim to the same wells. The Boran herders readily admit that the Rendille and Samburu used the water sites on Marsabit mountain long before they migrated from Ethiopia. On their side, Rendille/Samburu herdsmen admit that the Boran have improved the wells over a long period of time. Everyone in Marsabit knows that improving a well, and contributing labour and investments means the building up of use rights. This particular instance shows how in certain situations, resource scarcity can contribute to reconciliation and cooperation between otherwise antagonistic ethnic groups.

Evidence from the colonial records showed similar phenomena. Both in 1939 and 1955, which were drought years, it was reported that

> During part of the year it was common to find Boran, Rendille and Gabbra using common water holes, and surprisingly little friction occurred between them. (Marsabit District Annual Report, 1939: 7)

> There was no internal unrest; in fact relations between the three tribes were most friendly – which is most surprising in view of the severe drought conditions prevailing throughout the year. As with the Boran, the Rendille-Gabbra relations remain most friendly and have shared their water and grazing. (Marsabit District Annual Report, 1955: 7, 16).

It is of course very difficult to find out if these years are isolated cases, or if there is a pattern in the occurrence of violence and the ecological conditions in Northern Kenya. We therefore need an overview of all the years in which we had data at our disposal. In the following overview[7] all armed incidents that resulted in deaths or physical injuries that were registered are counted.

The data in Table 11.2 show an increase in absolute numbers of armed incidents over the years. However, the number of violent deaths has not increased over the long term. For instance, from 1990 to 1999 in total 337 people were killed in armed violent incidents. From 1950 to 1959, which were relatively prosperous years in the Northern Frontier District (MDAR 1950–59), at least 389 people were killed in armed violent encounters. This also implies that present armed encounters have not been more lethal than in the past; per incident less people died in the 1990s than in pre-independence time. One could

[7] In this study, we speak of armed violent encounters when those encounters result in death, abductions, torture or injuries, in order to avoid a subjective interpretation of concepts like competition, ethnic strife, verbal aggression and other behaviour that does not result in loss of life or physical injuries. The incidents counted in Table 11.2 are raids, armed attacks or murders. 'Raid' is an armed attack where livestock is involved, and 'murder' is an armed attack where one or two individuals are assassinated for various (usually political) reasons. The incidents in this list also have an 'ethnic' character, in the sense that virtually always the ethnic identity of the groups involved was reported where it seemed to play an important role. Included in the list of incidents are the abductions of Kenyan residents by the Ethiopian army. These abductions are 'violent' in the sense that weapons are used to threaten people, and when people are abducted, they are usually severely tortured. We included the violence used by the Ethiopian and Kenyan armies against Kenyan civilians because these incidents were often raids (or responses to raids), murder and rape, and have a strong ethnic component. Incidents involving the Ethiopian and Kenyan armies or police seem to have a 'multiplier' effect, and often occur (co-incidentally?) at the same time as other incidents. Other types of criminal or violent incidents (for instance a drunkard in town killing his neighbour) are not included in this table.

Table 11.2 Overview of registered numbers of violent ethnic incidents and death cases, rainfall and population numbers of Marsabit District per year

Year	Rainfall	Absolute no. of violent incidents	Absolute no. of violent deaths	Relative no. of violent incidents (incident/population x 10,000)	Relative no. of violent deaths (death/population x 10,000)	Population
A						
1929	596.14	1	3	0.8	2.5	12,229
1930	637.54	2	2	1.8	1.8	10,948
1931	1,372.87	3	4	3.3	4.4	9,017
1932	526.54	4	126	4.0	125.2	10,067
1933	661.67	1	2	1.0	1.9	10,547
1934	501.65	6	5	4.1	3.4	14,681
1936	910.34	3	1	1.8	0.6	16,825
1937	999.24	1	7	0.6	4.1	16,885
1939	629.16	0	0	.00	.00	15,895
1940	694.69	13	37	8.2	23.3	15,880
1941	1,029.72	11	66	6.9	41.6	15,880
1942	1,369.82	7	22	4.4	13.9	15,814
1943	847.60	11	409[8]	7.4	276.4	14,796
1944	856.74	6	30	3.9	19.3	15,519
1945	1,344.68	1	5	0.7	3.2	15,500
1946	452.88	3	4	2.0	2.6	15,396
1947	787.15	1	17	0.7	11.0	15,398
1948	983.74	2	6	1.3	3.9	15,478
1949	819.15	1	1	0.7	0.7	15,174
1950	370.59	4	21	2.5	13.1	16,000
1951	638.81	6	30	3.5	17.7	17,000
1952	1,037.59	2	77	1.1	42.8	18,000
1953	753.36	7	6	3.7	3.2	19,000
1954	1173.99	5	25	2.3	11.5	21,789
1955	804.67	2	10	0.9	4.6	21,789
1956	693.42	6	32	1.9	10.2	31,337
1957	1061.47	23	185	7.4	59.7	31,000
1958	757.68	2	0	0.7	.00	30,774
1959	769.37	3	3	1.0	1.0	30,774
B						
1990	412.10	1	1	0.1	0.1	133,140
1992	409.60	14	24	1.0	1.7	141,248
1993	539.30	3	11	0.2	0.8	145,485
1994	832.80	9	66	0.6	4.4	149,850
1995	736.50	4	2	0.3	0.1	154,345
1996	851.40	17	36	1.1	2.2	158,975
1997	320.80	5	66	0.3	4.0	163,745
1998	1489.30	24	93	1.4	5.5	168,657
1999	891.50	50	38	2.9	2.2	173,717

(Sources: Marsabit District Annual Reports 1929–99, Kenya Human Rights Report 2000, Marsabit Meteorological Station)

[8] Although the Second World War might have had an impact on the number of conflicts, the majority of the killings (451 in total) were caused by fights between the Gelubba (Dasenech) and Gabbra and Boran herdsmen in absence of police control.

also argue that the society has become less violent over the last century; in the 1990s on average only 2.1 persons per 10,000 inhabitants were killed annually, while from 1950 to 1959 on average 16.4 persons were killed per 10,000 inhabitants per year.

We should also take into account that the nature of incidents has changed over time. In the past, conflicts more often had the appearance of raids. The proportion of incidents in which the Kenyan and Ethiopian army was involved in the 1990s is quite substantial. For example, 23 of the 50 incidents in 1999 were caused by the Ethiopian militia against Kenyan civilians, causing eight cases of death and numerous abductions. In the same year, the Kenyan army was involved in nine incidents, in which 17 civilians were killed (in an alleged attempt to stop people from supporting the Oromo Liberation Front (OLF). In only 16 incidents, in which 12 people were killed, no army was involved.[9] The first conclusion that we can draw from these data is that, contrary to common belief, the number of violent conflicts in the course of last century has not increased proportionally to the population growth. The last decade shows an increasing trend, but still the level is not as high as in pre-independence years.

The second question, whether violence is related to scarcity of resources, is more difficult to answer. As we have seen, there is no long-term trend of increasing violence, which suggests that despite population growth people might have found ways to share and cooperate. However, how do people respond to short-term scarcity situations? Drought years are generally years of severe environmental and also economic scarcity. If such years showed higher death rates than wet years, one could conclude that violence might be induced by direct scarcity situations.

In the next section we will test the 'scarcity-causes-violence' paradigm, using drought as a scarcity indicator. Droughts in the rangelands as recorded in historical accounts of annual reports and by Sobania (1979) and Tablino (1999) in Marsabit District correspond fairly accurately with an annual rainfall of 700 mm or less on Marsabit mountain.

Figure 11.4 shows trends in absolute numbers of incidents, numbers of people killed and rainfall. In some years it looks as if the number of incidents is higher with increasing rainfall. Table 11.3 shows the average number of incidents and killings in wet, average and dry years of rainfall. 'Incident rate' and 'kill rate' is the number of incidents and killings divided by population numbers and multiplied by 10,000.

From Table 11.3 we can see that the absolute and relative numbers of deaths are higher for wetter years than for dryer years. The mean number of incidents does not show a clear trend. However, it is clear that twice as many people are killed in wet years (50.1 vs. 23.5) than in drought years, in both relative and absolute terms. It is possible to imagine a situation in which people might postpone violence until the first wet year after a drought. Surprisingly, wet or average years following a drought do not show an increase in incidents and

[9] In this respect it is interesting to note that in a recent report of the Daily Nation, the majority of firearms deaths in several Kenyan districts are attributed to police activities (Leyan 2002). 'Six out of every ten Kenyans who are shot dead are victims of police' says a new report. But the statistics rise dramatically in 2001, when the police shot dead nine out of every ten victims. The study, the first ever in Kenya done by medico-legal experts, attributes an average 60% of firearm deaths to police and 39% to criminals in the previous five years.

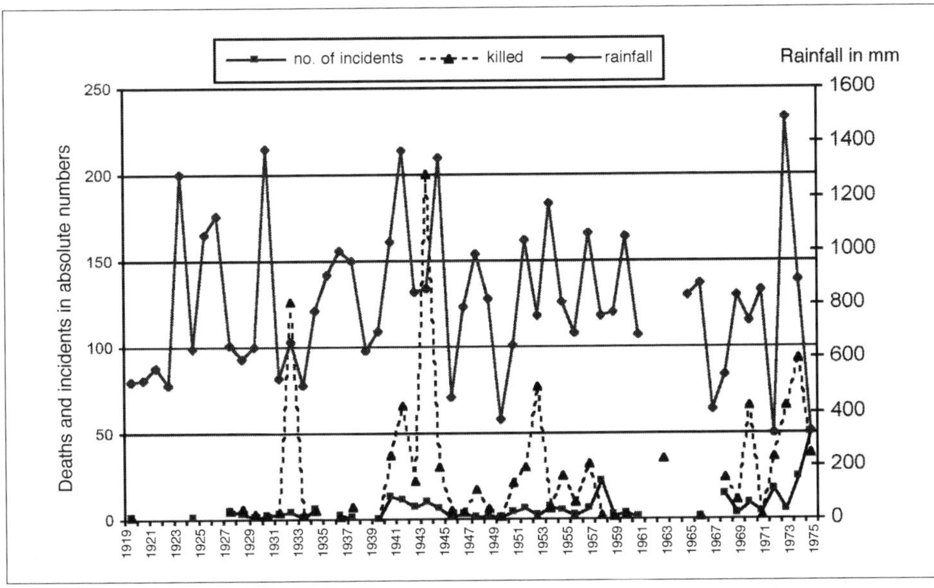

Figure 11.4 Absolute number of armed incidents, people killed & rainfall levels
(Source: This figure is based on Table 11.2[10])

Table11.3 Average number of killings in dry, average & wet years

	Drought years (n=13)		Average years (n=10)		Wet years (n=16)		Average & wet years following drought (n=8)	
	Mean	(st.dev)	Mean	(st.dev)	Mean	(st.dev)	Mean	(st.dev)
Incidents	7.6	(13.8)	6.2	(6.3)	6.5	(6.0)	5.5	(3.4)
Killed	23.5	(34.1)	40.1	(57.5)	50.1	(99.7)	23.4	(22.2)
Incident rate	1.5	(1.3)	2.4	(2.3)	2.7	(2.7)	2.8	(2.6)
Kill rate	12.7	(33.9)	14.3	(20.4)	26.3	(67.7)	8.0	(8.4)

(Source: based on data from Table 11.2)
Note 1: A drought year is rainfall ≤700mm, average year 701-850 mm, wet year ≥851 mm rain, and average and wet years following drought is >700 mm rainfall following years of ≤700 mm of rainfall.

killings. In fact, less people were killed (23.4) in wet years following droughts than in wet years in general (50.1). The standard deviation is however high, so we cannot make hard statements from these figures. The only statement we can make is that there is less violence in drought years than in wet years. That means that the violence occurring in Marsabit District is not related to drought-induced scarcity of resources. This is in line what the herdsmen at Bakato dam in 2000 already told us.

[10] In 1943 there were 409 people killed. This is omitted in the graph, for 'distortion of scale' reasons. In the calculations in Table 11.3 this number is included.

Explaining the decrease of violence in drought years

So, if it is true that violence has not increased over the last century, and there is less violence in drought years, this leads us to the question why violence diminishes in times of environmental stress.

Poverty & collective action

The herdsmen explained that more violent ethnic conflicts, especially armed raids, take place during wet years. They say that raiders like to attack during wet years, because the grass in the range is high, which is important for hiding before and after the attack. In addition, during wet years animals are strong enough to trek vast distances. It is of no use to steal weak animals from the enemy in a drought because it is not easy to feed and water them. In a wet year, there is the availability of surface water when rain has accumulated in pools, which makes it easier to trek with the animals. Such water sources dry up during droughts. Furthermore, when there is a drought it is very difficult to water a herd of animals at the well site because so much labour is needed when the water table is low. This was partly the explanation why poor herdsmen decided to reconcile in 2000.

The dilemma faced by the herdsmen at the well sites in 2000 resembles the Prisoner's Dilemma in 'game theory'. Forced by incomplete information about the other player's behaviour ethnic groups have to choose between either cooperation, avoidance or fights. Their choice depends on which situation is expected to offer most advantage. In the first type of collective action, people cooperate for example to use water jointly from a source. Information about the other player's behaviour is made optimal by a deal both parties make; if you don't cooperate this time, you may not use the well any other time. The pay-off is survival in hard times. This shows some similarities to the Folk Theorem in Game Theory where punishment among players guarantees compliance to the rules in collective action (see Gravelle and Rees 1992 for details on the Folk Theorem).

The opposite form of collective action is to fight. Groups of herdsmen raid each other's livestock and try to ban the other group from the water source. The payoffs vary from stolen cattle to blood revenge, honour and increased power and status for a local political leader.

The question now is which type of collective action is more likely to occur during droughts? The poor herdsmen implied that it was not rational to start fights during droughts. Drought years are very hard to survive anyway, so why would people incur extra costs with fighting? Our informants also raised the issue of poverty. Poor people especially would not profit from fighting during a drought, they asserted. During droughts, the poor herdsmen remain behind on the mountain, because they have too few animals to move. Herdsmen require a large herd and pack animals to make mobility worthwhile, and if they don't have those, they are forced to stay and reconcile in order to be able to use the pasture and water that is left. The poor herdsmen implied that the wealthy elite profits most from fights. The herdsmen that we interviewed suggested that it was more rational for the poor who stayed behind to cooperate and share their resources, in the absence of the wealthy elites.

The ultimate aim of each herder is that he and his livestock survive a drought. Negotiating access to a water source and cooperation around the maintenance of this well, even if it belongs to another ethnic group, will increase the chance of survival. The lack of information about the other parties' behaviour is limited because of the deal that is made: no cooperation during drought will mean a ban from the water place forever. It is thus more rational to stop fights during droughts.

Mancur Olsen (cited in Ostrom 1990) challenged the idea that if members of a group have a common interest or objective they would all be better off if that objective were achieved through cooperation individuals in that group would act to achieve that objective assuming they were rational and self-interested. He says that '*unless the number of individuals is quite small, or unless there is coercion or some other special device to make individuals act in their common interest, rational, self-interested individuals will not act to achieve their common or group interests*' (Olsen 1965 in Ostrom, 1990: 5–6). Although this can explain why people do not have the incentive to contribute to the common good, it also explains why violence is not likely to occur during droughts in Marsabit district. Violent ethnic conflict is a collective action from which the benefits (stock theft, praise, blood revenge and honour) to the group do not outweigh the costs of fighting (closing off water sources, revenge, general insecurity) that has to be carried by each individual. The advantages might be higher in wet years, when the costs of violence can be carried more easily. Therefore, violence occurs more often during times of abundant rain and grazing.

The fluidity of ethnic identity in migratory areas

Part of the explanation of why violence is reduced in times of scarcity lies in the social realities of present day migratory areas. Contrary to what is often believed, ethnicity does not play such a crucial role in the genesis of a conflict. Territory in an area like Marsabit mountain, but also in some places in the lowlands, is not so strict and permanently defined along ethnic lines as may appear at first glance. Similarly, the ethnic identity of an individual, or even a whole family, is not as strict as it might seem. So far we have dealt with 'ethnicity' as if it is easy to define and distinguish ethnic groups. Ethnicity seems to play a crucial role in explaining all sorts of problems in Africa, including violent conflicts, but what role does ethnicity actually play? Although individuals carry identity markers like beads of different colours and spears to show their present ethnic identity, it does not mean that all their relatives belong to that group only, or even that they are born in that ethnic group. For instance, anthropologists such as Schlee (1989) found that every ethnic group in this area has clans which consist of individuals that come from neighbouring ethnic groups. People can decide during their lifetime to move to a neighbouring ethnic group if that is advantageous. These clans of people who once belonged to another ethnic group seem to be quite large in the rural villages on the mountain; in Kituruni and Songa, for example, people have relatives in both Samburu and Rendille families. Also in Hula Hula, there are a substantial number of people who belong to the Odhola clan in Rendille, who have blood relatives in the Odhola clan among Gabra. There are many families who have blood relatives among other ethnic groups, but their precise number is not known. Neither do people like to emphasise this 'double-ness' in ethnic identity, so it is hard to find quantitative data on this topic. However, we have reason to believe that their number might be especially high in the Marsabit mountain area. Double ethnic identity is especially used or reinforced in times of stress, when people migrate and change their livelihood. Impoverished pastoralists have to depend on others for some time, until they are self-supporting. For instance, when pastoralists settle in Marsabit, some redefine their ethnic identity. They will adopt the ethnicity of the area where they are going to live. Such people do not profit from conflict at all, because it forces them to take sides and this reduces the chance of obtaining assistance from another ethnic group. We, therefore, think that although sedentarisation increased pressure on certain resources, it actually might also have increased the peacekeeping elements in the society. Because more households are settled and don't move anymore, they have to keep the peace in order to negotiate access to resources in times of environmental stress.

Even though this fluidity of ethnic boundaries is a characteristic of Marsabit District, it would be wrong to suggest that this phenomenon does not exist outside this area. Frederik Barth observed flexibility in ethnic identity in 1968 among the Basseri in South Persia (Jenkins 1997), Mohamed Salih observed ethnic merging and alliances in the Sudan and Nigeria (1999). Multiple ethnic identities might be a more common phenomenon than appears in studies, because the existence of a single ethnic identity is sometimes assumed. But as Markakis commented:

> A persistent confusion between form and substance has often confounded our understanding of social conflict in Africa. Ethnicity, for instance, is often the ideological form such conflict takes, but its substance is seldom a clash of cultures. Like all ideologies, ethnicity is a symptom of social disorder, not its cause. (in Mohamed Salih 1999: v)

The social reality is rather a dynamic and complex pattern of multiple and changing ethnic identities, where cultures, norms and values merge and change until conflicts create boundaries and ethnic 'clarity'. Therefore, in Marsabit District ethnic identity is more of a social resource that can be made of use, rather than something that restricts individuals from resource use. Even though ownership of water resources, for instance, is ethnically defined, this does not restrict resource use by individuals from other ethnic groups. The following section will illustrate this.

The governance of natural resources

Another salient feature that stands out is the way access to resources is organised. In Marsabit, despite poverty and population growth, it appears that strong common property regimes governing water resources not only cope well with increased water scarcity, but are also flexible enough to guarantee access to newcomers. An intensive study on water access rights, water resource management and water use carried out in 1998, 1999 and 2000 in Marsabit district revealed the importance of local governance issues in the discussion on resource scarcity and violence.

One of the most important types of waterholes on Marsabit mountain during the dry season is the hand-dug well on which the majority of the people and livestock depend. The property regime governing the well is a combination of a private and communal property system; the well itself is individually owned (by the person who dug the well or his sons who inherited it), but the water inside is communally owned. The owner of the well, *aba ela* (father of the well) is

Photos 11.1 & 2 Two wells on Marsabit mountain

In this well there are three men lifting water up to fill the basin.
Sagante wells, August 2000
(Photo © K. Witsenburg)

This trough was filled using two wells on both sides. About 2,000 cattle need water from this place every day. Karantina, August 2000
(Photo © K.Witsenburg)

responsible for repairs, de-silting and organising groups to help him with this. Everybody who contributes labour has rights to water their herds at the waterhole. The water users elect a manager who is responsible for the allocation of water rights, the *aba herega* (father of the watering rota). Decision-making power over water resources is thus spread over two individuals and controlled by the water users to avoid misuse of power by the well owner.

Due to scarcity of water, time and space not everybody can come with their animals to the same well on the same day. Herders come once in three days to water cattle, on which day the herdsmen are also responsible for filling the water trough and maintaining the well site. The filling of the trough is labour intensive. The deeper the water table is, the more labour is needed to lift up the water. Usually, about three to six people stand in a chain on a scaffolding of branches from the bottom up to the trough, and pass up buckets of water. The passing on of buckets is accompanied by rhythmic singing, to cheer up the heavy, monotonous work.

During water-allocation meetings at the onset of the dry season when water is needed most, well owners, managers and users of such water sites discuss the allocation of water per village. Everybody in these villages has a potential access right, irrespective of their ethnic identity. The basic idea is that 'water belongs to everybody', which ensures that the community has the obligation to make sure that no outsider will be denied access. Everybody who needs water that season can apply and will be scheduled, provided they contribute labour and adhere to the rules governing the water site.

Wells always carry the name of the owning clan or individual, but that does not prevent other clans from using them. On the contrary, during interviews at the well site it appeared that the schedules were purposely allocating water to different clans or ethnic groups. The diversity of clans using one well was felt to be an advantage, showing hospitality, good social relations, peace and cooperation.

What happens when the drought intensifies and water becomes scarcer? Generally, rich stock owners with large herds are expected to leave the area. Pasture is usually not adequate anyway, so most of them will have already moved before the water becomes too scarce. Well sites that have been no-go areas of violence and war in wetter times, open up and are rehabilitated for use to accommodate the increased demand for water. So it happened that the Bakato well site, located between two hostile groups, was re-opened during the worst of the drought in 2000.

The water management regime in Marsabit shows that water, as a scarce common property resource is not used as an open-access resource, because only through maintenance, labour or financial contributions can one build up use rights.

The fascinating aspect about the hand-dug wells in Marsabit District is that threats such as 'free riding', lack of maintenance and repair, and irresponsible use resulting in water pollution are absent. Free riders have very little chance because people cannot water their animals on their own. Somebody coming in the evening alone, to water his animals would face considerable difficulties, because of the low water table. In addition, the well site, being remote, is unsafe in the quiet evenings. After the watering day is over, the water trough and the basin are filled for the wild animals 'out of respect' as the herdsmen say. So it is possible that a single herdsman might also encounter wildlife (in Marsabit that means meeting elephants, leopards, buffalos) at the watering place. Every herdsman is thus dependent on others for watering his animals, not only for the labour requirements, but also for security reasons.

So we can say that where it is needed to avoid conflict, a strong enforceable property regime over natural resources exists, which does not change when population pressure increases. Interestingly, the opposite situation also arises in which common property systems seem to be vaguely defined in order to avoid conflict, as in the case of Bakato well site. This well site is a typical example of a case in which double ethnic use rights exist. Vaguely defined property systems leave room for opportunistic and temporary use rights through negotiation and can accommodate some flexibility, which is of crucial importance in ecosystems which are in disequilibrium.[11] It is important for outsiders to recognise that such

[11] The notion of 'disequilibrium ecosystem' refers to the extreme variable climatic conditions in sub-Saharan Africa where the so-called 'optimum vegetation' is not assumed. The main premise of the disequilibrium model is that resources are characterised by non-linearity and the oscillation of 'boom

'double-ness' exists not only to understand possible conflictual claims, but also for their potential peacekeeping functions during drought.

We therefore think that introducing new legislation that demarcates territory, like the issuing of title deeds to individuals or groups of people, can create conflicts in such areas.[12] This is in line with Platteau's warning: '*... titling opens up new possibilities of conflict and insecurity that can have disastrous consequences for vulnerable sections of the population at a time when their livelihood crucially depends on their access to land*' (1996: 45). Platteau suggested that attempts at land titling to benefit outsiders would face considerable difficulties because of various claims on ancestral lands and the lack of social legitimacy of such transactions. Even though it is difficult to speak of 'ancestral lands' in Marsabit, and probably in all other areas where people with different ethnic identities have been mobile and migrating, there are various groups who can claim to be 'the first migrants' in the area, depending on which reference point in time is taken. The introduction of title deeds in such areas with double ethnic use rights, would involve a fixation of what have been flexible boundaries and a reduced chance for use by other groups in future. The possibility of exclusion for certain groups and the reduced possibility of negotiating access to closed territory makes it perfectly rational to use violence and contest efforts at formal land adjudication.[13]

Challenging the scarcity-causes-violence paradigm we also suggest that poor people have developed institutions to cope with increasing scarcity of renewable resources in the short term, and cooperate rather than indulge in violence. Furthermore, if at any time a conflict over a scarce natural resource like water exists, it can be a sign that local resource users themselves have been made powerless and that their negotiation system has been paralysed, either by external agencies or by local elites. To use scarcity of resources to explain the resulting violence would then be an oversimplification of reality. Our contribution to the discussion is therefore that, unlike current assumptions made in the environmental security debate, the evidence of a causal relationship between population growth, environmental scarcity and ethnic violence is not strong.

However, even though it is valid to assume that at present, the traditional institutions can cope with short-term increasing resource scarcity, it is not possible to assess from the above results whether people in Northern Kenya have found new institutional solutions to cope with long-term increasing resource

[11] (cont.) and bust' cycles in production. The approach explicitly stresses dynamic episodes of peaks in production during good years and crashes in production during unfavourable years of environmental stress. Empirical work shows how natural resources are characterised by dynamic processes and continuous changes in flows, stocks, time, scope, scale, numbers and size. This line of thinking was developed by Scoones (1995); Behnke, Scoones and Kerven (1993); Oba (1996, 2001).

[12] In this respect it is worth mentioning that the recent 'water conflicts' along Tana River between Pokomo farmers and Orma pastoralists started after the government launched a land adjudication programme along the river (Daily Nation Team, 10 March 2001). Where vagueness in property rights along the Tana River existed, the attempt to define territory triggered violent conflicts resulting in at least 60 deaths and numerous injured and displaced families, yet it has been explained as a typical case of scarcity induced conflict.

[13] Unfortunately, it seems that many scholars and government administrators do not see these nuances in property systems and easily deny their existence. Policies that are based on the idea that individualisation of property rights is superior to customary rights to common property resources, often result in narrower definitions of ethnic territories and boundaries where previously double-ness existed. Ethnic violence resulting from land adjudication activities, for instance, may be reinterpreted in this light, rather than ethnic violence being attributed to a lack of ingenuity and institutions.

scarcity. Short-term responses to scarcity may be to share, cooperate and accept higher labour inputs generally, yet there is no evidence of sustainable institutional change in the long term.

Explaining the existence of ethnic violence

Rejecting one explanation for violence, however, does not mean that the gap in knowledge can easily be filled with another explanation. We certainly cannot fill this gap yet, although we can formulate some ideas to start filling in this gap in future.

Where violence is partly an institutionalised and organised pattern in society, the breakdown of traditional social institutions might mean that violence is reduced or changed in form. From the reports it can be observed that the character of conflicts has changed over the last century: the number of traditional raids in relation to other types of ethnic violence have decreased, while the violence during election time and during land adjudication programmes, or state-sponsored violence have increased.

We observed that in the genesis of a violent conflict, people consistently referred to resourceful and powerful individuals who seemed to orchestrate confrontations between less resourceful people. A study on the psychology of the sly and manipulative ways these leaders operate could illuminate much more on ethnic conflicts than a general 'scarcity-causes-violence' paradigm. This means that a study on the origin of violence should focus more on the people who own resources rather than on those who lack them, and on those who profit from violence instead of on those who suffer from it. At a local level of analysis, this implies that the role of traditional elders, the new political elites, the small-arms traders and the local police for instance, should be investigated. At a higher level what the role of the police, the army and business companies at district or national level should be analysed. At a global level, it means that an analysis of the role and profits of wealthy nations, international organisations, multinationals and the weapon industry could provide new insights.

As there is rationality behind all violence, the focus should change from 'those who fight in a conflict' to 'those who benefit from a conflict', because they are not necessarily the same. Behind all conflicts, there are individuals, groups, companies or nations who profit from the violence. A study of violence should thus focus on the 'flow of wealth' from and to areas of conflict. It means that the present focus on poverty and resource scarcity disguises the causal factors behind ethnic violence, because the 'resource owners' who coordinate the violence pass unseen.

The correlation between resource wealth and violence might, thus, be much more revealing than a focus on resource scarcity. A number of studies at a high level of analysis have been carried out in this context (Collier 2000, Collier and Hoeffler 1998, de Soysa 2002). De Soysa (2002) for instance correlated resource wealth and the occurrence of violent conflicts for 76 countries over 11 years, and found that:

> Despite testing numerous specifications and several sub-samples, at no time did natural resources, both renewable and non-renewable, come close to predicting conflict negatively, nor human and institutional development positively. The results find ample support for those who argue that greed rather than grievance (at least in terms of the availability of natural resources) is likelier to generate armed violence. (de Soysa 2002: 28–9)

In line with these results, it should be tested whether this relationship also exists at lower levels of analysis. A focus on the 'flow of wealth' to and from war-torn areas, and identifying those groups or individuals who benefit from conflict will offer better causal explanations for the occurrence of violence. As such a focus is much more difficult, and also dangerous for the researcher and his/her informants this could explain in part why there are not many such studies available as yet.

References

Adano, W.R. 2000. 'Costs and Benefits of Protected Areas: Marsabit Forest Reserve, Northern Kenya.' In C. Perrings (ed.) *The Economics of Biodiversity Conservation in Sub-Saharan Africa: Mending the Ark.* Cheltenham: Edward Elgar.

Adano, W.R and Witsenburg, K. 2005. 'Once Nomads Settle: Assessing the Process, Motives and Welfare Changes on Mount Marsabit.' In E. Fratkin and E. A. Roth (eds) *As Pastoralists Settle: Social, Health, and Economic Consequences in Marsbit District*, Kenya. New York: Kluwer Plenum.

Baxter, P.T. 2001. 'Immediate Problems: a View from a Distance.' In M.A. Salih, T. Dietz and Mohamed Ahmed (eds) *African Pastoralism, Conflict, Institutions and Government.* London: Pluto Press.

Berkes, F. 1989. *Common Property Resources: Ecology and Community-based Sustainable Development.* London: Belhaven Press.

Behnke, Roy H., Scoones, I. and Kerven, C. 1993. *Range Ecology at Disequilibrium: New Models of Natural Variability and Pastoral Adaptation in African Savannas.* London: Overseas Development Institute.

Bromley, D. 1992. 'The Commons, Common Property and Environmental Policy.' *Environmental and Resource Economics* 2 (1): 1–18.

Collier, P. (2000). 'Doing Well Out of Wear.' In M. Berdal and D. Malone (eds) *Greed and Grievance: Economic Agendas in Civil War.* Boulder, CO: Lynne Rienner.

Collier, P. and Hoeffler, A. 1998. 'On the Economic Causes of Civil War.' *Journal of Peace Research* 39: 417–33.

Daily Nation Team. 2001. 'Now 15 killed in water battle.' Daily Nation Team, 10 March 2001. Available at: http://www.nationaudio.com/News/DailyNation/10032001/News/News33.html.

Dietz, Ton, Nunow A.A., Adano, W. R. and Zaal, F. 2001. 'Pastoral Commercialization: On caloric terms of trade and related issues.' In M.A. Salih, T. Dietz, and G.M. Abdel (eds) *African Pastoralism: Conflict, Institutions and Government.* London: Pluto Press.

Fairhead, J. and Leach, M. 1996. 'Rethinking the Forest–Savannah Mosaic.' In M. Leach, and R. Mearns (eds) *The Lie of the Land.* London: James Currey.

Fratkin, E. and Roth, E. A. 1996. 'Who Survives Drought? Measuring Winners and Losers among the Ariaal Rendille Pastoralists of Kenya.' In D. G. Bates and S. H. Lees (eds) *Case Studies in Human Ecology.* New York: Plenum Press.

Gleditsch, N. 1998. 'Armed Conflict and the Environment: a Critique of the Literature.' *Journal of Peace Research*, Vol.35: 3: 381–400.

Government of Kenya. 1969. Kenya Population Census, 1969. Nairobi: Government printer.

Government of Kenya. 1979. Kenya Population Census, 1979. Nairobi: Government printer.

Government of Kenya. 1994. Kenya Population Census, 1994. Nairobi: Government printer.

Gravelle, H. and Rees, R. 1992. *Microeconomics.* London: Longman.

Homer-Dixon, T. 1999. *The Environment, Scarcity and Violence.* Princeton, NY: Princeton University Press.

Hussein, K., Sumberg, J. and Seddon, D. 1999. 'Increasing Violent Conflict between Herders and Farmers in Africa: Claim and Evidence.' *Development Policy Review* 17: 397–418.

Jenkins, Richard. 1997. *Rethinking Ethnicity. Arguments and Explorations.* London: Sage Publications.

Kahl, C. H. 1998. 'Population Growth, Environmental Degradation and State-sponsored Violence: The Case of Kenya.' *International Security*, Fall, Vol. 23, no. 2: 80. Available at: http://www.uky.edu/RGS/Patterson/

Kaplan, R. 1994. 'The Coming Anarchy.' *The Atlantic Monthly* 273: 44–76.

Kenya Human Rights Commission. 2000. *The Forgotten People Revisited. Human Rights Abuses in Marsabit and Moyale Districts.* Nairobi: KHRC.

Klem, B. 2003. *Dealing with Scarcity and Violent Conflict.* A background paper. The Hague: Netherlands Institute of International Relations 'Clingendael.'

Leyan, B. 2002, January 14. 'Sharp Rises in Killings by Police, Says Report.' Nation Insight Report. Available at: http://www.nationaudio.com/News/DailyNation/14012002/ News/Insight4.html

Lusigi, W. J. (ed). 1983. Integrated Resource Assessment and Management Plan for Western Marsabit District, Northern Kenya. UNESCO-IPAL. Integrated Resource Assessment Part 1; Technical Report, No. A-6.

Markakis, J. (ed). 1993. *Conflict and Decline of Pastoralism in the Horn of Africa.* London: Macmillan and The Hague: Institute of Social Studies.

Markakis, J. 1997. *Resource Conflict in the Horn of Africa.* London: Sage Publications.

Marsabit District Annual Report (MDAR)

1929 Marsabit District Annual Report, 1929, PC/NFD1/2/2, 1930–36.
1931 Marsabit District Annual Report, 1931, PC/NFD1/2/2, 1930–36.
1935 Marsabit District Annual Report, 1935, PC/NFD1/2/2, 1930–36.
1937 Marsabit District Annual Report, 1937, PC/NFD1/2/3, 1937–43.
1958 Marsabit District Annual Report, 1958, PC/NFD1/2/5, 1951–60.
1959 Marsabit District Annual Report, 1959, PC/NFD1/2/5, 1951–60.
1977 Marsabit District Annual Report, 1977. Unpublished report, 1977.

Marsabit District Handing Over Report 1922 Marsabit District (Gabra) Handing Over Report, 1916-1930, PC/NFD2/2/1.

Maxwell, J.W. and Reuveny, R. 2000. 'Resource Scarcity and Conflict in Developing Countries.' *Journal of Peace Research* 37 (3): 301–22.

McPeak, J.G. 1999. *Herd Growth on Shared Rangeland: Herd Management and Land-use Decisions in Northern Kenya.* PhD thesis. University of Wisconsin-Madison.

Mkutu, K. 2002. 'Pastoralism and conflicts in the Horn of Africa.' Africa Peace Forum. Available at: http://www.saferworld.org.uk

Oba, Gufu. 1996. 'The Range Degradation Debate and its Implications for the Drylands of Africa.' In A. Hjort-af-Ornas (ed.) *Approaching Nature from Local Communities. Security Perceived and Achieved.* Linköping: EPOS, Research Programme on Environmental Policy and Society Institute of Tema Research, Linköping University, Sweden.

O'Leary, M. 1990. 'Changing responses to drought in Northern Kenya: the Rendille and Gabra Livestock Producers.' In P.T.W. Baxter, and R. Hogg (eds), *Property, Poverty and People: Changing Rights in Property and Problems of Pastoral Development.* Manchester: International Development Centre.

Ostrom E. 1990. *Governing the Commons. The Evolution of Institutions for Collective Action.* Cambridge: Cambridge University Press.

Platteau, Jean-Philippe. 1996. 'The Evolutionary Theory of Land Rights as Applied to Sub-Saharan Africa: A Critical Assessment.' *Development and Change*, Vol. 27: 29–86.

Salih, M.A. Mohamed. 1999. *Environmental Politics and Liberation in Contemporary Africa.* Dordrecht: Kluwer Academic Publishers.

Schlee, G. 1989. *Identities on the Move. Clanship and Pastoralism in Northern Kenya.* Nairobi: Gideon S. Were Press.

Scoones, I. 1993. 'Exploiting Heterogeneity: Habitat Used by Cattle in Dryland Zimbabwe.' *Journal of Arid Environments* 29: 221–37.

______. 1995. *Living with Uncertainty. New Directions in Pastoral Development in Africa.* London: International Institute for Environment and Development – Intermediate Technology Publications.

Sobania, N.W. 1979. *Background History of the Mt. Kulal Region of Kenya.* IPAL Technical Report A-2. Nairobi: UNESCO/UNEP.

de Soysa, I. 2002. 'Ecoviolence: Shrinking Pie, or Honey Pot?' *Global Environmental Politics* 2, 4, November: 1–36.

Tablino, P. 1999. *The Gabra; Camel Nomads of Northern Kenya.* Nairobi: Paulines Publications Africa.

Tiffen, M., Mortimore, M., and Gichuki, F. 1994. *More People, Less Erosion – Environmental Recovery in Kenya.* London: Wiley.

World Bank. 2003. *Breaking the Conflict Trap: Civil War and Development Policy.* World Bank policy report. Available at: www.worldbank.org.

Index